The Paradoxes of Globalisation

Also edited by Eric Milliot and Nadine Tournois

LES PARADOXES DE LA GLOBALISATION DES MARCHES

Also by Eric Milliot

LE MARKETING SYMBIOTIQUE: LA COOPERATION AU SERVICE DES ORGANISATIONS

Also by Nadine Tournois

LE MARKETING BANCAIRE ET LES NOUVELLES TECHNOLOGIES

LA BANQUE (*with Guy Tournois*)

LA MARKETING FACE AUX NOUVELLES TECHNOLOGIES

LA CREATION DE VALEUR DANS LA BANQUE (*with Matthias Fischer*)

The Paradoxes of Globalisation

Edited by

Eric Milliot

and

Nadine Tournois

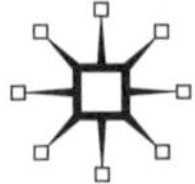

Selection and editorial content © Eric Milliot and Nadine Tournois 2010
Individual chapters © the contributors 2010
Preface © Jacques Barrot 2010

All rights reserved. No reproduction, copy or transmission of this
publication may be made without written permission.

No portion of this publication may be reproduced, copied or transmitted
save with written permission or in accordance with the provisions of the
Copyright, Designs and Patents Act 1988, or under the terms of any licence
permitting limited copying issued by the Copyright Licensing Agency,
Saffron House, 6-10 Kirby Street, London EC1N 8TS.

Any person who does any unauthorized act in relation to this publication
may be liable to criminal prosecution and civil claims for damages.

The authors have asserted their rights to be identified
as the authors of this work in accordance with the Copyright,
Designs and Patents Act 1988.

First published 2010 by
PALGRAVE MACMILLAN

Palgrave Macmillan in the UK is an imprint of Macmillan Publishers Limited,
registered in England, company number 785998, of Houndmills, Basingstoke,
Hampshire RG21 6XS.

Palgrave Macmillan in the US is a division of St Martin's Press LLC,
175 Fifth Avenue, New York, NY 10010.

Palgrave Macmillan is the global academic imprint of the above companies
and has companies and representatives throughout the world.

Palgrave® and Macmillan® are registered trademarks in the United States,
the United Kingdom, Europe and other countries.

ISBN 978–0–230–27868–4 hardback

This book is printed on paper suitable for recycling and made from fully
managed and sustained forest sources. Logging, pulping and manufacturing
processes are expected to conform to the environmental regulations of the
country of origin.

A catalogue record for this book is available from the British Library.

Library of Congress Cataloging-in-Publication Data
The paradoxes of globalisation / edited by Eric Milliot And Nadine Tournois.
     p.   cm.
  ISBN 978–0–230–27868–4
  1. Europe—Foreign economic relations—Developing countries.
  2. Developing countries—Foreign economic relations—Europe.
  3. Globalization.   4. Export marketing.   I. Milliot, Eric.
  II. Tournois, Nadine, 1954–
  HF1531.Z4D4464 2010
  337—dc22   2010027582

10   9   8   7   6   5   4   3   2   1
19 18 17 16 15 14 13 12 11 10

Printed and bound in Great Britain by
CPI Antony Rowe, Chippenham and Eastbourne

Contents

List of Tables, Figures, Box, Graph and Map

Tables

Figures

Box

Graph

Map

Preface

The people of Europe experience globalisation as a combination of hope, opportunity and threat. Hope, since for poverty is receding in the world thanks to the emergence of continent-states; and opportunity, because the interdependence of global economies and the multiplication of zones of prosperity are powerful levers of trade and growth for Europe. However globalisation also inspires fear: fear of a North–South divide that feeds extremisms; fear of the predominance of the Internet and real-time information (certainly a marvellous advancement, but one that also entails the risk of dangerous behaviours and organisations); fear in the face of climate imbalance; fear when confronted by the violent crises linked to the interweaving of economies which we were unable to anticipate: the oil crisis, the food crisis, the financial crisis.

It is in this context, by its very nature paradoxical, that the following book sets out the various studies that, through different fields of management, address the reality of international business.

After asking the fundamental question concerning the nature of globalisation, which combines economy, policy and even ideology, the concept of 'business boundaries' is then challenged. The book also tackles companies' strategic diversification, which supposedly enables all needs to be covered, but which today has resulted in the rediscovery of the virtues of specialisation. It furthermore demonstrates the supplementary paradox that the emergence of the 'global village' has also resulted in local cultures being rediscovered along with a stronger need to identify with them.

The contributors to this book also deal with the need for the comparability of companies' results at an international level, which has led to the setting up of a system of international accounting standards overseen by the Big Four who are both judge and jury. The financial crisis has highlighted the fragility of this system.

These perspectives show that the problem of globalisation must be, more than ever, tackled in terms of worldwide governance.

In the tormented period in which we live, it is clearly apparent that Europe can play a strategic role, a role of example. Located between the nation and the world, it offers a model of integration and close cooperation between states.

The stability arising from its strong internal market should enable it to impose an international system of standardisation and regulation. Throughout the crisis, we have seen how the united voice of Europe has been able to map out a global financial system – at once reformed, regulated and transparent.

In solving the paradoxes of globalisation, which constitute manyobstacles to a harmonious development of national economies, European added-value is undeniable. It knows how to combine economic efficiency with the respect for ethical values without which prosperity cannot have a solid basis. As such, the European Union is, as Jean Monnet said, 'a stage on the way to the organised world of tomorrow'.

Jacques Barrot
Former VP of the European Commission

Introduction: A Complex, Restrictive and Contradictory Globalisation of Markets

Eric Milliot and Nadine Tournois

For thousands of years, human activity has been characterised by the phenomenon of trade internationalisation. However, the concept of globalisation in Management Science is a relatively recent one. The first important academic works on this subject were written a few decades ago by Buzzell (1968), Barnet and Muller (1975) and Sorenson and Wiechmann (1975). Nowadays, globalisation is defined by the International Monetary Fund (IMF, 1997), as being

> the growing economic interdependence of countries worldwide through the increasing volume and variety of cross-border transactions in goods and services and of international capital flows, and also through the more rapid and widespread diffusion of technology. (p. 45)

This definition, which is widely accepted in institutional and professional circles, has three weaknesses for Management Science research professors.

i. In eliciting only one type of actors (countries), it implicitly eliminates companies, professional associations, international organisations, all of which, however, play an important role in the development of the supranational integration of economies. In 1991, Reich was already talking about the linchpin role of companies and the relative powerlessness of states in regulating globalisation.
ii. In focusing on the growth of transactions and the diffusion of technology, the definition ignores the new methods imposed by the opening-up of borders (inter-company cooperation, the breaking down and rebuilding of the value chain, relocation or outsourcing).
iii. By concentrating on the interdependence of countries, it neglects to underline the other section of its dynamic, namely the decompartmentalisation of national markets.

In order to respond to the limits of the IMF definition, this study interprets the meaning of market globalisation as

> a movement which facilitates the coordination and/or the integration of industrial and marketing operations beyond national borders, by generating the decompartmentalisation of markets and underlining the interdependence of the actors.
>
> (Milliot, 2005: 43)

A clear definition of the concept of globalisation is necessary in order to establish a base for analysis but is not sufficient for a clear presentation of paradoxes. This presentation must be associated with a precise framework. This is even more useful as the speeches about globalisation are numerous, and occasionally tackle a multitude of themes in a rather unstructured manner. The resulting confusion arises largely from the amalgamation of two types of market (products and capital) and two types of actors (the 'regulators', i.e. states, the World Trade Organisation, regional blocs; and the 'operators', i.e. companies, inter-company networks, pressure groups). The following table sets out the four main fields of discussion concerning globalisation:

	REGULATORS (states, WTO)	OPERATORS (companies, inter-company networks)
PRODUCT MARKETS (goods, services)	The field approached in Chapters 2 and 11	The field approached in Chapters 1–9 and the Conclusion
CAPITAL MARKETS (money, financial)	The field approached in Chapters 2, 10 and 13	The field approached in Chapters 2, 4, 10, 12 and 13

These four fields are not naturally impenetrable; each element interacts with the others. However, they enable the clarification of the level of reflection and the agreed upon key questions with regard to the economic integration of nations.

In order to avoid the pitfall exposed previously, the main analyses set out in this book concentrate on the real catalysts of markets; that is to say, the companies (operators). As Miotti and Sachwald (2006) emphasise, this choice can be justified by the fact that the internationalisation of markets is no longer led by developed countries, but by large companies that have been a driving force particularly since 2000. Their development strategies, which often ignore political boundaries, are more than ever before disrupting consumption habits, work organisation methods and states' political trends.

Having laid out the conceptual and analytical frameworks, it is now possible to introduce the key question dealt with in this book. Almost three decades after Levitt's seminal article appeared (1983), globalisation is far from having standardised most consumer products. The internationalisation of trade is experiencing an evolution which is often thwarted by various contradictory forces. For that matter, some authors talk about 'triumphs' and 'setbacks' (Bairoch, 1997), 'good fortune' and 'bad fortune' (Sur, 2006). This situation results from the complex web of different interactive ideas which give rise to numerous paradoxes. These paradoxes particularly affect, to varying degrees, companies' functioning and developing methods.

In fact, in reaction to globalisation, a growing number of consumers seem to want to return to the traditional products established in their country's culture. In a rapidly evolving world which does not always offer stable reference points, these products reassure people and allow them to lay claim to a certain identity. In France, for example, the impact of the 'Made In' label is escalating (Briard, 2007). There is a growing feeling of 'attraction-repulsion' in relation to products known as 'global products'. Consumers clearly want to be citizens of the world, but refuse any change to local particularities. They would like to have a society which is open to the world, but reject the idea of an environment without either depth or roots. This ambivalent demand challenges the companies that are perceived to be the principal vectors of globalisation.

Forced to reply to their prospective clients' demands and to submit to local regulations, companies are developing far fewer plans of action that are uniform on a global scale. To use Bartlett's (1986) terms, 'global strategy' is, or has been, abandoned by numerous companies (IKEA, McDonalds, Coca-Cola, for example). They are now trying to reconcile systems of standardisation and adaptation so as to confront complex market conditions. Thus for a large majority of sectors of activity, globalisation gives rise to new local working conditions.

In spite of the multiplication of identity demands, in order to set their strategy in motion many companies are approaching foreign markets while maintaining an ethnocentric profile. They place managers from their own countries at the head of their subsidiaries, regularly make reference to their culture of origin and transfer their management techniques abroad. This reflexive approach sometimes provokes reactions locally which, paradoxically, restrict companies' international development. These problems have, for example, been experienced in France by Disney, Pizza Hut and McDonald's.

At the industrial level, even if the phenomenon is in an embryonic stage, some companies are returning to their countries of origin in order to reduce their production costs, after having developed their operations abroad. Examples of French companies which have done this recently include Atol, Genevieve Lethu, La Mascotte and Samas. This return is justified in numerous ways: reduction of transport costs, simplifying of management systems, better productivity hours, improvement in product quality, proximity to prospective clients, economic patriotism. It conveys a movement against the current of globalisation which could develop in the future.

The paradoxes also concern the financing of companies. The pressures exerted by the all-powerful financial markets since the collapse of the Bretton Woods system mean that companies are increasingly restricted in the development of long-term operations (Artus and Virard, 2005). Indeed, for investors to be offered quick profitability, business leaders can no longer always finance projects, however essential these may be in the development of their organisation. They are turning towards value-creation strategies. This situation is accelerating financial globalisation, as speculators are looking for high yields on a planetary scale, but are simultaneously preventing companies from making the necessary investments for tackling international competition in good conditions. Financial globalisation thus seems to be eventually rendering fragile the economic units most committed to the global market. For example, to get round this contradiction, Legris Industries decided to withdraw from the Paris Bourse in 2004. A senior manager of the group (quoted by Du Guerny, 2006: 9) justified this choice by saying,

> Financial analysts misunderstand our jobs and their evolutions, even if we have a clear, long-term strategy.

From a more transverse point of view, it can be noticed that there is also a certain amount of ambivalence at the level of companies' social responsibility. Globalisation is partly based on the diffusion of information. Friedman (2006) puts forward the idea that *The World is Flat* to convey forcibly the fact that telecommunications and transport reduce the notions of time and distance. This ease of access to data puts companies under pressure as their actions are from now on scrutinised and analysed on a vast scale. If any breach of trust is spotted, clients and partners are very quickly informed. Now that companies are free to develop their operations across boundaries, they find that their hands are increasingly tied at environmental and societal levels.[1] The more internationalised they are, the more they are monitored by different civil organisations (Corporate Watch, Multinational Monitor, United Students against Sweatshops, for example). If they do not take into consideration the principles of social responsibility which are agreed upon today, then, like Nestlé, Nike and Wal-Mart for example, they risk their image being weakened in the eyes of prospective clients who are increasingly conscious of the issues.

As we can see, globalisation operates on complex and restrictive principles which companies have to identify and manage. In order to help them, this book proposes an analysis of the main logical contradictions which characterise the economic integration of national markets. As it is impossible to list all the contradictions (they may adjust to a context in various different ways), this study merely attempts to shed specific light on the main ambivalence of a phenomenon which has a high impact on a growing number of companies. In order to answer this objective, the various reflections presented here are grouped around three thematic keys:

i. General policy and strategy
ii. Marketing and logistics
iii. Accounting and finance

Before dealing with the paradoxes of the supranational integration of markets with regard to these fields of management, a preliminary chapter sets out the conceptual bases of 'globalisation'.

Note

1. In France, consider the New Economic Regulations Law (loi sur les nouvelles régulations économiques – NRE). On the international scale, there is the Global Compact, put forward by the UNO, which invites companies to respect the rights of man and certain work and environment standards.

References

Artus, P. and Virard, M.-P. (2005) *Le capitalisme est en train de s'autodétruire*. Paris: La Découverte.

Bairoch, P. (1997) *Victoires et déboires: histoire économique et sociale du monde du XVIème siècle à nos jours* (three volumes). Paris: Gallimard.

Barnet, R. and Muller, R. (1975) *Global Reach: The Power of the Multinational Corporations*. London: Jonathan Cape.

Bartlett, C. (1986) Building and managing the transnational: the new organizational challenge in M. Porter (ed.) *Competition in Global Industries*. Boston: Harvard Business School Press.

Briard, C. (2007) L'argument du 'Made in France' refait surface. *Les Echos*, 31 (January): 12.

Buzzell, R. (1968) Can you standardize multinational marketing? *Harvard Business Review*, November–December: 98–104.

Du Guerny, S. (2006) La mondialisation selon Legris. *Les Echos*, 23 (October): 9.

Friedman, T. (2006) *La terre est plate*. Paris: Editions Saint-Simon.

International Monetary Fund (IMF) (1997) *World Economic Outlook*, May: 45.

Levitt, T. (1983) The globalization of markets. *Harvard Business Review*, May–June: 92–102.

Milliot, E. (2005) Stratégies d'internationalisation: une articulation des travaux de Porter et Perlmutter. *Revue Management & Avenir*, 3 (January): 43–60.

Miotti, L. and Sachwald, F. (2006) Commerce mondial: le retour de la 'vieille économie'? *Les études de l'Ifri*, Ifri, Paris: 45.

Reich, R. (1991) *L'économie mondialisée*. Paris: Dunod.

Sorenson, R. and Wiechmann, U. (1975) How multinationals view marketing standardization. *Harvard Business Review*, May–June: 38–56.

Sur, S. (2006) Heurs de la globalisation, malheurs de la mondialisation. *Questions Internationales*, 22: 4–5.

Preliminary Chapter

What is Globalisation? The Paradoxes of the Economic and Political Substance of Markets

Yvon Pesqueux

The discussion of corporate activity globalisation is now questioning the national dimension of culture. Today, in multinational corporations and society, the vapid term 'glocalisation' is bandied about – think globally and act locally – but it is, rather, time to question the irreducible antagonism between the values of the geographic space of markets and those of the geographic space of nations. Indeed, globalisation backs up the assertion that the geographic space of markets must overlap that of nations. The result of the impact of multinational corporation activity tends to make the global market look like a private market where the norms these corporations propose (or impose) tend to create an actual mode of government. This leads to a shift from the 'local-general' that is appropriate for describing business activity to the 'specific-universal' that is appropriate for a political understanding of societies.

This shift is couched in the term 'globalisation', which tends to create confusion between globalism and cosmopolitanism, yet is considered as mercantile cosmopolitanism since it is designed towards the interests of the managers of these firms. The multinational corporation thus views itself as being nowhere 'foreign'; and yet, it cannot be the archetype of the founding institution of a universal culture appearing out of thin air. Its action raises the more general question of globalisation as a converging or diverging point between cultures. In fact, the development of communitarianism, based on group identification (and no longer on societies) – communities that invoke the cultural argument – seems to operate alongside the increasing internationalisation of economic activity, with the world as the benchmark (and no longer societies). Globalisation and communitarianism go hand in hand as they work to de-territorialise landmarks based on the logic of downgrading society and its geographic and political anchorage as a benchmark.

It should be stressed that globalisation ran throughout the twentieth century and not only in its current sense. Didn't two world wars take place in that century? In its current sense, globalisation is probably more informed by these than it appears to be.

In the strict sense of the term, globalisation is 'to be in the world' and the concept conveys the idea of gathering. Also, the American sense of globalisation encompasses the ideas of non-finality, unlimitedness, instability and abstraction. The term straddles the general and the worldwide, thus making a 'universal' combination.

Ferrandéry (1996) stresses that globalisation is a concept that emerged in the mid-1980s in US management schools and in the English-American press. It was then presented as a normal offshoot of technological evolution and later became the genuine catchphrase of free-market agitprop: towards an American-type western universal taking over from the European-type western universal as framed through colonialism. This shapes the geographic origin of this genuine heteronomous imposition towards self-government, with the market becoming the reference point of this imposition.

As Bellon (2004) stresses, however, 'that is forgetting that throughout human history other technological revolutions and discoveries of the boundaries of our space have not led to a dogmatic vision of the future' (p. 8). Globalisation is considered as non-imperialistic because it is grounded in the economy and free trade, compared with the imperialism of the Cold War which was linked to the Soviet Empire and grounded in force. It refers to a complex movement that opens up the economic borders, allowing CEOs of multinational corporations to justify the expansion of their scope across the world and leverage dynamics differences, while offering an overall vision of their action. This can be described as an international division of labour shifting towards an international division of production and business processes, dominated by finance. It can already be noted that globalisation encompasses the long-standing economic debate over the international division of labour which is somehow discursively 'cleared' by its underlying phrase 'globalisation of social and economic inequality'. The advantage to gain from this change of phrase is immediately apparent as globalisation then carries an essentially dogmatic ideological project. Such a project conveys a form of desire for the emergence of international law that is also normative because it is stateless and located outside any social perspective. Politically speaking then, it is about the replacing of the organs that stem from popular sovereignty with organs that are removed from the peoples, in the name of internationalism. Thus, its truths and dogmas should catch on without discussion.

The globalisation promoted by the CEOs of multinational corporations is about testing the general business organisation model, designed to standardise management practices, and those of organisations viewed as entities whose governance must flow from the instruments developed in businesses, against the social and political practices related to various cultural contexts depending on countries. But the universalist project of management processes is problematic in the sense that it involves generalising a management-type political ideology, that is, managerialism, which trumps political institutions per se in an ultimately totalitarian environment of 'monolithic thinking'. Monolithic thinking ties in with the fact that things could not be done otherwise and, by extension, that one cannot think in any other way but in accordance with the categories of corporate management. Should the line be blurred between capital internationalisation, corporate multinationalisation, globalisation and the advent of a global society described as 'multicultural' in order to keep up its democratic face?

This chapter will address the various senses of globalisation and propose different perspectives:

- A descriptive perspective linking globalisation with trade flows.
- A political perspective linking globalisation with the 'crisis' of sovereignty.
- A historical perspective taking up Fernand Braudel's argument about the 'world-economy'.
- A cultural and anthropological perspective based on Arjun Appadurai's argument about 'area culture'.

1   Different senses of the concept of globalisation

As the discussions in the 1960s and 1970s have already suggested, the first obvious sign of the interaction of a firm's international activity with politics was in the development of multinational corporations, which in turn raised the issue of the political dimension of the international activity of businesses. There is also an area in which this interaction was tested: technology transfers.

The realisation of the existence of original capabilities brought out how technology transfers in the chemical industry had been facilitated; for example, in North African cities where there was an existing wool-dyeing tradition. The idea growing out of these aspects is that culture (at least in its technical forms) is absolutely transferable, seemingly warning observers about potential inclinations to overstate factors of cultural difference. Globalisation, then, stems from a cultural reconstruction which is supposedly an outgrowth of the cultural breakdown, often stressed by dualist conceptions of international business activity – according to those conceptions, technologies and 'centre-based' modes of government tend to annihilate those on the periphery, to their advantage. Technology transfers first brought to the fore the issue of culture as an 'operator' of internationalisation, that is, ultimately, the prospect of a plan for a universal society dominated by technique.

In fact, just as the emergence of multinational corporations brought about the discussion regarding the essence of this multinational nature, the resulting globalisation may spring from their increasingly international activity, but it may also be of a different nature. It involves their relationships with local laws which they comply with, and leveraging the international nature of their activity in relation to the loopholes developing across those laws. In that way, they can pursue objectives such as tax optimisation, legal constructs (to profit from favourable legal gaps) or social dumping.

Accordingly, businesses and multinational organisations such as non-governmental organisations (NGOs) are confronted with the issue of the 'global' organisation model 'by nature' and 'out of necessity'. This in turn raises the issue of 'multinationality' as a specific cultural feature. The objective is to promote a multinational corporation as a 'federation free of any national dominant culture' (Darcourt-Lézat, 2002, p. 17) with a progressive undertone. The firm is then presented as the 'culturally fairest' breeding ground for this project of fusion between a mercenary managerial culture and traditional local cultures with which 'we do things together'. The 'global' firm somehow builds the 'future greener pastures' of the multinational corporation.

This also raises the question, more or less explicitly, of the political dimension of globalisation. Indeed, while the economic dimension of the phenomenon is recognised, the categories that help represent its political dimension remain inadequately constructed. Yet an examination of the social and political issues certainly makes it easier to grapple with them, as random examples show, including sustainable development, international security, health security and so on.

As to a conceptualisation of the political dimension, de Senarclens (2002) stresses three aspects:

i. The evolution of content and practices associated with the *raison d'état* (national interest), considering the expansion of the international sphere, towards a form of sovereignty limited by the recognition of expanding international trade – an expansion viewed as the 'superior' common good – as well as the development of beyond-state political bodies; for example, the European Union. This went hand in hand with the development of other worldwide-based bodies such as NGOs and predominant businesses. The shift in content that this brought to states' sovereignty appears to hinge upon this 'cohabitation'.

ii. The capacity of states and international institutions to cope with these political developments, considering, in particular, the political will of Organisation for Economic Co-operation and Development countries (OECD) to promote a capitalistic economy fixed on the expansion of trade in goods and services and financial flows. This will rest on political actions in trade liberalisation and the creation of commercial areas based on economic integration issues, and, more marginally, on political and social issues.

iii. The development of conceptual frameworks for environmental, health and security issues (for example, the ecological 'right of interference', humanitarian or even political interference towards dictators), and the attention paid to non-state-based agents whose expectations will be favoured.

Accordingly, there are at least six senses of globalisation to suggest, each of which has its own logic:

i. *An economic sense* mainly related to the consequences of the activity of multinational corporations.

ii. *A geographic sense* in which globalisation is a geography of flows tying together the footless activities of multinationals and their anchorage in a defined territory, independently of the nation state's categories. In fact, this is behind the creation of a new type of territory that is never quite localised and the implications of which are both financial (to profit from a labour-cost differential and, more generally, to improve the optimisation of the company's resources) and strategic (to open up to new markets and competencies) (Vashistha and Vashistha, 2006). Multinational corporations look upon the world's geography independently of the geographic space of nations, along the lines of region-based functionalism, 'regions' actually being sets of nations.

iii. *A political sense* that factors in the growing weight of 'supranational' organisations and the importance attached to transnational political issues (environment, health security and so on), thus substituting the organs stemming from popular sovereignty, with political organs remote from the peoples, and paving the way for the self-proclaimed influence of lobbies, independent of their representativeness. Globalisation then epitomises a kind of denial of people's sovereignty due to the emergence of European Union-type supranational groupings deflating the reference to the nation state, whether welfare state (as in developed countries) or developmentalist state (as in developing countries), for an organiser-state of globalisation expansion. Globalisation thus carries ambiguities (due to the state's loss of control over the processes of daily life) and contradictions (between external pressures and local social structures), introducing paradoxical impositions between the subject's political autonomy and the heteronomous pressures of the processes of his/her social life; paradoxes by creating unprecedented risks (appropriation of generated wealth for the benefit of outside agents, environmental risks, vulnerabilities of the poorest, while the exercising modes of political power remain rooted in the categories of the nation state).

iv. *A dogmatic sense* in which globalisation is a necessary doctrine or even, as Bellon notes, 'the natural consequence of technological evolution and the finitude of the world' (2004, p. 9). Globalisation is then conceived of as an external constraint limiting citizens' choices in the context of a fatalistic ideology, thus reducing political internationalism to mercantile cosmopolitanism. Based on this ideological perspective, it is possible to separate scholars' commentaries on globalisation into those of the sceptics, for whom globalisation is nothing but the dissemination of American values across the world, and those of the globalists, for whom globalisation is the expression of a structural change of political, social and cultural forms, due to its impact on economic life and daily life. However, it is also possible to consider arguments pertaining to a progressive ideology, in which globalisation is an 'upward competition dynamic', as demonstrated by China's and India's growth, and those pertaining to a critical ideology, in which globalisation is the expression of deregulation resulting in inequality and injustice. The proponents of the progressive ideology also view globalisation as a metaphor of affluence masking the construction of the inequalities of the free-market moment. Finally, the dogmatic sense of globalisation also contributes to articulating a connectionist ideology vindicated by reference to trade as well as to the information and communication technologies. The two rationales become mixed up (trade in commodities is worth as much as communication), but do not lead to a conception of totality. Yet, connectivity cannot just add up that easily, hence the dual reference to diversity. In conjunction with a proprietorist ideology, globalisation makes connectivity into a property of humanity, independently of any reference to nationality (hence its cosmopolitanism). However, in the light of an ownership right universally valid for 'to be in the world', one needs to have a property to trade for.

v. *A historical sense* in which globalisation is the current verbalisation of capitalism as a political order applicable worldwide, as well as in the current moment which legitimates the representation of the geographic space of markets as overlapping with that of nations. In that respect, globalisation is what happens post-colonisation and the East–West confrontation.

vi. *An organisational sense* which places at the core of organisational rationales a relational perspective that becomes whole in relation to outsourcing. Indeed, outsourcing leads to a reinterpretation of Marx's 'putting in' factory (in *The Capital*, Marx traces the history of the development of the factory as a place bringing in employees who were previously home workers, a situation he describes as the 'putting in' system), as a kind of 'putting out' of activities rolled out across the world, as well as a growing resort to external management. Globalisation is also a form of technostructure outsourcing, as the manager figure has shifted in relation to external experts, either on account of their independence or expertise.

Of course, the debate tends to combine these six senses with varying degrees of explicitness but with a view to mapping a geography that is no longer physical, economic or human. In contrast, it could be described as a 'deregulated geography', based on the freedom principle applied to the flow of capital, commodities and people, the deregulation imposition for work relations and the privatisation of society. This in turn results in the firm being institutionalised as a reference space, and the market being the ultimate stage of political and social organisation.

2   A descriptive perspective of globalisation

In the early twentieth century, European powers were already building their networks between countries, even when nationalism and protectionism held sway. This tendency was undermined by wars, then regulated through international authorities and agreements dominated by the United States. As early as the second half of the nineteenth century, the technical evolution of transportation had accelerated trade, first through steam, then through the internal combustion engine. Better communication of information also proved to be one of the major vehicles of globalisation. The revolution and impact of telecommunications on the economy and everyday life are merely working to build full-scale industrial expansion, as well as fostering the spread and upsurge of information transfers.

But this liberalisation and acceleration of international trade as an enriching factor operates on the basis of protectionism. The Bretton Woods agreements formed the basis for the crafting of the 1947 General Agreement on Tariffs and Trade (GATT), designed to facilitate trade. The GATT agreements, however, did not hamper the continuation of a veiled form of protectionism, and this calls for a larger discussion over the issue of the globalisation of economies, which is inadequately controlled by states. The International Monetary Fund (IMF) and later the European monetary fund also emerged out of this necessity to organise and facilitate trade expansion, as well as to ensure a country's economic independence and therefore helping to reduce the financing of deficits. Rounds of negotiation, usually led by the United States, extended the scope of the principles of free trade, spawning the World Trade Organisation (WTO). Concurrently, regional trade blocs also expanded, including, for example, the European Economic Community, Council for Mutual Economic Assistance, North American Free Trade Agreement and Association of South-East Asian Nations. These help facilitate trade within a particular area and reorganise a protectionist or preferential space. In this way, globalisation can be regarded as a geography of flows.

3   A political perspective of globalisation: globalisation and sovereignty

If we investigate whether globalisation is a metaphor, then like any metaphor, it is about deciding what the image stands for. It certainly calls into question the sovereignty of the nation state where geographic space and institutional territory of sovereignty merge. It is worth noting that sovereignty operates through the expression of an authority using formal instruments of government which produce a priori control.

This crisis of the nation state is one characteristic of the free market moment, whose deterritorialisation brings about four senses of sovereignty, besides the one that remains for the nation state, including two economic senses, one political sense and one that is both political and territorial in the geographic sense of the term.

Corporate governance constitutes the codified form of sovereignty within an economic territory, the large corporation – the materialisation of economic inter-regulation – against market governance, which constitutes the non-codified form and thus developing faster in another territory, the financial markets – the materialisation of a posteriori self-regulation. In the broad sense of the term, governance constitutes the form of sovereignty within the framework of a new political territory, supranationality; that is, the territory of such institutions as the European Union, the World Bank and the OECD, which benefit from a democratically uncontrolled handover of sovereignty from the states – the materialisation of political inter-regulation. Also, governance constitutes the form of infranationality, including regions that do not necessarily correspond to administrative regions (for example France's south-east regional grouping 'Pays de l'Adour', job pools and so on) – the materialisation of self-regulation. The sovereignty underlying infraterritories can be linked to the notion of *terroir* (see Chapter 5), considering its geographic location, and the notion of cluster, considering its social and economic dimension. This double dimension of ethnicity and authenticity on the one hand and expertise on the other is probably what most shapes the social and political construction of the infraterritory. The partial and slanted sovereignty of corporations corresponds to market sovereignty, adding to the sovereignty of supra- or infranational political territories, since these also benefit from a handover of sovereignty that is just as democratically uncontrolled (for example, associations of local governments in France). These four 'new' levels of sovereignty are in tension with one another and with the residual sovereignty of the nation state. In this respect, it is worth stressing the difference between the European nation state and the American nation state, whose nature differs from the previous ones. With its continental size and its political power, the American nation state does not come to grips with the crisis of the nation state or the other areas of sovereignty in the same fashion as Europe does. It could be said that emerging continental powers such as China and India will probably follow the same course. The implications of supranationality and infranationality are less significant, and the continent-wide sovereignty of the nation state, in light of its interests, can also regain part of the sovereignty handed over to economic territories. This may explain the sense that globalisation is a form of extension of Americanisation.

In fact, the crisis of the European nation state is specific in that it builds on Arendt's critique (1972), which pointed out the congenital vice of European nation states created after the First World War due to the existence of significant national minorities in some of the states (for example, Hungarians in Romania), a situation repeated during decolonisation and the collapse of the Eastern bloc. In the wake of these developments, the political, social and ultimately ethnic sense of the nation state was undermined, owing to the existence of groups of immigrant populations in Western European countries. This crisis adds to the previous one, with the current tension operating between this area of sovereignty and the new areas of sovereignty.

All these tensions lead from independence-type sovereignty to interdependence-type sovereignty, or even dependence applicable to each of the sovereignty types discussed above, hence the current interrelation of deregulation – expressing the tension between the economic and political areas of sovereignty – and governance, which covers the tensions related to interdependence between those various areas. This interdependence-type sovereignty can be defined as the capacity to produce something but in relation to the other areas, hence the legitimacy assigned to soft law over hard law. It could also be referred to as negotiation sovereignty; that is, a situation where the legitimacy of the area is not questioned, whereas the content of sovereignty it produces interacts with the other contents produced by the other areas. The governance at stake can then be described as 'negotiation machinery' (hence the importance attached to deliberation). The consequences are just as important in terms of citizenship. According to the institutional territory that is referred to, and considering the confusion in terms of the territorialisation, one is led to refer to 'nomadic citizenship'.

Globalisation is not solely the devaluation of the nation state as a major political identification focus, but also the addressing of interactions now operating between the national levels of political, social, cultural and economic life, and global players with varying degrees of influence (multinational corporations, NGOs, media and so on).

The challenging of the territory of the nation state's sovereignty has a major impact on the substance of the sovereignty of the new territories, mainly on the nature of the community resulting from it. It should be noted that the community formed around the nation state consists of two defining aspects, one side related to identification (the nation is the major place of citizen identification) and the other related to solidarity. The latter was characterised by the development of the Welfare State or what Castel describes as 'social property' (2003), a counterpart of private property for the social classes deprived of it. The new territories propose new content for these two aspects of identity and solidarity. Regarding identification – except for the geographic communitarian infraterritory which becomes a narrowed locus of positive identification – the new territories lead to a collapsed vision of identification, as if the nation state, a locus of positive identification, was no longer necessary. The reference to globalisation is particularly revealing in this respect, with the figure of the world customer substituting for the cosmopolitan figure of the world citizen, the multinational corporation never 'foreign' anywhere, and so on. Regarding solidarity, the 'insurance-based utopia', mercantile by nature, is considered as capable of replacing the political aspects of solidarity. No wonder then that the communitarian identification based on primordialism (race, gender, age, religion and moral values) is thriving.

A closer look at the firm as an institutional territory suggests that the issue of its sovereignty, of legal inspiration (corporate governance), has been 'outpaced' by outsourcing rationales leading to organisational governance. This marks the dissociation between the firm's legal area, its economic area and its social area. Indeed, outsourcing has organisational consequences in terms of strategy (which then holds for the firm's economic area and no longer its legal area alone) and technostructure (part of the technostructure is outsourced with the resort to consultants and various experts, and so on), hence the phrase 'extended firm'. This can be easily illuminated by recalling how much the economic area of a multinational corporation differs from its legal and social areas in so far as the subcontractors are actually firms providing work. This perspective is one aspect of globalisation generally anchored to the organisation. Also, it is worth pointing out the geographic anchorage of outsourcing. Strictly speaking, this is referred to as globalisation because it involves acknowledging that the firm's activity is performed within the geographic space of markets, which differs from that of nations.

4   A historical perspective of globalisation: the argument of Fernand Braudel

Braudel (1988) articulates a broader argument, looking at pre-capitalistic development described by Marx as the phase of primitive accumulation of capital. He presents, in three volumes (*Les structures du quotidien, Les jeux de l'échange* and *Le temps du monde*), the argument that trade, specifically long-distance trade, would play a crucial role in the development of capitalism as it seeks to alter life and society from the perspective of the production and sale of commodities. The development of capitalism interfered structurally with the political dimension of nations. Braudel relates how it is possible to pin down the birth of world economies as early as the thirteenth century in Amalfi (Italy), and refer to them through the existence of a trading centre. The centre of the world economy consists of the city, which gains considerable economic importance due to the competences that it has, and its capacity to use and develop specific know-how in the commercial and financial fields. This importance can be measured through the flows resulting from the city concerned. Braudel chronicles the ebb and flow of dominations worldwide (Venice, Bruges, Geneva and Amsterdam) and national economies (France and England) but within a space – that of the world economy – reaching beyond the space of nations. He also argues that capitalism has a long-standing history and has aimed, since its inception, to prevent the development of competition. By separating trade from the market, Braudel offers a conception of the market that differs dramatically from the conception that currently prevails in economics. It is a market that seeks to transcend national borders as well as to reduce competition in order to guarantee high profits.

Braudel discusses the irreducible duality of human activity which is performed, in its daily manifestations, within political spaces and the geographic space of markets, independently of political boundaries. This activity operates on the basis of profit-seeking, in particular high profits connected to long-distance trade and speculation. But it is also the moment of technology transfers across continents (from China and the Islamic world to Europe in the fourteenth and fifteenth centuries, for example) as well as population transfers (from Africa to America in the eighteenth century, for example). His premises are as follows:

- History can be understood only through a global dimension that factors in geography, economics, politics, social sciences and culture.
- The rules specific to human activities organise space which varies slowly.
- Time cycles, ranging from a few years to a century, punctuate time.

World economies present similar characteristics: production surpluses occur, markets form, trade expands, a monetary system is set up, followed by bills of exchange and credit, and merchants shift from trade to finance, labour division follows growth and is an indicator of its progress. The secondary and service sectors add to the primary sector. The development of the service industry is an indicator of a developing society.

A world economy consists of a dynamic central area and a periphery comprising a lagging area and people it exploits. It leans towards a monopolistic status, its instruments of domination having shifted from the canon to new products and credit. The centre of a world economy first consists of cities, then territorial states which – taking more time to become established – will have more resources and extend their domination across the world. The industrial revolution that follows is the outcome of all the previous steps leading to growth, which becomes ongoing. All the sectors of the economy are set in motion without any of them being a bottleneck.

The various areas of a world economy are prioritised and converge towards their centre. Over centuries, local and regional market chains are set up. Markets are gradually incorporated into a city or a dominant area. The pattern of domination rests on a dialectic wavering between a nearly self-developing market economy and an overarching economy. Any world economy is an interlocking, a juxtaposition of interrelated areas at different levels. Its core includes the most advanced and diversified features. The central area holds only some of those strengths. The periphery is vast and diffusely peopled, and archaism and exploitation by others are standard practice. The world economy constitutes an order against other orders and does not rule society single-handedly. The political, social and cultural elements also dictate priorities to society and act on the world economy.

Braudel's argument helps in examining today's society according to a time division, other than one based on economic factors. Capitalism is then considered as a set of economic, geographic and social hierarchies. To refer to this argument is also to argue that there is no globalisation in the specific sense of the term in the late twentieth century, but rather the continuation of a movement whose current contours go as far back as the Middle Ages, as a result of the breakdown of the tenets of the domanial economy dating from classical antiquity. Reconsidering this perspective of globalisation in light of history puts its relevance into context, and at the same time it emphasises the continuity of the phenomenon, thus providing a different focus on the perspectives of the activity of multinational corporations. It is also one way to address the issue of how economic activity – operating in the geographic space of the markets – interferes with citizen life operating in the geographic space of nations.

5   A cultural and anthropological perspective of globalisation and Appadurai's model of the area culture

Mattelart (2008) devoted his article *Encyclopedia Universalis* to the subject of the relationship between globalisation and culture, exploring whether humanity settles into monoculture under the pressure of the symbolic universals of mass consumption and networks. Against this argument he proposes an observation of social and economic divides and identity-driven claims.

In the process, he indicates that this perspective is correlated with the Industrial Revolution, with the development of technical networks and their supposedly aggregating power. This approach to globalisation goes hand in hand with the issue of the dominant lingua franca, English, because language is considered as the ultimate locus of cultural identity. However, observing, as Braudel does, that today New York's financial quarter is the centre of the world economy, can globalisation not be interpreted along the lines of Americanisation? Is the diagnosis of 'civilisation's illness', which makes up American centrism viewed from outside, adequate to gain an understanding of the features of globalisation? This is not what Appadurai (2001) articulates in his anthropological perspective of area culture.

To come to grips with the concept of culture it is necessary to address anthropology as its reference point, even though it later spread across other disciplines. Appadurai's anthropological interpretation of culture in the globalisation era – the area studies – is probably one of the most seminal today, particularly as it seeks to address territories based on a model that is specific to them, even though the multinational corporation does not appear per se in his exploration. But the very title of his book, *Modernity at large: cultural dimensions of globalisation*, suggests that globalisation remains a relevant talking point from an anthropological viewpoint; that is, an anthropology in which culture remains a key notion.

Appadurai points out that 'the electronic means of communication and mass migrations thus emerge today as new forces, but not so much on a technical level as on the imaginary level' (2001, p. 42), noting that in another of his writings (Appadurai, 1990), he had named 'affective community' the fact that a group of individuals begins to share their dreams and feelings as a transborder phenomenon, made possible by the media (satellite TV, the Internet and so on). This, he argues, is what leads to an updating of how culture can be understood from a new diasporic perspective which challenges the categories of acculturation and therefore assimilation. In the process, he grounds a new appreciation of multiculturalism that, if not irreducible, is at least a lot more robust in the era of globalisation. This allows him to reinterpret bi-, inter- or multicultural into categories that break out of the usual culturalism (it should be noted here that culturalism rests on the premise of the understanding of our behaviours in relation to the culture we belong to).

He performs this reinterpretation – based on the duality 'nostalgia–imagination' – by building on a critique of primordialisms that underlie the culturalist perspective in which one is encouraged to refer to items, including ethnicity, religion and so on, to delineate the contours of groups and understand their meaning. It should be recalled how much primordialisms ground the ideology of 'localism', thus combining the two synchronic (in light of primordial values) and diachronic (in light of a territory, its history and traditions) determinisms. Arguably, primordialisms tend to act like prejudices. The term 'Islamist' is a glaring case in point, whose inherent racism is concealed by bringing forward a territorialised religious characteristic. To choose primordial characteristics is also to construct a value judgement. That is, while culturalism is 'the conscious mobilisation of cultural differences in the service of a larger national or transnational politics [...] frequently associated with extraterritorial histories and memories, sometimes with refugee status and exile, and almost always with struggles for stronger recognition from existing nation states or from various transnational bodies [...], culturalist movements (because they almost always focus their efforts on mobilization) are the most common form of the work of imagination' (Appadurai, 2001, p. 50). This leads Appadurai to reinterpret, with regard to the categories of globalisation through the concept of cultural area, the concept of the nation state. He proposes looking at the essential agency of imagination feeding off images for which he provides a form of programmatic classification as will be seen below. Imagination is effectively a driver of identification processes as well as of the loyalty process whose biasness should be mentioned. To be loyal is indeed to pick one's side, one's friends, and so on, and therefore also to pick one's enemies. The argument is that there is still production of locality today, however, on the basis of totally updated neighbouring structures due to the use of mass communication resources.

The cultural area thus provides a basis for anchorage to a locality that no longer has to be spatially determined. For example, the same French agent may be pursuing an imperialistic course (that of the top management of the company he or she represents) and a diasporic course (that of the Frenchman/woman abroad), based on two fairly distinct cultural areas. With globalisation, the here-and-now tends to take on an entirely new meaning, which leads Appadurai to propose a 'post-patriotism'. Nevertheless, the postcolonialism of today's globalisation remains indebted to the movements of ideas, populations and individuals of 'eurocolonial' worlds to which we owe the 'imagined communities of recent nationalisms'. Immigrant communities also carry transnational loyalties. The weight given to the concept of community should be noted here; a concept that is also found at the core of communitarianism but viewed here in relation to a 'deterritorialised' collective.

If a global cultural system is actually emerging, it remains 'filled with ironies and local resistances' under the cover of unfettered adherence to the consumption modes of Western objects. This leads Appadurai to consider imagination as a social fact central to all forms of action. Homogenisation and heterogenisation thus work together.

To explore these disjunctures, Appadurai proposes the following concepts (disjunctive among one another, having unpredictable relationships, and thus unable to help design a genuine infrastructure) to challenge the misguided simplifications, so he claims, of primordialisms due to the deterritorialisation of individuals.

- *Ethnoscapes* consisting of individuals who are shaping today's shifting world (tourists, immigrants, refugees and so on), conducive to deflating the stability of communitarian, kinship and residency links, and so on, and having to address their localisation dreams. However, *ethnoscapes* stimulate the elements of primordialism.

- *Technoscapes*, which help factor in the 'global, also ever so fluid configuration of technology' (Appadurai, 2001, p. 50), both high and low, leading, for example, to the export of Indian chauffeurs to the Emirates and Indian software engineers to the United States.
- *Financescapes,* which factor in the fluid disposition of global capital that is never located.
- *Mediascapes* represented by electronic capabilities which make it easy to produce and disseminate information, providing individuals spread across the world with 'repertoires of images, narratives and "ethnoscapes" in which the world of commodities and the world of "news" and politics are profoundly mixed' (Appadurai, 2001, p. 51). They provide fodder for their imagination. They play a major role in a project to pacify separatisms in the name of the 'majoritarianisms' they carry, yet driving separatisms dialectically. They are grounded in a conception of image, which can be compared to that held by de Castoriadis (1999), pointing out its interaction with representation: 'Representation, imagination, imagery have never been viewed for themselves but always in reference to something else – sensation, intellection, perception, reality – subjected to the normativity built into the inherited ontology, brought to the standpoint of truth or falsehood, hijacked into a function, means judged by their contribution to the possible achievement of an end, truth or access to the other' (p. 25).
- *Ideoscapes* are a set of images 'often political and [which] frequently have to do with the ideologies of states and the counter-ideologies of movements explicitly capturing state power or a piece of it' (Appadurai, 2001, p. 52), consisting of elements including freedom, welfare and sovereignty with regard to the meaning assumed by their original location. This is where the issue of communication fits in.

The suffix '-scape' indicates that it does not involve 'objectively given relations which look the same from every angle of vision. These landscapes thus are the building blocks (…) of imagined worlds, that is, the multiple worlds which are constituted by the historically situated imaginations of persons and groups spread around the globe' (Appadurai, 2001, p. 52). This leads Appadurai to criticise – due to the volatility of links of all kinds, as stressed above – the acculturation process which implies the transgenerational stability of knowledge. Tradition and the categories of cultural reproduction are thus reinvented, anchored in 'spatially fractured arrangements' (p. 52). It is important to stress the potential of this kind of concept to account for the substance of the multinational corporation, and its project of homogenising world culture while producing diversity in a dialectical fashion. The most significant outcome of this interplay of '-scapes' is the birth of fetishisms. Appadurai singles out a few of them, including global production fetishism, the fetishism of the global consumer figure, the fetishism of a reference to a culture that cannot be grounded on a general theory.

6 Conclusion

The term 'Americanisation' was coined in the wake of the Second World War and it is used as a reference for analysing the cultural offshoots of the Marshall Plan, with the emergence of the social category of the senior executive, as Boltanski (2008) observes. The response to Americanisation reached its apex in May 1968 (a period of strikes in France, Germany and the US), and in the US with the protest against the Vietnam War. This protest, more broadly, translated into a solidarity effort towards Third World countries, argued to be more exposed than others to US economic and cultural domination. Also, it effectively paved the way for a larger ideological perspective which can be described as 'Third Worldism', with all the simplification and wishful-thinking attributes specific to an ideology.

The fact that companies – mainly American ones initially – are becoming multinationals obliterates the larger debate that was initiated with the culturalist commentary on mass production and consumption after 1945. The utopian perspective of globalisation then finds its ideological outlets with such phrases as 'global village' and 'earth spacecraft', which tend to eliminate the dividing line previously established between a culturally hegemonic power and the others, and designed to smooth out differences. By foregrounding the economic nature of the perspective (before its cultural side), the objective is to paint a credible picture of a fair and universalist situation, involving all producers and consumers. In this respect, mass consumption plays a specific role as a homogenising factor of a medium purported to be neutral, transparent and universal and empowering, hence the project to smooth out cultural differences. Similarly, the subtle connections between culture and ideology find themselves obliterated, encouraged by the peremptory claim of the end of ideologies, political revolution as a form of protest and, by extension, the end of the core of cultural differences. There has been constant reference to the cultural determinism of a new socio-technical system of an essentially global economic nature. The United States is represented as the first society of this kind, fatefully placated after the end of the Vietnam conflict, which eliminated any reference to the imperialistic character of its power towards building a new consensus. It is all about market places, as an extension of this global village, and the construction of large free trade spaces. The perspective of universal cultural symbols – essentially business-based – followed in its wake, de facto transforming representation within categories operating in a vacuum and obliterating the world's profound inequalities.

Besides, the categories of globalisation go hand in hand with a form of cosmopolitanism, a kind of counterpoint to a world deprived of the cosmopolitanism of communist political thought. The cosmopolitanism of globalisation is viewed as the project to reduce the diversity of groups which must then be homogenised. But this probably leads to the dual quest for differentialism, which could be justified by the reference to their dimension (numerical criteria) and their principles (axiological perspective built on a value hierarchy).

Globalisation points to the existence of an essentially economic perspective, a kind of metaphor of the New World, a vast and untapped commercial El Dorado. Also, the term masks the existence of a frantic race for the exploitation of new commercial opportunities. This race has, in turn, caused a greater push for short-term profitability and competition, leading many companies to disregard, overlook or refuse to address factors of environmental risks, cultural diversity, outrageous exploitation of the least-protected workers (including children), and to support, directly or indirectly, dictatorial regimes which are enforcers of labour docility. The comparative advantage of nations, a notion inherited from mercantilism, seems to correspond to the competitive advantage of multinational corporations in a continuum of some kind. This mercantilist advantage that those multinational corporations are recognised as having corresponds to a form of communitarian perspective which recognises them as having specific rights independently of their representativeness. It is through these manifestations that multinational corporations highlight the question of the political substance of economic activity. In fact, they highlight the question of its critique whose ideological cooption turns it into alter-globalisation over, as would have been normal, anti-globalisation or even cultural revolution.

Globalisation also grounds the dogma that the activity of multinationals supposedly benefits workers and citizens of developing countries more than the activity of 'normal' companies does, based on an argument that certainly needs to be further investigated. The argument is that, in the collapsed institutional framework in which they operate, the great autonomy of the subsidiary translates into greater autonomy of the worker who works in it. Basically, this logic is an implicit free market theory of exploitation.

Globalisation as a historical moment also raises the issue of the entropic conditions of its exhaustion and reversibility. Thus, the indicators that need to be tracked are those of the geographic space of nations, including imperialistic wars, rise of nationalisms, trade disputes, social claims, economic and environmental disruptions, growing regulation of financial markets and matters environmental and so on. These indicators are indeed representative of contradictions that challenge formal modes of cooperation (cooperation between states, for example OECD, EU and so on) as well as informal modes (business alliances), and thus the governance systems that underpin the world order. This provides a basis for discussing deglobalisation, even though this book as a whole is more geared towards the sense of globalisation than the one addressed in this text.

Bibliography

Appadurai, A (1990) 'Topography of the self: praise and emotion in Hindu India' in CA Lutz and L Abu-Lughod (eds) *Language and the Politics of Emotion*. Cambridge, Mass: Cambridge University Press.

———— (1996) *Modernity at Large: Cultural Dimensions of Globalisation* (Public World Series). Minnesota: University of Minnesota Press.

———— (2001) *Après le colonialisme – Les dimensions culturelles de la mondialisation* (French translation: Bouillot, F). Paris: Payot, Paris.

Arendt, H (1972) *Le système totalitaire* (collection Points politique). Paris: Seuil.

Bellon, A (2004) Dieu créa la mondialisation . . . *Le Monde Diplomatique*, November: 4–9.

Boltanski, L (2008) 'Cadre' in *Encyclopedia Universalis*. Paris: Encyclopedia Universalis.

Braudel, F (1988) *Civilisation matérielle, économie et capitalisme, XVème-XVIIIème siècle* (3 volumes). Paris: Armand Colin.

Castel, R (2003) *L'insécurité sociale* (collection La république des idées). Paris: Seuil.

Castoriadis, C (1999) *L'institution imaginaire de la société* (collection Points – essays, No. 383). Paris: Seuil.

Darcourt-Lézat, Y (2002) Essai sur l'entreprise multiculturelle, *Quaderni*, 42 (Spring): 16–23.

Ferrandéry, J-L (1996) *Le point sur la mondialisation*. Paris: Presses Universitaires de France.

Mattelart, A (2008) 'Mondialisation' in *Encyclopedia universalis*. Paris: Encyclopedia Universalis.

Senarclens de, P (2002) *La mondialisation – Théories, enjeux et débats*. Paris: Armand Colin.

Vashistha, A and Vashistha, A (2006) *The Offshore Nation*. New York: McGrawHill.

Part I
General Policy and Strategy

1
The Paradoxical Dynamics of Globalisation

Eric Milliot

The phenomenon of the globalisation of markets is not a new one. For several hundred years, regular, cross-border exchanges of goods and knowledge have been organised between human groups (tribes, cities, communities).[1] To illustrate this we can look at the famous Silk Road, already being used by trade caravans in the second century BC. In contributing to the weaving of political and cultural links between remote groups, this route went beyond the mere scope of trade and the simple distribution of products. It is also noteworthy that, before 1914, the exchange of merchandise was facilitated by the freedom of people. Travel in Europe was generally not controlled (no passports, no work permits, no immigration policies).

The First World War put an end to this movement of opening-up and encouraged the adoption of protectionist measures. The results of this policy were so disastrous that after the Second World War, the allies decided to introduce an international plan of monetary stability (the Bretton Woods agreements, 1944) and one of free trade (General Agreement on Tariffs and Trade, 1947).[2] These efforts allowed the progressive resurgence of a cross-border economy.

The resulting decompartmentalisation of markets would lead one to suppose today that companies have never been so free to operate on a world-wide scale. In fact, since the middle of the twentieth century, the flow of cross-border freight traffic has been accelerating,[3] the number of industries affected by international trade has been increasing, and the importance of foreign operations carried out by companies has been growing constantly.

In combination with the emergence of the information society, it would seem that the actors' geographical, strategic and operational freedom is particularly strong. A more precise analysis of the operating conditions of businesses suggests that this should be put into perspective. The decompartmentalisation of markets undoubtedly broadens the field of industrial and/or commercial opportunities, but, at the same time, imposes numerous constraints on companies, limiting their autonomy and their independence.

In order to understand this paradox, this chapter first of all studies the dynamics that fuel the phenomenon of globalisation and, second, analyses the ambivalent nature of the driving forces of globalisation. Third, the industrial and geographical characteristics that redefine the field of action and the freedom of the actors are examined and, finally, the necessary compromises developed by companies to cope with the forces that are imposed upon them.

1   A twofold political–economic sphere of influence

As stated in the introduction, globalisation consists of a dual dynamic: the decompartmentalisation of markets and the interdependence of actors. These two symbiotic rationales generate a complex system of dualities which must be understood in order to appreciate the real degree of freedom that companies have.

1.1   The decompartmentalisation of markets

National markets are seeing their borders becoming more and more permeable to foreign economic activities because of globalisation. Concretely, tariff barriers (customs duties, compensatory taxes, anti-dumping duties), non-tariff barriers (standards, quotas, import licences), regulatory barriers (exchange controls, currency repatriation, local participation) and cultural barriers (traditional trade values, specific purchasing habits, particular conditions of use) are all becoming progressively blurred.

The phenomenon is becoming more marked with the multiplication of free trade areas, customs unions, common markets and economic unions. The number of regional trade agreements, notified to the General Agreements on Tariffs and Trade (1948–1994) or to the World Trade Organisation (WTO), has grown from 100 in 1990, to 421 in December 2008 (WTO, 2010). The virtually exponential increase of this type of agreement is the result of the very distinct commercial opening-up of countries which allows company managers to reconsider their fields of exploitation and to embark upon new markets.

1.2   The interdependence of actors

Thanks in particular to the decompartmentalisation of markets, globalisation emphasises the interdependence of actors (nations, companies, non-governmental organisations (NGOs)). More than ever, it suggests that the world should be analysed systemically so as to identify the complex interactions and interrelations of the international community members. This idea can be illustrated in an anecdotal manner by the chaos theory and its butterfly effect. According to the meteorologist Lorenz (1979), the flapping of a butterfly's wings in Brazil may ultimately set off a tornado in Texas. This idea of extreme dependence between elements enables the underlining of the impact of globalisation on the actors, whatever their size and geographical position. A very small Brazilian company specialising in cutting-edge technology may, in fact, due to one major innovation, put a multinational implanted in Texas into difficulty by rapidly rendering its key products obsolete.

1.3 A paradoxical link

The two forces just described complement and fuel each other. Their association engenders an energy that profoundly modifies the working and functioning methods of businesses. At the same time, a paradox is created by associating the idea of freedom (decompartmentalisation of markets) with that of loss of autonomy (unilateral, bilateral or multilateral dependence of the actors). Let us develop this contradictory rationale.

Since the First World War, companies have never been in reach of so many opportunities at the international level as they are now. The partial or total elimination of trade barriers today allows them to have an extremely vast and varied field of action. Along with this expansion, companies are tending to become very dependent on a heterogeneous group of organisations. Being unable to do everything and, indeed, to do everything well in a growing market that is becoming more and more competitive, they are called upon to specialise and to multiply partnerships which restrict their strategic and operational autonomy.

Globalisation thus offers a framework of functioning and growth in which contrary rationales are addressed. In embarking upon new markets, companies are seizing opportunities that force them to lay themselves open to specific risks (transfer of know-how, sharing of information, partial privatisations) and to depend on other structures (suppliers, intermediaries, competitors). The following explanations attempt to present this paradoxical sphere of influence in a more precise manner.

2 Ambivalent driving forces

In order to understand the phenomenon of the economic integration of countries, the forces leading up to its origins and development need to be studied. With this intention, our analysis is based on the work of Yip (1989, 2003) who identifies four groups of elements (linked to governments, markets, competitors and costs) so as to appreciate the functioning conditions of the global economy.

If the framework of reference proposed by Yip cannot be ignored, it can be completed with a fifth group of forces, linked to time. It also can be clarified by distinguishing between those factors which render the internationalisation of companies possible and those factors which render it obligatory (Table 1.1). In fact, commitment at the international level is not always an

Table 1.1   Ambivalent nature of driving forces

Drivers	Facilitating international action (examples)	Imposing international action (examples)
Linked to state powers	Denationalisation of state-owned companies	Public companies used to showcase technology
Linked to market	Relative standardisation of needs for certain goods and services	Global demands made by certain key clients
Linked to competition	Facilitated contracts with the best subcontractors to reinforce competitive advantage	Installation abroad to pre-empt development of competitors
Linked to costs	Reduction of transport and communication costs	Increased importance of fixed costs as opposed to variable costs
Linked to time	Distribution of information in real time	Shorter life cycle of products

Source: Adapted from Yip (1989, 2003).

option; it is sometimes a necessity. This is of a dual nature for the active forces listed.

2.1   Governmental drivers

The authorities contribute to the elimination of trade barriers by means of different measures: implementation of a free trade policy, adoption of international technical standards, relaxing of employment laws, passing of common trade regulations, signing of regional trade agreements.

They also facilitate international operations by privatising public companies. These decisions lift the restrictions on the international movement of capital and products, and offer the possibility of seizing new opportunities for expansion.

At the same time as barriers are eliminated, countries can oblige public companies to move into certain countries for political reasons or to showcase developed technology. Areva serves as an illustration of the volition of the French authorities. Although this group is capitalising on a vast field of action, its internationalisation is strongly encouraged by the state executive authority.

2.2   Market drivers

These materialise in the convergence of purchasing powers (in industrialised and newly industrialised countries), in the relative standardisation of lifestyles, the homogenisation of consumption requirements, the geocentric attitude of buyers, the development of international distribution channels and the transferability of commercial policies. These factors offer new working conditions which undeniably facilitate the globalisation of numerous industrial and commercial activities.

Over and above this field of possibilities, the global demand of certain client companies sometimes forces suppliers to become implicated in very specific countries. When Peugeot established itself in Wuhan in the People's Republic of China, it was in the best interests of its main equipment manufacturer, Valeo, to follow too. The question of setting-up was never really asked. Internationalisation, in this case, was absolutely necessary to the retaining of a key client.

2.3   Competitive drivers

To cope with their competitors, companies are increasingly called upon to refocus on their core business. They therefore have to outsource a good number of operations and sign contracts with the best subcontractors whatever their nationality and geographical location. Globalisation thus offers the possibility of incorporating strong complementary skills so as to develop or reinforce competitive advantages.

Symmetrically, the economic integration of countries gives a worldwide dimension to competitiveness. Companies are then obliged to act on a global level to prevent direct competitors from using a new geographical zone as a platform for growth. In the automotive industry, the competitive game illustrates the need for having a presence on several continents. This presence allows, among other things, the pre-empting of strategic implantation movements made by rival firms.

2.4   Cost drivers

The economies of scale and of scope, the learning effects, the drop in logistic costs (container ships, omnimodal transport), the cost differentials between countries, the unequal distribution of resources, monetary instability, the increasingly heavy burden of research and development, all call upon companies to internationalise and to concentrate their innovation efforts on a standardised product rather than on several products that have been adapted to local markets.

Simultaneously, the increasing size of fixed, or partially fixed, costs[4] obliges the actors to work on an enormous scale in order better to face up to crisis situations. In fact, when the cost structure is dominated by variable costs, a company can confront temporary difficulties by reducing its purchase of raw materials and of inputs. On the other hand, when the variable costs have already been greatly constricted and the fixed costs are in the majority (automation, computerisation), a company has only one solution to limit the effects of the crisis: to increase its sales in the foreign countries that are least affected by the crisis. Here again, internationalisation is no longer an option, but a certain obligation in order to split the risks and ensure the durability of a company.

2.5 Temporal drivers

The elements that make time into a catalyst for globalisation must be added to the first four groups of factors identified by Yip.

The reduction in travel time, the rapid evolution of technology, the virtually instantaneous circulation of information all mean that companies can practically manage their relocated operations in real time. Since distance is no longer associated with time (Cairncross, 1997), constraints linked to geographical distance are put into perspective. As a consequence, internationalisation is becoming easier to manage (videoconferences, electronic mails).

At the same time, management of delays is becoming a strategic consideration owing to the shortening of product life cycles. In order to absorb the costs of research and development quickly, companies very often are obliged to play the globalisation card. Take the example of the automotive sector. In the 1950s, a vehicle was designed to be sold over a period of ten years or so. Nowadays, a manufacturer tries to achieve a return on investment after about four years. Having spent 1,125 million euros on developing the 407, Peugeot knew that it was well-nigh impossible to recuperate this amount by selling the product on a few national markets. Over a relatively short period, Peugeot had to act on several continents.

These five groups of factors demonstrate that the markets' globalisation not only offers companies some options, but also specific functioning conditions. It is thus essential to understand this phenomenon well, so as to identify the key success factors, develop competitive advantages and measure the constraints that limit the decision-making freedom of business leaders.

3 Dictated industrial and geographical fields of action

The globalisation of product markets is only at an intermediate stage of development.[5] There are still very great disparities between nations concerning the price of comparable products, the costs of production and tax policies. If globalisation had really matured, these different variables would have an identical value worldwide. The disparities would then, for the most part, be justified by reasons of quality (Hirst and Thompson, 1996).

The process of globalisation comes up against different elements once more:

- National economies remain partially state-controlled (public companies, banks under local authority control).
- Countries continue to develop veiled protectionism (standards, subsidies).

- Companies' capital is generally held by investors from the country of origin.
- Some consumers give priority to the purchase of local products (economic patriotism, dietary customs).
- Different occurrences regularly expose the dangers related to globalisation (unemployment, crises).

In order to estimate the potential evolution of globalisation and its consequences on firms' development methods, the nature of international competition must be studied at the business and country levels.

3.1   A predetermined degree of industrial globalisation

Sectors are confronted with a particular level of opening-up of markets. This means that, depending on the activity, globalisation imposes itself on companies to one extent or another. Paradoxically, once more, the actors' strategic freedom is put into perspective by the international dynamics of the industry in which they are involved.

Using information collected from the World Bank, the United Nations Organisation and McKinsey & Company, Fraser and Oppenheim (1997) have drawn up a table that enables the assessment of the extent of globalisation reached by different industries for 1995.

Even though some industries have largely developed since then,[6] Fraser and Oppenheim's study allows an understanding of the necessary level of internationalisation for certain operations. Four groups of activities have been identified.

3.1.1   *Globalised activities*

The physical commodities (oil, ore, timber), the manufactured commodities (refinery products, aluminium, steel sections) and the scale-driven business goods and services (aeronautical engines, construction equipment, semiconductors) have already gone global and in 1995 represented 22.83 per cent of the gross world product value.

The companies involved in these activities possess a virtually predetermined operational spatial field. As a result, they have to work at a very great geographical scale except when, whenever it is possible, they opt for a niche marketing strategy.

3.1.2   *Activities going global quickly*

At the time the study was undertaken, the following businesses represented 15.36 per cent of worldwide production and were enjoying a growing globalisation:

- Labour skill or productivity-driven consumer goods (computers, televisions, cars).

- Brandable, largely deregulated consumer goods (non-alcoholic beverages, shoes, luxury goods).
- Professional business services (bank investment operations, legal services, consulting services).

In this context, it is clearly in companies' best interests to prepare for the escalation of international competition. This transitory phase generally obliges the actors to play the internal or external growth card (mergers, acquisitions) and also that of inter-company cooperation agreements (alliances, partnerships).

3.1.3   *Activities with low levels of globalisation*

In 1995 the following goods and services were beginning to open up to globalisation and represented 50 per cent of world production:

- Hard-to-brand globally, largely regulated consumer goods and services (food products, private individual financial services, television programmes).
- Local (unbranded) goods and services (building materials, education programmes, medical care).

The companies involved in the types of industries outlined above, are under less pressure to settle abroad. However, it is strongly advised that they seize the opportunities of cost reduction and of differentiation linked to international operations.

3.1.4   *Non-global activities*

Government services (public administration, national defence, justice) represented 11.81 per cent of world production in 1995 and are closed to market globalisation.

In theory, globalisation brings only a slight influence to bear on the functioning methods of entities implicated in these activities. Here the actors behave according to the logic and principles appropriate to the local context. However, this presentation needs to be put into perspective when a country embarks on a regional trade agreement with strong economic integration. The case of the European Union demonstrates clearly that, here too, supranational influences and regulations have distinct identifiable consequences for the different member states.

Fraser and Oppenheim's study demonstrates that the phenomenon of market emergence is developing in a sequential manner. Several decades will need to pass before a high level of economic integration in the vast majority of industries appears. According to Bryan and Fraser (1999), the share of worldwide production affected by a high level of globalisation should increase from 22.83 per cent in 1995 to more than 80 per cent in 2027.

Although this estimate has to be taken with a great deal of caution,[7] it would appear that companies from industries little affected by worldwide forces (packaged foods, household services, real estate transactions) will very shortly be concerned by competition which transcends a country's borders. There again, companies' strategic freedom is being reduced as they have to prepare to confront markets that are developing well beyond the commercial framework they know today.

3.2   An unexpected redefinition of national borders

For several decades, the globalisation of markets has essentially affected the Triad countries (the United States, Western Europe, Japan). The circle is widening from now on to integrate progressively three supplementary categories of actors:

- newly industrialised countries (Israel, Singapore, Taiwan);
- rapidly emerging markets (Brazil, China, India);
- former member countries of COMECON (Council for Mutual Economic Assistance) – repealed in 1991 (Hungary, Poland, the Czech Republic).

Although the phenomenon of globalisation affects the majority of countries nowadays, the notion of national trade borders is, however, still a topical one. This notion, under pressure from a contradictory dialectic, takes on a new dimension that must be identified.

3.2.1   *The enhanced prestige of identity roots*

In eliminating traditional tariff and non-tariff barriers, regional trade agreements are going beyond the political boundaries of countries. Paradoxically, this decompartmentalisation of markets is generating the rise to power of certain distinctive cultural identities. Individuals are (re)developing some traditions and claiming identity characteristics due to a fear of losing their identity to hybridisation. The resurgence of cultural boundaries is thus reinforced by countries' economic integration. Mongin and Bayart (in Beckouche, 2001) think that the internationalisation of trade reinforces indigenous values. Geschiere and Meyer (1999) even go as far as saying that globalisation provokes the production of cultural differences. A redefinition of borders would thus be founded on the refusal of syncretism and cultural integration. This prestige of origins in Europe is characterised by a revival of the vernacular languages, traditional local recipes and folk dancing. This paradox is a supplementary challenge for companies' development policies.

3.2.2 *The importance of cultural proximity*

The notion of geographical proximity is put into perspective by the notion of cultural proximity. In the era of the information society, companies are recording problems caused by this behavioural and emotional discrepancy.

The relocating of call centres to developing countries illustrates this phenomenon. If distance no longer poses a problem in terms of management (collaborative software, broadband internet connections), it is nevertheless a source of interpersonal difficulties with clients. For operations requiring a good knowledge of the business context and the adherence to certain values (understanding customers' expectations, a suitable definition of quality), the reversed relocating of service providers' work to the home country illustrates the need for identity references that are understood and shared.

These few elements of reflection, concerning the evolution of the industrial and geographical frameworks of companies trading internationally, convey the necessary adaptation of managerial rationales. Let us now look at the nature of the answers to the challenges of economies' supranational integration.

4 An increased strategic and operational dependence

Globalisation conveys new rules of functioning which are, at times, contradictory. It offers a geographically enlarged field of transaction which, in an unexpected manner, gives birth to new borders. At the same time, it occasionally imposes actions requiring a lot of resources that limit the independence of actors.

To understand the impacts of these paradoxes, the following explanations deal with the dual managerial rationales fuelled by globalisation and with the contractual forms enabling related specific challenges to be answered.

4.1 A dynamic source of dualities

The parallel movements of integration of markets and of interdependence of actors give rise to a business context characterised by numerous paradoxes. Consider the following different contradictions that companies must learn to combine:

- Development of a strategic reflection at the level of several countries (for more synergies, more profitability) and application of the resulting policy at the level of a particular market (for more dynamism, more understanding of the prospects).
- Association of the principles of standardisation (to benefit from scale economies, to facilitate the control of operations) and of adaptation (to benefit from legitimacy in prospects' eyes, to give value to skills within subsidiaries).

- The need to establish actions undertaken on global resources (financial flows, databases) and local resources (human skills, marketing techniques).[8]

Ruigrok and Van Tulder's (1995) idea of 'glocalisation' illustrates this ambivalent paradox. Rosenau (2003) talks about the 'distant proximities' that characterise what he calls 'fragmegration'. This neologism underlines the original interweaving of the local forces of 'fragmentation' and the global ones of 'integration'.

Whatever terms are used, these different dualities convey the phenomenon of globalisation as a complex group of varied dynamics (mobility of production factors, economic integration of nations, increased interdependence of activities).

Before concluding this point, it must be noted that this group has evolved over time. For O'Rourke and Williamson (1999), there are two waves of globalisation characterised by particular rationales of functioning. The first wave, which they place between 1870 and 1914, was based on the mobility of factors and on international trade;[9] the second, beginning at the end of the Second World War, is marked, over and above market forces, by the strong organisational coordination between different types of actors (nation states, international organisations, companies and NGOs).

To better understand the latter dynamic, it is necessary to study its impacts on the strategic and operational choices of business leaders.

4.2 A reticular response

Companies have developed certain practices in order to deal with the supranational integration of economies. One of these consists of multiplying cooperation agreements with legally independent entities. Bamford and Ernst (2002) point out, moreover, that most large-sized firms, which, in general, are more likely to have dealings internationally, are nowadays involved in more than 30 alliances.[10]

This cooperation strategy, underlining as it does the previously identified idea of dependence between companies, is of a varied nature. One typology (Milliot, 1999) enables the estimation of the resulting degree of strategic and operational freedom (Figure 1.1). This typology is based on two axes.

i. The first axis presents the possible links between the partners' fields of activity. A link is proved to be true when the operations carried out by the collaborating companies are similar or complementary.
ii. The second axis shows the links between the market segments targeted by the different actors. A link is established when companies are interested in the same group of customers.

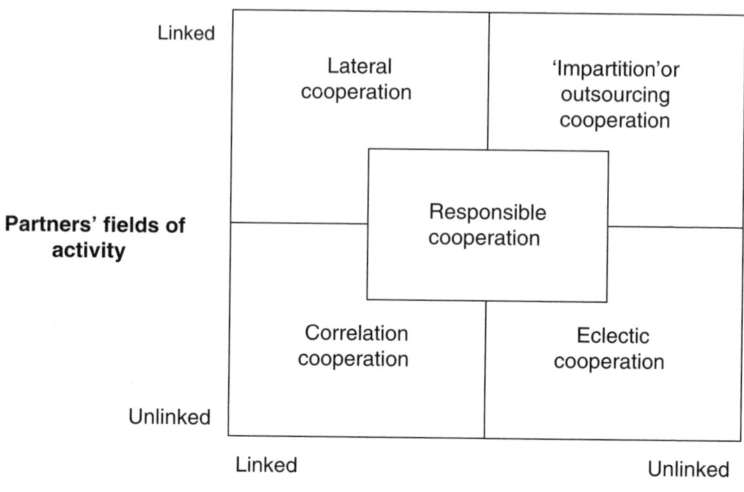

Figure 1.1   Typology of interorganisational cooperation
Source: Adapted from Milliot (1999).

The crossing of these axes allows five types of inter-company cooperation especially adapted to international operations.

4.2.1   *Lateral cooperation*

As its position on the matrix indicates, this form of connection concerns partners who have interrelated fields of activity and market segments.[11] In concrete terms, it is about alliances that have been signed between direct and indirect competitors.

The factory common to the Toyota and PSA Peugeot Citroen groups illustrates this type of agreement. This production unit, which was established in the Czech Republic and opened in 2005, aims at confronting growing competitive pressures in the small urban car segment.

The two partners are well known for their long tradition of independence which makes their sharing of the industrial plant even more surprising. Pressures of globalisation have, however, pushed them to change their strategies and to accept the loss of part of their operational autonomy. For example, the French constructor has had to bow to its Japanese partner's production rules.

4.2.2   *'Impartition'[12] or outsourcing cooperation*

This partnership concerns companies having a related field of activity, but not, in theory, targeting the same markets. Principally, it allows the association of firms having complementary competences and resources on the vertical plane.

The subcontract agreements signed between major groups and their principal suppliers can be referred to as an illustration of this cooperation. For example, Bell Canada signed a contract with Manuvie for a network management department to be completely outsourced by using internet protocol.

This is an asymmetrical form of cooperation as the power of negotiation of one of the partners is generally superior to that of the other partner. The strategic freedom of the relatively dependent partner is thus reduced. This company is subject to the user requirement specifications, to the conditions of payment and to the delivery rhythms imposed bythe supplier or the customer.

4.2.3   Correlation cooperation

This connection rationale concerns companies that are targeting the same market segment, but which are in different lines of business. Here the main objective is to improve the selection of products that are offered to the prospects.

Philips, for example, sells an electric toothbrush with Procter & Gamble toothpaste to certain markets. This co-branding enables a more precise commercial response in a mature market.

In general, the signatories of the agreement are sure of strategic and operational autonomy thanks to the actors' specific skills and assets. However, co-branding is not without dangers. In associating their images, one partner may suffer from the industrial or marketing malfunction of the other.

4.2.4   Eclectic cooperation

This agreement is somewhat atypical as it brings together companies that have no links in terms of activity or market. It is often used to ensure a positive transfer of image and/or competence between the signatories to the agreement.

In this particular context, the partners are so complementary that, in principle, they retain great freedom of action. This freedom is nevertheless reduced in combined operations to be run collectively. The premature end of the cooperation may be brought about in the event of a profound disagreement. This is exactly what happened between Mercedes and Swatch when they designed and built the Smart car. Strategic, marketing and cultural differences led the two companies to resume their independence. Nowadays, only the German Daimler group (Mercedes) is in control of the company which manufactures small urban cars.

4.2.5   *Responsible cooperation*

This final type of cooperation is of a transverse nature. It can be superimposed over the four connections we have just looked at. Its distinctive feature is that it uses and/or defends causes such as the protection of the environment, the protection of minority rights and so on.

In this context, a company will sometimes carry out a responsible action by working with a respected non-governmental organisation. This type of connection reduces the independence of the guaranteed multinational. In order that the partnership can be possible, the multinational must comply with the precise and sometimes restrictive user requirement specifications it is subjected to.

An illustration of this type of agreement is the collaboration between Pierre and Vacances and the World Wide Fund for Nature (WWF). The French holiday specialist has been committed to improving its environmental performance and to increasing its employees' and clients' awareness of ecological issues since 2005. Although the group is motivated by this approach, it has to be accountable and show itself to be worthy of the support of WWF.

These different logics of cooperation, which can complement and hinge on each other, are a partial answer to the challenges of globalisation (Milliot, 1998). In particular, they enable a better understanding of the environment, the development of synergies, the sharing of certain risks and the reduction of unitary costs. Sometimes they also allow the critical mass to be reached and to reinforce the competitive position of the agreement signatories. At the same time, they bring about a loss of independence and autonomy which may constrict the flexibility and reactivity of the committed companies.

5   Conclusion

Globalisation offers companies numerous opportunities (extending the markets, transfer of new know-how, lowest possible supply costs). These various opportunities, which are linked to the ease of movement of factors and products, imply that companies have never before had such strategic and operational freedom. Although not inaccurate, this needs to be seen relatively, since globalisation calls upon its actors to submit to its dynamics by imposing certain methods of functioning.

If companies' freedom of movement and action is confirmed, the strategic and operational constraints that are brought into existence with the integration of economies are profound (the search for external synergies, the need to acquire critical mass, the sharing of know-how). By redefining the domain of work and that of the management methods of companies, this movement puts the idea of managerial autonomy into perspective. In order to improve efficiency at the local and global scale, to face up to national and international competition and to meet their prospects' ethno-centred and geocentred expectations, firms are progressively called upon to get organised in a series of complex agreements. This process gives rise to a paradoxical argument: the progressive elimination of the trade borders of countries is bringing about the progressive elimination of the physical and legal boundaries of companies.

Notes

1. The concept of *nation* is a relatively recent one. It appeared at the end of the sixteenth century in the West, but did not adopt an essential dimension until the beginning of the French Revolution (Zarka, 2007).
2. Some authors talk of two globalisations (O'Rourke and Williamson, 1999; Schularick, 2006). The first runs from 1870 to 1913; the second from 1950 to the present time.
3. In 2004, 28 per cent of the gross world product (GWP) was affected by international trade, as opposed to 8 per cent in 1950 (Adda, 2006).
4. For example, these costs represent about two-thirds of Saint-Gobain's total expenditure.
5. Foreign Policy, in collaboration with AT Kearney, calculates a globalisation index in order to estimate a country's degree of integration (www.foreignpolicy.com).
6. At the time of publication, McKinsey & Company has not yet brought this table up to date. It is noteworthy that businesses that were considered as being relatively little affected by countries' economic integration are now experiencing a growing internationalisation; for example, financial services, higher education programmes, military operations.
7. Since the publication of these works, numerous events have occurred that have got in the way of the development of globalisation: a temporary worldwide trade reversal after 11 September 2001, blocking of the WTO negotiations (Doha round), concern by a growing number of prospects to revert to more traditional products.
8. According to Boccara (2005) territorial roots of industrial activities enable resources usable at the international level to be obtained. These new global resources then help the reinforcement of operations carried out locally. This systemic approach would explain, for example, why the intragroup trade in big American companies has been reaching a plateau for several years.
9. This phase illustrates the famous Heckscher-Ohlin-Samuelson model (HOS).
10. Ernst (2002) makes clear that the number of alliances has increased by more than 20 per cent per year during the last two decades.
11. This form of connection refers to the concept of 'coopetition' which was developed by Brandenburger and Nalebuff (1996).
12. The term 'impartition' is used in the sense coined by Barreyre (1968). It consists of a vertical lasting cooperation founded on the principles of trust and sharing.

References

Adda, J. (2006) *La mondialisation de l'économie: Genèse et problèmes.* (7th ed.) Paris: La Découverte.

Bamford, J. and Ernst, D. (2002) Managing an alliance portfolio. *The McKinsey Quarterly*, 3: 29–39.

Barreyre, P.Y. (1968) *L'impartition. Politique pour une entreprise compétitive.* Paris: Hachette.

Beckouche, P. (2001) *Le royaume des frères. Aux sources de l'Etat-nation.* Paris: Grasset & Fasquelle.

Boccara, F. (2005) A la recherche de la firme globale : localisation industrielle et globalisation financière des multinationales. *L'industrie en France et la mondialisation.* Paris: Ministère de l'Economie, des Finances et de l'Industrie.

Brandenburger, A. and Nalebuff, B. (1996) *Co-opetition.* Welwyn Garden City: Doubleday.

Bryan, L. and Fraser, J. (1999) *Race for the World.* Boston: Harvard Business School Press.

Cairncross, F. (1997) *The Death of Distance: How the Communications Revolution Will Change Our Lives.* Boston: Harvard Business School Press.

Ernst, D. (2002) Give alliances their due. *The McKinsey Quarterly*, 3: 4–5.

Fraser, J. and Oppenheim, J. (1997) What's new about globalization? *The McKinsey Quarterly*, 2: 168–79.

Geschiere, P. and Meyer, B. (eds) (1999) *Dialectics of Flow and Closure.* Oxford: Blackwell.

Hirst, P. and Thompson, G. (1996) *Globalisation in Question.* Oxford: Blackwell.

Lorenz, E. (1979) 'Predictability: does the flap of a butterfly's wings in Brazil set off a tornado in Texas?' (Address to the annual meeting of the American Association for the Advancement of Science, 29 December.)

Milliot, E. (1998) *Le marketing symbiotique.* Paris: L'Harmattan.

——— (1999) Les modes de fonctionnement de l'entreprise informationnelle. *Revue Française de Gestion*, 125 (September/October): 5–18.

O'Rourke, K. and Williamson, J. (1999) *Globalization and History: the Evolution of a Nineteenth-Century Atlantic Economy.* Cambridge, Mass.: MIT Press.

Rosenau, J. (2003) *Distant Proximities: Dynamics beyond Globalization.* Princeton: Princeton University Press.

Ruigrok, W. and Van Tulder, R. (1995) *The Logic of International Restructuring.* London: Routledge.

Schularick, M. (2006) A tale of two globalizations: capital flows from rich to poor in two eras of global finance. *International Journal of Finance and Economics*, 11:339–54.

World Trade Organisation (WTO) (2010) *Regional Trade Agreements.* www.wto.org.

Yip, G. (1989) Global strategy . . . in a world of nations? *Sloan Management Review*, Fall: 29–41.

——— (2003) *Total Global Strategy.* (2nd ed.) Englewood Cliffs: Prentice Hall.

Zarka, Y.C. (2007) Nationalité et citoyenneté. *Cités*, 29 (1): 3–5.

2
Local Authorities and Foreign Companies: The Paradoxical Issue of FDI Towards Fast-Growing Economies

Jean-Paul Lemaire

The insertion, accelerated over the last two decades, of the emerging economies, and particularly the fast-growing economies (more than 5 per cent growth per year), into both the flow of trade and international investments,[1] underlines the growing involvement of these countries in globalisation. This, however, evokes paradoxical aspects regarding the attitude of both the authorities of host countries, in their involvement with foreign investors, and of the investors themselves.

For local authorities, the desire to attract investment flows leans in favour of those deploying policies to upgrade the level of infrastructure, and adjusting regulatory frameworks is not without restriction. If the primary purpose of these policies is to maximise the expected benefits in terms of inflow of financial resources, job creation, technology transfer and upgrading of local managerial practices, they could bring nothing less than tangible limits susceptible to the contrary which may upset, or even discourage, foreign investors. These policies present paradoxes. On the one hand, there is the will to protect local actors from stiff competition from the outside, which could lead to their exclusion from certain sectors with high-growth potential, by depriving them of the possibility of their own future opportunities in the foreign markets. On the other hand, there is the willingness of the local authorities to preserve tight control of strategic sectors, for example public utilities, banking, natural resources, distribution, which could, in the event of excessive control of foreign players, jeopardise the direction of the economy and even national sovereignty.

For foreign direct investors eager to commit the necessary resources, these newly opened opportunities also entail higher risks than those faced in other areas. The size and potential of many of them, and the natural resources, both physical and human, that are available, often at a very attractive cost, are incentives to expand with a view to winning market shares ('horizontal-isation'), or to optimising their international value chain ('verticalisation'). These investors are nevertheless concerned, on the one hand, about minimising their exposure by limiting the assets, both tangible and intangible, potentially subject locally to structural risks as well as cyclical, lowering exit barriers; in other words, costs and losses they have to bear in the event of withdrawal. On the other hand, their concern is having the ability to benefit from immediate opportunities that arise, or to respond most effectively to new constraints likely to appear, while retaining, in an increasingly dynamic context, the highest level of flexibility.

This double problem for both local authorities and foreign direct investors did not always arise in identical contexts from an emerging economy to another. The problem may, in fact, be seen in the context of a 'structured opening', such as is demanded by the long process of accession to an international or regional organisation, that will lead to an intensification of trade flows and international investments. It can also be raised, more brutally, by the occurrence of 'conjunctional shocks', usually of an economic nature, a result of difficulties in controlling the effects of very strong growth. Therefore it is no longer insertion into, but reintegration of the economic space concerned in the flow of trade and international investments.

For this reason, and by way of illustration, two representative cases can be explored, one of each of the two contexts: namely, Vietnam's accession to the World Trade Organisation (WTO), and the gradual reopening of Argentina after the crisis of December 2001.[2] The process of these two fast-growing economies can be analysed in parallel (Figure 2.1).

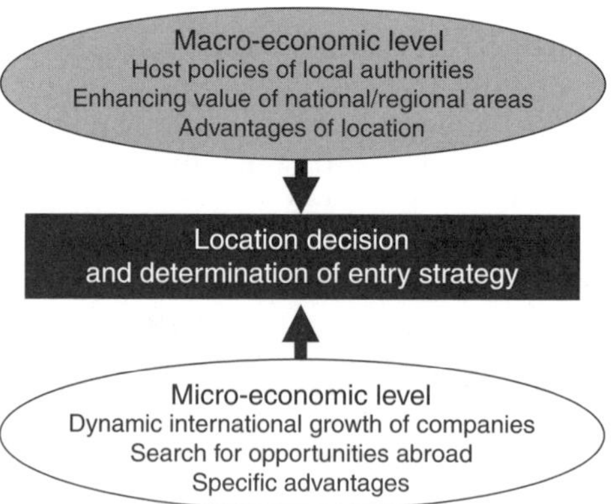

Figure 2.1   Location incentives
Source: Based on Dunning's OLI (Ownership, Location, Internalisation) theory (1988)

The factors to be considered should be taken into account in a structured manner:

- starting from the external pressures of various kinds which are applied at the macroeconomic, supranational or national level, on every economic area in question;
- measuring consecutive impact of these pressures on the sectors, in particular those most likely to attract foreign direct investors;
- determining the often-paradoxical options faced by both local authorities and foreign enterprises.

1 The paradoxes facing the stakeholders of foreign direct investment

Moving beyond the traditional approaches to international specialisation, the development of foreign investment in fast-growing economies requires more specific approaches that focus on the new redistribution of production at the global level (Lemaire, 2003).

The field of international business, which is concerned with the interaction between enterprises and economic areas (Ricart et al., 2004), relates to the search for symmetric competitive advantages which are relevant to activities, resources and knowledge.[3]

For the company, ownership and development abroad of a number of its activities (strategic business units) is the key to benefiting from the resources (financial, technical, managerial), enabling them to be mobilised and allocated, making the best use of the know-how (technological, marketing, organisational) available to the organisation, and which it should renew and expand. For the economic areas, endowment of both tangible elements (space, natural resources, quality and cost of labour) and intangible ones (political stability, market maturity, and the willingness and ability of the economic actors to open up) is crucial in order to encourage the development of specific activities initiated by foreign investors.

However, more paradoxical attitudes of both local authorities and foreign companies would appear to be related to their belonging to the most widely differentiated zones; i.e. mature/industrialised in one instance, emerging/fast growing in others.

The literature understood in the broadest sense, from international economy to international management, illustrates a diversity of approaches which already permits the identification of a series of paradoxes. These are related to the opening up of both economic areas and foreign direct investment, seen from the perspective of the local authorities as well as the companies. The approaches reveal, in addition, a significant and recent development of the incorporation of the geoeconomic context of rapid growth that enables to change the traditional approaches of international investment which, so far, does not differentiate much between the target zones, industrialised or emerging, for foreign direct investments (FDI).

1.1   The paradoxical aspects of current thinking regarding FDI

The theoretical basis of this consideration leading to the environmental analysis for decision-making and drawing the path of convergence between foreign direct investors and local authorities can be driven, on the one hand, by the school of thought focused on the opening of economic zones and, on the other, by the current focus on the dynamics of the internationalisation of businesses (Lemaire, 2003).

1.1.1   *The opening of economic zones*

The focus on the opening of economic zones can be distinguished by

- either, the approaches that tend to explain or appreciate the attractiveness of economic areas, relying more on objective factors, such as those which explain international specialisation,[4] than on more intangible contextual factors, such as those used by Porter (1991) (for example, domestic rivalry, domestic demand conditions);[5]
- or, those who legitimise new forms of protectionism (beyond List's arguments [1851]), in particular to preserve the 'infant' industries (which could apply now to 'declining' industries, especially in mature economies). Krugman (1991), among others, highlights the development of 'strategic trade policies'.[6]

1.1.2   *The dynamics of the internationalisation of businesses*

The focus on corporate internationalisation dynamics can be distinguished by

- the approaches that rely, as précised by Dunning (1988), on the search for new development potential outside expanding companies' mature area of origin and/or for the production factors (natural resources, knowledge, skills and so on) they are lacking (Arnold and Quelch, 1998);
- the approaches following Prahalad and Doz (1987) or Kogut (1995a and b), optimising the deployment of corporate value chain, taking into account the evolution of the international environment.

These approaches lead to arbitrating between various possible locations,[7] as well as between various entry strategies, referring to such external issues as the level of risk, as well as to internal corporate issues, like cultural proximity[8] and language.

1.2 The paradoxes of geoeconomic contexts of FDI development

These different contributions highlight the paradoxes in the attitudes of local authorities and those foreign companies which are likely to apply to both industrialised areas and emerging areas. Nevertheless, a number of factors are included, where the result can be measured through indicators published by various specialised agencies[9] assessing the risk of each country. These indicators include a wide variety of criteria which, *inter alia*, emphasise that the delay in growth of emerging countries, even fast-growing ones, is noted compared with the industrialised countries; they also emphasise the elements of attraction they present for investors. The differences between the two types of areas, in terms of the intensity and nature of risks as the degree of attractiveness, can be significant, making the decision of implantation particularly difficult and, beyond that, the choice of a mode of presence and its development in the emerging areas of rapid growth also difficult.

Furthermore, the characteristics of these emerging areas are beginning to be identified in finer detail (London and Hart, 2004) in terms of the interest they generate on the part of companies from industrialised areas. They are ceasing to be seen as areas of simple mismatch of maturity, thus the gap would be reduced naturally by adopting Western-style patterns of development. However, taking into account the specifics of their environment (Meyer, 2004), in other words the political realities, local regulations, economic, social and technological issues suggesting more suitable approaches (for example, the 'bottom of the Pyramid'[10]), has recently struck many Western companies looking to exploit the considerable potential offered especially in the fast-growing economies.

Finally, the capacity and speed of change in the environment of emerging countries constitute another important factor for the evaluation of and comparison between different localities by business decision-makers. For them, there is an increase in the attractiveness of a country when its local authorities are determined to accelerate the development and improvement of the local structures, i.e. the infrastructure, legal and regulatory framework, financial institutions and practices of economic agents, in order to support and sustain growth by promoting openness. However, the converse is true when the progress made by a country during earlier periods declines because of the strength of past practices and setbacks caused by political instability or economics; the occurrence of crises, the consequences of imbalances involved with accelerated growth which are, in most cases, the cause of such reversals, are then called into question.

It is therefore necessary to take into account the approach of each foreign direct investment, both for the local authorities and for the plans of the foreign companies, to consider or expand their settlements, an approach that combines all the elements conducive to achieving the most positive outcome for both parties involved. This would entail

- the authorities welcoming foreign investment by providing the licence or permit for implantation, and giving favourable and reassuring conditions, in the short, medium and long term, without, however, abandoning the collective priorities and the benefits expected from the local economic actors;
- the business venture capitalist, after properly defining the project in order to reconcile both its own interests and that of the host country, mobilising sufficient resources in this regard, within the most appropriate legal and economic framework.

2   The paths of convergence: from the environmental analysis to the decision of FDI location: the implementation of the PREST model nationally

Reconciling the interests and contradictory expectations of the two types of stakeholders leads to highlighting the determinants of their respective positions in order to achieve the projected investment in a way that is acceptable to both parties, developing a 'funnel' approach, following the logic of the PREST model[11] at three successive levels.

i. *The macroeconomic level*, supranational or national, at which the 'external pressures', structural or cyclical, are identified pertinent to both the local authorities and the foreign investors; pressures that stimulate and also those that hinder, delay or suspend the opening of the area in question, thereby affecting the achievement and sustainability of FDI.
ii. *The meso-economic level*, multisectoral or sectoral, at which the impact of these pressures on the different sectors is evaluated, which will be more or less affected, positively or negatively, according to their respective characteristics; this evaluation is in order to determine what sectoral or multisectoral 'challenges' the respective stakeholders will have to tackle.
iii. *The micro-level* of the actors, local authorities on the one hand and foreign companies engaged in a process of investment on the other, at which the key sectors best suited to host FDI are selected; these are the sectors with the most appropriate entry modes, in determining the strategic 'levers' most likely both to facilitate the deployment and to maximise the benefit of the various stakeholders involved.

The successive stages of this process in the two selected economic areas are discussed in parallel (Lemaire and Bui, 2008; Lemaire and Lopez, 2008).

i. Vietnam, as a 'transition economy', heir to a centralised and autarchic system,[12] is envisaged in the perspective of its entry to the Word Trade Organisation which was concluded in January 2007.[13]

ii. Argentina, as an example of a liberal country, involved in a process of reintegration into the international trade and investment flows after the harsh crisis of December 2001 due to the accumulation of fiscal and external deficits.[14]

2.1   The identification of 'external pressures' to be taken into account by relevant stakeholders

From the perspective of the development of foreign investment in a specific economic area, analysis of the environment takes into account a number of factors regarding the national or supranational area. These factors are considered as having a possible direct or indirect influence on the attitude of both local authorities and that of foreign firms seeking to expand their direct investments. These 'external pressures' can be either favourable or unfavourable with respect to the development of foreign direct investment, in the eyes of local authorities and/or the eyes of corporate decision-makers. Depending on the situation, they may also include a cyclical or structural element determining the effects more or less rapidly, and more or less sustainably, in certain sectors. Finally, while both local authorities and foreign companies may have similar perceptions of these pressures, whether positive or negative, they may view the pressures differently; in other words, positively by some, negatively by others.

For fast-growing economies, the same kinds of pressures will be reflected. However, they will have to be evaluated as specifically from one country to another, as from one period to another. They can thus provide a useful point of reference for the construction of a monitoring system adaptable for use in significantly different contexts, such as Vietnam and Argentina, on condition, of course, that they are periodically reviewed and updated, to reflect the rapid transformations in the national and international environments.

2.1.1   The political and regulatory pressures

The political and regulatory pressures constitute, particularly in these two emerging zones of high growth, the most decisive elements of the environment for the direction of foreign investment flows.

In the case of Vietnam, these are the structural pressures favourable to its opening up, thereby increasing the attractiveness of the country for foreign investors, of which there are many. These pressures included the plan for opening up, the progressive upgrading of the legal and regulatory frameworks, the fight against corruption, and the improvement of public infrastructure, at the initiative of the public authorities. Without them the resumption of foreign investment, after initial progress in a remarkably short time, would not have been possible.[15] However, trade unions, representatives of the centralised economy, and even business leaders of the new private sector expressed some concern about the country's capacity to face foreign competition (Lemaire and Bui, 2008).

In the case of Argentina, throughout the 1990s seen as the 'star pupil' of the IMF and the World Bank (Bertone et al., 2003),[16] political willingness regarding its opening up and the liberal foundations of the political and economic systems were not questioned because of initial concern about the country's inability to rebuild a local economy in full recession, where the accumulated structural deficits could no longer justify parity along with many foreign investors (Rolland et al.: 203).[17] *This means that you differenciate figure as the previous illustration and the tables like the following ones. Why not?* (Table 2.1)

Table 2.1   PREST: the political-regulatory pressures

Structural pressures affecting (+/−) the opening of the location under consideration	**Cyclical pressures affecting (+/−) the opening of the location under consideration**
• National will and capacity to fit into a large, regional (e.g. ASEAN, Mercosur), supraregional or global group (WTO). • Permanence of practices distorts free competition (e.g. corruption, systematic bias in favour of local actors). • Nature of political relations and economic links with neighbouring countries, partnering countries and multi-governmental organisations.	• Stability of the political system as a team in power, continuity of economic policies initiated. • Behaviour of political leaders (opportunism shown vis-à-vis foreign companies). • Sensitivity to political tensions (cross-border, terrorism) and/or economically from the region or beyond.
Structural pressures affecting (+/−) the framework of economic and legal infrastructure	**Cyclical pressures affecting (+/−) the framework of economic and legal infrastructure**
• Measures of deregulation or re-regulation designed to adapt the framework within which FDI is likely to develop. • Measures of privatisation and restructuring of the public sector and/or previously nationalised industries. • Adjustment policies of the major infrastructure sectors (transport, financial services, distribution, etc.).	• Occurrence of natural disasters and climate change. • Changes in the creditworthiness of the country vis-à-vis the international community and debt capacity / placement. • Resistance from pressure groups hostile to the projected development, strikes and social movements, interethnic tensions, xenophobic outbreaks.

Source: Lemaire (see note 11).

Despite Argentina's strong recovery, recorded since 2003, both the disadvantage of governmental instability, which has been long extended, and the return to populist behaviour on the part of the country's leaders, have delayed the return to confidence vis-à-vis foreign companies, some of which had served as scapegoats for the country's mismanagement.[18]

2.1.2 *The economic and social pressures*

In both Vietnam and Argentina, the economic and social pressures figure equally prominently among the determinants of the attitudes of both the local authorities and the companies envisaging developing their investments locally.

Vietnam's acceleration of growth was determined within just a few years by a significant increase in demand, coupled with rapid social changes. However, these were unevenly distributed between urban and rural areas, showing new expectations on the part of local consumers. At the same time, local supply could boast about cost competitiveness, in spite of low levels of training and a poor command of management techniques, the infrastructure deficit being still sensitive and the lengthy process of the privatisation of state enterprises. All these elements in the process of rapid improvement, however, could be combined with the advantage of the change in exportation related to the dollarisation of the economy (Schwartz, 2005) and the climate of security and social stability, generally higher than that of its main neighbours.

With respect to Argentina, it was necessary to restore confidence in a disorganised economy (Tresca, 2004) that had lost much of its productive structures before the crisis of December 2001, particularly in industry, considered inefficient compared with imported products. The use of the advantages of foreign exchange resulting from the depreciation of the peso has not provided a complete clean-up of the situation, especially as world market prices, particularly for agro-food products, are significantly more attractive than domestic market prices. In a context of social instability, the local producers' preference has created a shortage of domestic sourcing and generated some inflationary pressures. Taxes on exports decided by the government have not successfully improved this situation and, more generally, not permitted a fairer distribution of the products of the recovery (Table 2.2).

2.1.3 *The technological pressures*

These probably constitute the category of environmental factors that is the least sensitive to economic cycles, in contrast to the other two types do pressures, even though here, too, the changes occur at quite a rapid pace.

What characterises Vietnam above all, is the considerable need for transfer of technology in all fields, not only technically, but also managerially and organisationally. The shift from a planned economic system, centralised

Table 2.2   PREST: the economic and social pressures

Structural pressures affecting (+/−) supply and demand in a quantitative way	Cyclical pressures affecting (+/−) supply and demand in a quantitative way
• Growing population stimulating local demand and constituting a reservoir of cost-effective labour. • Rising purchasing power, rapid development of the middle class and reduction of the population living below the poverty line. • Increased availability and accessibility of resources from the soil and subsoil, existence of large spaces available for activities. • Sensibility to currency fluctuations and changes in world prices of raw materials and commodities.	• 'Bottlenecks' in some sectors of production and inflationary pressures. • A heightened sensitivity to the crises affecting neighbouring or distant countries, having established relations of exchange with those countries. • Interruption of transfers between the country and abroad as a result of a sharp depreciation of the currency. • Abrupt withdrawal of the country's foreign liquid assets and interruption of foreign financing for the benefit of local banks.

Structural pressures affecting (+/−) supply and demand in a qualitative way	Cyclical pressures affecting (+/−) supply and demand in a quantitative way
• Changes in consumption patterns, higher levels of local and foreign consumer demand. • Higher sensitivity to respect for the environment and ethical production conditions. • Increase in education level and development of competencies among local staff.	• Influence of patterns and versatility of consumer tastes, preference for foreign products and services. • Loss of confidence by foreign partners in the country's economy resulting from impromptu economic or political events (e.g. bursting of the bubble of speculative real estate).

Source: Lemaire (see note 11).

and, more importantly, widely autarchic, to a liberal and open system, emphasised the deficiencies in the infrastructure, such as production structures (and not only at the institutional level: see section 2.1.1), and the consequent need to upgrade them. The capacity of the country to integrate into the international supply chain is dependent on this upgrading, and this integration is necessary for the development of its flow of imports and exports, and the development of investments to be realised from the perspective of both horizontalisation and verticalisation. The development of information systems is, undoubtedly, an accelerator to learning, but it

Table 2.3   PREST: the technological pressures

Pressures affecting (+/−) the dissemination of technology	**Pressures affecting (+/−) the upgrading of technology**
• The existence of local competencies developed in a functioning educational system (or benefiting from effective external support), in terms of both production techniques and management and organisation. • Access to and ability to benefit from the development of distribution systems (e.g. broadband internet) and the intensification of information flows (existence of capacity for treatment). • The ability to assimilate technology originating from exterior sources, to adapt and/or transform technology in light of the constraints of their local or regional implementation. • The presence or potential of the development of resources and structures of local R&D related to international research networks.	• The ability to assimilate and to achieve international standards of quality, environment and safety (see ISO standards). • The ability to achieve compliance for local products and services with the most demanding certification systems (US and EU). • Taking into account the infrastructure level (roads, telecommunications, energy supply, in water, port and airport facilities) of the new production constraints and international logistics (control of the supply chain, just-in-time, traceability).

Source: Lemaire (see note 11).

reaches only a small fraction of the population and productive entities, mostly in the cities, making the differences in terms of level of education especially sensitive. Moreover, despite factories proudly displaying their ISO certification on their walls, compliance with the standards and the ability to certify their products and services are still very limited. Finally, as in many other Asian countries, industrial and intellectual property remains very little respected (Table 2.3).

Argentina, however, is among the world leaders in the field of education, with an exceptional percentage of literacy, and displays an impressive level of higher education proportionate to its total population.

Nevertheless, it lost control of a number of industrial sectors where the country could have achieved better results, as a result of the relatively small size of its domestic market, of a certain lack of entrepreneurial spirit, as well as of the presence of world leaders in the sectors where it could ambition to perform. But Argentina's ability to acquire and master technology-based activities is most promising; it has already begun this, for instance in the field of dematerialised distant services, notably engineering. The identification of all these pressures led local authorities as well as foreign firms to better appreciate the main challenges of assessment in the context of an intensification of investment flows. Their respective analyses offers the following, largely converging, conclusions:

- for the local authorities, the challenges are first, to better exploit and to upgrade local production factors; second, to maximise the country's competitive advantages; and finally, to increase the country's attractiveness on a general level;
- for the companies, the challenge is to take full advantage of these local assets, in order to improve their overall industrial, commercial and financial performances (Figure 2.2).

2.2   The resulting challenges to be raised by local authorities and foreign firms in the perspective of intensified FDI

Taking into account the different categories of external pressures, these three challenges are based on a logic that impacts on local authorities, as well as on foreign firms:

- The challenge of adaptation means adjusting and swiftly developing the local offer. Emerging countries that have companies settling in them, must follow and accompany the pace of both domestic and international environment changes.
- The challenge of redeployment invites both categories of actors to permanently reconsider their activities, as well as favourable geographical opportunities. They must take advantage simultaneously of the improvement in production factors and of new opportunities offered both domestically and abroad.
- The challenge of competition encourages both parties to find convenient development processes in order to better face both local and international competition.

2.2.1   *The challenge of adaptation*

The challenge of adaptation depends initially on the supply of the stakeholders of both parties. With regard to the local authorities, the most important adjustment is the upgrading of the infrastructure. This includes the politico-regulatory elements, the public utilities and education, in an environment that appears increasingly attractive and favourable to foreign investors. With regard to foreign companies, this means adapting to the local conditions of production and to the needs and expectations of both domestic and international demand, and locally produced services.

In relation to the respective context of each of the two economic areas identified, the challenge of adaptation facing the local authorities would

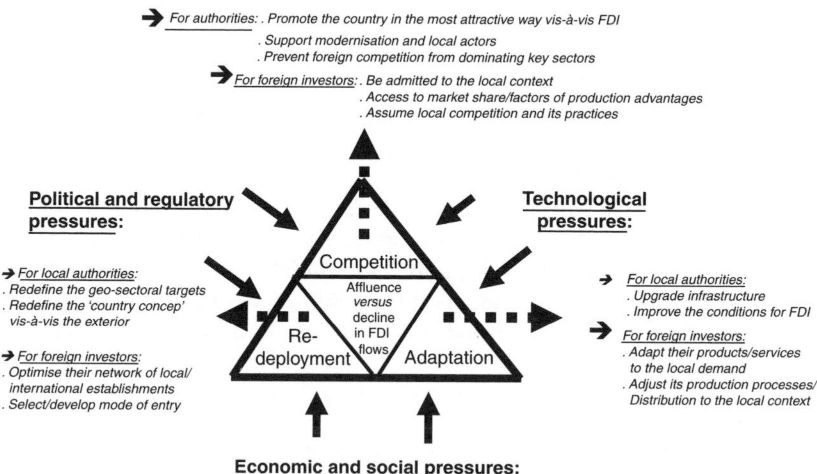

Figure 2.2　The challenges faced by local authorities and foreign companies
Source: Lemaire (see note 11).

seem, a priori, to be the most difficult for Vietnam to face, given the many structural handicaps the country has to overcome. The Argentine authorities, on the other hand, have to consider fundamental changes that touch the very foundations of the country's economic system and, above all, the behaviour of economic agents; all this despite the cyclical nature of the crisis that the country has to overcome.

Vietnam, as a priority, focused on areas as diverse as regulation, public utilities and education, in order to promote its economic space. The nation was able to rely, in this regard, on its impressive ability to mobilise its resources, and to act pragmatically, in order to achieve significant results in a relatively short time, by making rapid progress[19] This was demonstrated by its ability to overcome the long process of joining the WTO, in which it now features as a 'model pupil', while being able to avail itself of a growth which, since 2003, has remained buoyant.

Argentina, on the other hand, after a period of remarkable recovery,[20] revealed that the structural weaknesses and attitudes of its past have not disappeared, despite its undeniable assets. These unhelpful elements include maintaining a large proportion of private assets abroad, the weakness of national solidarity, the rise of inflation[21] and the recurring characteristic social unrest.[22]

Accordingly, foreign companies have to take into account the very different constraints. In Vietnam, various external pressures are a matter of concern. These include the attitude of the authorities which enables them, and even encourages them, to subscribe to a long-term approach to horizontalisation as well as to verticalisation (including highly capital-intensive activities). Although the many factors of instability and the strict attitude of the local authorities remain, particularly in the heavily regulated sectors such as financial services, the reforms encourage investors to study the opportunities offered (Vu, 2005). In Argentina, in spite of largely favourable fundamentals, its persistent instability, as well as the behaviour of the government, means scrutinising very carefully the unpredictability of the political and social environment, and the difficult steering of the economy (Peltier, 2006). It also involves taking advantage of the immediate benefits offered by the country, notably the excellent qualification level and advantageous cost of the local workforce, and activities requiring little capital, except for those that are turned resolutely towards external markets (verticalisation).

It is the combination of this double counting of external pressures, by the local authorities on the one hand, and by foreign companies on the other, in order to adjust their bids, that will suggest guidelines likely to be approved, both for the activities and for the geographical locations to be retained.

2.2.2   *The challenge of redeployment*

The challenge of redeployment, in effect, led the stakeholders to review, respectively, their portfolio of activities and the structure of their supply chain and production, as well as their portfolio of holdings. For local authorities, this meant reconsidering the major sectoral guidelines of the country and/or its regions, and even to change their image by creating a 'concept' with which to be associated.[23] For foreign companies, this meant justifying and upgrading their presence, on the one hand in terms of the local potential (opportunities and resources) and on the other, by maximising their effectiveness (overcoming constraints such as cost, compliance with deadlines, risk reduction), compared with the internationally dynamic overview of the firm that commands continual improvements in its deployment internationally.

The benefits that a country has to offer, as well as the handicaps that need to be dealt with, associated with the efforts to adapt that the authorities have committed themselves to, should be clear signals to foreign companies, so allowing them to position themselves in the most harmonious way possible.

In Vietnam, all infrastructure sectors related to production (electricity, transport, telecommunications and so on), as well as services (financial services, postal and so on), now offer considerable opportunities for foreign players, despite the control and presence of the state which traditionally has been strong, justified by the desire to preserve national sovereignty.[24] These priorities are imposed and are associated with long-term prospects, even if, in parallel, investment can be encouraged to become involved in the internationalisation of the production processes of certain players anxious to take advantage of particularly favourable labour costs. This does not exclude heavy investment in consumer capital, for example in electronics manufacturing.

Conversely, in Argentina, infrastructure sectors have experienced a genuine reflux of foreign investors that the government had not supported during the crisis period and beyond. At the initiative of the foreign companies, a series of 'traditional' investments have been maintained since December 2001, more 'horizontal' than 'vertical', such as automobile assembly lines and components manufacturing,[25] hyper- and supermarkets, and even vineyards. But those which have been developed as a priority are mainly low capital consuming, with minor 'barriers to exit', valuing a highly qualified local workforce more, targeting customers from abroad, in a 'vertical' perspective (for example, software design, research department) and, as such, generating a high quality price ratio.

Thus deployment or redeployment emerges, sharply contrasted to the activities of fast-growing economies, in regard to the role of foreign firms responding to the attitudes and decisions of local authorities.

This should, therefore, lead Vietnam to seek to meet the needs of local infrastructure before accelerating the production activities intended to serve international demand; and, in a longer timeframe, to offer products and services in original sectors, to give the greatest possible added value to the most original and increasingly well-controlled local competitive advantages. Argentina, conversely, should limit local instability, still poorly controlled by the authorities, to encourage foreign investments. It should also avoid infrastructure sectors, and not consider investment in consumer capital, other than in the context of a well-understood verticalisation,[26] while retaining those who are as insensitive as possible to local demand, thus giving up only a little control to shifts in national policies. This amounts to combining the best access to the best local resources for services primarily aimed at foreign markets, with, if necessary, the participation of local investors, since capital is important to consider; provided, however, that they agree to engage.

But it is the competition and its evolution that will feature within the host country, but also, more importantly, abroad, in the main international markets as additional decisive elements of the decision of FDI location.

2.2.3   *The challenge of competition*

The competitive challenge is to identify internal and external actors, assess the rival countries vis-à-vis international investors, and also the competing companies that could operate in the same sectors and the same target areas in the world. This requires a high reactivity, equally on the part of both actors. The local authorities need to attract, more than other comparable countries, the investments best suited to facilitate the development of their economy, while helping local businesses to succeed in their breakthrough abroad. The foreign companies need to be accepted locally by all economic agents, and to expand their market share, both in the country, as quickly as possible, and abroad, in order to benefit from the attractive aspects of the local competitive advantages.

The path to international openness changes rapidly, in response to the developing characteristics of the international environment and, hence, to those of the competition. It challenges the permanent positions earned by players operating in an environment which is increasingly integrated; location must be dynamically subject to adjustments and permanent challenges.

Thus, Vietnam, on the one hand, long neglected by international investors, has benefited, in addition to its determination to remove the remaining barriers hindering its entry to the WTO, from the interest of many investors not overly concentrating their activities in China. Offering benefits comparable to those of its larger neighbour, Vietnam has been able to encourage the establishment of certain stages of the production process of some foreign companies, as part of their verticalisation policy. Nevertheless, as a result, the emergence of some 'bottlenecks' has created some difficulties for the foreign firms involved: for instance, in the labour market, the scarcity of local talent encouraged one-upmanship, and dramatically increased specific technical or managerial specialities, turnover rates and labour costs. Under the development of their local market share (horizontalisation), foreign direct investors may have to tolerate increasing competition from local players encouraged by government policies and, in extreme cases, be forced to withdraw (Bui and Lemaire, 2008).

Argentina, however, faces increasing competition from its neighbours and partners in Mercosur *(it is not an acronym)*, to attract investors who, despite the cultural proximity it offers, have overcome their infatuation with the great liberal period of the 1990s, which created many disappointments for them, the European investors in particular. The domestic competition, too, in areas where technology transfers are quickly assimilated and there is abundant local expertise, can be fierce,[27] and calls into question the maintenance of the investor, especially if instability in domestic demand or the regulatory framework reduces the expected profitability.

Ultimately, everything has to be earned in the context of emerging countries with high growth, neither for local authorities, nor for foreign companies; perhaps because the increasing openness of these economic areas occurs in a context of accelerated internationalisation, making it constantly changing from environmental pressures, internal and external, opportunities and threats will evolve continuously making it difficult to control the situation, the respective interests of the parties and, therefore, the continuity of the commitments made.

From this analysis and observation of the dynamic characteristics of these two areas of reference, a framework for decision-making can be put forward that can be applied to FDI, which is oriented to one area as to the other and, possibly to others with comparable characteristics, that is to say those whose rapid growth is the main attraction in common vis-à-vis foreign companies.

By combining elements of synthesis generated at successive levels of the PREST analysis and taking into account the concerns and observed attitudes of local authorities such as direct investors, this framework focuses on two axes.

i. *The degree of upgrading infrastructure* envisaged in a broad sense (politico-regulatory, economic and social, technological), particularly through the structural work of local authorities, which will allow investors to specify the nature of their FDI: namely, to identify priority sectors where local needs are felt and appreciated, while simultaneously recognising the reception conditions that could bring reservations; and to determine in what perspective, horizontalisation and/or verticalisation, their local investment could be envisaged.

ii. *Sensitivity to instability and economic crises*, as well as the ability of the authorities to control and limit the effects of conjectural pressures, which would allow investors to clarify, in an optimal combination, their entry strategies: namely, acceptable levels of capitalisation, to minimise the exposure of their investment to risk, locally and internationally; and the level of control and sharing of such risks as capital costs, when considering partnerships with local actors.

In such a context, when following the designation of the fastest-growing economies, corresponding to each of the four quadrants of Figure 2.3, the two countries chosen can be positioned quite logically.

Vietnam, which is characterised by a still-limited level of infrastructure and by an appreciable economic and political stability, but with local authorities led with great determination, could be included in the *Insistent* category, with the prospect of developing, ultimately, to the *Indisputable* group. What presently encourages foreign investors to become involved in the infrastructure sector (including industrial streams to restructure and upgrade, such as energy, tourism and food production), however, is that the authorities are opening their doors in an attractive way. This could also be envisaged for investment in sectors where demand is currently strong, along with the rising standard of living, particularly in urban areas (for example cars, motorbikes or motorcycles, household equipment, consumer goods, modern distribution and so on), with, however, the risk of local actors climbing to power with the support of the authorities.

Argentina, benefiting from a level of infrastructure of reasonably good quality, but generally suffering, however, from chronic instability created more by the behaviour of political and economic actors than by the

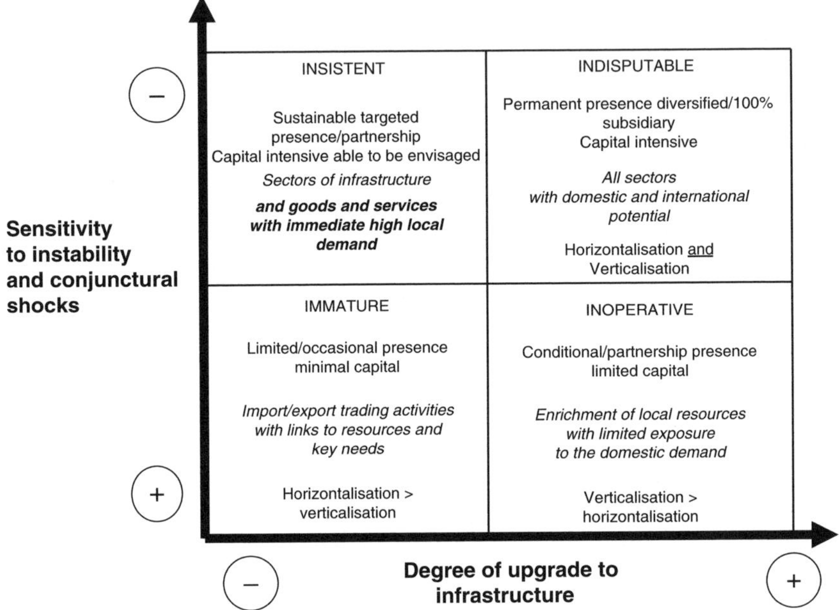

Figure 2.3   '4 × i scheme' (Lemaire © 2009)

instability of the external environment, could be placed among *Inoperative* countries. Investors should instead move towards structurally exporting sectors (mining and primary processing, agro-food, or even value-added technology), where fluctuations in domestic demand would have relatively little impact. In other sectors, the prospects are more uncertain, at least as long as the guidance of local authorities remains unpredictable vis-à-vis investors.

Conclusion

The fastest-growing economies provide international direct investors with particularly attractive targets. These include the development of domestic demand, such as rapid changes in their economic framework, combined with still-limited labour costs, and stimulate their interest even more when the investors' economies of origin no longer offer sufficient growth.

However, paradoxically, these opportunities are coupled with differentiated risks, while affecting all open economies. These differences result from the heterogeneity of maturity and instability levels among countries or regions. Another paradox stems from the lowering of national barriers for trade and finance, as well as from the wider dissemination of the market economy. As a result the transmission of crises is becoming increasingly rapid and economic cycles are expected to be less and less differentiated.

Consequently, it appears even more difficult than in the past for foreign firms to take on the specific uncertainties of these unfamiliar economic areas, and to select without too much risk of error, their countries for localisation. The analytical approach presented here seeks to facilitate the incorporation of the most external factors that could determine the attitude of local authorities as well as foreign direct investors. Taking into account the challenges that these two groups have to face, it leads to a framework permitting the classification of the various emerging economies compared with each other, and suggests the types of investments and input modes that investors could prioritise, in relation to the policies developed by the authorities and the behaviour of local actors.

However, this overall approach, as a tool for analysis and decision-making, is not to be applied only to these two fast-growing economies of average size, which are, of course, very different from one another and comparable to many other economies. It should, however, ensure that other factors, foremost among them the size of the country (based on demographics, GNP, the main economic aggregates), its growth rate, its geographical location and so on, should not be introduced into such a decision model. In the same way, and even beyond their sector of membership, the characteristics of the business (quantitative: size and growth rate; and qualitative: international experience, national culture and technique, mode of governance) could make for a symmetrical object of comparison. These corporate characteristics could be explored in a symmetric way. Then, such an analysis focused on the business could be a useful complement to the above one focusing on economic areas.

Notes

1. The stock of outward FDI almost doubled from 1980 to 1990 (Ramamurti, 2004). In 2006, it exceeded \$12,000 billion, of which 25 per cent was in emerging markets and 75 per cent in industrialised countries (the proportion was 20 per cent and 80 per cent respectively in 1990). Pace of growth, despite some irregularity, has accelerated in recent years. FDI inflows have been a growing part of FDI for the third consecutive year, exceeding \$1300 billion, an increase of 38 per cent compared with 2005 (UNCTAD, 2007).

2. In December 2001, multigovernmental organisations (International Monetary Fund and World Bank) triggered an abrupt and steep depreciation of the Argentinean peso by declaring that the increasing level of the country's debts and its persistent budget deficits no longer justified the one-to-one parity between the US dollar and the Argentinean peso. The questionable initiatives of local authorities and continuing internal tensions did not contribute to a re-establishment of foreign investors' confidence.

3. The ARK model (Activities, Resources, Knowledge) developed by Enright connects these three dimensions in a symmetrical manner; on the one hand, for businesses, and on the other, for economic areas (Ricart et al., 2004).

4. Analysed by Hecksher, Ohlin and Samuelson (1933), supplemented and précised by Stopler and Samuelson (1941), and Léontieff (1953).

5. See Porter's *diamond* concept (1991).

6. Not only in the industrialised countries willing to maintain and develop global oligopolies in certain key sectors, such as aeronautics, pharmaceuticals and semiconductors, but also, increasingly, in fast-growing economies: after Japan, the 'dragons' and 'tigers' of South East Asia, before, more recently, Brazil, Russia, India, Mexico, China (BRIMC), which can claim to imitate these predecessors.

7. See, notably, the CAGE model of Ghemawat Cage (2001).

8. The importance of psychic distance, which was originally highlighted by Johanson and Vhalne (1977), constitutes one of the axes used particularly for determining the choice of implantation at the enterprise level.

9. Among these include organisations of credit insurance covering the transactions and international investments (for example, COFACE, Ducroire, ECGD, Hermès, SACE), the credit rating agencies which measure country-risk (for example, Fitch), or even the specialised agencies in the approach to emerging countries for exporters and/or investors (for example, North South Export).

10. The huge market of low-income consumers. For details of consumers whose annual income in terms of purchasing power parity is less than $1500 see Prahalad and Hart, 2002.

11. The PREST model (Political-Regulatory, Economic and Social-Technological; see Lemaire, 1993, 1997, 2000, 2003), initially designed to identify the determinants of the strategic decision for a company operating in a geographical environment which is most often supranational (regional, continental, multi-continental or global), is here envisaged in an interesting broader perspective involving, at the same time, businesses and local authorities, in view of the decision to set up foreign investment.

12. Like China and even India, Vietnam has clearly decided to become a member of the WTO. Unlike Russia, which is still outside this organisation, due to pressure groups linked to powerful sectoral interests (oil and gas) that have more to lose than to gain by joining the WTO (Dyker, 2006), to be compared with other emerging countries like Algeria, which is still in the antechamber of the WTO, are also subject to contradictory influences.

13. Vietnam had previously joined the regional economic union, ASEAN, where it is the tenth country member.

14. Due to persistent internal and external deficits, Argentina has been hit hard by a devaluation that provoked the sudden rupture of relations with its external economic partners and, therefore, has been faced with the need to rebuild and restore

confidence with its foreign partners, including investors (Apaix, 2003; Carrera et al., 2003).

15. In the early 1990s, FDI had increased remarkably to reach an annual rate of $9 billion in 1996, which fell back down to $2 billion in 1999 (Lemaire and Bui, 2008).

16. This was after having, in particular, carried out the privatisation of many businesses and public services to demonstrate its willingness to rebalance public finances and to liberalise the country's structures, while eliminating most of the barriers to financial flows between countries and the exterior, and unilaterally establishing a fixed link between the peso and the dollar with a parity of 1 dollar to 1 peso (the currency board). See Gabetta, 2002; Krueger, 2003; Stiglitz, 2002.

17. In particular those who had invested heavily, such as European companies providing electricity, telecommunications and water treatment, which were heavily indebted to Western markets in hard currency and had found themselves also facing declining consumption, and therefore declining income, and, most importantly, having to honour repayment deadlines with hard currency incomes not indexed in the significantly depreciated local currency.

18. In response to the ban on increasing its fares, in September 2005, Suez announced the withdrawal of Aguas Argentinas (the company in charge of sanitation and the distribution of water in the Greater Buenos Aires area). The government put an end to its concession in March 2006 and transferred its assets to AySa, a newly created state-owned company, in accord with a movement that had already been under way for several months, of recovery by the state of public service companies. Incidentally, the retailers Carrefour and Casino were accused by President Kirchner, in the context of a high-profile, anti-inflation campaign, of not 'paying enough attention to the Argentines wallet' (Lemaire and Lopez, 2008).

19. 'The traditional comparative advantage based on natural resources and low labour costs is diminishing in importance. Knowledge and skill become determinants of competitiveness. The big challenge to latecomer countries is how to continuously improve their comparative advantage and dynamic competitiveness, created by human beings in an integrated environment, under the impact of economic globalisation [...] The overall target of Vietnam now is to successfully implement the transition and development. The first task is to transform the centrally-planned economy into a market economy with socialist orientation. The second is to transform the traditional peasant economy into a modern industrialized economy, moving from extensive to intensive development, with improved competitiveness and higher quality of economic growth' (Do Hoai Nam, 2005, cited in Lemaire and Bui, 2008).

20. If one now speaks of the 'three glorious' (2003–2005) after the '20 horrible' (1982–2002) years, it is perhaps a little early to assume that this dark page of Argentine history has been turned. The economic fundamentals have certainly improved considerably: during these three years, growth was 9 per cent on average, the three major sectors of activity advanced almost in parallel, at 11.9 per cent for agriculture, 7.7 per cent for industry and 8.3 per cent for services. Significantly, the best performance recorded is in the construction sector, with an increase of 20.4 per cent. For its part, unemployment decreased significantly, to below 12 per cent between 2004 and 2005, and even below that at 10 per cent the following year. This prompted a resumption of consumption, promoted by an increase in real wages close to 5 per cent on average; exports increased in 2005

by 13.8 per cent at fixed cost, while the trade balance, although slightly bending, remained at more than \$12 billion (Trucy and Planque, 2006).

21. The evolution of consumer prices translates to a decrease of 1.1 per cent per annum on average in 2001, then an increase of 25.9 per cent in 2002, to 13.4 per cent in 2003, 4.4 per cent in 2004, then rose again to 9.6 per cent in 2005, but with underlying inflation already approaching 14 per cent (source: Embassy of France in Argentina, Economic Mission).

22. As evidenced by the difficulties in accepting an increase in export taxes, intended to avoid draining the domestic supply for the benefit of external demand. This provided improved margins and the refilling of the coffers of the state, and gave support to the most disadvantaged populations and sectors, as evidenced by the 'arm-wrestling' which was started in March 2008 by President Kirchner with producers of agro-food products.

23. In the same way that China has been regarded as 'the factory of the world', Brazil is seen as 'the farm of the world', and India as the 'back office' of the world; this does not mean that this image is only tolerated and definitive, since, for example, India strives to position itself now as an 'office of studies' or global 'research centre', at least for certain sectors such as IT or generic pharmaceuticals.

24. Note, especially for financial services, that the issuing of currency (the right to print money) which falls under the control of banks is true of the central bank, which constitutes, with the army and police, one of three pillars of national sovereignty.

25. Thus Peugeot Société Anonyme (PSA) has not hesitated to expand its assembly plant in the suburbs of Buenos Aires. Renault, it is true, chose not to increase its local capacity, preferring to develop other locations elsewhere in the Mercosur (Lemaire and Lopez, 2008).

26. For foreign direct investors, access to Mercosur can be an additional incentive to locate in Argentina, insofar as it offers, in a context of 'enlarged horizontalisation', access to nearby markets multiplied by reports of the potential of the country.

27. As in the domain of large-scale distribution (Hagemann, 2003).

References

Apaix, O. (2003) Le long déclin de l'Argentine. *Alternatives Economiques*, 214 (May): 72–5.

Arnold, D. and Quelch, J. (1998) New strategies in emerging markets. *Sloan Management Review*, 40 (1): 7–20.

Bertone, L., Lagadec, P. and Guilhou, X. (2003) *Voyage au cœur d'une implosion*. Paris: Eyrolles.

Carrera, A., Mesquita, L., Perkins, G. and Vassolo, R. (2003) Business groups and their corporate strategies on the Argentina rollercoaster of competitive and anti-competitive shocks. *Academy of Management Executive*, 17 (3): 32–44.

Dunning, J.H. (1988) *Explaining International Production*. New York: Unwin Hyman.

Dyker, D.A. (2006) Russian accession to the WTO: why such a long and difficult road? *Post Communist Economies*, 6 (March): 3–20.

Gabetta, C. (2002) Le naufrage du 'modèle FMI', crise totale en Argentine. *Le Monde diplomatique*, January.

Ghemawat, P. (2001) Distance still matters: the hard reality of global expansion. *Harvard Business Review*, 79 (8): 137–47.

Hagemann, B. (2003) Les distributeurs se serrent la ceinture. *LSA*, 1797 (16 January): 18–19.

Johanson, J. and Vahlne, J.E. (1977) The internationalisation process of the firm: a model of knowledge development and increasing foreign commitments. *Journal of International Business Studies*, 1 (8): 277–83.

Kogut, B. (1995a) Designing global strategies: comparative and competitive value-added chains. *Sloan Management Review*, Summer: 15–28.

——— (1995b) Designing global strategies: profiting from operational flexibility. *Sloan Management Review*, Fall: 27–38.

Krueger, A. (2003) Le FMI et l'Argentine comment prévenir et résoudre les crises. *Commentaires*, 100 (Winter): 831–42.

Lemaire, J.P. (2000) 'Measuring the international environment impact on corporate marketing and strategy: the PREST model.' 16th International Marketing and Purchasing Group Conference, Bath, UK (7–9 September).

——— (2003) *Evolution de la réflexion sur l'internationalisation*. Paris: Dunod.

——— (2005) 'Dynamic cross-border positioning of emerging countries companies: from environmental analysis to corporate internationalisation incentives.' Paper presented at the International Conference on Marketing Paradigms for Emerging Economics, Indian Institute of Management, Ahmedabad, India (12–13 January).

——— (2007) 'International champions from large fast growing economies: Brazil's corporate emergence dynamics compared with China's and India's.' Paper presented at the 33rd conference of the European International Business Academy, Catane, Italy (13–15 December).

Lemaire, J.P. and Bui, L.H. (2008) 'Vietnam, le défi de l'OMC'. Business case study. Centrale des Cas et des Moyens Pedagogiques (CCMP)/École Supérieure de Commerce de Paris- Ecole Européenne des Affaires (ESCP-EAP – now ESCP Europe)/Centre Franco Vietnamien de Formation à la Gestion (CFVG).

Lemaire, J.P. and Lopez, D. (2008) 'Argentinean Promises'. Business case study, CCMP/ESCP-EAP (see above).

List, F. (1851) *Système national d'économie poilitique*. Paris: Capelle.

London, T. and Hart, S.L. (2004) Reinventing strategies for emerging markets: beyond the transnational model. *Journal of International Business Studies*, 35: 350–70.

Meyer, K.E. (2004) Perspectives on multinational enterprises in emerging economies. *Journal of International Business Studies*, 35: 259–76.

Peltier, C. (2006) La stratégie à haut risque du Président Kirchner. *Problèmes Economiques* du 22 Septembre repris de *Conjoncture BNP Paribas*.

Porter, M.E. (1991) *The Competitive Advantage of Nations*. New York: The Free Press.

Prahalad, C.K. and Doz, Y. (1987) *The Multinational Mission*. New York: The Free Press; London: Macmillan.

Prahalad, C.K. and Hart, S. (2002) The fortune at the bottom of the pyramid. *Strategy and Business*, 26: 2–14.

Ramamurti, R. (2004) Developing countries and MNEs: extending and enriching the research agenda. *Journal of International Business Studies*, 35: 277–83.

Ricart, J.E., Enright, M.J., Ghemawat, P., Hart, S.L. and Khanna, T. (2004) New frontiers in international strategy. *Journal of International Business Studies*, 35: 175–200.

Rolland, D., Chassin, J., Pinot de Villechenon, F. and Morand, P. (eds) (2003) *Pour Comprendre la Crise Argentine*. Paris: L'Harmattan.

Stiglitz, J. (2002) Leçons d'Argentine. *Les Echos*, 21 January.

Schwartz, A.J. (2005) Dealing with exchange rate protectionism. *Cato Journal*, 5 (1): 97–106.

Tresca, G. (2004) *El collapse de la convertibilidad y el Nuevo modelo de desarollo argentine.* Buenos Aires: Realidad Argentina.

Trucy, J.P. and Planque, M. (2006), 'Economic situation of Argentina', publication of the French Embassy in Argentina, Economic Mission: Spring.

United Nations Conference on Trade and Development (UNCTAD) (2007) *World Investment Report, Transnational Corporations, Extractive Industries and Development.* Geneva: United Nations.

Vu, B.T. (2005) *L'impact de l'adhésion du Vietnam à l'OMC sur le secteur bancaire vietnamien: le cas de la Banque de l'Investissement et du Développement.* Unpublished thesis for Professional MS Management of International Projects. Paris: European School of Management (ESCP-EAP).

3
The Paradox Between Global Efficiency and Local Responsiveness: The Case of French Multinationals Established in China

Jacques Jaussaud and Johannes Schaaper

On the basis of Burns (1963) and many other contributions to the academic literature, mechanisms that support efficiency often lead to reduced flexibility. Bartlett and Goshal (1987, 1989), however, have emphasised how multinational companies (MNCs) have developed new organisational solutions at a regional or a global level to make efficiency and local responsiveness compatible. This chapter investigates how such an attempt translates in China.

China has been chosen because MNCs have been attracted there by low production costs (efficiency perspective), but they face high growth, new opportunities and permanently emerging new competitors, which calls for local responsiveness.

On the basis of a series of twelve qualitative interviews with expatriate managers of French subsidiaries in China, the authors examine how coordination and control mechanisms implemented by multinationals can be associated in order to reconcile global efficiency and local responsiveness. All the MNCs of the sample have developed a sophisticated formal control of their subsidiaries in China. However, instead of rigidifying the organisation, this strong formal control becomes the support of intense exchanges between the headquarters, the Chinese subsidiaries and other units of the multinational, reinforcing the aptitudes of the subsidiaries for local responsiveness.

Every firm has to look for efficiency, i.e. the relationship between what it produces or sells and the resources it uses for this purpose (Bouquin, 1986; Johnson et al., 2005). Multinationals do not escape this requirement, especially because low production costs often constitute a competing advantage on world markets. A company is said to be efficient when it reaches an objective with reduced consumption of resources (natural, human, financial, technical and so on). It is useful to make a distinction between efficiency and efficacy. Efficacy, or effectiveness, is the ability to produce a desired amount, or succeed in achieving a given goal, without taking into account the amount of resources spent. Being efficient is being efficacious while minimising the use of resources. For instance, a car is efficacious when it allows movement from one place to another; the car becomes efficient when this displacement consumes the least fuel possible. The concept of efficiency is at the heart of the multinational's preoccupations when their resources are scarce, expensive and difficult to acquire.

For three decades, multinational firms have been fragmenting their production processes internationally. They have multiplied the number of their subsidiaries abroad, and frequently resorted to outsourcing part of their activities near companies located in foreign countries. In order to preserve the global efficiency of the network of their subsidiaries and subcontractors, the head offices often implement strong centralised coordination. But being more centralised, the multinational is likely to have difficulties in adapting quickly to the local environment of the countries where their subsidiaries are established. Moreover, these environments are very different and in perpetual evolution. An expatriate in charge of a subsidiary in China, who was interviewed for this research, explained that its 'head office negotiates overall agreements, which are reflected locally; then here in China, we learn the terms of the agreement which we have to apply, which poses problems; for example, the prices negotiated up there are not often accepted by the local partners'. The subsidiaries abroad have to deal locally, every day, with legal, technological and social constraints. Another expatriate in charge of a subsidiary in China, in the medical sector, said 'our customers are the Chinese hospitals; their needs are often very different from those of the traditional customers, which leads us to reconsider the business model'.

Managers in charge of overseas subsidiaries, who are closer to the local environment, can identify local opportunities much more easily than managers in the headquarters. For instance, an expatriate in charge of a subsidiary in China, which is a second-rank subcontractor of a French car manufacturer also established in China, explained that he has to deal with production fluctuations, varying from simple to triple. The reason is that the initial project of its client, the French car manufacturer, did not reach initial expectations. So, in order to use better its productive capacities, he approached local companies of both the car industry and of other industries. The head office did not even realise that those local clients existed. In the end, the subsidiary obtained a whole series of contracts with small local Chinese firms.

As can be understood through these examples, to address local constraints and to seize local opportunities, subsidiaries must be responsive. This implies that the multinational should maintain a flexible structure, and grant to the managers of its subsidiaries abroad a certain degree of autonomy in their action. The subsidiaries can thus optimise their own activity and contribute positively to the total efficiency of the multinational.

The paradox dealt with in this chapter can be stated as follows: is the objective of efficiency in the worldwide network of a multinational firm compatible with the need for granting autonomy to managers of subsidiaries abroad? Following the reasoning of Burns (1963), the choice for a multinational seems to oscillate between, on the one hand, strongly centralised coordination aiming at global efficiency and, on the other, more autonomy for the overseas subsidiaries to increase their responsiveness to local conditions. The limits that each of these choices implies (low reactivity or, on the contrary, potentially higher costs and prices), force multinationals to search for new solutions. Bartlett and Goshal (1987, 1989) observed that certain subsidiaries manufacture components and products that they provide to other units of the multinational, which are acting on a great number of different markets worldwide. These production subsidiaries, whose sizes are no longer limited to the market of the country where they are established (logic of efficiency), are strongly controlled and staffed with a large number of experts. These reinforced teams are able, at the same time, to negotiate with other units of the multinational, to analyse the threats and opportunities in their local environment and then to react (logic of flexibility). Bartlett and Goshal (1987, 1989) call these organisations 'transnational firms'.

This chapter explores how the paradox of efficiency versus flexibility is translated concretely using China as a field study. With the goal of efficiency, China has constituted, since the beginning of the 1980s, a production base at reduced cost for many multinationals. But the Chinese environment has been so dynamic since the beginning of the 1990s that it requires considerable capacities of responsiveness. For this reason, the authors hoped to observe the efforts French subsidiaries make and the mechanisms used to aim at reconciling the search for global efficiency and strong local reactivity.

The chapter first illustrates the means mobilised by the French multinationals at the service of efficiency, while underlining their limits. Second, it analyses how rigidities resulting from the use of efficiency mechanisms are overcome in order to maintain local responsiveness, a significant requirement in China.

1 French subsidiaries in China: mechanisms of global efficiency

Section 1.1 presents the empirical research design which enabled better identification of the sources of efficiency for the French multinationals in China. Then Section 1.2 highlights the main sources of efficiency revealed by qualitative interviews held with expatriates in China.

1.1   Empirical design for the research

The research is based on a series of twelve interviews which were conducted in 2005 with expatriates in charge of production subsidiaries established in China by French multinationals. The research is qualitative and exploratory in nature. It is not the number of cases that matters but the diversity of the answers, which is necessary to understand the phenomenon under investigation (Symon and Cassel, 1998). The sample comprises subsidiaries of multinationals of varying sizes, having different experiences in China, of different branches of industry, producing equipment or consumer goods. The authors visited expatriates of these subsidiaries established in various Chinese provinces, in particular Beijing, Shanghai, Wuhan and Nanchang. At the request of the majority of the interviewees, the names of the companies remain anonymous. Although confidential information was not accessed, authorisation of the head offices to publish the names of the companies would have been, in certain cases, difficult or lengthy to obtain. The final sample of the subsidiaries is presented in Table 3.1.

Quantitative empirical research methodology offers several well-established advantages. In particular, it allows generalisation through statistical inference. However, it also has well-known methodological limits. Although it visualises and quantifies phenomena, it does not provide underlying answers. Quantitative methodology and the inherent statistical analysis provide data about the research problem that help quantify facts and provide answers to questions such as 'How many?' However, the questions 'Why?' and 'How?' often remain unanswered. Conversely, qualitative research methodology, in particular personal in-depth interviews, offers potential underlying explanations for observed facts.

The interview guide reviewed the main instruments of coordination and control studied by the academic literature in international management (Geringer and Hebert, 1989; Martinez and Jarillo, 1989; Kumar and Seth, 1998). The interview guide started with two opening questions about the history of the firm in China and the entry modes (that is WOS or IJV), for both the interviewed subsidiary and the other subsidiaries of the MNC in China. Then, sixteen open-ended questions asked managers to explain how and why their MNCs use various mechanisms and instruments to control their subsidiaries in China, looking especially at the share of capital, the number and the functions of expatriates and of local Chinese managers, reporting procedures, formalisation of the organisational structure and the training of the Chinese employees. Finally, during the discussion, the topics were broadened towards subjects concerning efficiency and local responsiveness.

After the interview, the replies of the expatriates were fully transcribed. Then, the twelve interviews were gathered, topic by topic, into a two-dimensional grid (the topics in rows, the twelve cases in the columns). Thematic content analysis of the themes enabled an initial understanding of how the multinationals use the various instruments and methods

Table 3.1   Sample of the interviewed French subsidiaries in 2005

ID	Size MNC[1]	Branch of industry	Nature of the subsidiary[2]	Age of subsidiary	Number of subsidiaries in China	Number of employees[3]
A	Rather small	Automobile equipment	IJV (63%-37%)	2	2	44
B	Giant	Electric and electronic components	Holding, 5 WOS and 17 IJVs	20	22	6,000
C	Giant	Optics	100% WOS	9	1	750
D	Big	Automobile equipment	IJV (50%-50%)	11	8	150
E	Big	Chemistry	IJV (52%-48%)	9	3	1,000
F	Big	Chemistry	Holding, 8 WOS and 7 IJVs	25	15	3,000
G	Rather small	Automobile equipment	IJV (75%-25%)	9	1	25
H	Giant	Automobile equipment	IJV (75%-25%)	9	7	250
I	Giant	Chemistry	Holding, 18 subsidiaries,	15	18	1,000
J	Big	Pharmacy	100% WOS	13	2	64
K	Rather small	Automobile equipment	100% WOS	7	1	84
L	Giant	Electric and electronic components	Holding, 13 WOS and 7 IJVs	19	20	6,000

[1] 'Giant' refers to multinationals among the first in their industry, present in a large number of countries; 'rather small' corresponds to multinationals established industrially in a small number of countries (fewer than 10); 'big' multinationals cover the intermediate cases.

[2] WOS (Wholly Owned Subsidiaries) are subsidiaries of which the capital is 100% held by the multinational; in the case of 'the joint ventures', the first percentage figure corresponds to the share of capital held by the multinational, the second to that held by the local Chinese partner. IJV = International Joint Ventures.

[3] These data refer to employees of the subsidiary, and in the case of a holding, the number of employees that it manages in China.

to coordinate their activities worldwide, and keep control over their subsidiaries in China. But the content analysis also allowed an understanding of multinational attempts to reconcile efficiency and local reactivity, which is the central paradox of the research.

1.2   Sources of efficiency reconsidered in the light of the interviews

According to the abundant literature, efficiency can be reached by various means such as the rationalisation of the organisation, the standardisation of products and procedures, formalisation of the organisation, the accumulation of experience, economies of scale, training of the employees, technological progress and so on (Taylor, 1947; Burns, 1963; Mintzberg et al., 1998; Johnson et al., 2005). These means were addressed throughout the interviews, in particular the accumulation of experience and economies of scale, standardisation and formalisation, the international localisation of activities and the centralisation of the decision-making process.

1.2.1   *The accumulation of experience and economies of scale*

The concept of economies of scale should be distinguished from the concept of economies of growth (Parent, 1975). Economies of scale correspond to a reduction of unit costs related to an increase in the production capacity. How can the unit cost decrease, and thus efficiency improve, when the size of production capacities increases? The interviews recognise two causes classically identified in the academic literature (Parent, 1975; Morvan, 1991).

First, when a firm invests in a new production plant, the unit costs decrease automatically when the output increases more quickly than the costs of structure. This occurs in particular when the investment integrates technical progress. For instance, equipment that is 20 per cent more expensive can be 30 per cent more productive. This effect occurs in particular in industries requiring heavy investment. Second, when the size of the plant increases, production can be organised differently and the production operations broken down more thoroughly into basic tasks. During the visits to factories, which were carried out at the time of the interviews, it was noted that 'Taylorisation' of production is still massively applied in China, particularly because the wages of the Chinese workmen are still very low and do not encourage the automation of production.

All the interviewees who took part in the research insisted on the need for attaining a sufficient scale to reduce the unit costs. Some of them, however, underlined that they had difficulties in producing at the full capacity of their plant in China, particularly when they had been established in China to follow a main industrial customer (Cases A and K). This problem will be discussed later.

When the size of a production plant increases, however, it becomes more complex to manage, particularly when the number of production sites and product lines grows: over-consumption, malfunctioning due to bad coordination and, as a result, poor quality may occur. To face this growing complexity, multinational firms add intermediate levels of coordination and control. Five of the twelve multinational firms that were interviewed had recently created holdings in China (Cases B, C, F, I and L), including three with a more regional focus, supervising subsidiaries in other Asian countries (Cases B, C and I). But one must be aware that these new coordination structures increase the fixed costs and consequently the unit costs; they thus generate diseconomies of scale.

Economies of scale are often associated with economies of experience, which consist of a reduction of unit costs thanks to the accumulation of experience, usually measured by the total cumulated production since the launching of a product. This phenomenon occurs at different degrees according to sectors. The unit costs decrease when experience is gained, thanks to the lessons drawn from errors, the reconsideration of working methods and the introduction of new procedures, which improve the organisation of the firm and its level of efficiency. Moreover, training is necessary to transfer experience. Training contributes to the improvement in the productivity of managers and workers at all the levels of the company. The interviews show that training of local staff and workers is absolutely necessary; all the more so when production subsidiaries must reach high levels of quality to answer international standards, whereas they are located in a country, China, where labour is still often insufficiently qualified.

This accumulated experience might be difficult to transfer in very different contexts, for example the Chinese one. The two key elements of experience, the organisational learning and the acquisition of new skills by employees, are to be rebuilt in a host country. This is not always easy, in particular when a multinational firm sets up a production plant for the first time, in a country like China. Consider the case of Subsidiary A, which is a subcontractor of a multinational in the automobile sector. This automobile multinational decided to open a factory in China and required its subcontractors to follow. 'If you do not conform, your client throws you out of its worldwide network,' said the CEO of Subsidiary A. In order to start its production in China quickly, the multinational A bought a Chinese factory on the spot, whose production technology was rather obsolete. All the production knowhow had to be rebuilt. Two years after the purchase of this Chinese factory, the French expatriate was very proud to show the organisation of its production in small islands according to the model of the factory in France. The experience gained by the multinational in France was finally able to be transposed.

The expatriate in charge of Subsidiary D acknowledged that when its firm set up the first production unit of the group in China, in 1995, 'we did not know how to do it'. Therefore, the group chose to set up a joint venture with a Chinese partner, who would be able to solve all the problems of conducting businesses in China. The CEO of Holding F corroborates this: 'My group, present in China for more than 25 years, has now acquired the necessary experience that enables us to create only wholly-owned subsidiaries in this country.'

1.2.2 *Standardisation and formalisation of the organisation*

Standardisation consists of harmonising the products, the production processes and work procedures according to standards that establish technical specifications, criteria, methods, processes and practices. Formalisation, for its part, consists of structuring and organising the firm, or the subsidiary, by resorting to written documents. Formalisation is in fact written standardisation. For a multinational, formalisation includes the description of jobs and functions, control and reporting documents, as well as administrative procedures, on a worldwide scale.

Mintzberg (1982) underlines that when a firm grows in size, the number of hierarchical levels increases naturally, and the procedures are accordingly more systematically formalised. The interviews corroborate this very clearly. For Multinational B, 'everything is written: broadly the rules are the same everywhere, except for small local adaptations'. Multinational H, although of French origin, standardises its procedures in English so that they can be circulated throughout the subsidiaries worldwide. The reporting of Multinational E is on intranet: 'from Buenos Aires to Wuhan, everyone fills in the same documents'. The expatriate in charge of Subsidiary L says that the business practices in China are a 'copy-paste' from what happens in France.

The interviews show several reasons why multinationals, even the smallest ones, standardise and formalise massively. First, when a product is sold on the world markets, the standardisation of production and marketing makes it possible for the multinational firm to benefit from economies of scale, source of efficiency, and to guarantee a better regularity of the quality of their products. Second, most of the subsidiaries are certified (ISO 9000 or ISO 14000, GMP (Good Manufacturing Practices) or other certifications according to sectors), which requires that the functions and procedures are written very specifically. Third, when the production is fragmented between several production sites dispersed throughout the world, the standardisation of components facilitates the final assembly and allows changing of supplier. The expatriate in charge of Holding B (the Holding in China of Multinational B), whose group wishes to build a multinational of world standard, affirms that 'excellence needs written rules [...and that] the Chinese are happy to have these rules'. Multinational I, whose production requires the handling of dangerous products, resorts to written procedures 'to guarantee the transfer of unified practices within the group because of the industrial risks'.

However, standardisation and formalisation, if they are pushed too far, can also bring disadvantages. First, the standardisation of products, especially in consumer markets, does not allow an easy response to specific market requests. Also, formalisation rigidifies the organisation as a whole, ossifies the roles of everyone, reduces the space for acting, and thus reduces the reaction capacity of subsidiaries when they face local constraints or opportunities. The expatriate in charge of Subsidiary G states that 'one cannot apply in China all the functions and procedures decided at the head offices in France'; he advises that 'one should not transpose, but has to modify and adapt standards to local practices'.

1.2.3 *International localisation of production*

Multinationals break down their production processes into subsets of components which are manufactured in various countries according to the costs of production factors. These components are then assembled elsewhere, before being re-exported to final markets. The reduction of customs duties and other barriers to trade, as well as the development of new technologies of information and communication (NTIC), favour this long-term tendency. The geographical localisation of their activities by multinationals, which is done on a worldwide scale, is of prime importance in their search for high efficiency.

The interviews show why multinationals locate their production activities in China. First, production with strong labour intensity is transferred to China because of the low wages of workers there. The subsidiaries of the sample confirmed this emphatically. Multinational B even seeks to benefit from the relatively weak wages of Chinese engineers, who are employed in their delocalised research and development centres. In the same way, Multinational C delocalised its engineering centre to Thailand. Nowadays, in a number of countries in rapid economic transition, multinationals can benefit from qualified personnel who are modestly remunerated. So multinationals also transfer more and more sophisticated production and development activities to China.

Second, some multinationals moved towards their suppliers, themselves established in China. Multinational F created a network of joint ventures to provide rare raw materials which are available in certain areas of China. The expatriate in charge of the regional seat of Multinational B explained that its multinational set up production plants in China in particular, because of the advantageous prices of intermediate components.

Third, a certain number of multinationals went to China to be closer to their customers. Subsidiaries A, D, G and H, all four subcontractors in the automobile sector, followed their principal client, who established a factory in China to serve the local Chinese market. Multinational B considers that the Chinese market is its largest product market in the world, larger than the North American or European markets. With the goal of being closer to their consumer markets, they set up large factories in China. Multinational I handles dangerous products which are expensive to transport. In order to cover the Chinese territory and reduce transportation costs, it established a network of eighteen subsidiaries in China.

However, the fragmentation of the production process and the international localisation of the value chain pose some serious problems, which could harm the efficiency goal. The breaking up of production into components, produced here or there, requires a strong standardisation. The end product in some cases can no longer be adapted to the specific demand of consumers of specific countries. This is, for example, the case with the clothes industry, certain segments of which are very sensitive to the phenomena of trends. The clothes produced in China and transported to Europe cannot be adapted quickly to the fast changes of demand. This is why certain firms in the clothing industry, constantly renewing their collections, maintain production plants close to their consumer markets.

Moreover, the international breaking down of the value chain requires strong and centralised coordination of the fragmented tasks carried out in various multicultural contexts. It means the multinational firm must increase its control over its worldwide delocalised activities.

1.2.4   *The centralisation of the decision-making process*

In order to maintain the overall efficiency of the organisation, the fragmentation of its value chain around the world requires that multinationals centralise the coordination of the decision-making. If, for example, the components of a product, manufactured in various production sites or by different subcontractors, do not arrive at the appropriate time at the assembly factory, costs of disorganisation appear (delay, none delivery, none quality, increasing inventories, and so on), which are in opposition to the search for efficiency. The interviews in China confirm clearly that the French multinationals have a strong tendency to centralise the decision-making and control procedures. Multinational E practises 'worldwide piloting by activities'. Multinational J has set up in China a steering committee, which includes the expatriate CEO and managers from the headquarters in France, among them the chairman and managing director of the whole group. This committee takes all the strategic decisions relating to China. The interviews show that in most cases, local decision autonomy in China is bordered and limited 'to daily management' (Case C), 'the operational management of the subsidiary' (Case I) or 'inside an envelope that head office gives to the subsidiary' (Case E).

What is the goal of such strong centralisation? The expatriate in charge of Holding F explains that 'it is necessary to guarantee coherence in the strategy of the multinational worldwide'. Indeed, the centralisation of information and decision-making contributes to the avoidance of waste and uncoordination and, a priori, to strategic coherence and, therefore, to the global efficiency of the multinational. More fundamentally, the centralisation of the decision gives control to the central headquarters, and power to its managers who supervise the subsidiaries in the world.

However, strong centralisation generates some major disadvantages. When a multinational firm grows in size, and when this growth goes with a higher number of interconnected production units and intermediate coordination levels, the increasing complexity of decision-making reduces the flexibility and ability to react to local situations. The managers at the central headquarters lose contact with the realities of the local environment of the subsidiaries. In turbulent and dynamic economies like that of China, the response speed between a subsidiary and its head office, especially when the hierarchical layers are multiplied, can be insufficient to face difficulties or to seize opportunities locally.

2   Reducing the paradox between global efficiency and local responsiveness: some answers provided by French multinationals in China

The authors reiterate that the central issue is as follows: how can multinationals allow a sufficient level of local reactivity to their overseas subsidiaries and simultaneously conserve their global efficiency? The second section of this chapter develops answers provided by the subsidiaries of the sample for the specific Chinese context in which they act daily.

The central research question, as developed in the introduction, can now be reconsidered. In the first section, it was stated that the essential sources of efficiency, because they rigidify and complicate the organisation, potentially reduce the reactivity of subsidiaries abroad when they face local constraints and opportunities. The need for ensuring global efficiency, while simultaneously maintaining the autonomy of decision required for local reactivity, led to the search for new solutions. The interviews identified four groups of solutions:

i. recourse to experts, travelling from one subsidiary to another on short-term assignments;
ii. enhanced informal exchanges developed thanks to formal reporting procedures;
iii. development of new intermediate structures, such as holdings or regional headquarters;
iv. development of a common corporate culture within the multinational, extended to the Chinese employees.

2.1   The recourse to experts on short-term assignments

An expert can be defined as a person who has a high level of competencies in a technical, administrative or commercial field. Some multinationals in the sample have massive recourse to experts, who travel intensively on short-term missions. Subsidiary C receives 'an expert every two days, for very different missions'. Multinational I has a network of experts with strong technical skills on which its subsidiary can rely 'as soon as we do not find somebody locally to solve a problem'. Other subsidiaries in the sample receive fewer experts, and when they do come to China, it is essentially for technical issues such as the setting up of new equipment or the development of new programmes. In most of the subsidiaries, the expatriate CFO or the person responsible for the financial reporting is assisted by experts with expertise in finance, reporting and auditing.

In all cases, the experts bring skills to the subsidiary that it lacks or solutions that it doesn't have yet or has not mastered entirely. This is often the case for reporting, in particular when the multinational is listed on the stock exchange (7 cases out of the 12 of the sample). Experts constitute a considerable source of flexibility since, according to the difficulties faced, the subsidiary can call upon their expertise, which is available within the network of the multinational. In Multinational F, 'the experts are carrying technologies which they spread throughout the whole world'. The expatriate CEO of Subsidiary I, for example, frequently sends out a request for assistance through the worldwide network of his group. In most cases, experts reply themselves or are identified by another staff member. The interviewee affirms that 'this network of experts with strong specialised and technical skills constitutes a crucial asset when problems must be solved'. According to the expatriate manager of Subsidiary D, 'experts who come from the headquarters are in contact with the principal clients in France; as those clients standardise their methods on a world level, when the experts come to China to solve problems, they have already solved similar problems in France or elsewhere. A Chinese manager can never do this job.'

2.2   Formal control and informal exchanges

Cases A, K and I bring complementary lessons to the paradox of global efficiency as opposed to local responsiveness. These three subsidiaries were initially established in China to follow their large European or Korean clients. Once in China, they had to find new Chinese clients. For Cases A and K, in particular, finding new Chinese clients quickly was imperative, because the sales of their main French client were taking too long to get going in China. Such shifts in marketing approaches towards local customers testify to a strong local responsiveness. How was such reactivity developed? In each of these three cases, according to the interviewees, the prospecting of new customers was decided with the support and heavy involvement of the managers at the head office of the multinational. The replies of the interviewees reveal that they are in permanent contact with their head offices, or with the regional headquarters, especially for formal reporting procedures. Those contacts use a whole set of informal means of communication, such as telephone, email and face-to-face discussions. These informal exchanges were initially based on the data from the reporting documents, but then were extended to other dimensions of the activity of the subsidiary, in particular its difficulties and its strategy in relation to new clients. Similar developments were made apparent during interviews with the managers of Subsidiaries B, C, F, J and L.

It appears that formal control, conceived in the logic of efficiency, generates intense informal interactions. The topics under discussion during these informal exchanges are not limited to the results of formal control only, but involve other aspects of the activity of the subsidiary, its difficulties and new projects. These informal exchanges contribute to the enhancement of the subsidiary's responsiveness when it faces turbulence within the local environment, and thus, in a wider sense, to the reactivity of the multinational as a whole.

2.3 The creation of intermediate structures: China holdings and regional seats

To face increasing complexity related to the increase of its size and the number of operations that result from this, any organisation naturally introduces additional hierarchical levels of coordination. The headquarters coordinate and control an intermediate level, which in turn coordinates and controls lower levels. Five of the twelve multinationals interviewed have created a holding in China to supervise their subsidiaries (Cases B, C, F, I and L). Three of these (Cases B, C and I) even act as regional headquarters and control the activities of subsidiaries in several Asian countries. These three regional headquarters belong to the largest and most globalised of the multinationals in the sample.

The expatriate CEO of Holding F stresses that the strategy of his group remains strongly centralised 'because it is necessary to ensure a worldwide coherence'. But he adds that it is highly important to also introduce 'a decentralised dimension to the structure'. According to him, the country holding he manages benefits from a relatively large freedom of action 'within the limits of the rules of conformity, which are non-negotiable, and this across the whole world'. For example, Holding F searches for potential local partners and can bargain new contracts and partnerships.

Holding I, which employs fifteen expatriates, supervises all the subsidiaries that the MNC has established in China, Taiwan and South Korea. Previously, this supervision was localised in Paris. The reporting documents of the subsidiary are now sent to, and reviewed by, the regional office. If differences between reported results and objectives appear, the CEO of the subsidiary provides explanations to the managers at the regional office, with a joint search for solutions. According to the CEO of this holding, this 'rather decentralised decision process with a mutual adjustment works very well in the group'. He underlines, however, that 'to be very precise, the regional seat is not a decision-making body; at the end, the person in charge of the subsidiary in China has to assume his responsibilities'. The regional office of Multinational I has as a simple objective, to facilitate the working of the subsidiaries. Its main task is to intermediate between the subsidiaries in China and the seat, but also between the subsidiaries in China and local authorities, as well as between the subsidiaries of the regional Asian network. Lacking real decentralised decision-making power, the regional headquarters in this case contributes only slightly to the increase in local responsiveness.

The expatriate CEO of Holding B explains that at the time of his arrival in China he realised 'that there was too much autonomy in China and that it was a weakness'. Consequently, its MNC created three regional offices as intermediate levels between the head office in Paris and the three great zones of activity where the MNC has its activities, which are the American, European and the Asia-Pacific markets. The regional seat in Shanghai (Case B) looks after all the important topics and takes the decisions, while the head office in Paris keeps an eye on these. All the main decisions are discussed during monthly meetings by video conference, which can last up to two days. It can be observed here that, contrary to Case I, the regional office of Multinational B benefits from a real decentralised decision-making power, under the control of its head office. This decentralisation contributes favourably to an increase in local responsiveness.

Multinational L created an Asia-Pacific division in Hong Kong, which replaced its former international division, localised in Paris. The Chinese subsidiary sends its reporting documents directly to the Asia-Pacific division. The first role of this regional office, therefore, consists of maintaining a high degree of efficiency of the multinational. However, it also has an objective to increase local reactivity, and this in two ways at least. First, the expatriate CEO of the China Holding L said that its group seeks to develop and offer less-sophisticated products which are better suited to the Chinese market. To do this, as the China holding is closer to local demand, takes the initiative of acquiring Chinese companies, in agreement, of course, with the management of the Asia-Pacific division and the head office in Paris. Second, Holding L looks for opportunities to produce locally, certain products which, so far, are imported. The China holding informs the Asia-Pacific division of these opportunities, and the division then makes a decision in coordination with the head office in Paris. It can be observed here that the regional intermediate management has, as a double objective, to maintain a high degree of efficiency, by means of direct supervision of the subsidiaries in China and in other countries of Asia, and to contribute strongly to the development of reactivity towards the local constraints and opportunities.

These examples (Cases F, B, L and I) show the advantages for a multinational of creating a China holding or a regional office. Such intermediate structures control a fewer number of operations and the decision-making process becomes less complex. If information and decisions circulate quickly, which is possible thanks to NTIC, as the video conference (Case B) suggests, the speed of response improves. At the same time, the seat retains the possibility of centralising the essential decisions, which contributes to the optimisation of the total efficiency of the multinational. The creation of a holding or a regional office thus constitutes a good way of reducing the paradox between total efficiency and local responsiveness. However, in practice, two types of limits can appear. First, these additional intermediate structures increase fixed costs, to the detriment of global efficiency. Second, in a turbulent and dynamic environment, the speed of response between a subsidiary and its head office, when the hierarchical layers multiply, can still be insufficient to deal with certain difficulties or to seize local opportunities. This is the case with certain regional seats in the sample, which still remain highly dependent on the central seat.

2.4   The development of a common corporate culture within the multinational

Multinational F defined a set of rules of behaviour to be respected by any employee of the group. Within these rules, the managers of subsidiaries are free to take decisions. But how can the head office be sure that local managers who benefit from such decentralised decision-making power will comply with the rules? How can the head office be sure that managers with decentralised power will behave in conformity with the interests of the company? According to the agency theory (Jensen and Meckling, 1976; Fama and Jensen, 1983), answers to these questions are related to the concepts of control and incentives. A whole set of formal and informal control mechanisms are massively mobilised by the multinational firms in the sample. However, because of the high cultural and geographical distances between France and China, the expatriate interviewees insisted on the importance of shared values. These shared values are part of the wider concept of corporate culture (Schein, 1985). Top executives and middle managers who have integrated the culture of their company are highly likely to comply with company rules, including the most implicit ones, when negotiating, for instance, in differing cultural contexts or when facing unforeseeable situations.

In order to ensure the worldwide coherence of the multinational, nearly all the interviewees in the sample stressed the importance of corporate culture. Multinationals develop various complementary actions to reinforce the corporate culture and to enable it to be shared by the Chinese employees. Subsidiary A, for example, sends Chinese managers to France, 'so that they can feel the French culture, which somehow influences the culture of the company'. The expatriate CEO of Holding B stresses that its group is European and not French: 'such is the culture and it should be shared with the local employees'. The CEO of Subsidiary C says its group 'is a social company with a very strong company culture'. In Multinational E, 'the young future managers must be immersed in the culture of the group before being given managerial functions with important responsibilities; if not, there are potentially conflicts'. The CEO of Subsidiary I, more precisely, calls upon the need to transfer the culture of quality and safety on which the corporate culture of its multinational is founded. The CEO of Subsidiary H says that its multinational 'strongly inculcates the culture of the group through many signs such as, for example, diagrams in the work rooms'. He adds that 'all expatriates have assimilated the company's culture; they are selected because they have this culture: you think "H is our company"; this is even a recruitment criterion'.

3   Conclusion

From the point of view of Burns (1963), the search for global efficiency and the development of local responsiveness do not seem easily reconcilable. However, multinational firms gain a lot by trying to make them compatible. Therefore, they invent solutions, as analysed by Bartlett and Goshal (1987, 1989), such as equipping certain subsidiaries to produce not only for the market in the country of their establishment, but also to produce products or components for other units of the multinational, established in several markets. These subsidiaries, on the one hand, obtain economies of scale and, on the other, are able to employ human resources with rich and diversified skills, stimulating flexibility and local reactivity.

The research was aimed at understanding how the efforts for conciliation of two, a-priori opposite logics are translated into operational answers. China was chosen for the field study since multinationals, aiming at efficiency, have invested massively in China, in order to benefit from cost reduction. At the same time, the dynamism of the Chinese economy offers a lot of new opportunities, which also enhances the emergence of new competitors, requiring strong and quick local responsiveness. We interviewed the expatriate CEOs of twelve subsidiaries or country holdings established in China by French multinational companies.

Most of the mechanisms identified by the literature that are usually implemented to attain the greatest efficiency, have been identified in our sample: the accumulation of economies of scale, the experience curve, standardisation of products and procedures, formalisation of the organisation, international localisation of activities and the centralisation of decision-making. These mechanisms normally cause organisational rigidity. But the interviews identified various ways of maintaining a sufficient level of flexibility, especially through short-term missions of experts travelling around the network of subsidiaries of the multinational, intensive informal exchanges at reporting sessions, decentralisation of decisions by the creation of intermediate structures, China holdings or regional offices, and the development of a strong corporate culture within the multinational, extended to Chinese employees.

Formal exchanges, initially supporting the search for global efficiency, seem to play a key role in reducing the paradox 'efficiency against local reactivity', while formalisation creates enhanced informal exchanges, which are a main source of a high-level of responsiveness. Informal exchanges resulting from control procedures and formal coordination are, in the opinion of the expatriates interviewed, extremely time- and energy-consuming. The managers of the headquarters cannot devote as much attention to all the subsidiaries worldwide. It seems that the strategic character of China for these multinationals, and the fact that their future is to a great extent at stake, explains why managers at the head office give such an amount of attention to their subsidiaries in China (Jaussaud and Schaaper, 2006). Finally, this is how, in the Chinese context, multinationals reconcile efficiency and local reactivity. It could be that in other less crucial parts of the world, formal control does not lead to such rich informal exchanges between the head office and its subsidiaries. This point, however, deserves more precise research.

References

Bartlett, C.A. and Goshal, S. (1987) Managing across borders: new organisational responses. *Sloan Management Review*, Autumn (Fall): 43–53.
——— (1989) *Managing Across Borders: The Transnational Solution*. Boston, Mass.: Harvard Business School Press.
Bouquin, H. (1986) *Le Contrôle de Gestion*. Paris: Presses Universitaires de France.
Burns, T. (1963) Industry in a new age. *New Society*, 31 (January): 17–20.
Fama, E.F. and Jensen, M.C. (1983) Separation of ownership and control. *Journal of Law and Economics*, 26: 301–26.
Geringer, J.M. and Hebert, L. (1989) Control and performance of international joint ventures. *Journal of International Business Studies*, 20: 235–54.
Jaussaud, J. and Schaaper, J. (2006) Entre efficience, réactivité et apprentissage organisationnel: une étude qualitative sur le cas des filiales françaises en Chine. *Management International*, 11 (1): 1–13.
Jensen, M.C. and Meckling, W.H. (1976) Theory of the firm: managerial behaviour, agency cost and ownership structure. *Journal of Financial Economics*, October, 3 (4): 305–60.
Johnson, J., Scholes, J. and Whittington, R. (2005) *Stratégique* (7th edn). Harlow, Essex: Pearson Education.
Kumar, S. and Seth, A. (1998) The design of coordination and control mechanisms for managing joint venture – parent relationships. *Strategic Management Journal*, 19: 579–99.
Martinez, J.L. and Jarillo, J.C. (1989) The evolution of research on coordination mechanisms in multinational corporations. *Journal of International Business Studies*, Autumn (Fall): 489–514.
Mintzberg, H. (1982) *Structure et dynamique des organisations*. Paris: Les Editions d'Organisation.
Mintzberg, H., Quinn, J. and Ghoshal, S. (1998) *The Strategy Process* (revised European edition: Prentice-Hall Europe). Harlow: Pearson Education.
Morvan, Y. (1991) *Fondements d'Economie Industrielle* (2nd edn). Collection Gestion. Paris: Economica.
Parent, J. (1975) *Les firmes industrielles*, Collection Thémis, Volumes 1 and 2. Paris: Presses Universitaires de France.
Schein, E. (1985) *Organisational Culture and Leadership*. San Francisco: Jossey Bass.
Symon, G. and Cassel, C. (1998) *Qualitative Methods an Analysis in Organisational Research*. London: Sage Publications.
Taylor, F.W. (1947) *Scientific Management*. New York: Harper and Row.

4

The Paradox of Honesty: How Multinationals Contribute to the Spread of Organised Crime

Philippe Very and Bertrand Monnet

Drug trafficking, arms trafficking, prostitution, money laundering, organ trafficking: these are the traditional activities of organised crime. Carried out by mafias, cartels and other criminal groups, these activities seem at first so remote from the concerns of multinational corporations that they are often referred to as the 'parallel world'. Our economy is perceived by many as being split into two separate worlds: the legal and honest sphere made up of, and involving, the operations of respectable enterprises, and the parallel sphere, made up of illegal, largely underground activities.

In this chapter, we will show that this vision of the world no longer exists, and that the interaction between these two spheres extends to such a point that the boundaries have become blurred.

The events of 11 September 2001 contributed greatly to this situation. The attacks on the World Trade Center, which caused nation states to focus their attention on, and commit significant resources to, fighting terrorism, have had three major consequences:

i. The emergence of numerous groups claiming links to al-Qaeda, mostly outside the United States due to the reinforcement of security measures within the US.
ii. The expansion of criminal activities by organised groups who, under less scrutiny, have expanded their territories and prospered; Naim (2007) shows the expansion of these transnational outfits which have replaced, or co-opted, local groups and gangs.
iii. The diversification of criminal group activities with the identification of legitimate companies as easy targets for enrichment, as our discussion will show later.

Before 9/11, the adoption of a capitalist economy by countries previously under the control or influence of the Soviets allowed local criminal groups in many areas to expand and profit from the changing world order in the wake of the fall of the Berlin Wall. In some countries, such as Bulgaria, the rise of corruption in national administrations also contributed to an increase in criminalisation. In Nigeria, a significant portion of oil company profits legally ends up in the hands of local government officials. These profits rarely trickle down to the populations of the Niger Delta who, in turn, resort to preying upon the multinationals to compensate for this perceived injustice.

In fact, the globalisation of business has brought about the simultaneous internationalisation of criminal groups, which also has translated into an increasing exposure of multinationals to these criminal groups. The paradox of this situation is that by contributing to the economic development of emerging countries, multinationals contribute, often involuntarily, to the spread of organised crime. A substantial portion of the newly created wealth from these emerging economies ends up in the hands of criminals, and we have a situation where the honest enrich the dishonest.

Our research on this phenomenon sheds some light on this complicity, which is often coerced (Very and Monnet, 2008). We have studied the attacks on companies since 11 September 2001 and have identified for each attack the criminal elements, their motivations and their methods. We will first present a typology of existing criminal actions, then analyse the repercussions of attacks on multinational companies, and finally discuss the managerial consequences of these acts.

1   Typology of criminal action against multinationals

1.1   Types and strategies of organised crime

The United Nations Convention (Palermo, 2000, Article 2: Terminology) defines organised crime as 'a structured group of three or more persons, existing for a period of time and acting in concert with the aim of committing one or more serious crimes or offences established in accordance with this Convention, in order to obtain, directly or indirectly, a financial or other material benefit' (p. 2). Relying upon this definition, we can break down organised crime as a whole into the following groups:

- mafias, or the 'aristocracy of crime' (Raufer, 2005);
- cartels and other transnational groups, such as the Colombian drug cartels;
- street gangs, such as biker gangs, which are heavily involved in drug trafficking;
- tribes, clans and local communities organised in a deliberate way to commit systematic and repeated criminal acts, such as the Ijaw and Itsekeri communities in Nigeria;

- armed groups that began as revolutionary armies and have abandoned their initial political ambitions to pursue economic gain through criminal activity, such as the FARC (Revolutionary Armed Forces of Colombia – People's Army) in Colombia;
- organised terrorist networks.

Similar to companies, these groups develop strategies to meet their goals, whether economic – as in the case of the first five groups – or political or ideological, as in the case of terrorist networks. Criminal groups use four types of strategies to target multinationals: predation, diversion, destruction and competition. These categories can be further divided into eight tactics which are presented in Table 4.1.

1.1.1   Type 1: Predation

When using predation, a criminal group aims to capture the wealth of the targeted victim by using one of four tactics:

  i. treasure hunt
 ii. product hunt
iii. personnel hunt
iv. knowledge hunt.

1.1.1.1   Treasure hunt.   The aim of treasure hunts is to get rich directly at the expense of a company. Italian mafias practise the *pizzo*, a simple extortion system applied to any business operating on the criminal group's territory. In the dangerous Strait of Malacca, some attacks on ships are carried out simply to steal the cash onboard, as criminals are not necessarily interested in the merchandise. But treasure hunts can be more elaborate, involving forced employment of ghost workers or forced sale of services. For example, many oil companies operating in Nigeria employ members of local communities,

Table 4.1   Typology of criminal activity affecting multinationals

Strategy	Tactic	Examples
Predation	Treasure hunt	Extortion, forced sale, forced employment
	Product hunt	Theft, road and maritime piracy
	Personnel hunt	Kidnapping for ransom
	Knowledge hunt	Espionage, counterfeiting
Diversion	Parasitism	Use of company logistics to launder money
Destruction	Symbol hunt	Murder, destruction of sites
Competition	Property hunt	Business takeover
	Market hunt	Market takeover

even though most of them have never set foot there. If a company tries to resist this practice, its oil fields or refinery sites can be attacked, looted or even destroyed.

Regarding the practice of forced sale of services, foreign companies operating in parts of Russia, for example, are often obliged to use a 'recommended' security company to monitor their facilities.

1.1.1.2 Product hunt. A product hunt includes thefts and acts of piracy with the intent of appropriating company products and physical resources.[1] In Nigeria, oil 'bunkering' is mostly controlled by rebels of the NPDVF (Niger Delta People's Volunteer Force), or other armed factions. Bunkering consists of drilling a hole into an oil pipe and stealing the leaking oil. With this strategy, criminals grow rich by selling the stolen oil.

Piracy is practised on both the road and the sea. The trend is to steal merchandise during transportation, where protection is more difficult, rather than when secured at company sites. As criminal groups generally operate on their own territories, product hunts require previous knowledge of multinationals' transportation and logistical arrangements.

1.1.1.3 Personnel hunt. Personnel hunt is another type of extortion often referred to as 'kidnapping for ransom'. Criminal groups receive payment in exchange for the release of kidnapped hostages. This practice is widely used in Latin America, particularly in Colombia and Mexico, in Russia and in many other countries. Expatriate multinational managers become the targets of choice for kidnappers and live with this lethal threat on a daily basis.

1.1.1.4 Knowledge hunt. Knowledge hunts refer to acts of espionage and counterfeiting which increasingly are carried out by organised criminal groups. Spying consists of stealing a secret or know-how, with a view to selling it to competitors or other interested parties. Counterfeiting involves diverting a secret or some intangible asset (such as a brand) to produce imitations of the original product. Spying to produce counterfeit weapons, luxury goods or cigarettes is just the tip of the iceberg: these illicit practices now extend to many industries (Saviano, 2007). The software, automobile and aeronautical spare parts industries are particularly exposed to this type of risk.

These four predation tactics have direct consequences on the financial results of companies. They result in a loss of earnings and can lead to cash flow problems. They also have psychological consequences, particularly in the case of personnel hunts, as they add a danger factor to the daily lives of workers. Predation tactics also have an indirect economic impact related to the costs of developing and implementing solutions to anticipate or respond to such attacks. However, predation does not represent a threat to the survival of targeted multinationals. As criminal groups tap into and depend on company resources through predation tactics, it is in their interest that the companies they prey upon continue to grow, so that they can pursue their lucrative illicit activities.

1.1.2   Type 2: Diversion

Criminal groups employ a second strategy which consists of diverting the organisational and logistical capacities of a business in order to fulfil their needs. Here, criminal groups do not act as predators, but as opportunists who use companies for their illegal trafficking activities: money laundering or trafficking in drugs, arms or people. The target becomes an attractive substitute for the ad hoc development of a logistical system by the criminal group.

This strategy is called 'parasitism'. Just as the tapeworm lives inside the human body, the criminal group feeds off its target. The banking industry is particularly threatened by the laundering of dirty money. International transportation and logistics companies (road, rail, sea or air) are attractive for other forms of trafficking. A mining company had one such experience: they discovered that one of their ships was being used to transport cocaine from the Caribbean Islands to North America. This incited them to outsource sea transportation in the area. Therefore, an indirect consequence of parasitism is the economic cost of the resources put in place to combat it or avoid it. But such diversions also have a direct impact on companies, as they raise the issue of their legal liability, and that of their managers who run the risk of being accused of complicity when the trafficking is discovered.

1.1.3   Type 3: Destruction

The third strategy, destruction, is mostly used by terrorist groups who carry out an ideological combat on behalf of a religion, a political objective (to overthrow a government, for example) or, more generally, against capitalism. Seeking to destroy the very symbols of what they despise, their targets are primarily companies that represent a way of life that the terrorists want to eliminate: Western multinationals (for example, the attacks against the Marriott Hotel in Jakarta, McDonald's in Asia, employees of the Direction des Chantiers Navals in Karachi), or oil conglomerates (for example, the attack on the oil tanker *Linburg* in Yemen).

According to a report from the British insurance group Lloyd's (2007), 20 per cent of terrorist attacks after 11 September 2001 have targeted businesses, resulting in the death of about 2,000 employees. Direct impacts of these attacks translate into the loss of physical resources such as buildings, properties, equipment, and the loss of human life. Security costs are twofold: costs related to security measures required by the government (for American companies, for example), and costs arising from the implementation of solutions specific to each multinational. In these cases, the survival of the attacked multinational is threatened, at least locally, as such actions can push a company to pull out of a country.

1.1.4   Type 4: Competition

With the fourth strategy, competition (as seen from a company standpoint), businesses find themselves actually competing with an organised criminal group. This is the case when a criminal organisation seeks to create a respectable façade or benefit from a lucrative legal market, which leads it to use two tactics:

  i. property hunt
 ii. market hunt.

1.1.4.1 Property hunt.   Property hunts consist of taking control of a company using one of two techniques based on the level of economic development of the country: pressure on top executives or predation of privatised companies. Favoured by mafias in industrialised countries, the first strategy uses an array of methods to force executives to hand over the reins: private loans at usury rate, threats on the families of executives and shareholders, destabilisation or infiltration of the board of directors. In Japan, the Yakuza regularly applies this type of hunt; for instance, creating turmoil during a general assembly (Pierrat and Sargos, 2005). In developing or emerging countries, criminal groups take advantage of privatisation operations to take over a company. By corrupting local governments, they succeed in gaining control of companies coveted by honest, legitimate competitors. This essentially leads to the integration of criminal groups into the legitimate business world.

1.1.4.2 Market hunt.   Market hunts consist of seizing a market at the expense of a legitimate company. Common in public tenders (for example, parking lots or waste management), it implies that the criminal group already runs a 'respectable' company. With the help of accomplices within the government, the criminal group is selected for the public tender. Such a situation hinders the international development of multinationals and often leads to their failure to penetrate some national markets which, in turn, leads them to re-examine their expansion strategies. Another impact is the arrival in the competitive arena of rivals directly connected to criminal groups.

With these two tactics, multinationals now face unfair competition with 'businesses' which may not respect the rules of fair competition. A mafia organisation can take control of a company and use it, either to develop its criminal activity, or to have a respectable façade. Whatever the motivation, the controlled company can then exert pressure or use violent means to develop its legal activities.

1.2   Cybercrime

The term 'cybercrime' is commonly used to describe various realities: the spread of viruses over the Internet, destruction of websites, hacking into IT systems and so on. We examine these different criminal activities below.

To commit their crimes, criminal groups need information about their targets. By connecting to the computerised address book of an expatriate worker, a gang can anticipate his moves and prepare a kidnapping (personnel hunt). Criminal groups penetrate information systems and access R&D projects which can then be sold or used for counterfeiting (knowledge hunt). They can learn about shipping routes to organise a drug trafficking move (parasitism). They may also use phishing techniques to get information about company customers or steal their identities to carry out financial transactions (treasure hunt). The cost to American banks of such methods reached US$1.2 billion in 2003 (*Wall Street Journal*, 2004).

In summary, intrusion into information systems is an efficient way to obtain useful information in order to carry out any type of crime. In this case, the expression 'cybercrime' can be defined as a means to put into place a predation, diversion, competition or destruction strategy using information-based technologies.

'Global-born' businesses specialising in online trade (sale of merchandise, banking activities, games, gambling, auctions and so on) are also particularly vulnerable to extortion: company servers are flooded with an enormous information inflow which results in a denial of service to legitimate customers until a ransom is paid. Organised criminal groups behind such practices are often based in Eastern Europe (*Wall Street Journal*, 2007). Such practices show that criminal groups possess the technical resources to completely paralyse the operations of a 'global-born' company, or that they can oblige computer scientists to work for them.

To summarise, cybercrime is one tool criminal groups can use to implement the diverse strategies discussed in this chapter.

2   Impact of criminal action on competition

The increasing vulnerability of multinationals to criminal activity has various impacts on competition depending on the type of crime committed or the tactic used by the group. For each type or tactic, these consequences can be direct (specifically related to the crime committed) or indirect (related to the policies put into place by states to deal with specific threats) (Spich and Grosse, 2005).

2.1   Consequences of predation

Resource predation has a direct impact on company accounts. Treasure hunts (extortion, forced sales, forced employment) generate the payment for undue or exorbitant services, thus increasing expenses in the profit and loss account and leading to potential cash flow problems.

Product hunts result in a predictable increase in the cost of insurance, which protects companies against theft and piracy, or in an increased quantity of unsold merchandise when companies are not insured.

While personnel hunts have financial consequences related to the payment of a ransom, they also generate human resource management problems as kidnappings carry psychological consequences not only for the hostage and their family, but also for the other employees. It can become difficult for companies to find employees willing to work in regions where kidnapping is a potential threat. Another added expense for companies is risk premiums paid to expatriates, which increase significantly following a kidnapping. Moreover, when a hostage is killed, questions on the legal liability of companies or their CEOs can arise.

Knowledge hunts result in the loss of a competitive edge (espionage) or market share (counterfeiting). More than the other predation tactics, knowledge hunts have a direct impact on a multinational's competitiveness and can cause a company to redefine its strategy.

Additional costs are those related to the implementation of solutions, either internal or external, which include onsite security measures, protection of expatriate workers and their families, services to fight illicit use of a company's intellectual property and so on.

In Nigeria, one of the world's leading oil-producing countries, production costs have doubled in the past few years as a result of criminal activity, including product hunts ('bunkering' of oil pipes, onsite destruction and looting and so on), treasure hunts (forced employment, extortion), personnel hunts (kidnapping for ransom), as well as costs incurred to deploy solutions to fight these activities.

2.2 Consequences of diversion

The use of a multinational's logistics operations to develop a criminal activity a priori has no direct effect on its bottom line. The criminal group simply transits drugs, weapons, human beings or money through the company's pipeline, and even surreptitiously contributes to increasing its productivity! However, financial, law enforcement, customs and judicial institutions in many countries have forced some industries to set up strict monitoring systems to avoid becoming ensnared as accomplices to such criminal activity. On top of these indirect compliance costs, there is the risk of them being accused of criminal complicity with organised crime groups (Bauer, 2005). For example, bankers are often brought to justice for complicity in dirty money laundering operations.

2.3 Consequences of destruction

The attacks committed against multinationals' facilities, or the murder of their employees, have various consequences. Business activity can be paralysed for long periods in the event of site destruction, resulting in a loss in turnover. Insurance costs may also increase, and the legal liability of the company or its managers can be called into question (Collard, 2005).

Countries such as the United States have introduced anti-terrorism policies requiring companies to set up costly security systems which, in some instances, can lead them to change their logistic operations. For example, the control policy put into place in American ports has led to increased costs and longer delays for merchandise transiting through these ports.

2.4   Consequences of criminal competition

By exercising market predation and gaining control of legitimate businesses, criminal groups gain entry into the competitive arena. The first consequence is on the multinational strategy (Very and Ivanova, 2005). These criminal practices put constraints on a company's international development and prevent it from penetrating specific countries or regions. The second consequence has to do with the increasing uncertainty in interpreting the competitor's behaviour as it is difficult to define the genuine motivations of the criminal organisation. Do they want to use this company to carry out their activities, or create a façade of honesty? In the latter case, will they develop their activities using legal competition weapons, or will they resort to corruption, pressure and coercion on the targeted markets? Could companies find themselves no longer fighting on equal terms?

3   Summary of the repercussions

The research-based developments discussed above show the extent of the problems created by the increased illicit activities perpetrated by organised criminal groups in the sphere of legitimate business. For multinationals, the impact is not just limited to cost increases, either direct or indirect. It may also take several forms, and oblige companies to redefine their internationalisation strategies, review their human resources and logistical system management policies, protect themselves against any accusations of complicity and better protect their competitive advantage. Also, companies that fall victim to a criminal act are fearful for their reputation and image. Public knowledge of a crime has several potentially harmful effects.

Financial markets can penalise a multinational unable to extricate itself from a criminal group. Companies can also suffer from recruiting problems if they are perceived as incapable of guaranteeing the safety of their personnel and operations. It is precisely to preserve their reputation that few companies publish information about crimes committed against them. There is, however, one exception: counterfeiting of luxury items, which has the dual effect of penalising legitimate sales, and of spreading the brand and even reinforcing its positioning in the luxury sector.

3.1 Managerial implications

The investigations carried out on types of criminal activities raise important questions about the evolution of the business world. While the encroachment of organised crime into the business world has increased since the 9/11 attacks, the resources allocated to security have focused mainly on one type of threat: terrorism. But, protection from destruction means taking all the necessary measures to avoid a future attack or loss of life. Unlike destruction, predation, diversion and competition translate into criminal acts which affect a company with varying frequency. Therefore, the objective is not to avoid a future threat, but to manage an existing one that may have potentially harmful consequences.

As a result, we can no longer talk about two parallel worlds, a legal one and an illegal one, as they are clearly intertwined. The most structured criminal groups, mafias, cartels and other transnational actors, enter the legal sphere in various ways. By buying companies and taking over markets, they become rivals of existing competitors in their operating territories. When they divert logistical capacities, they use legal channels to carry out their illicit trafficking. The interaction between criminals and multinationals is complex. They compete with each other or use the same resources. By practising espionage and the resale of secrets or know-how, criminals have influence on the relative competition between the actors of a given industry.

This last point leads us to question the frontier between 'good' and 'evil': stealing an industrial secret is attractive if it can be resold. In other words, the buyer also commits a crime, and the world of the 'good' is polluted with businesses using criminal methods. The fact that espionage has always existed does not mean it should simply be ignored.

Multinationals need to understand that today's business environment includes criminal elements and these elements need to be considered when formulating any development strategy. Some companies have adopted advanced management systems to deal with criminal threats and have adapted their solutions to the type of criminals they encounter, the local area they operate in and the crimes committed. When faced with treasure hunts in African or Asian communities, they set up local sustainable development policies. If they are dealing with structured and hardened criminal groups, they deploy other solutions: avoidance, risk transfer, assessing and acting on the cause and so on. For example, when faced with a kidnapping risk, human resources departments are mobilised to inform expatriates and their families, and teach them the right attitudes and behaviours. Such risks can usually be covered by an insurance company. As the solutions must address specific problems, the costs can vary widely.

From a management standpoint, the main consequence of international development for businesses is to anticipate criminal threats as much as possible by integrating them into their investment plan, forecasting the related costs and calculating the profitability of such a project through a risk assessment. Companies also need to notify and prepare their various divisions on how to react when they encounter such threats. Lastly, they must make sure they contribute as little as possible to the achievement of the objectives of criminal organisations.

4   Conclusion

In many areas of the world, multinationals are of great interest to organised criminal groups. The international expansion of these companies is increasingly hindered by problems arising from illegal practices used by more or less structured groups that operate in domestic or transnational territories. Human, technological and financial resources, logistical systems, markets, strategies, the integrity of justice and even control of their capital, are all in jeopardy. Multinationals are increasingly vulnerable to this interpenetration and these increasing intrusions. It even becomes difficult to define a clear boundary between the legal and illegal world. As a result, criminal risk moves from being a peripheral risk to a systemic risk.

In order to succeed in a sustainable way and remain competitive, multinationals need to consider the aspect of criminal organisations in their strategic thinking process. Through their development of international sites and the power of attraction they represent, they create local wealth which contributes not only to a country's economic growth but also to the growth of the criminal sphere. Multinationals no longer simply encounter organised crime; they operate in a criminalised world, where honesty does not pay, and where, paradoxically, crime contributes to its prosperity.

Note

1. Criminals even succeed in stealing electricity! Very and Ivanova (2005) describe the case of a European electricity company that acquired a Brazilian company and then discovered that one third of the clients were unknown to them. Electricity was being diverted by local gangs who organised and managed their own distribution network in poor neighbourhoods.

References

Bauer, A. (2005) Sécurité, crime et entreprises: le nouveau chaos mondial. *Défense Nationale et Sécurité Collective*, 3 (Supplément Spécial): 9–16.
Collard, C. (2005) Terrorisme et engagement de la responsabilité de l'entreprise et de ses dirigeants. *Défense Nationale et Sécurité Collective*, 3 (Supplément Spécial): 33–42.
Naim, M. (2007) *Le Livre Noir de l'Economie Mondiale*. Paris: Grasset.
Lloyd's (2007) *Under Attack? Global Business and the Threat of Political Violence*. London: Economist Intelligence Unit Ltd and Lloyds.
Pierrat, J. and Sargos, A. (2005) *Yakusa*. Paris: Flammarion.
Raufer, X. (2005) *La Camorra*. Paris: La Table Ronde.

Saviano, R. (2007) *Gomorra: dans l'empire de la Camorra*. Paris: Gallimard.

Spich, R. and Grosse, R. (2005) How does homeland security affects US firms' international competitiveness? *Journal of International Management*, 11: 457–76.

United Nations (2000) *United Nations Convention against Transnational Organised Crime*. December. Palermo: Italy.

Very, P. and Ivanova, O. (2005) L'action criminelle, entrave au développement de l'entreprise. *Défense Nationale et Sécurité Collective*, 3: 27–32.

Very, P. and Monnet, B. (2008) Quand les organisations rencontrent le crime organise. *Revue française de gestion*, 3 (183): 179–200.

Wall Street Journal (2004) *A Special Report: E-Commerce – Something's Phishy: Online Identity-Theft Scams are So Effective That They Threaten to Steal a Vital Ingredient of E-commerce: trust*, 15 November: 8.

——— (2007) *Email Scheme Targets Executives*, 10 October: B5.

Part II
Marketing and Logistics

5
The Taste of Industrialised Societies for Traditional Products: Socio-Cultural and Economic Paradoxes

Nathalie Prime and Mitsuyo Delcourt-Itonaga

The post-industrial countries, or the Triad societies (Europe, Japan, United States) (Ohmae, 1985), marked by the continuous growth of international exchanges after the Second World War, represent the heart of the global economy. In all of these societies, independently from the cultural areas of origin, a common phenomenon can be observed: the wish to revive traditions that were thought lost, as well as the products of *terroir*[1] and other authentic products (Warnier, 1994). After decades characterised by a zealous rush for progress and profit-seeking, new values seem to be of major interest to well-off consumers in contemporary societies; for example, a quest for being at ease with oneself, with others and the world by connecting with traditions in areas as different and various as food, health, cosmetics, living and leisure (Eschwège and Charpentier, 2005).

Traditional hand-crafted products of ethnic origin from a specific region, or *terroir*, are perceived as authentic and desirable. They are associated with a specific and unique region, era and culture, and as such they satisfy our senses. As opposed to industrial products, which imply the concept of 'to have', traditional goods correspond to the concept of 'to be', allowing for the identification and differentiation of the individual consumer (see Section 2.1, Fromm, 1978). Today, one willingly admits that the limits of the standardised globalisation of markets (Levitt, 1983) are numerous and that the 'global village' founding myth of globalisation (McLuhan, 1962) must be nuanced. We are rather living in 'global villages' (Usunier and Lee, 2008) by keeping our identities and our values while at the same time participating in – for the affluent, it is true, but also for an increasing number of individuals – the global community.

Economic globalisation is therefore paradoxically the source of new differentiations. Furthermore, the consumption patterns in the Triad economies are converging towards a renewed interest in traditions that had been neglected, and can even become fashionable.

This chapter explores the reasons that help to explain the taste of industrialised societies for traditional products, and the paradoxical dynamics that accompany this renewed interest in their consumption. From the socio-cultural point of view, traditional products are not limited to an expression of the past but indicate the future as the renewed interest in them contributes to coping with multiple disparities, created in the contemporary societies of over-consumption and over-production. These disparities occur between the countries of the south and those of the north, between remote regions and more developed areas, and between the inequality between craftsmen and industrialised production. If the consumption of such products raises the question of the value of a past-future link in modern societies, it also creates – as a result of the appreciation of both past and future – a fertile hybridisation between tradition and modernity. This creates a synthesis which helps to bring about a general ecology of life, and which guarantees a better future for balanced human societies. Also, from the economic point of view, the taste of industrialised societies for traditional products raises the paradox of a skilful union between traditional know-how and innovation throughout the process of production and commercialisation. Therefore, if traditional products are by definition rooted in *terroir*, their economy, from design to distribution, is not rigidly set in the past, but leans heavily on innovative values and tools, particularly from the commercial point of view (craft marketing).

1   The taste for traditional products in the industrialised societies: a remarkable convergence among open societies

The taste of industrialised societies for traditional products is particularly remarkable. The diversity of examples referred to below, in various countries and fields (not limited to hand-crafted products) proves how widespread and common this taste is between countries. We will look at Japan, the United States and France in turn.

1.1   The various forms of the need to revive traditions

In Japan today, young people without the experience of the traditional Japanese lifestyle enjoy wearing a kimono. It's an integral part of their fashion experience. Freed from complex traditional codes, the wearing of the kimono has been re-invented, partly for fun but also as a reflection of their interest in tradition. In the field of entertainment, one of the most popular radio programmes downloaded by the young generation is *Rakugo*, a solo-narrative art of fast-paced humorous stories dating back to the seventeenth century. The stories in general deal with everyday family or neighbourhood life with unexpected, humorous endings.

Traditional floral art, *ikebana*, is also making a surprising renaissance. Previously considered as an obligatory part of a woman's education, it is now practised widely by middle-aged businessmen to express their individual creativity and to relax after work (*Nihon Keizai Shimbun*, 2006). Moreover, the red *furoshiki* (a traditional Japanese square fabric to wrap and carry things) named 'happiness' has been launched by the retail association of Toshima-ku, one of the twenty-three districts of Tokyo, in order to promote ecological issues. This *furoshiki* is made from recycled plastic bottles. The number of plastic bags provided at shops is about 30 billion annually, 230 on average per inhabitant in Japan. The eco bag, or *furoshiki*, is now a necessary item for Japanese women. Furthermore, *Kyosei* (cohabitation or symbiosis), a concept proposed by the architect Kisho Kurokawa in 1980 is steadily developing. More than cohabitation, it's a symbiotic relationship between different world cultures, between man (technology) and nature, between history and the present. One example is housing: important efforts are undertaken in the restoration of old wooden houses, in order to preserve the local landscape and to avoid important CO_2 emissions (which is an estimated 15 tons per house if destroyed and burned). For two decades, a new technology based on the analysis of the structure of old houses has allowed local people to more easily integrate the traditional wooden architecture, which is more adapted to the local climatic and economic environment, while using modern construction materials.

In the United States, other traditional behaviours are seeing a revival. Midwifery and home births, practices that almost disappeared in the 1950s, are experiencing an upturn in popularity, avoiding the excessively high involvement of technology when giving birth in hospital. In business, a combination of religious aspiration and management is in fashion: books with evocative titles such as *Leading with Soul*, *The Healing Manager* or *Managing from the Heart* appeal to the importance of the human side of management practice. The benefit of teamwork in those countries with a culture of individualism (Surowiecki, 2008) is being re-evaluated. In the past, the popular strategic texts of *Art of War* influenced management practices. Now a new theory of management, based on core traditional philosophies like the Indian philosophy of Bhagavad-Gita, is finding an echo in American business schools (*Business Week*, 2006). The concepts of personal satisfaction, of a symbiotic relationship between business partners, and of the relations between consumers and the social responsibility of companies, are also praised in the development of good managerial practices.

Finally, in France, the reproduction of iconic products of the past including furniture, food and clothes, has been gaining popularity. For example, the reissue of vintage perfumes represents a return to real values in the context of standardised market offers. This trend can also be observed in the viticulture industry where a number of chateaux and other producers have chosen to cultivate their vineyards using organic or biodynamic techniques.

In France again, from recycling to vintage, the recent fashion is for 'intelligent consumption'. The magazine *Aladin* highlights the wide interest of consumers of different ages in vintage products. This magazine provides comprehensive information about forthcoming exhibitions and sales events, about regions and their traditional products, about traditions and popular art museums, but also about trends in design, collectors' interests (from old comic books to expensive furniture) and so on. Although representing a niche market (with a circulation of 60,000), the popularity of this magazine reflects the trend of consumers searching for unique or original objects with imaginary and timeless value, accompanied by the almost playful pleasure of treasure-hunting. A boom of garage sales also shows the pleasure that goes together with the practices of 'anti-leaky basket' (i.e. control in spending money).

This nostalgic trend is expressed by Reflets de France, a private label of the hypermarket Carrefour, created in 1996, which relies on the taste for *terroir* by offering a large range of traditional regional food products that reflect the art of traditional French cooking. Over 250 articles are produced locally by 140 producers allowing this brand to gain popularity among consumers. The concept of this product range is locally adapted in other European countries under the brand name of De Nuestra Tierra in Spain, Souvenir du Terroir in Belgium and Terre d'Italia in Italy. Italy is particularly receptive to the concept of *terroir*. In 1989, in the Torino region, the Slow Food movement that is today worldwide was born, in reaction against the rapid Italian lifestyle and monotonous fast food. This movement intends to preserve eco-regional cooking and the shared gustative memory. Eataly, a store that brings together small agricultural producers throughout Italy has also been opened in Torino and Milan. It promotes artisan-made and eco-friendly products.

Product marketing reflects these tendencies. So jeans, a symbol of Western pop culture, never stop being re-invented or rediscovered in the various offers coming from all brands worldwide, Levi's 501, launched originally in 1873, keeps its popularity, and vintage jeans are sold by eBay or even by auction houses that more usually sell art. At the same time, a new trend of manufacturing that is more ecological and sustainable (organic cotton, natural indigo, reduced use of water and energy, recycling of fabrics and so on) is set by new brands such as Gilded Age (*WAD*, 2008). Finally, marketing through advertisements has become the vehicle of this re-invention of the tradition that features nostalgia relating to the quality of work in the past, brought into the present. For example, Samsonite luggage promotes timeless design and durability for an entire lifetime; the Italian tailor Ravazzolo emphasises that skilful hands make their clothes; Isetan (a Japanese department store) advertises a men's umbrella with a bamboo handle, lacquered using traditional 300-year-old techniques.

1.2   Artisan and diverse products of *terroir*

Among traditional products are hand-crafted goods. When we try to define these products, we realise that there are no homogeneous international standard or shared norms. These products are not quantified in the statistics of international trade, including the major international system of trade statistics (Le Système harmonisé de désignation et de codification des marchandises [SH]), the harmonised system of designation and codification of merchandise. However, the International Chamber of Commerce (CCI, 2003) underlines the following features: traditional products are mainly hand-made products whose roots are often cultural, exhibiting a distinctive quality based on inherent characteristics, mainly aesthetic appeal, in particular visual, but also sometimes touch and smell. Craft products can also be functional and/or useful (*'l'art utile des artisans'*), which is not the case of the visual arts (decorative art created principally for pleasure).

From a geographic point of view too, the definition of *terroir* products is very specific and uneven across countries. However, these different approaches to definitions which express different cultural backgrounds come together in the agreed definition, adopted by forty-four countries who participated in the international symposium 'Crafts and the International Market – Trade and Customs Codification', held in Manila in October 1997. This definition is as follows:

Hand-crafted products are those produced by craftsmen, either completely by hand, or with the help of hand tools or even mechanical device, as long as the direct manual contribution of the craftsman remains the most substantial component of the finished product. These are produced without restriction of quantity. Even when craftsmen produce the same model in a large quantity, pieces are never exactly identical. They are produced by using raw materials from sustainable resources. The special nature of hand-crafted products derives from their distinctive features, which can be utilitarian, aesthetic, artistic, creative, culturally attached, decorative, functional, traditional, religiously and socially symbolic and significant. (CCI, 2003: 6).

Traditional products are, therefore, extremely varied, but they are all products of *terroir*. These products are always characterised by three key dimensions (Bérard and Marchenay, 2000; Fort and Fort, 2006):

i. a territorial dimension that gives specificity to the raw material or know-how (i.e. rooted in a precise geographic area);
ii. a temporal dimension (i.e. rooted in know-how established over time, either at national or regional level, or through an enterprise, or by an artisan);
iii. a cultural dimension that connects the two previous dimensions (i.e. rooted in the habits acquired over years, and valid for the area and

community concerned; rooted in the traditional usage that gives sense
to the product and its consumption).

Created in this way, essentially hand-made with the help of appropriate
technologies, either manual or mechanical, traditional products reflect the
psyche of a people. The intensity of these roots can vary according to the
product, endowing a traditional product with a *terroir* root that is more or
less strong in one, two or three dimensions (Aurier et al. 2004). The wine
of *terroir* typically illustrates these three dimensions of anchorage that is territorial, temporal and cultural. The 2004 documentary film *Mondovino* by
Jonathan Nossiter demonstrates that in parallel to a merchandising of marketed wine (an industrial approach used for predominant wine in the New
World), the sensorial dimension of taste prevails when a New York wine mer-
chant speaks of *terroir*. His liking for French wine can be explained precisely
because it's a wine of *terroir*.

2 Socio-cultural reasons of the taste of the industrialised societies for traditional products

Several theoretical contributions can shed light on the principle reasons for
this renewed taste for traditional products in the industrialised societies. The
pressures created by a standardised globalisation based on optimised productivity, on quantification and industrial conformity (the 'McDonaldisation of
society' according to Ritzer, 2004), have never been as strong as today. In a
wider area, these pressures also accompany the evolution of urban zones of
emerging economies. We will illustrate three needs of industrialised societies
that help to explain the renewed interest for the consumption of traditional
products: the quest for harmony between technology and culture, the quest
for a rediscovery of roots and the quest for sense-making through material
culture.

2.1 The quest for harmony between technology and culture: the consumption of High Touch products, a source of balance in a High-Tech addicted society

The phenomenon previously described in different industrialised societies
directly recalls the work of John Naisbitt (2001) on the duality of High Tech–
High Touch perspectives concerning the co-evolution of technology and
culture. Today, several symptoms reveal High Tech addiction, even an alien-
ation of modern society and the way that technology impacts on lifestyles
when used in excess. Thus, High Tech society is marked by the following
symptoms:

1) We favour the quick fix, from religion to nutrition; 2) we fear and
worship technology; 3) we blur the distinction between real and fake;

4) we accept violence as normal; 5) we love technology as a toy; 6) we live our lives distanced and distracted.

(Naisbitt, 2001: 13)

Yet, humans instinctively seek a balance between the social changes brought about by new technology and other human aspects of life. The concept of High Touch offers an important counter-balance to the accelerated impact of technology in our everyday life.

Our relation to time is particularly affected by the intrusion of technology into everyday life, pushing us towards acceleration and instantaneity. High Touch time is slow and circular, so is abundant because 'time comes back'. In contrast, High Tech time is rapid, counted, optimised and economised. It's a monetary time associated with a permanent shortage of time. It is the time of machines (which is linear, uniform and continuous), typical of industrialised societies where individuals lose contact with nature, then with themselves and ultimately with others (Prime, 1999). High Tech products or those produced by machines, reflect this monetary value of time, whilst High Touch products, made manually with care by a craftsman, provide us with a human touch which, in turn, gives a sensation of deep pleasure.

For Fromm (1978), uniform time (that of the machine) is the time of 'to have'. The logic of 'to have' has supplanted that of 'to be' in every section of our lives; this dates back precisely to the rapid industrialisation in European societies during the nineteenth century. Everything tends to be viewed under the prism of 'to have', and our linguistic expressions particularly reflect this: we *have* children (it could be said that we *are* parents); we *have* problems (it could be said that we *are* worried).

The technologies eventually end up diminishing productivity when what promised to gain time consumes more of it: to acquire products of mass consumption products, the High Tech perspective compels us to be capable of defining our priority needs, to select brands, to buy, to install and to maintain these products, and often to update them. We sometimes spend more time trying to gain time.

It is not surprising that, in this context, a growing number of consumers have started to doubt the sophisticated, complicated or gadget-like high-tech products that don't necessarily bring them real satisfaction or benefits, especially when the access cost, and usage and maintenance costs, exceed the final benefits obtained. Also, a real crisis of value (the one perceived by the consumer), associated with the crisis of values (those resulting from the standardised over-consumption and lack of meaning) are commonly seen among consumers of industrialised societies. The Voluntary Simplicity Movement, based more on an individual than an institutional approach, advocates the search for reducing the dependence on money and speed (Martin, 2007). It's about a way of life characterised by material simplicity, by freeing time for oneself and for the community, rather than using time for making money. It is about encouraging practices which are both ecologically and socially responsible.

This movement has many shapes, however. Its origin can be found in Europe in the writings of Tolstoi and Ruskin (*Unto This Last*); in the United States, in those of Thoreau (*Walden*); and in Quebec, in the work of Mongeau and in the publication of *Ecosociété*. They advocate sustainable growth, eco-citizenship and 'consum'action'.[2] Zavestoski (2002) studied the psycho-social stresses related to living in a consumer society. On the basis of interviews with followers of Voluntary Simplicity, he suggests that their motivation comes from their difficulties of feeling true to themselves by their over-consumption. On the west coast of the United States, a certain wave of anti-consumption (named 'Compact') tries to compress rubbish to a minimum in order to decongest the planet. The English-speaking world refers to 'downshifting' when speaking of this movement against hyper-consumption. A similar movement has developed in 'Bobo' ('Bourgeois Bohême' lifestyle) areas of American, European and Japanese cities, that of 'Lohas' ('Lifestyles of Health and Sustainability'). Coffee shops, magazines, organic products and websites have grown in number, creating a specific and transnational market segment (for example, www.lohas.com). The generation of 'less is more' praises the less, using the phrase often associated with Ludwig Mies van der Rohe (1886–1969), one of the founders of modern architecture and an ardent promoter of simplicity and clarity in design. Concerned about environmental issues, poverty or excessive capitalism, this generation modifies its lifestyle without necessarily being militant. Others develop a committed approach by resistance to consumption (ICAR, 2008).

In response to these evolutions of consumers, a simpler approach to technology appeared when some renowned brands re-focused their offers. In electronics, for example, the message of Philips from September 2004, entitled *Sense & Simplicity*, clearly shows the company's strategy to create technologies that have real meaning to their consumers and simplicity of use. Reflecting this approach, Philips's corporate campaign in 2004 and 2006 articulates innovation and care to consumers in different scenes of daily life, from lighting to television sets to medical equipment, with images of a brand that can offer a softer lifestyle with electrical appliances. We can see in the IT sector, the phenomenon of EeePC, a mini PC launched by the Taiwanese company Asus. Due to its low price and weight (less than 1kg), and the ease of use, it appeals to consumers who want to go online at any time or to those who simply wish to learn to use a computer. As for Mac, an innovative niche product (6 per cent of the PC market) can be High Tech and High Touch at the same time, the aesthetics of its design reflecting the long-time practice of calligraphy by its inventor Steve Jobs.

2.2   The quest for a rediscovery of roots: the consumption of products for rediscovering roots in the search for lost links

Consumption is embedded in the characteristics of society (Granovetter, 1985). If contemporary society (of industrialised economies) was largely analysed sociologically, the current situation is sometimes difficult to read. Until today, many spoke of 'postmodernity' (Lyotard, 1979), a phase of modernity cut off from the fundamentals of the first modern revolution, fundamentals that prevailed approximately from the eighteenth century to the 1950s, promoting the ideas of individualism, of the market and dynamics of the techno-science world. Postmodernity represents the failure of grand narratives (Lyotard, 1979), these messianic narratives which lost all credibility with the disasters of the twentieth century. Postmodernity is indeed characterised by the rise of scepticism, but also by the spectacular transformation of behaviours and lifestyles in the years 1950–1960 (Lipovetsky, 1989). Although the counter-balance of the ancient institutions (the state, the church, the family) still endure, in this era there was a revolution of consumption and mass communication, a promotion of hedonistic values and of the futile, a cult of leisure, the sexual revolution, the feminist and homosexual movements. All these are the ingredients of a society focused on the individual, the material well-being and self-fulfilment, the here and now.

A significant change occurred in the 1970s when the state lost ground, when the influence of the religion and the family diminished (at least in Europe and Japan), and when the market society spread. The notion of hypermodernity then emerged to describe the recent disruption of contemporary society. As modernity rid itself of its traditional oppositions (the state, the church, the family) it became a superlative force (Aubert, 2004; Lipovetsky, 2004). In the hypermodern society, everything is 'hyper' (hyper-consumption, hyper-power, hyper-individualism, hyper-capitalism, hyper-anxiety, hypermarket and even hypertext and so on); in other words, everything is excessive or too much. It is an exacerbated modernity where individuals function more on the logic of excess than on one of harmony. Nevertheless, if the postmodern society could be called euphoric, the hypermodern society sees the reappearance of a generalised insecurity created by the permanent search for performance. This happens within the context of everything becoming vulnerable: work, family, health and the natural environment. From this point, contradictory behaviours are sometimes shown by the same individuals according to the situation. We live in the present worrying about the future; we are under the influence of media but we filter their messages; some abandon politics while putting a lot into volunteering. In his study of lifestyles, Mermet (2007) summarises the worldwide significant sociological evolutions from the 1970s (individual freedom), to the 1980s (material well-being where money is the measure of success and happiness), to the 1990s (identity and the search for meaning), to the beginning of the twenty-first century (search for harmony as each individual is increasingly responsible for his or her destiny).

In the absence of traditional referents and faced with the difficulties of achieving self-liberation, in the end, the self-identity is damaged and needs to be restored. In the flood of merchandise and information, the construction of identity takes place in a permanent contradiction between self and another (Appadurai, 2001). Consumption can play a privileged role in this quest for identity. The use of products helps to make up for the underdeveloped socialisation of individuals and contributes to the construction of multi-faceted identities where the need for rediscovering roots is realised by the three following links (Cova & Cova, 2001):

i. a return to the community (in opposition to the individual)
ii. a return to the past (culture of nostalgia opposed to the worship of newness)
iii. a willingness of appropriation (consumers have become actors of their consumption instead of being only passive).

The traditional products, as products of *terroir*, are associated with these three aspects of rediscovering roots.

i. *Return to the community*: A return to the community expresses itself in a desire to find solidarity, even a somewhat spiritual relationship, with the artisans of the rural, underprivileged communities of the developing countries, who open themselves to international distribution through fair trade or tourism.
ii. *Return to the past*: Return to the community also refers to the original communities of the rich countries, insofar as the artisans connect the consumers with their ancestral past. The consumers of traditional products feel nostalgia for those lost traditions now revived, as well as a desire to be global citizens.
iii. *Willingness of appropriation*: Finally, the rediscovery of roots through appropriation can also occur through the rituals of purchase and usage; for example, the return to the traditional ways of celebrating annual festivals.

The local revitalising movement 一村一品 'one village, one product', launched in 1979 in Oita prefecture (in the south of Japan) is illustrative of this need to rediscover roots by the production and consumption of traditional products of *terroir* in Japan. With the three principles promoted (Initiative, Independence and Innovation), it was meant to encourage the inhabitants to rediscover their own resources, both natural and traditional, within their community. This was done by creating or re-launching traditional products in order to revitalise the region which was suffering from depopulation, and to establish a certain economic autonomy *vis á vis* the central government. This movement played an important role in motivating people to work for a common project and to take pride in it. It helped make them aware of the importance of cultural and environmental preservation, and helped children to discover the value of their community. Three hundred and thirty-six products have been launched, of which the total annual turnover amounts to 14 billion yen (about 90 million euros). A product of this movement also implies activities under the slogan 'creation of product, education of man': 148 community establishments, 111 cultural activities and 80 environmental activities were listed as members of this movement in 2002. The movement also stimulated the development of mail-order selling of *terroir* products nationwide. This concept has now been adopted in other Asian countries and in Africa, and local-to-local exchanges have increased between Japan and other industrialised countries; for example, with California in the USA or Rhône-Alpes in France.

In the cinematographic field too, this search for links is very well illustrated by the overwhelming success of Danny Boon's film *Bienvenue chez les Ch'tis* (2008) that attracted an audience of 18 million in France alone. The film is an extraordinary sociological phenomenon that presents a world without gimmicks or gadgets, where speed and efficiency are dethroned in favour of a revival of traditions. Paradoxically, this national massive hit of a very French regional storyline allowed this film to become a success on the international cinema circuits. Similarly, Michel Gondry's comedy *Be Kind Rewind* (2008) shows how members of a small video club made their own versions of commercially produced, successful films, which were so enthusiastically received by their fans that everybody in their neighbourhood made films of their own story, which really interested them and concerned them all.

2.3   The quest for sense-making through material culture: the consumption of authentic products, or a meaningful material culture

Material Culture studies can start from two opposite points: representations of objects or the substance of processes; yet, for the moment, the tools of the study of material cultures is essentially focused on representations (Warnier, 1999). The links between the mechanisms of culture and representations created by use of objects can be traced to the approaches where material culture is considered as a communication system and the object as a sign, built on a *signifié* (what is meant) and a 'significant' (how it is meant) (Barthes, 1957; Baudrillard, 1968).

The anthropology of consumption (Douglas, 1979; Appadurai, 1988; McCracken, 1991; Miller, 1998) suggests that objects contain embedded meanings and values, allowing individuals to use them for communication. The act of buying is the starting point of the life of an object that will be transformed and invested with a new meaning, contextualised within the personal environment of the buyer, and contribute largely to shape the individual and collective identities. Material possessions are an 'extended self' (Belk, 1988) and intrinsically help to define a large part of identity, and also reflect it.

In modern societies, the very new fact in history (Warnier, 1999) is that money (the logic of 'to have') rather the social condition (logic of 'to be') of the subject, now provides the ability to access material resources. Three categories of action have been identified that allow us to de-merchandise and then to domesticate the acquired objects produced by mass-economy.

i. Unpacking (and installation in the personal environment).
ii. Commoditisation (the object is acquired by a system of supplies: from production and large, specialised distribution, to being 'finished' by the consumer).
iii. Incorporation into the physical movements of individuals (a number of objects are types of prostheses).

However, despite the practices of unpacking, commoditisation and incorporation, as modern societies are highly under the influence of social standardisation, an imaginary of 'authentic' merchandise was developed in various sectors by taking the opposite course (Warnier, 1994). Marketing of authentics has therefore to be subtly managed, for there could be a perceived paradox of producing authentic products with mass production methods (Cova & Cova, 2001).

Contrary to an object of consumption non-identified (OCNI) (Fischler, 1990), produced by unknowns in unknown places and sold anonymously through a large distribution channel, namely standardised and without identity, an authentic object is characterised by three specific kinds of value:

i. it comes from elsewhere (it is exotic)
ii. it comes from the past (another time)
iii. it comes from the future (another time).

These three kinds of value can be juxtaposed in the same material object, notably exotic value and the past value in the case of products of *terroir* in the industrialised societies (Warnier, 1994), whilst in the developing societies, this juxtaposition can often be found between the future (time) and elsewhere (exotic), referring to Western modernity.

3   Economic paradox of the revival of traditional products: the link between traditional and innovative know-how

It may be instructive to compare the current revival of authentic traditional products in the process of globalisation with the Arts and Crafts movement, created by William Morris in the 1880s as a counter-balance to the fast pace of industrialisation in England, at that time the most advanced in the world. This movement of aesthetic, moral and social ideas was aimed at preserving both the know-how of traditional craftsmanship, such as the use of natural materials, and the existence of craftsmen who were confronted with increasing power of mass-production. Influenced by John Ruskin's writing that happy workers produced beautiful things, Morris attempted to increase their enjoyment and productivity by ensuring they were fully involved in taking responsibility for all stages of production (Livingstone & Parry, 2005).

Furthermore, this period coincided with the World Expositions: places of international exchange and the discovery of aesthetics from elsewhere. The Arts and Crafts movement spread to different parts of the world: Art Nouveau in Europe and in North America (with influence of the culture and crafts of the native Americans); and the 'Mingei' (Folk Crafts) in Japan (1920–45) that became a nationwide movement for the recognition of historical folk crafts during the period of accelerating modernity (meaning Westernisation at that time). Invited by the Ministry of Commerce and Industry as an adviser of industrial design (1940–42), Charlotte Perriand, one of the major interior designers and architects of the twentieth century, advised Japanese craftsmen eager for modern innovation rather than the reproducing of (Western) models (Perriand, 1998). The movement contributed to structuring the sector of traditional products for today, and also promoted a form of international urban modernity by designing modern living space and objects with traditional techniques and materials.

This example illustrates well that the revival of traditional products originates from an economic paradoxical approach in which traditional know-how and modern, innovative know-how, work together throughout the process of production, from the phase of research and development, to the conception of products and their launch on the market, where typical marketing tools are used.

3.1   Traditions and innovations in Research and Development and the conception of traditional products

Firstly, at the beginning of the production process, traditions and innovations can be observed in the phase of research and development (R & D), and that of the conception of the products. During this phase, the integration of the company with different stakeholders of the environment can take various forms; for example, collaboration with other companies, with public institutions, with associations and with other professionals (tourism).

In this way, traditional products help to revive regions and their dying traditions. It may be worth citing here the successful example of the Laguiole knife. The community of Aubrac, perched on the plateau of Aubrac, 1,040m in southern France, worked as seasonal sawyers in Spain, when one of them bought a Navaja, a Spanish folding flick knife. The knife traditionally used by the Aubrac community had a fixed blade, riveted to a piece of beech wood. This encounter of two cultures of knife gave birth to the first Laguiole knife in 1829, of which the famous hallmark appeared in 1840 and the corkscrew in 1880. In 1920, the automation of manufacturing knives on the industrial site Thiers in the neighbouring region caused the decline of the artisan production of Laguiole knives. However, a couple of local artisans carried on the prestigious production and repair service. The local councillors of the rural community of 1,240 inhabitants decided to re-launch and promote this local economy by creating the association Couteau de Laguiole (knife of Laguiole), with its first mountain workshop producing under the brand name Couteau de Laguiole in 1981. Remaining for a long time within the locality of Paris, to where many of the regional community had moved, the Laguiole knife then became internationally *à la mode* at the end of the 1980s when Philippe Starck and Sonia Rykiel revamped it. The tradition was thus re-launched and updated for today's tastes, while the Laguiole is sold in museums, on the Internet, and is copied in Asia and Spain (*La Terre*, 2006).

In the textile sector, one can cite the example in India of the brand Fabindia (www.fabindia.com), created by the American John Bissel in 1960, to target first the domestic market. Today, this brand has ninety-seven shops in over forty cities and subsidiaries in Rome, Dubai, Bahrein and Qatar. Its success comes neither from a revolutionary way of management, nor a frantic pursuit of profit, but from the entirely artisan production, which combines Indian traditions and objects of everyday life. More than 20,000 weavers, cabinetmakers and dyers use their skills for the company. The originality of Fabindia is also to maintain strong and fair ties with its suppliers and artisans. By means of a cooperative system, created by the company, the artisans take advantage of the benefits of the group. They also set up a financial base that is more secure for the company as, being stakeholders of the company, it follows that they are concerned about the quality of their production.

In Japan, the excellence of manual work is perceived as an invaluable good and there is no clear distinction between crafts (tradition) and industry (modernity). Handwork allows the production of what the machine can't make, improves the aesthetics and performance of products, and in the end, increases productivity. In addition to the title of 'Living National Treasure' (highly distinguished master craftsmen/artists), every year since 1967, 150 people who contributed to technological innovation, improvement of product quality or that of the transfer of know-how are awarded the title of *Gendai no meikô* (contemporary master artisan) by the Ministry of Labour. Twenty industrial sectors are chosen, such as metallurgy, electrical construction, architecture, cooking and textiles.

A second aspect of the link between traditional know-how and technological innovation lies in the conception of eco-friendly products, this often by economic necessity. In Nancy (eastern France), Revelor (the Lorrain network of glassmakers), with the aid of the European Regional Development Fund (FEDER), seven research laboratories such as the Laboratory of Energy and Theoretical and Applied Mechanics (LEMTA), the Centre of Petrographic and Geochemical Research (CRPG), and three platforms of technological associates, brings solutions to the local glassmaking industry (Baccarat, Daum, Saint Louis): computer modeling the shape of the glass, calculating the resistance of lead-free crystal to thermal shocks and so on. This collaboration contributes to the reduction of flaws in the production, to the creation of sophisticated products of high added value and finally to the preservation of local employment.

In Ishikawa prefecture (Japan), the local R & D centre has found the solution for manufacturing the ceramic *Kutani-yaki*, known for its polychromic decorations, which adheres to the new hygiene regulations. Mercury-free paints were created that can reproduce the brightness of the traditional paintings by a good balance in the composition of various minerals contained in them.

3.2   Tradition and innovation: craft marketing

The liberalisation and the deregulation of global commercial systems have stimulated the circulation of merchandise and services. This imposes on the creators and suppliers of all types of traditional products a professionalism in confronting the intensifying competition. Faced with the enormous choices offered to consumers, craftsmen and visual artists and all the intermediate persons of the supply chain have to continuously make efforts to improve the quality of their products and services, their process of production, the identity of their brands and the efficacy of their marketing strategies. Competitive marketing is a condition for success in the commercial development of the traditional products within a global and more open environment.

The marketing approach places the client at the centre of both consideration and action of the company. The knowledge of demand is, therefore, essential, in particular that of markets abroad that are less familiar (Prime & Usunier, 2004). Marketing aims, therefore, to firstly promote the creativity and talents of artisans who confer on their products a 'flavour' that is traditional, cultural, symbolic or distinctive. This value arouses interest among consumers, and corresponds to the emotional needs and aesthetic tastes of demanding clients who can be found in the specialised segments of domestic or export markets (Delcourt-Itonaga, 2006).

In the area of luxury goods, Hermès is distinguished as an exceptional crafts business (*Maison d'artisanat d'exception*, Libération, 2008). In this way, they gain the respect of consumers. Their marketing is rather traditional, since it is the 'handwork' involved in the production and the word-of-mouth of clients that make the brand grow (*Stratégies*, 2005). In Japan, *Wajima-nuri* is lacquerware produced with the most elaborate techniques of lacquer-application; it is famous for its aesthetic quality and the durability of the products. The process involves two years of preparation of the stands for drying the wood, then between seventy-five and 100 successive coats of lacquer; in total about 120 processes of fabrication are ensured at each step by artisans who are shared out between 11 different divisions of work. The distribution method practised from the eighteenth century is also applied today, namely door-to-door sales by the craftsmen themselves. The direct contact with users allows them to design customised products, meeting the specific needs and desires of the customers.

The development of the Internet strongly supports the marketing of traditional products, either as the vehicle of information and communication, or as the support for distance sales. The Internet allows access to information about taste, and thus its dissemination (Auray & Gensollen, 2007). This geographically enlarged distribution allows the preservation of niche markets in a great number of countries. The Internet is also a practical tool for the education of younger generations. The website Craft in America provides educators with a guide on three themes: memory, landscape and community (www.craftinamerica.org). In the same way, Ishikawa prefecture in Japan has created a website, dedicated especially to children, about the arts and craft heritage of the region.

Commercial innovation too, has had to resolve the growing issue relating to the protection of intellectual property when craftsmen are faced with counterfeit products, when they are not used to thinking about this question. In this respect, the glassmakers' consortium Promovetro (Murano in Italy) and the Chamber of Commerce of Wajima (Japan) organise seminars on intellectual property rights while working on the labelling of their products. Similar organisations are now aware of the importance of this subject. The emerging economies, notably China, are sensitive to this matter and actively apply for patents.

New problems of intellectual property rights have become an essential element of the marketing of traditional products as the links between intellectual property, economic development and marketing exist throughout the commercial cycle. Commercial successes of traditional products are numerous, thanks to a consistent marketing approach, focused on the high value attached to intellectual property. Furthermore, the development of brands and their advanced communication allow them to create high awareness and strong images (CCI, 2003).

The case of Maquí is a representative example of this approach. The Equadorian producer of handmade straw hats (known worldwide under the name of 'Panamas'), has registered in Equador the brand Maquí, which means 'hand' in the Quechua language. The sign (Maquí) was selected with great care so that it could be easily recognisable. Being a registered trademark on the targeted markets, it has progressively become a known brand in its sector thanks to its effective use. To commercialise hats, Maquí progressively launched advertising programmes of the crafts communities of Equador, by highlighting the quality and style of its handmade hats. In twenty years of existence, Maquí has gained a good reputation worldwide. Thanks to the advertising campaigns, consumers are effectively able to easily make a distinction between different straw hats and buy the one they desire. By advertising its brand, Maquí is obliged to maintain a certain quality. The brand is known as one of the most reliable and prestigious on the international market. The brand guarantees to consumers that every hat is unique, and respects the traditional Equadorian art of weaving and braiding, and is made of straw of high quality. Since Maquí benefits from its brand awareness, its importance on the market has been continuously increasing, together with its brand value.

4 Conclusion

Traditional products, among the products of *terroir*, account for an important revival of consumption in contemporary industrialised societies. Associated with a balance between High Tech and High Touch perspectives, vehicles of the revival of roots in a community, and the past and personal experience, they convey an authentic source of meaning and well-being to consumers that industrialised, highly standardised products do not have the ability to fulfil. The taste of industrialised societies for traditional products also contributes to the development of the economy where the traditional know-how relies on various innovations in order to conceive, produce, distribute and protect these products, sometimes on a global scale.

One can see in this way that the revelation of the power of local identities can paradoxically drive them to an integral development of the past and the future. Similar to the theories of acculturation (Berry, 1980), it is possible in contemporary consumption to connect the value of maintaining traditions with that of maintaining the link with modernity (Table 5.1).

The importance given to the traditions and to the construction of the world of tomorrow through the use of traditional products could go beyond the paradoxical value given to the past in the global contemporary consumption. It could rather highlight a fertile hybridisation between the know-how of the past and the consideration of the future. The consumption of traditional products in industrialised societies therefore responds to an increasing demand for the ecology of a more balanced life for the future, which is based on personal responsibility and the principle of sustainable development, more than on the actualisation of old-fashioned traditionalism which is locked into itself or purist.

Table 5.1   Value of the past-future link and contemporary consumption

		Value of maintaining the link with the tradition (the past, the ancient, the premodern)	
		Weak	**Strong**
Value of maintaining the link with modernity (the future and the new)	Weak	Postmodern consumption (presentism)	Traditionalist consumption (purism)
	Strong	Hypermodern consumption (always more tailormade, novelty)	Ecology of life (products of sustainable development, harmony)

Finally, the consumption of traditional products (lasting, repairable), which accompanies everyday life has become apparent in the reaction to disposable products. It creates favourable conditions for discovering different world cultures, and, therefore, different values. It further helps develop the cultural side of this consumption, a major issue of living together in more open contemporary societies.

Notes

1. *Terroir* is the concept that products from a particular region or locality have specific characteristics which reflect the region of their origin. In Britain these would be sold as 'local products' or 'locally produced'.
2. 'Consomm'acteur' is a composite word of 'consommateur' and 'acteur' meaning the consumer that is not only passive but also active.

References

Appadurai, A. (1988) *The Social Life of Things: Commodities in Cultural Perspective.* Cambridge: Cambridge University Press.
——— (2001) *Après le Colonialisme.* Paris: Payot & Rivage. (English language edition [1996] *Modernity at Large.* Minnesota: University of Minnesota Press.)
Aubert, N. (ed.) (2004) *L'individu Hypermoderne.* Collection Sociologie Clinique. Toulouse: Editions Erès.
Auray, N. and Gensollen, M. (2007) Internet et la synthèse collective des goûts, in Olivier Assouly (ed.) *Goûts à Vendre, Essai sur la Captation Esthétique.* Paris: L'Institut Français de la Mode.
Aurier, P., Fort, F. and Siriex, L. (2004) Les produits de terroir du point de vue des consommateurs: sources perçues et associations au terroir. Paper given at the 20th Congress AFM, 6–7 May, Saint Malo.
Barthes, R. (1957) *Mythologies.* Paris: Seuil.
Baudrillard, J. (1968) *Le Système des Objets.* Paris: Gallimard.
Belk, R. (1988) Possessions and the extended self. *Journal of Consumer Research*, 15 (September): 139–68.

Bérard, L. and Marchenay, P. (2000) Le vivant, le culturel et le marchand: les produits de terroir. *Autrement*, 194: 191–216.

Berry, J.W. (1980) Acculturation as varieties of adaptation, in A. M. Padilla (ed.) *Acculturation: Theory, Models and some New Findings*. Colorado: Westview Press.

Business Week (2006) (issue date 30 October 2006, web version 19 October 2006) 'Karma Capitalism': 86–91 by Pete Engardio and Jena McGregor.

Centre du Commerce International (CCI) (2003) Le marketing des produits de l'artisanat et des arts visuels, le rôle de la propriété intellectuelle. *Guide Pratique*. Geneva: CNUCED-OMC-OMPI.

Cova, V. and Cova, B. (2001) *Alternatives Marketing*. Paris: Dunod.

Delcourt-Itonaga, M. (2006) How can traditional products play a role for the future? Case studies: Murano Glassware and Wajima Lacquer ware. *Thèse Professionnelle*, Mastère Spécialisé Marketing et Communication. Paris: ESCP-EAP.

Douglas, M. (1979) *The World of Goods: Towards an Anthropology of Consumption*. London: Routledge.

Eschwège, A. and Charpentier, A. (2005) Bien-être avec soi, bien-être avec les autres. *Marketing Magazine*, 99, 1 November. www.emarketing.fr/Magazines.

Fischler, C. (1990) *L'Omnivore: Le Goût, la Cuisine et le Corps*. Paris: Odile Jacob.

Fort, F. and Fort, F. (2006) Alternatives marketing pour les produits du terroir. *Revue Française de Gestion*, 162: 145–59.

Fromm, E. (1978) *Avoir ou Etre?* Paris: Robert Laffont, Collection Réponses. (English language edition [1976] *To Have or to Be*. San Francisco: Harper and Row.)

Granovetter, M. (1985) Economic action and social structure: the problem of embeddedness. *American Sociological Review*, 91, November: 481–510.

ICAR (2008) *The International Centre for Anti-Consumption Research*. University of Sidney, 4–5 December.

La Terre (2006) Les ombres chinoises sur les Laguioles, 2 October. www.laterre.fr.

Levitt, T. (1983) The globalization of markets. *Harvard Business Review*, May–June: 92–102.

Libération (2008) Le luxe flashy finira par lasser (interview with Patrick Thomas). *Next* (supplement in *Libération*), 9 June.

Lipovetsky, G. (1989) *L'Ere du Vide: Essai sur l'Individualisme Contemporain*. Paris: Folio.

Lipovetsky, G. with Charles, S. (2004) *Les Temps Hypermodernes*. Paris: Grasset.

Livingstone, K. and Parry, L. (2005) *International Arts and Crafts*. London: Victoria and Albert Museum.

Lyotard, J.F. (1979) *La Condition Postmoderne, Rapport sur le Savoir*. Paris: Collection Critique, Editions de Minuit.

McCracken, G. (1991) *Culture and Consumption: New Approaches to the Symbolic Character of Consumer Goods and Activities*. Indiana: Indiana University Press.

McLuhan, M. (1962) *The Gutenberg Galaxy: The Making of Typographic Man*. Toronto: University of Toronto Press.

Martin, H.-R. (2007) *Eloge de la Simplicité Volontaire*. Paris: Flammarion.

Mermet, G. (2007) *Francoscopie*. Paris: Larousse.

Miller, D. (1998) *A Theory of Shopping*. Oxford: Polity Press.

Naisbitt, J. (2001) *High Tech, High Touch*. London: Nicholas Brealey.

Nihon Keizai Shimbun (2006) Ikebana, otoko mo necchû (Ikebana, men are also enthusiastic), 21 April.

Ohmae, K. (1985) *Triad Power: the Coming Shape of Global Competition*. New York: The Free Press.

Perriand, C. (1998) *Une Vie de Création*. Paris: Odile Jacob.

Prime, N. (1999) Cultures et mondialisation: l'unité dans la diversité. *Expansion Management Review*, September: 53–66.

Prime, N. and Usunier, J.-C. (2004) *Marketing International* (2nd edn). Paris: Vuibert.

Ritzer, G. (2004) *Tous Rationalisés! La McDonaldisation de la Société*. Paris: Alban.

Stratégies (2005) Grand Prix du luxe: marketing artisanal. 1 December.

Surowiecki, J. (2008) *La Sagesse des Foules*. Paris: Editions JC Lattès.

Usunier, J.-C. and Lee, J. (2008) *Marketing Across Cultures* (5th edn). London: Harlow Pearson.

WAD (2008) The history of a legend. *Denim*, 44–55, 61, 72.

Warnier, J.P. (1994) *Le Paradoxe de la Marchandise Authentique, Imaginaire et Consommation de Masse*. Paris: L'Harmattan.

——— (1999) *Construire la Culture Matérielle: l'Homme qui Pensait avec ses Doigts*. Paris: PUF.

Zavestoski, S. (ed.) (2002) Anti-consumption attitudes. *Psychology & Marketing*, special issue, 17 (2): 121–6.

6
Paradoxes of International Marketing in Developing Countries

Svetla T. Marinova and Marin A. Marinov

Marketing ethics has always been viewed in the context of business ethics or morality, as marketing is a business function that identifies, anticipates and satisfies customer requirements profitably, thus creating and maintaining the interface between consumer preferences and companies' market aspirations. Baumhart (1961) and Tzalikis and Fritzsche (1989) among others have pointed out that marketing is perceived as the most problematic business function concerning morality. Research has questioned the ethics of marketing, mostly related to its role in promotion and sales where public trust is relatively low. Pires and Stanton (2002) suggest that marketing ethics should be treated as social responsibility, or what is 'good' for society in general and consumers in particular. However, there is no uniform philosophical argument of what is 'good' and 'ethical' and whether 'good' and 'ethical' have identical meanings.

The views of Kant (1997) on ethics are utilitarian and deontological, based on reason, intention and duty. According to him, duties cannot be associated with self-interest expressed in expected payoffs or rewards. Thus, companies should exist to satisfy the needs of society, and firms have a duty, a moral obligation, to deliver benefits to society. Such an argument establishes firm gains as a function of the social wealth and development they create and the consumer satisfaction they deliver.

Consequently, the social cause is paramount in a company's conduct. Taking Kant's ethical concept as a reference point, it can be argued that it pays for companies to *appear* ethical and for their expectations of increased sales, market share and, most of all, profitability to *appear* as motivated by objectives different from self-interest (Yeo, 1988). Such an approach can bring higher payoffs for a company because consumers will perceive its operations as ethical. Therefore, if companies appear to be ethical, following ethical codes and norms regulating their self-interest, they will be rewarded by the consumers. The real issue is whether companies want to *appear* ethical or whether they can *commit* to a marketing behaviour that will place consumer welfare before their own self-interest.

John Mill's ideas on ethics (Mill, 1863) are utilitarian, based on the consequences of action indicating that business ethics should maximise the total amount of pleasure in the world and minimise the total amount of pain, thus augmenting the scope of beneficiaries. Mill's understanding of ethics is intrinsically associated with the 'common good' rather than with a company's self-interest. According to Nantel and Weeks (1996), considering all functional business areas as marketing management represents the most disputed area in terms of utilitarian ethics. They argue that the implementation of ethics in marketing is a paradox in itself, as the definition of marketing, which is predominantly utilitarian, provides marketing managers with a justification for ethical conduct when they ensure that the consequences of their behaviour are moral. However, utilitarian views do not always result in ethical marketing conduct. Mill's notion questions whether marketing activities are to be limited to an increase in the market share or profitability of a single company, or whether they should deliver benefits to a greater number of people not involved in a company's decision-making processes. The problem is that the 'common good' has various interpretations and its scope is vague and not at all explicit. Should the common good be applied to a target market segment, to the mass market, to various social groups or to society as a whole? Moreover, in international marketing the issue becomes complex and acute, as the common good should transcend country borders and nationalities. Will the common good reflect the 'good' for home and host countries, for companies that engage in international marketing activities and for consumers in their domestic and international markets? Mill's response to such questions would probably be that national, geographical and political categories are not an objective basis for ethical values. The greatest happiness principle, on the other hand, builds upon values that are universal to everyone – pleasure and pain. So the only consistent general moral principle must be 'Seek the greatest good for the greatest number'. The difficulty arises when companies need to decide what the greatest good is, what the greatest number is, and how marketing can really deliver the greatest good to the greatest number.

1 Ethics relativism and marketing

The marketing concept implies that companies need to satisfy various consumer preferences based on the needs and wants of those consumers, and should also generate profit. The idea of a company's self-interest of profitability is apparently difficult to justify in Kant's view, but is acceptable in Mill's understanding of utility. The application of the marketing concept should, therefore, 'put the customer first' and deliver benefits to the individual consumer, society as a whole and the company itself.

Ethical relativists accept that moral absolutes do not exist and therefore the definition of what is moral is based on the social norms of the society in which they are practised. Hence, there are no universal moral standards applied to all peoples at all times. In marketing terms, ethical relativism can justify different ethical standards applied to various countries and evolving over time. Such an interpretation of morality allows for various interpretations of ethical norms that reflect a diversity of cultures and practices. Moreover, this creates a need for marketing adaptation within a particular market over time as the societal culture, knowledge and technology change, as well as across markets at a given point in time. If moral relativism is accepted as a basis for the international marketing activities of companies, there can be no common framework for resolving moral disputes or for reaching agreement on ethical matters between companies and different societies. It can only nurture flexibility, which creates rather complex relationships with consumers in the home and foreign markets with no common reference point. Thus, the arguments for its implementation into the marketing of companies create unease, and question the core universal values that transcend national borders.

2 Multinational corporations and consumers in developing countries

The need for addressing the issues of international marketing ethics arises from the increased internationalisation of multinational companies (MNCs) and the process of the globalisation of business (De George, 1986; Hoffman *et al.*, 1986). Extant research on international marketing ethics has been focused mostly on developed economies, while developing countries have received limited attention (Donaldson, 1985; Rogers et al., 1995). This chapter addresses controversial issues in the marketing ethics of MNCs serving consumers in developing countries, where the most important matters are projected in the four elements of the marketing mix. As in business-to-consumer markets, consumer support is of crucial importance for the success of marketing activities, and companies' profitability ethical conduct towards consumers is the most critical area of business ethics (Crane and Matten, 2004). This chapter questions whether consumer satisfaction in developing countries is aligned with the interests of the MNCs. There is a paradox caused by globalisation, emphasising that the satisfaction of consumers in developing countries and the interests of MNCs in them are impossible to synchronise. The paradoxical relationship between marketing ethics and company opportunism at the international level will be focused upon. Thus, the role of consumer sovereignty in terms of capability, information and choice is examined in relation to companies' profit maximisation interests.

Big and powerful MNCs in developing countries often have bargaining power greater than that of national governments. Companies such as Coca-Cola, Nokia, General Electric, Citigroup, Wal-Mart, Microsoft, General Motors, Pfizer, Royal Dutch/Shell, HSBC, BP, Toyota and many others appear to have turnover and value-added greater than the GDP of many developing economies. For example, the size of ExxonMobil with an estimated value-added of $US 63 billion in 2000 was bigger than the GDP of economies such as Pakistan or Peru (Onkvisit and Shaw, 2004). Developing economies are vulnerable and rather exposed to unethical marketing because of their economic potential, low bargaining power and lack of legal framework and law enforcement to protect domestic companies, consumers and the society as a whole. This makes consumers in such countries less likely to benefit from the common good. Moreover, Friedman (1970) argues that the goal of business and, hence, marketing activities should be to maximise profit within the law. If the driving force of a company is to generate and maximise profit, its behaviour in the marketplace should also be based on universal ethics for ensuring good for the society at large. How can we define what the limits of ethical behaviour are? The question is whether profits should be maximised in environments where law protection is weak or non-existent.

The legal framework for regulating company-consumer interface is usually asserted on the conception of a company's interest for profit maximisation, subject to legal constraints, which is reflected in the position of *caveat emptor*. Consumers in developing countries have few rights of moral treatment by MNCs that are legally safeguarded. Consequently, the responsibility for ensuring and regulating the ethical behaviour of MNCs lies with the consumer whose rights barely exist, whose bargaining power is extremely low and whose sovereignty is rudimentary.

Determining and delivering value to consumers should lie at the heart of marketing strategy. Finding a balance between consumer welfare and profit maximisation in companies' marketing strategies has proved to be challenging and in many cases illusive. MNCs expand into developing markets seeking new market growth potential, creating new market segments and penetrating existing ones, extending the product life cycle of outdated products, introducing new products, and acquiring and upgrading existing local brands, thus offering more choice to consumers and satisfying both existing and unmet needs and wants.

Before MNCs get a grip of the market in developing countries, they focus on the satisfaction of the company's primary needs, which relate to financial improvement and stability. Thus market development strategy is often associated with unethical marketing behaviour. For example, in order to develop the market for tobacco products in Taiwan, cigarettes have been freely distributed to consumers, regardless of their age and gender, by fashion models and beautiful young girls in order to lure consumers into usage. Such an approach has been common for market penetration strategies as well. For instance, when the transition from central planning to a market-led economy started in the Ukraine, MNCs were quick to engage in delivering packed cigarette gifts to consumers with the intention of increased product usage. While cigarette sales have been controlled and limited in many developed countries, the market share of American and British cigarette producers in markets such as Russia, China and South Africa among others is on the rise.

The moral issues in developing and implementing marketing strategies are associated with the definition and serving of target segments. Serious ethical concern arises from the approach of MNCs to target poor and illiterate consumers in developing countries with unaffordable prices, thus either excluding them from the market or driving them into consumption that can deprive them from satisfying their basic necessities. An illustration of this are the prices of life-saving medication, or the practice of introducing brands as substitutes for generic commodities.

MNCs in developing countries control more than the elements of their marketing mix. They play a crucial role in changing social structures, shaping political power, knowledge transfer, and even determining economic development and competitive structures. This power and control create major disadvantages for the developing states as they need to regulate the marketing and investment behaviour of big MNCs. Under such conditions, one would expect that MNCs should not justify their behaviour as legal, but that they should set and maintain high ethical standards. The expectation that MNCs can act as self-regulators has often been riddled with flaws even within the developed economies. Hence, it would be unrealistic to expect that companies will be effective in the application of self-regulatory measures on their own, in an environment where consumer legal protection is weak. In addition, consumers in developing countries have limited consumer sovereignty and this restricts or eliminates their role in regulating unethical marketing practices of MNCs.

3 Ethics and the marketing mix of MNCs in developing countries

Laczniak and Murphy (1993) suggest that the ethical marketing behaviour of companies should be evaluated using the elements of the marketing mix. This has been the approach adopted by a number of researchers studying marketing ethics in developed market economies (Schlegelmilch, 1997; Smith, 1995), whereas in developing country contexts marketing ethics has been mostly limited to analyses of business ethics and environmental impact, or with the specifics of a social contract between the transnational corporations and societies (Rogers et al., 1995). Consequently, some key concerns about the marketing ethics of MNCs are discussed in relation to products, distribution, prices and promotion they apply to developing country markets.

3.1 Products

Marketing ethics should not necessarily be confined to legal regulations. Marketing claims to put consumers first, which implies a moral obligation to deliver products and services that will safeguard consumers against any harm. The paradox is that instead of putting the consumer as the focal point, it is market expansion, market growth, new market development and tapping into emerging markets with high-growth potential that often become more important.

The ethical problems in developing countries are associated with companies' attempts to expand their sales of socially controversial products that are known to harm people's health, with marketing morally and physically obsolete products, or products that can harm the environment or mislead consumers, promising to achieve something they aspire to but the product cannot really deliver. The likelihood of introducing and marketing such products without any limitations is much higher than in the developed markets. The attempts of developing countries to attract foreign direct investments to spur economic development, coupled with endemic widespread corruption among government officials, can provide additional fruitful opportunities for unethical product offers.

Product safety in developed economies is strictly regulated by law and yet there are occasions when knowingly harmful products slip through the regulatory net. A specific illustration is the recent scam with the Sudan 1 health hazardous colouring that was found only after UK-produced food was exported to Italy. Whilst the likelihood of selling harmful or substandard products in developed countries is severely curbed by competitive pressures and regulation, in developing economies competition is less intense and MNCs control the lion's share of the market. The rather limited purchasing power, information exposure and education level of consumers in such markets represent a serious constraint in buying decisions concerning product safety, quality and usage. An illustration of this problem is Nestlé's infant formula being sold in Africa and Asia to women who didn't need it, couldn't afford to buy or prepare it, and could hardly read the directions for making it (Bar-Yam, 1995), which led to massive numbers of child deaths. Similarly, Imodium of Johnson and Johnson, while banned in the US, was sold to infants in developing countries, causing severe intestinal problems and consequent death (Scanlan, 1991).

The role of documented or implicitly stated warranties when marketing products in developing countries is rather obscure. The product performance benchmark is not clear to consumers, nor are the additional obligations and responsibilities of sellers and manufacturers explicit or easy to enforce. On the one hand, there exists a perception that companies can sell substandard products or offer rather limited after-sales service, as consumers in developing countries are hardly sophisticated in their requirements and expectations. On the other hand, many retailers appear and die quickly, so the seller as a consumer reference point can disappear, while the wholesaler or manufacturer does not offer a customer support network.

Another major problem is the limited, if at all available, consumer protection from product failure and related injuries that exists in the form of strict liability in developed economies. The likelihood of improper use of products in developing countries is higher because consumers are less informed, and the information for product usage is insufficient or presented inappropriately for their understanding, thus more easily causing physical, emotional, financial or psychological harm. If one views the same issue from the perspective of companies, the question that can be raised concerns the degree of their moral responsibility in such circumstances. In 2002, Bayer packaged a pesticide marketed under the name of Folidol to small farmers throughout Peru, the great majority of whom spoke Quechua only and were illiterate. The pesticide resembled powdered milk and had no strong chemical odour. It was distributed in small plastic bags, labelled in Spanish and displayed a picture of vegetables. The labels provided no usable safety information, such as pictograms and little indication of the danger of the product. It was mistakenly used as powdered milk causing death and digestive disorders in children.

Consumer product awareness and bargaining power in developing markets is much lower, and the institutional support for consumer rights is either non-existent or rather limited. While consumers in developed countries can easily use the legal system, consumer protection agencies, international courts for human rights and other defence mechanisms, consumers in some developing countries may theoretically have access to protection but in reality it is often out of their reach due to information, legal and means deficiencies.

Labelling of products is of common concern for consumers in developing countries. For example, in countries where an international code and national laws for marketing breast milk substitute products exist, MNCs continue to produce labels that fail to comply either with the code or with national laws. They ignore provisions on information to be included on labels, idealising their products by comparing them favourably with breast milk, use pseudo-scientific claims or fail to use appropriate language.

Although branding practices in emerging markets call for special attention, it is worth mentioning the acquisition of local trade names and unbranded products by MNCs in developing countries that enhance them marginally and promote them as value-added branded goods sold at a higher price. Moreover, many of these acquisitions result in replacing local generic products with MNCs' own brands. Recognising the limitations of purchasing power, global brands are being sold in big emerging markets, such as L'Oreal in India, in tiny packs that create an illusive impression of low-priced products, yet that still ensure high unit profits for the MNCs.

3.2 Distribution

Big foreign retail chains have enormous power in the underdeveloped distribution systems in developing countries, as they can oust local small retailers or retail chains that do not enjoy economies of scale and are thus have limited financial and marketing resources. The advancement of powerful international retail chains creates opportunities for other foreign companies to enter new markets or expand their market presence. The bargaining power of these wholesalers and retailers *vis-à-vis* consumers is immense. Consequently, most products sold by international retailers are aimed at profit maximisation and feature to a limited extent locally sourced, generally cheaper, traditional produce. Such practices can have a dual impact. On the one hand, they can lead to the disappearance of local producers or to a decrease in their profits, but on the other, they do not necessarily satisfy existing consumer wants and needs, rather they try to shift consumer preferences towards foreign-branded product categories that will increase retailers' profits. The ethical issue is mostly associated with the responsibility of companies, manufacturers and retailers for pushing the boundaries of shifting consumer needs and wants in an aim to create conformity that can additionally support global players in their foreign market presence, while limiting actual consumer choice and destroying local businesses. Thus, marketing activities can be seen as efforts to reduce competition, which finally result in a tendency to increase the probability for unethical behaviour of companies (Smith, 1995).

3.3 Pricing

Pricing in developing countries is greatly dependent upon the limited purchasing power of the large part of the population. In countries where the majority of people earn less than $US 1 a day, it is very difficult to accept the price-value relationship as prophesied in developed economies. The divergent interests of MNCs and consumers are most obvious and explicit in such contexts, as MNCs' attempt to maximise sales revenue and profits, whereas consumers strive to obtain the highest-quality products at the lowest possible price. Price sensitivity is of paramount importance in developing countries where the majority of consumers occupy 'the bottom of the pyramid' (Hart and Christensen, 2002; Prahalad and Hart, 2002).

Fair price is usually thought to be a result of a mutually acceptable consent between the exchange parties under the conditions of a competitive market. The question one may ask is about the existence of competitive market conditions for MNCs serving consumers in developing economies. To what extent do MNCs compete in or define and control the market? For example, the brewing industries in many Central and Eastern European countries are partially or fully controlled by between one and three large MNCs, some of which have a national market share of 40–70 per cent, thus limiting competitive pressures and creating better conditions for price fixing. In an attempt to protect low-income consumers from the multinational super- and hypermarket chains, the Venezuelan government has recently established the Mercal grocery stores chain to provide basic foodstuffs at an average of 50–70 per cent lower than in multinational supermarkets that have driven the 'abastos', small traditional local shops, out of business. The paradox is expressed by the question, 'Which pricing approach is fair and for whom?'

When MNCs establish production facilities in developing countries, thus lowering the overall cost of production compared with the cost of the same goods when imported from developed countries, this often does not lead to cost savings for consumers. In such cases MNCs tend to charge a comparatively high price in order to ensure consistency across markets. This is particularly the case with branded goods having worldwide recognition. For instance, the yogurt produced by Danone in Bulgaria with added starch, is probably not of a higher quality compared with local non-branded or yogurt that is without additives. Thus a paradox appears, as while organic products in the developed markets occupy the premium end of the market due to their perceived health benefits, Western brands not only push local organic produce to the low end of the market, but can also make such products extinct from the marketplace in developing countries.

The role of marketing in the introduction of highly priced items is associated with reshaping social structures and creating difficult-to-justify spending aspirations. In their attempt to conquer developing country consumers, MNCs apply pricing policies that intentionally limit consumer abilities to buy. In such a way, MNCs create an artificial market for the privileged few. This is a rather unethical and dangerous approach when applied to pharmaceutical products, and especially to life-saving drugs.

MNCs, using their power and marketing capabilities, can exploit low pricing to enter a developing market to build a customer base and eliminate competition. When the beer brand Amstel was introduced by Heineken in Bulgaria, it was priced substantially lower than locally produced beers, playing on its brand name and foreignness. As Amstel made gains in the Bulgarian market, having stolen market share from mostly domestic competitors, it was re-priced. Similar strategies have been used by foreign retailers setting foot in Poland, Bulgaria, Slovenia and other countries.

Pricing techniques in combination with marketing communications approaches are also used to mislead, if not intentionally deceive, consumers. For instance, in Slovenia, consumers find the price quotations in the catalogues of the MNCs Neckermann and Quelle misleading. The practice of making the lowest price more noticeable is confusing buyers because it is not immediately obvious that this is the price for a very small proportion of the goods sold (Makovec Brencic and Rojšek, 2005).

3.4 Promotion

Promotional ethics has two main levels of concern, namely individual and social. On the individual level, promotional practices and especially advertising are blamed for creating false beliefs and unrealistic expectations concerning particular products, thus increasing the likelihood of purchases. On the social level, concerns are associated with the social and cultural impact of advertising changing social consumption patterns and cultural values, with the ultimate aim of increased consumerism that can support companies' expectations of market share, higher prices, brand enforcement and profitability growth.

Developing countries are either traditional or transitional societies where cultural traits and values are not based on materialism. Rather, social behaviour has been driven by religious beliefs, family and community spirit, close contact with nature and harnessed drive for material possession. MNCs, with their high advertising propensity, make any effort to form new consumer wants and needs, mostly emphasising cosmopolitan aspirations and values (Cannon and Yaprak, 2002).

The ethical concern associated with promotion stems from the fact that marketers' perceive it mostly as a persuasive rather than an informative marketing tool. Consumers in developing countries in general do not enjoy a high degree of sovereignty, and are highly susceptible to the impact of advertising as they perceive its role mostly as informative, thus *helping* them make 'informed' buying decisions. Hence, the probability for an unethical impact of persuasive advertising in such contexts is much greater.

The borderline between persuasive and deceptive, and intentionally misleading, advertising is vague. Whilst presenting products and companies in the most favourable way is essential in marketing promotions, it is the content of the persuasive message that can create ethical problems. An advertisement can probably be regarded as ethical if its content is informative, not misleading and does not create unrealistic expectations. In developing country contexts where consumers are less experienced, it is more likely for advertising to create misleading consumer expectations because of message interpretation and associations, as people have been exposed to marketing communications techniques only recently. Apparently, consumer sovereignty and particularly consumer capability, in terms of experience and vulnerability in developing countries, is substantially different from those in developed economies; this difference needs, therefore, to be carefully considered by MNCs that wish their marketing communications programmes to be perceived as ethical.

Pollay (1986) suggests that marketing communications strengthening consumerism and materialism in society aim to establish societal beliefs that consumption can lead to happiness. Thus consumerism pervades all aspects of life in the developed modern societies. However, creating happiness based on consumption has proved to be illusive. This is not necessarily positive either for the society as a whole or for the individuals in it. While offering more products to consumers can increase choice, excessive manipulative marketing communications can create feelings of insecurity, guilt, constantly increasing dissatisfaction with consumed products and unfounded aspirations for a better life. One might argue that the real drive behind persuasive and manipulative marketing communications is MNCs' continuous efforts to constantly increase profits. Such practices in developing markets have been an intrinsic part of MNCs' struggle for new market access and increased market presence that can bring higher profits. Corporations flood consumers in developing countries with 'feel-good' images that could form new consumer segments or expand international and global consumer clusters, ensuring higher financial returns for the companies. While proponents of such practices may support their ethical nature, the impact of these practices on social norms and structures – transforming traditional beliefs and value systems, and creating aspirations for happiness founded on consumerism and material possessions – does undermine the equilibrium of the inner self of *homo sapiens*. This is not an argument against advertising in its fair, informative format that aims to create consumer choice and satisfaction. Rather it is an argument questioning the degree to which MNCs can enforce self-constraints on persuasive and manipulative campaigns and the feasibility of self-control. Therefore, it is not consumer sovereignty on its own, but coupled with consumer protection legislation and practices, that can limit the negative effects of marketing communications on consumers.

4 Conclusion

The marketing ethics of MNCs in developing countries appear to be largely skewed to the position of *caveat emptor*, where profit maximisation within an accepted legal framework favouring the company's own market growth interests underpins their marketing practices. This opportunistic behaviour has been made possible via the globalisation process, thus creating a paradox, i.e. globalised successful business is only the big business, not the business originating from various parts of the world, simultaneously making the consumer in developing countries more confused and less well off.

This paradox sets the core question of the marketing ethics: 'Under such circumstances should consumers expect companies to inform them about packet size changes, glossy and exaggerated statements, price increases, product suitability and so on, or should it not be the consumers who can assess and realise the nature of company marketing behaviour, therefore conscientiously safeguarding themselves from the unethical impact of company marketing practices?' One core problem associated with this paradox is that consumer sovereignty is a concept associated with free market economies where '...all authority rests with the sovereign consumer operating through the impersonal mechanism of the market' (Galbraith, 1984: 87), and the society creates some regulatory and consumer protection mechanisms, empowering individual consumers to exercise their rights. However, Galbraith also suggests that even in free market economies the power of MNCs to set and influence prices and to manipulate consumer response is disguised 'by the mystique of the market and consumer sovereignty' (Galbraith, 1984: 89). Following Galbraith's assertion that MNCs create artificial needs for unwanted products (Galbraith, 1974), one can argue that this is even more the case in developing economies where consumer rights are not protected or guaranteed by social and legal structures, thus increasing consumer vulnerability and the probability of MNCs to manipulate consumers by producing artificial demand for products they do not need.

Consumers in developed countries have a low individual bargaining power but a relatively high degree of consumer sovereignty, and are thus able to exercise much more power on companies' marketing ethics. However, in developing countries the trends are that the marketing environment is corrupt and does not offer the necessary consumer protection. The ethical norms applied by companies in developed markets should be used as a benchmark for assessing their marketing behaviour in developing countries. Thus, to diminish the paradox of marketing ethics in developing countries, when consumer satisfaction becomes paramount for MNCs' utilitarianism and relativism, they should not contradict each other in setting and meeting ethical standards; rather they should be congruent to and complementary with one another, with the objective of enhancing consumer welfare.

References

Bar-Yam, N. (1995) 'The Nestlé boycott: the story of the WHO/UNICEF Code for marketing breastmilk Substitutes'. *Mothering*, winter.

Baumhart, R. (1961) 'How ethical are businesses?'. *Harvard Business Review*, July/August (6): 6–19.

Cannon, H. and Yaprak, A. (2002) 'Will the real world citizen please stand up!: a critical review of cosmopolitanism as a consumer behavior construct'. *Journal of International Marketing*, 10 (4): 30–52.

Crane, A. and Matten, D. (2004) *Business Ethics*. Oxford: Oxford University Press.

De George, R. (1986) 'Ethical dilemmas for multinational enterprise: a philosophical overview' in M. Hoffman, A. Lange and D. Fedo (eds) *Ethics and the Multinational Enterprise*. Washington, DC: University Press of America.

Donaldson, T. (1985) 'Multinational decision making: reconciling international norms'. *Journal of Business Ethics*, 15 (4): 357–66.

Friedman, M. (1970) 'The social responsibility of business is to increase its profits'. *The New York Times Magazine*, September 13.

Galbraith, J. (1974) *The New Industrial State*, (2nd edn). Harmondsworth: Penguin.

———— (1984) *The Anatomy of Power*. London: Hamish Hamilton.

Hart, S. and Christensen, C. (2002) 'The great lap: driving innovation from the base of the pyramid'. *MIT Sloan Management Review*, fall: 51–6.

Hoffman, M., Lange, A. and Fedo, D. (eds) (1986) *Ethics and the Multinational Enterprise*. Washington, DC: University Press of America.

Kant, I. (1788) (reprint 1997) *Critique of Practical Reason*. (Edited by Mary J. Gregor). Cambridge: Cambridge University Press.

Laczniak, G. and Murphy, P. (1993) *Ethical Marketing Decisions: The Higher Road*. Boston: Allyn and Bacon.

Makovec Brencic, M. and Rojšek, I. (2005) 'Marketing in Slovenia: changes and challenges' in M. Marinov (ed.) *Marketing in the Emerging Markets of Central and Eastern Europe: The Balkans*. Basingstoke: Palgrave Macmillan.

Mill, J. (1863) *Utilitarianism*. (1987 edn). Loughton: Prometheus Books.

Nantel, J. and Weeks, W. (1996) 'Marketing ethics: is there more to it than the utalitarian approach?'. *European Journal of Marketing*, 30 (5): 9–19.

Onkvisit, S. and Shaw, J. (2004) *International Marketing: Analysis and Strategy*. (4th edn). Abingdon: Routledge.

Pires, G. and Stanton, J. (2002) 'Ethnic marketing ethics'. *Journal of Business Ethics*, 32 (1/2): 111–18.

Pollay, R. (1986) 'The distorted mirror: reflections on the unintended consequences of advertising'. *Journal of Marketing*, 50: 18–36.

Prahalad, C. and Hart, S. (2002) 'The fortune at the bottom of the pyramid'. *Strategy and Business*, 26 (January): 54–67.

Rogers, H., Ogbuehi, A. and Kochunny, C. (1995) 'Ethics and transnational corporation in developing countries: a social contract perspective'. *Journal of Euro-marketing*, 4 (2): 11–38.

Scanlan, C. (1991) 'Medicines banned at home sold by US makers abroad'. *The Miami Herald*, May 29: 11A.

Schlegelmilch, B. (1997) *Marketing Ethics: An International Perspective*. London: International Thompson Business Press.

Smith, N.C. (1995) 'Marketing strategies for the ethics era'. *Sloan Management Review*, 36 (4): 85–97.

Tzalikis, J. and Fritzsche, D. (1989) 'Business ethics: a literature review with a focus on marketing ethics'. *Journal of Business Ethics*, 8: 695–743.

Yeo, R. (1988) 'Genius, method, and morality: Images of Newton in Britain, 1760–1860'. *Science in Context*, 2: 257–84.

7
International Distribution: The Paradoxical Logics Developed by Retail Groups

Ulrike Mayrhofer

In the past, the majority of retail chains operated in their regional, perhaps national territory, essentially because of the complexity of the supply chain, consumer demand and regulatory constraints (Lehmann-Ortega and Schoettl, 2004; Mayrhofer, 2004). It was only from the end of the 1980s that retail chains began to significantly strengthen their international expansion. In the first instance, the movement involved the food sector, before expanding into the non-food field. The 1990s saw an intensification of the phenomenon, accelerated by the increasing numbers of mergers and acquisitions. Today, the internationalisation of activities has become a top priority strategic objective for a large number of distributors. Against the background of the globalisation of markets, competition between retail groups has now moved to the world stage (Dupuis and Fournioux, 2005; Meier, 2006).

However, the strategies adopted by retail groups are multiple and may appear to be contradictory. This paradoxical logic is seen especially in four areas: the choice of geographical market (focus on a limited number of countries or presence in a large number of markets), the pace of international expansion (country-by-country development or simultaneous conquest of several markets), the choice of mode of entry (setting up retail outlets from scratch or cooperative operations) and the degree of standardisation or adaptation of activities. The aim of this chapter is to explain these four paradoxes in order to contribute to a better understanding of the choices made by retail groups.

First of all, we shall seek to highlight the factors that explain the international development of retail groups. Then, we shall analyse the main development strategies implemented.

1 The internationalisation of retail chains: an opportunity or a constraint?

Over the last few years, a large number of retailers have strengthened their presence in international markets. The internationalisation of activities has often been announced as a top priority strategic objective, but it seems necessary to evaluate the real importance of the sales that retail chains make in foreign markets.

1.1 The importance of sales made in a foreign country

According to a study carried out by the consultant company Deloitte Touche Tohmatsu (2007), in 2005, the 250 biggest retail groups made 14.4 per cent of their turnover in foreign countries (against 12.6 per cent in 2000). Among the 250 companies identified, 143 retailers (57.2 per cent) have expanded into international markets, although thirty-five of them operate in only two bordering countries. These figures show that the relative weight of sales made by retail groups remains lower than in sectors qualified as 'global', such as the automobile and pharmaceutical industries (for example, the fifteen biggest companies in the pharmaceutical sector make almost 70 per cent of their sales abroad). The move towards internationalisation among retail groups seems more limited, even if a certain number of companies in the sector have heavily accentuated their presence in foreign markets (KPMG, 2006).

Available statistics reveal significant disparities depending on the retail group's country of origin. German and French groups seem to be the most internationalised: they make respectively 36 per cent and 34.8 per cent of their sales abroad. With regard to the geographical spread of their activities, it can be noted that German companies operate, on average, in 12.7 countries, and French companies in 15.7 countries. The international development of German and French retailers can be explained by the characteristics of their domestic market; specifically by the moderate household consumption, heavy domestic competition and a relatively restrictive regulatory environment. In contrast, American, British and Japanese companies seem to have more interesting development prospects in their home countries: the weight of international sales is 6.2 per cent for American retailers (with a presence on average in 3.7 countries), 14.6 per cent for British retailers (7.6 countries) and 1.2 per cent for Japanese retailers (2.6 countries). It can be noted, however, that the most highly internationalised companies have experienced higher growth rates than those who have chosen to concentrate their activity in the domestic market: the annual growth rate for companies which make more than 25 per cent of their turnover abroad (2004–05) was 15.3 per cent, against 7.6 per cent for their counterparts who operate only in their domestic market (Deloitte Touche Tohmatsu, 2007).

The ranking of the world's twenty leading retail groups enables us to better understand the choices made by the companies. As shown in Table 7.1, the world retail market is dominated by American, French and German companies: among the top twenty retail groups, ten are American, five are German and three are French. For several years now, the American group Wal-Mart has been the biggest global retailer, followed by the French group Carrefour and its American counterpart The Home Depot. The majority of retail groups have managed to increase their turnover, particularly thanks to their development in international markets. However, the amount of foreign sales varies significantly from one retailer to another. The Ahold group makes 77 per cent of its turnover abroad, Carrefour and Metro both make 52 per cent, Aldi and Auchan 45 per cent, and Lidl and Schwartz 43 per cent. Among the ten biggest American retailers, five operate only in the domestic market, and for Wal-Mart and Costco, international sales represent 'only' 20 per cent of their turnover. These data show that the performance of retailers does not seem to be linked to their degree of internationalisation. For example, the net profit announced by the Ahold group is lower than that made by the American companies that operate only in their domestic market. On the other hand, other highly internationalised groups like Auchan and Carrefour have a satisfactory profitability. These statistics suggest that the internationalisation of the activity does not always lead to an optimisation of the performance of retail chains (Ubifrance, 2006).

Compared with other sectors of activity, the move to internationalisation among retail groups is relatively recent. Although a large number of companies now give increasing importance to international markets, it seems that their degree of international development shows strong variation, depending on the country and the players. In order to understand these variations, it is necessary to examine the factors that explain the internationalisation of retail groups.

1.2   Explanatory factors for internationalisation

As with all businesses, the international expansion of a retail group can be attributed to a combination of several factors, such as the possession of a concept or brand with a strong potential, the desire of the management team, or the search for economies of scale and experience. However, in order to understand the movement to internationalisation among retailers, it is important to highlight four specific factors:

  i. the saturation of the national market
 ii. the opening up of markets
iii. the homogenisation of consumer needs
iv. increased competition.

(Mayrhofer, 2004)

Table 7.1 Ranking of the 20 biggest global retail groups (2005)

Group	Country of origin	Main activity	Sales ($ billion)	Sales growth 2004–2005	% Inter-national sales	Net profit ($ billion)
1. Wal-Mart	United States	GRFNP	312.4	+9.5	20	11.2
2. Carrefour	France	GRFP	92.7	+2.5	52	2.2
3. The Home Depot	United States	DS DIY	81.5	+11.5	6	5.8
4. Tesco	United Kingdom	GRFP	79.2	+27.1	20	4.1
5. Metro	Germany	Cash & carry	69.3	−1.3	52	1.2
6. The Kroger Co.	United States	GRFP	60.6	+7.4	0	1
7. Ahold	Netherlands	GRFP	55.3	−14.5	77	0.2
8. Costco	United States	Cash & carry	52.9	+12.3	20	1.1
9. Target Corp.	United States	GRFNP	52.6	+12.4	0	2.4
10. Rewe	Germany	GRFP	51.9	+2.3	31	ND
11. Sears Holdings	United States	Dept Store	49.1	−12	8	0.9
12. Lidl & Schwartz	Germany	Maxi-discount	45.8	+7.5	43	ND
13. Aldi	Germany	Maxi-discount	45.3	+5.3	45	ND
14. Lowe's Cos.	United States	SR DIY	43.2	+18.7	0	2.8
15. Walgreen Co.	United States	SR Health & Beauty	42.2	+12.5	0	1.6
16. Auchan	France	GRFP	41.8	+12	45	1.2
17. Edeka Zentrale AG	Germany	GRFP	41.3	+5.1	7	ND
18. Alberton's	United States	GRFP	40.4	+1.3	0	0.5
19. Safeway	United States	GRFP	38.4	+7.3	13	0.6
20. ITM Entreprises	France	GRFP	37.7	−20.2	10	ND

SR = Specialised retailing.
GRFP = General Retail, Food Predominating.
GRFNP = General retail, Food Not Predominating.
Source: Ubifrance (2006), *Les 100 Leaders Mondiaux de la Distribution.*

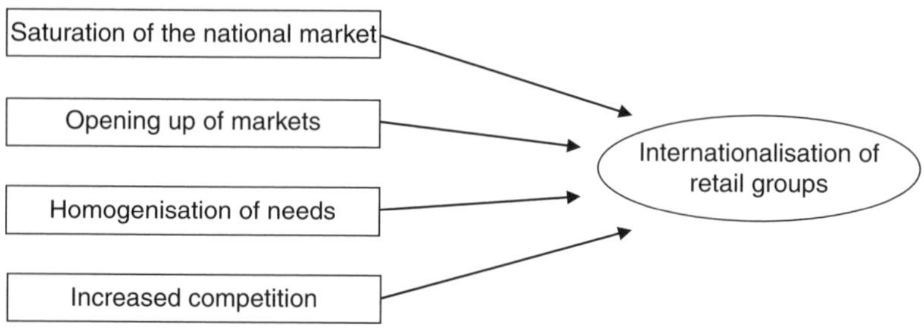

Figure 7.1   Explanatory factors for the international expansion of retailers
Source: Mayrhofer (2004).

Figure 7.1 shows their influence on the internationalisation of retail groups.

The saturation of the national market is the first reason explaining why retail groups have developed their activities outside their national base. A historical analysis of the movement reveals that internationalisation initially concerned retailers who had achieved a significant size in their domestic market (for example, the American retailers Wal-Mart and Woolworths, the French retailer Auchan), and those who were operating in a market with a limited size (for example, the Austrian retailer Julius Meinl and the Dutch retailers Ahold and Makro) (Colla, 1996). Today, the prospects for development in mature markets seem limited. The restrictive legislation in force in certain countries, limiting the creation of new retail outlets (for example the Royer and Raffarin laws in France), can also be an incentive to develop activities abroad (Lehmann-Ortega and Schoettl, 2004). Adopting a global view, some retailers have also noticed that foreign markets offer more interesting growth prospects, and are more profitable than their original market. As an example, we could cite the Spanish retailer Zara (Inditex) which makes bigger profits in most of its foreign markets than in its domestic market.

Secondly, the international development of retail groups has been made easier by the increasing opening up of the markets. In fact, for a long time, the regulatory framework in force in their various countries hampered the international expansion of retail groups. The movement towards liberalisation of world trade, reinforced by the construction of integrated economic areas has considerably reduced the barriers to entry for retail groups (Lehmann-Ortega and Schoettl, 2004). Today, emerging markets that are characterised by strong demand and a fragmented retail sector offer new prospects for development. We might mention, in particular, the countries of Central and Eastern Europe, Russia and China, which are attracting a growing number of retailers. However, it should be noted that, in a large number of countries, the defence of independent retailers is a priority, and regulations may seek to impede certain retail groups from attaining dominant positions. Moreover, several countries, like India, limit the possibility of making direct investments, and they oblige foreign retail groups to enter into association with local partners. Among the Western companies, the Metro group is one of the first to have set up in the Indian market (KPMG, 2006).

Thirdly, the growing homogenisation of consumer needs has boosted the movement towards internationalisation of retail groups. In spite of the existence of socio-cultural differences, consumer needs tend to coincide, at least in certain geographical areas and for certain categories of products (Ohmae, 2005; Townsend et al., 2004). The standardisation of the products and services offered renders their international circulation easier and enables retailers to make economies of scale in their supplies (Colla, 1996). Moreover, the emergence of global segments offers new opportunities for international development. Several companies, such as H&M (Hennes & Mauritz), IKEA and Toys 'R' Us have recognised the value of working in these segments. The growing mobility of consumers undoubtedly favours the success of the formulas adopted.

Finally, the intensification of competition in the retail field also explains the movement to internationalisation of retail groups. As in other sectors of activity, the search for critical mass seems to have become an important key factor for success. In fact, competition between the big groups is now played out on the world stage. A large number of players are extending their international expansion with the aim of becoming big enough to remain competitive (Dupuis and Fournioux, 2005). Although the increase in competition initially concerned mature markets such as France and Germany, which are characterised by a high level of concentration, we should note that, in certain emerging markets, the presence of a large number of retail groups has considerably increased the competitive pressure. In this regard, the example of the Czech Republic seems particularly interesting: because of the competitive pressure, several retailers, including Carrefour, Edeka and Julius Meinl have recently decided to withdraw from this market (KPMG, 2006).

Although the factors mentioned above favour the international expansion of retail groups, these groups nevertheless have to overcome a number of obstacles in order to ensure the success of their international operations. The experience of the different groups, in fact, leads to rather contrasting results. Some companies achieve enviable performances in foreign markets (for example, IKEA and Zara), whereas other retailers have faced difficulties in their international expansion (for example, Gap and Wal-Mart). What are the reasons which can explain these divergences in performance achieved via international development? To answer this question, we shall analyse the strategic choices made by the main retail groups.

2   The internationalisation strategies of retail groups: a paradoxical logic

When a retail group expands into international markets, there are four decisions which take on a special importance:

i. the selection of the geographical market: focus on a limited number of countries or presence in a large number of markets?
ii. the pace of the international expansion: country-by-country development or simultaneous conquest of several markets?
iii. the choice of mode of entry: setting up retail outlets from scratch or cooperative operations?
iv. standardisation or adaptation of activities?

2.1   The selection of the geographical market: focus on a limited number of countries or presence in a large number of countries?

If they are to conquer new markets, retail groups must make a wise choice of the countries in which they want to set up. A historical study of the internationalisation of retail groups shows that, as a rule, they favour markets which are just across the border, and large markets. Thus, French companies initially focused on the Spanish and American markets, German retailers on the Austrian and American markets, and British retailers on the American, Irish and Spanish markets. In this respect, we might note that the geographical and cultural proximity of markets generally makes it easier to set up new outlets. In this way, Auchan succeeded in developing the concept of the hypermarket in Spain, and Aldi successfully introduced the hard discount formula into the Austrian market (Colla, 1997). It is true that choosing markets in neighbouring countries enables the retailer to reduce the cost involved in entering a new market, particularly the costs of the supply chain and those linked to the transfer of know-how and communication (KPMG, 2006).

Some retailers have decided to focus on a limited number of relatively nearby markets, whereas others have sought to penetrate more distant geographical areas. Over the last few years, several French and German companies have tried to strengthen their presence in emerging markets, particularly the countries of Central and Eastern Europe, and China. As an example, we may cite the Carrefour group, which successfully set up in the Chinese market and which, thanks to its expansion into a large number of markets, has risen to the rank of world number two in the retail sector. In this regard, it should be remembered that presence in a large number of countries enables a company to limit the risks associated with the adverse development of certain markets.

2.2 The pace of international expansion: country-by-country development or simultaneous conquest of several markets?

Against the background of the globalisation of markets and competition, the majority of the big retail groups tend to accelerate the pace of their international expansion. However, the approaches they adopt can contrast quite widely. Some companies have favoured progressive internationalisation (country by country). An example of this is the American clothing retailer Gap (see Box 7.1). This approach enables the company to limit the risks associated with international development and to benefit from the international experience gained in other markets. However, it does not favour rapid development, which might be thought essential in order to succeed in highly competitive markets.

Box 7.1   The internationalisation of the American retailer Gap

Founded in 1969 by Donald G. Fisher, the American company, Gap Inc. is based in San Francisco, California. The initial idea was to offer a wide range of Levi's jeans in city centre outlets. In 1974, the company created its own brand and, since 1990, its shops only sell products with the Gap brand name.

After establishing a large number of shops in the American territory, the retailer decided to expand into foreign markets. Initially, it favoured countries that have a certain cultural affinity with the United States: in 1987, the first shop was opened in Britain and in 1989 one was opened in Canada. Having reached a satisfactory geographical coverage in these two markets, the company opened its first shop in France in 1993. In 1995, the company tackled the Japanese market and, in 1996, an outlet was created in Germany. These countries were selected because of their size and their level of economic development, but also because of the predisposition of these consumers to buy American sportswear. In each country, the company set up a subsidiary responsible for creating and managing the outlets.

The manufacture of the products is subcontracted to more than 700 suppliers, of whom the majority are in the United States or Asia. To ease the international distribution of its products, the company has set up distribution centres in the United States, Canada and Europe.

In the 1990s, this approach enabled the retailer to achieve satisfactory performances. However, due to the intensification of competition in the chosen markets, the company has had to face difficulties that have led it to reduce the number of outlets in Britain, Canada, France and Japan, and to withdraw from the German market.

Source: Gap Inc. (2006) *Annual Report*.

In the textiles and clothing sector, several retailers have chosen to expand simultaneously into a large number of markets so as to become major global players. This strategy enabled Zara (Inditex group) to establish outlets in sixty-eight countries and join the biggest companies in the sector. In this regard, it should be noted that the idea of critical mass has become a major challenge for retail groups. However, it is true that, having achieved a certain size, these groups have an increased negotiating power with producers and can achieve economies of scale and experience in the supplies area, but also with regard to logistics and communication (Colla, 1997).

In Europe, the introduction of the euro put heavy pressure on prices and led a large number of retailers to set up central purchasing groups at the European level, with the aim of obtaining better terms (Tordjman, 1999), which gives an undoubted advantage to retail groups present in a large number of markets.

2.3   The choice of mode of entry: setting up retail outlets from scratch or cooperative operations?

Any retail group wanting to set up in foreign markets is faced with the choice of mode for setting up shops. It can favour the creation of outlets from scratch or opt for an association with local retailers (Doherty, 2000; Gielens and Dekimpe, 2001). Creation of shops from scratch offers better control of international development operations. The company can in this way choose the place to set up and check all the operations carried out in foreign markets. As the creation of new outlets is generally costly, and because it can take a long time to implement, the retailer is often obliged to opt for progressive internationalisation of its activities. In order to persuade consumers to change their buying habits, the retailer must be able to offer a significant advantage compared with local competitors. Offering quality products at reasonable prices, the Swedish company IKEA thus succeeded in imposing itself as the specialist for furniture in kits and household equipment. After opening its first shop in Sweden in 1958, the firm expanded into other Scandinavian markets before progressively exporting its know-how throughout the world.

The association with local players generally provides better knowledge of the specificities of foreign markets. Compared with the creation of outlets from scratch, it can generally lead to a more rapid development of international activities. If the company chooses to cooperate with a local partner, it can share the costs and risks associated with international retailing activities. The retail groups who want to set up outlets in a number of countries often use the franchise method, as this form of cooperation enables them to quickly conquer new markets while limiting the costs associated with the creation and management of shops. Thanks to this formula, the Italian brand Benetton successfully set up in a large number of foreign cities. Companies who opt for this strategy can also decide to acquire the activities of a foreign retailer. In this case, it can take advantage of the reputation of the local retailer and more rapidly attain a dominant position in the target market (Mayrhofer, 2001). In countries where legislation in the retailing field is rather restrictive, companies often choose to ally themselves with local players. For example, in order to win over the Italian market, Auchan entered into an alliance with the Italian group Rinascente (Colla, 1997).

It is the same for markets which are difficult to access, such as the Chinese market, where cooperation with a local partner can make relations with local authorities, suppliers and employees easier (Laprès, 1996). When it has entered into association with local partners, the company must nevertheless pay particular attention to the management of the cooperative relationship and, if necessary, to the integration of the units purchased. The difficulties Wal-Mart has recently faced may also be explained by its confrontational relationship with some of its local units. The American group had, in fact, attempted to impose its management style on the employees of the companies it had taken over (Mayrhofer and Roederer, 2007).

2.4   Standardisation or adaptation of activities?

For a large number of retail groups, the internationalisation of their activities now represents a top priority strategic objective. The experiences of companies in this sector show that success or failure in foreign markets is determined by the choice of an appropriate retailing policy. In particular, the company must decide whether it wants to standardise its international activities, or whether it plans to adapt to the specificities of the local market. This choice is closely linked to the company's field of activity. Although in the food sector it is often necessary to adapt to the socio-cultural differences of a country, in the non-food sector a large number of retailers successfully apply a global retailing policy.

In the food sector, retailers must pay special attention to the different purchasing and consumption habits of the local population. These differences, which can be attributed to socio-cultural characteristics, explain why certain retailing formulas have not had the success expected in other markets. As an example, we might recall the difficulties encountered by Auchan, Carrefour and Leclerc in the United States. For these companies, the adventure of conquering the American market ended in failure, principally because Americans are not used to buying food and non-food products in the same retail outlet (Barth et al., 1996; Colla, 1996). Similarly, Carrefour's expansion in Japan was not a success, as the company was not able to differentiate itself sufficiently from local competitors to persuade Japanese consumers to change their buying habits (Prime and Delcourt-Itonaga, 2008). The example of the German retailers Aldi and Lidl is also worth mentioning. Although French consumers at first had reservations about the concept of hard discount, preferring to do all their shopping (everyday products) in a single outlet where a wider assortment of products was available, the more recent success of this formula seems to show that behaviour has changed. Despite the socio-cultural differences, several food retailers have succeeded in setting up in other markets. In the food sector, the adaptation of the assortment of products to the expectations of local consumers, however, is a necessity, even if it limits the possibility of making economies of scale in the supplies area (Meier, 2006).

Although in the food sector differences in buying and consumption behaviour remain, in the non-food sector it is possible to identify the emergence of global segments, at least for certain categories of products. The existence of these relatively homogeneous groups of consumers enables companies to implement a global retailing strategy. The advantages associated with such a strategy are many: negotiating power with producers, economies of scale, international brand awareness, uniform image. The majority of retail chains who have used this strategy with success are from Western countries. They have tried to export their retailing know-how to a large number of countries. They are essentially specialised superstores and chains of specialised shops. The superstores generally have greater negotiating power with producers than national retail groups, which makes it possible for them to offer very competitive prices (for example, Castorama and Obi in the do-it-yourself sector, Darty and Media World in the household electrical and electronic goods sector, Toys 'R' Us in the toys field, Fnac and Virgin Megastore in books and records). The shops, which generally target relatively specific segments, offer a narrower range of items, and are often located in city centres or in shopping malls (examples are Benetton, Cyrillus, Laura Ashley and Stefanel in the clothing sector, or The Body Shop in the field of cosmetics). Other retailing formulas have experienced a more limited level of internationalisation. We might cite Printemps, which has exported the department store concept to Asia and the Middle East, and such mail-order businesses as La Redoute, Otto Versand and Quelle, which have expanded into other European markets. The retailers mentioned above use the same concept at the international level and try to standardise the assortment of products they offer in order to make economies of scale. However, in practice, it often proves necessary to adapt what is offered so as to meet the demand of local consumers (Barth et al., 1996; Colla, 1996).

The developments presented above highlight the paradoxical logic of the strategies used by the big retail groups. They show that success in the international marketplace is not associated with one particular strategy. Our analysis is consistent with that proposed by Berger (2006), who based her work on a study carried out by researchers at the Massachusetts Institute of Technology (MIT), involving 500 businesses in North America, Europe and Asia. It shows that, if the world economy obliges companies to review their development strategies, it also offers a multitude of viable possibilities, sometimes within the same sector and for the same product. Our study suggests that retailers can also choose from a variety of options to succeed in foreign markets. Observation of practice in this area, however, indicates that the international success of a retail group is generally founded on the existence of a specialised know-how originally developed in the domestic market. This know-how can be, for example, a new shop format (the French concept of the 'hypermarket' or the German 'hard discount' concept), a retail brand which is innovative (the Spanish brands Mango and Zara), or exclusive (Cartier, Hermès, Louis Vuitton), and/or offer a competitive edge in terms of price (the Swedish retailer H&M – Hennes & Mauritz).

3 Conclusion

Economic globalisation has accelerated the move towards internationalisation in the retail field with, as a consequence, an intensification of competition, in particular in mature markets. Against this background of strong competition, it has become even more difficult for a company to conquer foreign markets and to differentiate itself from other companies. An analysis of strategies used by big retail groups shows that globalisation, although it is in fact a unifying force (Ohmae, 2005), does not impose any single model for development. Indeed, the strategies favoured by retail groups are various, and the performances they achieve through their different choices are diverse.

Although the globalisation of markets and of competition leads to a certain harmonisation of retailing systems, particularly within integrated economic areas such as the European Union, it is important to stress the fact that the world's economic environment remains deeply heterogeneous, with regard to both supply and demand. Thus, retailing systems continue to be highly differentiated. For example, in the majority of emerging countries, retailing remains highly fragmented and rather basic, despite the penetration achieved by certain foreign groups (Allix-Desfautaux, 2006; Schlosser, 2001). The same can be said of consumer behaviour, where different habits abound, although they will be likely to change (Dussart, 2006). As a consequence, the building of an appropriate strategy for international development remains difficult and it is probable that the choices made will retain a paradoxical character, at least in the near future.

References

Allix-Desfautaux, C. (2006) 'Franchise internationale et marchés émergents: un éclairage sur l'Inde'. *Décisions Marketing*, 43–4: 109–21.
Barth, K., Karch, N.J., McLaughlin, K. and Smith Shi, C. (1996) 'La distribution passe entre les frontiers'. *L'Expansion Management Review*, 83: 79–83.
Berger, S. (2006) *Made in Monde: Les Nouvelles Frontières de l'Économie Mondiale*. Paris: Editions du Seuil.

Colla, E. (1996) 'Les stratégies d'internationalisation des entreprises commerciales'. *Revue Française du Marketing*, 157–8: 133–59.

—— (1997) 'Les tendances de la distribution: évolution du secteur et stratégies des enterprises'. *Revue Française du Marketing*, 164: 103–20.

Deloitte Touche Tohmatsu (2007) *Global Powers of Retailing: The Search for Sustainable Growth*. Washington DC: Stores Magazine.

Doherty, A.M. (2000) 'Factors influencing international retailers' market entry mode strategy: qualitative evidence from the UK fashion sector'. *Journal of Marketing Management*, 16 (1–3): 223–45.

Dupuis, M. and Fournioux, J. (2005) 'Internationalisation du distributeur: de l'avantage compétitif à la performance'. *Décisions Marketing*, 37: 45–56.

Dussart, C. (2006) 'Les trois "A" de la globalisation'. *Décisions Marketing*, 43–4: 221–5.

GAP Inc. (2006) *Annual Report*. San Francisco: GAP Incorporated.

Gielens, K. and Dekimpe, M.G. (2001) 'Do international entry decisions of retail chains matter in the long run?' *International Journal of Research in Marketing*, 18 (3): 235–59.

KPMG (2006) *Trends im Handel 2010*.

Laprès, D. (1996) 'La distribution en République Populaire de Chine'. *Revue Française du Marketing*, 157–8: 171–203.

Lehmann-Ortega, L. and Schoettl, J.M. (2004) 'Distribution et modèles d'internationalisation'. *L'Expansion Management Review*: 75–83.

Mayrhofer, U. (2001) *Les Rapprochements d'Entreprises, une Nouvelle Logique Stratégique? Une Analyse des Entreprises Françaises et Allemandes*. Bern: Peter Lang.

—— (2004) *Marketing International*. Paris: Economica.

Mayrhofer, U. and Roederer, C. (2007) 'De la difficulté d'aborder le marché allemand: le cas de Levi Strauss Signature®'. *Regards sur l'économie allemande*, 8: 27–34.

Meier, O. (2006) 'Comment les groupements de distributeurs indépendants s'adaptent à la globalisation: une lecture du Mouvement Leclerc à l'international'. *Décisions Marketing*, 43–4: 175–90.

Ohmae, K. (2005) *The Next Global Stage: Challenges and Opportunities in our Borderless World*. Upper Saddle River: Wharton School Publishing.

Prime, N. and Delcourt-Itonaga, M. (2008) 'Cas "Carrefour au Japon"' in S. Hertrich and U. Mayrhofer (eds) *Cas en Marketing*. Colombelles: Editions Management & Société.

Schlosser, A.-M. (2001) 'Le destin des marques locales face aux marques internationals'. *L'Expansion Management Review*, 102: 88–94.

Tordjman, A. (1999) 'Les distributeurs, les industriels et l'euro'. *Revue Française de Gestion*, 124: 128–32.

Townsend, J.D., Yeniyurt, S., Deligonul, Z.S. and Cavusgil, S.T. (2004) 'Exploring the marketing program antecedents of performance in a global company'. *Journal of International Marketing*, 12 (4): 1–24.

Ubifrance (2006) *Les 100 leaders mondiaux de la distribution*. Paris: Ubifrance.

8
Medical Tourism: Paradoxes of Globalisation and Ethical Issues

Loïck Menvielle

The globalisation of markets has brought many benefits to companies as well as to consumers. Even with reservations, it should be recognised that globalisation can bring[1] 'a growth and an economic development which have as much interest for the rich countries as for the poor countries' (Reddy and Vyas, 2004: 166). One of the most important examples illustrating this is the internationalisation of the tourism industry, which has developed enormously both economically and socially. Sustainable tourism, cultural tourism or, even more surprisingly, medical tourism (or healthcare tourism) are some examples of the development of the sector. Globalisation of the tourism industry, however, has also resulted in limits and paradoxes (Azarya, 2004), which will be discussed further. Among them, medical tourism can be put forward as a paradoxical entity in itself. Indeed, the health sector, previously protected by the authorities or states, is now considered to be an emerging and lucrative industry among the new 'international businesses'.

However, influenced by various elements such as the development of socio-cultural trends, the healthcare sector has become, in the rich countries, a true consumer item or goods, similar to any other. This situation raises numerous questions – ethical, moral, legal and marketing – that should be addressed.

In the first part of this chapter, we will examine the various areas of the tourist sector, its main trends and the diversification it is undergoing. In the second part, we will focus on the area of my research, medical tourism, in order to define it, and to analyse the ethical implications of the health market at the international level.

1 The tourism industry: the part it plays in contemporary society

This section presents an overview of the development of tourism and the various issues with which it is currently confronted. In spite of the many constraints on the sector (for example, terrorism, which constitutes one of the most restricting factors in this industry's development), the tourist market has never before known such progress. Means of transport became more easily available to a greater number of customers and, at the same time, the strong demand of the generation of 'baby boomers' enabled this development to be maintained. In any case, the market is changing completely, and we now see the appearance of diversified offers, in order to meet customers' requirements. In this race (you could even say this frenzy) for 'avant-garde tourism', many paradoxes can be highlighted, particularly at the level of medical tourism.

1.1　High numbers and the development of the sector

The tourism industry has recently experienced strong development. Between 2006 and 2007, the number of international tourists increased by 6 per cent, from 846 million to 898 million arrivals according to the World Tourism Organisation (WTO, 2008a). Although the leading countries in the sector retain their attraction (France, Spain, the United States, Italy and China), it should be stressed that new geographical areas are showing the potential for interesting development. Indeed, of the 52 million additional arrivals between 2006 and 2007, the countries in the process of development record the highest increase. The economic development of Asia, pushed by countries like China[2] and India, but also Singapore, is the origin of the increased competitiveness of their tourist offers. Similarly, the Middle East showed the strongest progression (nearly 13 per cent according to this same study). Although the geopolitical tensions are strong in this region, the attraction of Saudi Arabia and Egypt remains; good quality offers and good professional skills on the part of the personnel make it possible to compare them favourably with other 'safer' destinations.

Internationalisation of tourism, according to projections by analysts of the World Tourism Organisation (WTO), shows changes in the market shares of international tourist arrivals, calling into question the current situation of the market in favour of other continents such as Asia-Pacific. Graph 8.1 is an illustration. However, it would seem that the financial crisis of 2008 will lead to a total deceleration of tourist consumption, particularly in the short term (2009/2010), while maintaining a certain degree of confidence for 2020 (WTO, 2008b).[3]

In the face of this increase of tourist demand, new developments have appeared that are related to an intensification of competition, the democratisation of tourism and the means of transport. Our own analysis as consumers, the works of academics such as Cohen (2004) and Conrady and Buck (2007), as well as recent various industrial advances such as the Airbus[4] 380, provide us with numerous examples that are related to the development of tourism and the diversification in this sector. This diversification is also evident by the level of the diversity of destination offers, and of the multiple expectations of the consumers (or companies).

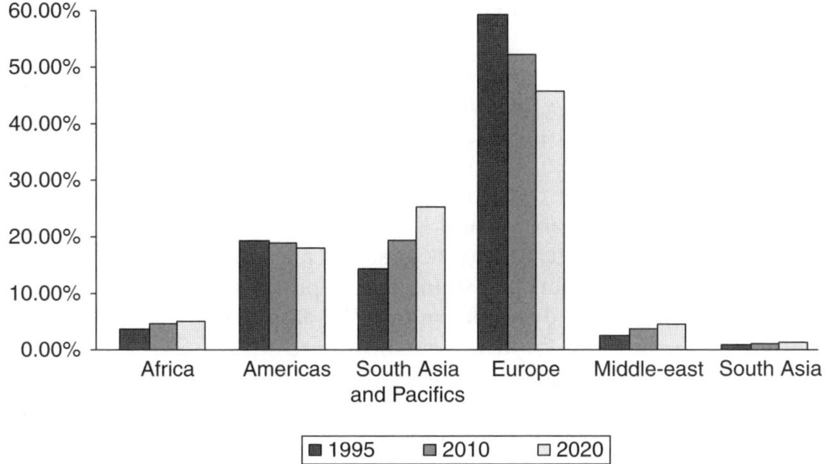

Graph 8.1   Potential Development of the market shares; projection of international tourist arrivals to 2020

Source: World Tourism Organisation (2005).

1.2   Diversification of tourism

The diversification of tourism is incontestably the fundamental characteristic of its development. Cazelais (1991), Hut (1996) and Spindler and Durant (2003) all emphasise the importance of this diversification that, as with industrial tourism,[5] constantly offers different and richer tourism experiences. For example, within the field of religious tourism, there has been an increase of Muslim pilgrims to Mecca while the Vatican has inaugurated an airline (Mistral Air) under the aegis of the Holy See especially to go to Santiago de Compostela in Spain or to Lourdes in France, at reduced prices. Cultural tourism, yachting or even rural tourism, are further offers, less unusual, but answering real economic, geographical and socio-cultural stakes.

Similarly, sustainable tourism, together with interdependent tourism which both share the same philosophy of protecting the environment and respecting other cultures and economic development – are now being researched by both academics and tourism companies, so are stimulating much debate (Cerina, 2007; Lozato-Giotart and Balfet, 2007). Of course, this new market segment, like the majority of the market segments relating to the commercial exploitation of sustainable development, fair trade or more general business ethics, is not without strong criticism. Wheeler (1995) and Mowforth and Munt (2003) do not hesitate to label it as a 'marketing stratagem'. Doubts can be raised, therefore, about the development of interdependent and sustainable tourism, both considered wrongly as a simple commercial tool by certain companies of hotel industry.

It is true that the consumer's behaviour in regard to this is very contradictory, particularly when they do not hesitate to use air transport to reach their destination, so creating additional pollution. In the same way, when we analyse the situation from the companies' point of view, we can legitimately question whether there really is altruistic and ethical behaviour on their part (Caire, 2004; Lansing and De Vries, 2006). Furthermore, we could wonder whether, in reality, this new concept is promoted with the intention of attracting new customers and so increasing profits.

In the context of these dynamic commercial offers a new area is emerging: healthcare tourism, also known as medical tourism. It is not a traditional market segment for several reasons. On the one hand, mainly in the Western countries with their ageing populations, medical needs are increasingly important in terms of both the number of interventions and rising medical costs. On the other hand, there are notable failures in some occidental and non-occidental medical healthcare systems. According to experts, the twenty-first century will see an explosion of government health budgets: companies and tour operators have already started considering medical tourism as commercially viable. Thus, medical tourism has been born; it will create, without doubt, a profitable market, as envisaged by Goodrich and Goodrich (1987).

2   Medical tourism

One of the first paradoxes to be highlighted relates to the name and the concept of medical tourism in itself. The *Petit Larousse* dictionary gives the following definition of tourism:

> The action of visiting a site for pleasure and activities.

The concept of tourism, therefore, seems almost paradoxical with that of medicine. The fact of creating such a market segment simultaneously presents both the challenge and the paradox.

Moreover, the perception of this segment by the majority of the consumers in France is rather paradoxical, as it is associated mainly with plastic surgery (i.e. not a priority medical concern), whereas, as the statistics show, plastic surgery is only a tiny part of the world market. It should also be noted that the media very often present this type of tourism in a superficial way, depicting medical tourism as something new, as a trend created by the pressure of seeking the extreme criteria of the perfect body, and emphasising the element of snobbery involved. In fact, the reality is very different, as we will now explore.

2.1   A millennium tradition of medical tourism

The origins of medical tourism are obscure for many people. However, history shows that this type of tourism has developed from our earliest civilisation. The Egyptians first used the curative benefits of the sea in order to ease pain and to cure other health disorders. However, it is to the Greeks and Romans that we owe the long tradition of hydrotherapy, of the exploitation of medicinal springs or hot water, according to Smith and Kelly (2006). This type of tourism 'is one of the most ancient forms of tourism if one considers the scrupulous attention paid to well-being by Romans and Greeks' (p. 1). The search for well-being and the possibility of being able to cure diseases judged at the time as 'incurable' encouraged the nobility and the aristocrats to move quite far within the Roman empire in order to be appropriately healed, or at least to acquire the perception of being so. Medical tourism as we know it is the result of this situation.

The spirit of hydrotherapy, thalassotherapy (water therapy) or the use of natural sources and its properties, were widely exploited until the Middle Ages. However, the backwardness of contemporary thinking greatly interfered with the development and use of the medical benefits that one could get from natural resources.

Society, therefore, had to wait for Renaissance period, and it was only in the eighteenth century that the virtues of 'modern' medicine were rediscovered, with an effect on medical tourism. Hydrotherapy in the town of Bath in England is the perfect illustration of this according to Boyer (1996). Both English and European aristocracy learnt to relax and look after themselves. Under the influence of Napoleon III and his family, the thermal spas benefited massively from this trend. And, from the end of nineteenth century, the nobility enjoyed the benefits of the French Riviera; a finding confirmed by Smith and Kelly (2006) and Proulx (2005). This then was the period of transition to 'modern medical tourism', which certain authors such as Boyer (1996) put forward as evidence when they speak of these places as existing both for health purposes and meeting points for the European aristocracy.

In Figure 8.1 we can clearly see the development of medical tourism and consumers' expectations over the centuries. The main dates show the main trends or the major changes in this type of tourism. In addition, the most significant changes of the twentieth century appear after the Second World War, highlighting an important rise in tourist activities, entertaining and leisure, according to Gartner and Lime (2000).

Two important periods are apparent. Firstly, there are the ancient developments and the benefits of the natural elements. The exploitation of thermal springs and natural resources (mud, clay or plants) characterises this basic stage in the evolution of tourism of health. Secondly, there is the period with an important degree of technicality. The deepening of medical

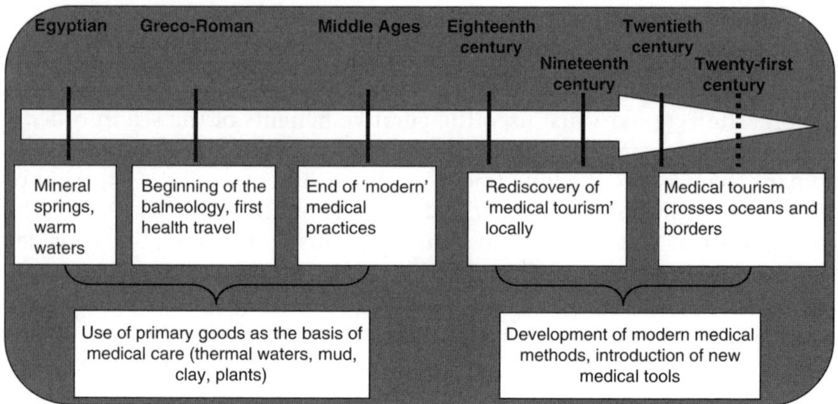

Figure 8.1   Historical development of medical tourism
Source: Menvielle (2009: 175).

knowledge brought to the sector new aspects to looking after patients. Moreover, the incentive to cross borders to profit from this care is explained by other important variables such as the cost of medicine or the length of the waiting list.

Technological developments (especially easier transportation), the progressive revival of economies, and the popularisation of tourism and leisure activities all support this rise of mass tourism as we now know it. It has developed as a consequence of the ability to travel further and under better conditions, which has pushed back the limits of national borders. Obviously, this is to be correlated with the appearance of the railway, vehicles and aviation. The development and the popularisation of these means of transport are at the origin of the blurring of the distinctions between the elitist customers and the working classes, or at least towards a generalisation of this mode of tourism (Gilbert, 1954).

Thus medical tourism passed from that instigated by the large Western hospitals (the American Hospital of Paris, the private clinics of Harley Street in London and so on), offering care for the privileged and wealthy, to medical tourism relying on private clinics in developing countries. What was a reserved privilege for certain people, became a need and an ultimate means for others. The management of risk by this kind of consumer is very different because he/she is willing to fly without having the benefit of any medical care beforehand. This could result, in some cases, in an increase of the risk of an incident during the trip (for example, phlebitis or a pulmonary embolism). Therefore, the ultimate aim of being operated on quickly can have disastrous consequences – an example of paradoxical behaviour.

2.2   The modern version of medical tourism

We have seen that medical tourism is not new, but has witnessed an expansion only during recent years. The dominant error in this field is the misunderstanding of the variables of medical tourism, and there is a lack of academic research. Medical tourism has nowadays to be considered with different variables. Garcia-Altes (2005) emphasises how large the sector of medical tourism is, but he includes all the various fields of healthcare. Using the generic term 'health tourism' would be very limiting and therefore, according to Connell (2005), the distinction between welfare tourism and medical tourism is necessary. Health tourism can be considered as falling into three categories (Mueller and Lanz Kaufmann, 2001; Menvielle and Menvielle, 2007) which can be described as follows:

- *Wellness tourism*: this does not require a heavy medical infrastructure, such as spas, hydrotherapy and thalassotherapy (water therapy). It can include leisure tourism, closely connected to nature and sustainable tourism; in this context, welfare tourism can be developed within the hotel infrastructure, which is part of durable development (Grell, 1994).
- *Rehabilitation tourism*: this aims to offer to a 'tourist patient' post-operative care or specific care such as anti-ageing treatments or treatments for dependency (drugs, alcohol and so on).
- *Treatment and surgery tourism*: this requires a heavy medical infrastructure with surgeons and qualified personnel; it is the field most widely known about from the consumer's point of view thanks to plastic surgery (cosmetic surgery), laser treatment (eye surgery), dental surgery, cardiothoracic surgery and treatment for cancer.

Wellness tourism can be described as 'healthy medical tourism', while rehabilitation and treatment tourisms can be described as 'sick/vital medical tourism'. Figure 8.2 illustrates this. The areas highlighted by Mueller and Lanz Kaufmann (2001) have been adapted to refer to health tourism. By this adaptation, the different degrees of involvement in the available medical offers of the consumer/tourist/patient have been integrated into the analysis. Therefore, this refers to the type of care desired by the consumer: preventive, palliative or curative. Within these three concepts the level of participation of the consumer is inferred, with a graduation of risk perceived and suffered. In contrast to Mueller and Lanz Kaufmann, Menvielle and Menvielle (2007) show the importance of the elements that have directly impacted on the moral, psychological and physical integrity of the consumer/patient, and thus emphasise the global participation of the consumer in the process of purchasing particular services.

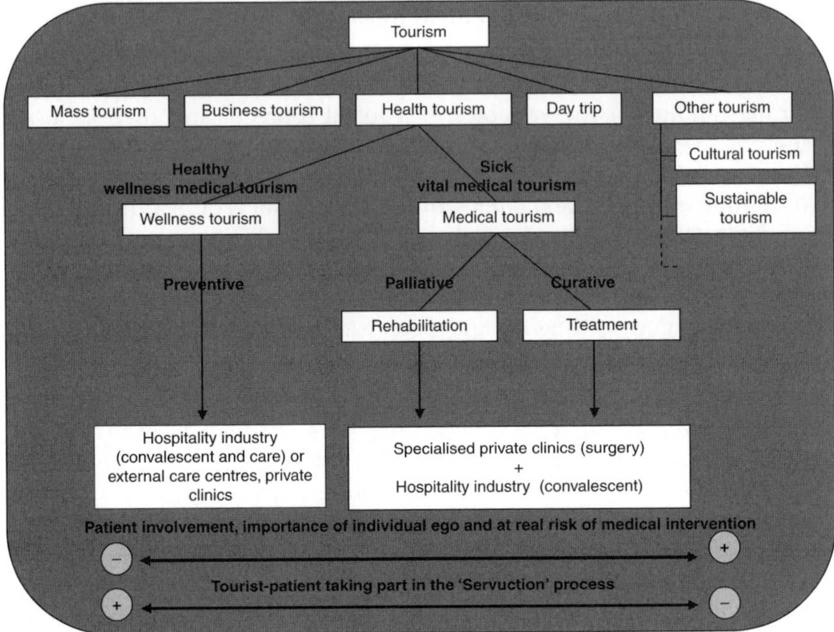

Figure 8.2   The various areas of medical tourism
Source: Mueller and Lanz Kaufmann (2001) (adapted by Menvielle and Menvielle, 2007).

Receiving the consumer under the best conditions (for example, more contact than usual with care personnel), considering them as a privileged guest or 'substituting' relatives with escorts, all help to flatter the patient/consumer (Zeithaml et al., 1985; N'Goala, 1997; Bendapudi and Leone, 2003).

Based on these different concepts, various marketing strategies and adapted combinations of marketing result. One of the main marketing questions that arises is to know how to reduce the perception of risk in the commercialisation of such packages. This question is all the more important as it touches the service area, which is characterised by its inviobility and constitutes a first factor of risk. This has been pointed out by Bauer (1960), Flipo (1984, 1988) and Laroche et al. (2003), to mention only the main researchers. The difficulty consists in how to manage these variables to bring about positive behaviour. On the one hand, the medical sector can provoke within the consumer a kind of repulsion, on the other, the tourism side also entails risks as perceived by the consumer, in particular with regard to the geopolitical variables, or the increase of insecurity created by the globalisation of terrorism according to Bianchi (2006). It is therefore necessary to do the utmost possible to find a relational concept that creates confidence between the service provider and the future tourist-cum-patient.

2.3   Ethical questions

Without creating an epistemological debate,[6] we notice that many observers and consumers are concerned with the association of ethical and marketing terms. However, it is important to note that medical tourism, more than any other form of tourism, involves ethical issues. The problem is certainly not limited to the actions of marketeers who, to some extent, are aimed at first. This situation also includes practitioners, lawyers (Grant et al., 2005) and, more generally, political and institutional leaders.

In France, the social reform policy proposed by the government is directed towards a social and medical protection that will gradually be managed by private insurance companies. If this proposal is confirmed, a good portion of the health system would be called into question. As with patients of certain Anglo-Saxon countries, people would then be tempted to be hospitalised or looked after in foreign countries. It is important to note that the French phenomenon of medical tourism relates mainly to aesthetic tourism (comfort) but could, following this financial change to social security, encourage patients requiring care to go elsewhere to obtain these services (for example, to Hungary, Poland, the Czech Republic and so on, where the cost of healthcare, glasses and prostheses is very attractive).

At the heart of this debate is the state's responsibility to provide health services. Rawls's works (1971, 1993) seem to apply more than ever. 'Primary goods' (Rawls, 1971) such as health or education are considered by Rawls to be non-financial goods and acknowledged as necessary to the well-being of all, as fundamental and vital, and as a necessary part of the principle of equal basic rights and liberties.

Hence, is it still possible to guarantee that individuals will have equal access to healthcare? The privatisation of the medical sector, particularly in Anglo-Saxon countries, allows us to predict certain fundamental limitations, as spelled out by Rawls, i.e. the development of an unequal society in which it is not possible to guarantee equality based on social justice or to establish true access to care for everybody. Would medical tourism be the result of a possible failure of the state's social system? If so, would developing or emerging countries, not yet able to ensure their own mission of justice in terms of primary goods, provide a solution, through medical tourism, for rich countries to address this failure? This would, indeed, be a very paradoxical situation.

Many other contradictions emerge, such as the installation of an equitable distribution policy in a society that is considered to be liberal. A thorough analysis of questions that apply to the sphere under discussion will be offered.

- What is the state's role with regard to the responsibility of access to healthcare for all its citizens?
- Does the state have to offset market failures of the healthcare system by making it necessary for individuals to consider the social responsibility of their acts and consequently their choices (Dworkin, 1981)?
- Can we reconcile ethics and economic rationality (Sen, 1987) in the context of medical tourism? Would this be purely utopian, while at the same time developing a selection of patients and allowing certain individuals to benefit from healthcare abroad?

It seems that the theories developed by Rawls's society and predictions assume a certain degree of idealism. However, when faced with reality, this idealism turns the medical healthcare market into ordinary goods. This discussion of political philosophy mixes ethics and justice, and confronts two economic schools of thought. It positions thinkers like Rawls on one side, which defends the state's intervention in an individual's life (Keynes, 1936, 2002), and puts, on the other side, the stakeholders for a more independent state where individuals would be responsible for their actions (Hayek, 1944; Friedman, 1971; Nozick, 1974). Nozick may be considered one of the most important anti-Rawlsian thinkers, foreseeing an aberration in the system and denouncing the outrageous interventionism of Rawls. For Nozick, *Theory of Justice* (Rawls, 1971) violates the basic rights of individuals by not allowing them to enjoy their freedom, thus disputing the existence of social rights. The great debate between orthodox and heterodox is reintroduced, with the globalisation question regarding the healthcare market raised via medical tourism. In any event, it is the problem of the governance of this globalised market that is raised.

Rather than create controversy, we wish to underline the interest we have in increasing our knowledge in a field of research that has not yet been greatly investigated. To demonstrate that this form of tourism is a great opportunity for consumers without measuring consequences and failures would be detrimental to the consumer. On the contrary, to state that this emerging sector infers only risks and prejudices for the tourist-patient hospitalised in India or in Morocco would be a hazardous approach.

If we analyse the concept of medical tourism and its marketing setting, we conclude that there are two opposing concepts. By definition, medicine is a discipline that raises and imposes ethical and deontological issues, while, on the other hand, marketing is often criticised for its failures on these levels (Flipo and Revat, 2003). Taking into account the phenomenon of globalisation induced by the concept of tourism itself, could a discussion on ethical marketing in connection with this activity be helpful? If we take into account certifications which are gradually set up, more and more guarantees are given to consumers (i.e. hygiene, technical procedures, surgical equipment and so on). These variables help influence consumer behaviour and will increase the degree of trust between the consumer and the medical infrastructure. Under the seal of institutions such as International Medical Harvard, standards are used to allow a certain transparency in the commercial processes and development of the servuction phase (Eiglier and Langeard, 1987) that guarantees doctors' commitments to their patients, thus allowing them to initiate an ethical process. At the same time, if principles are adopted by national institutions such as the National Consultative Committee of Ethics (CCNE), specifying the necessity 'to guarantee a person's dignity through anonymity and the assertion of the principles of exemption from payment', or that specifying that there is 'no availability of the body' (1994), it is not less true that there exists, at the international level, a body of governance and control that allows this market to function under satisfactory conditions from an ethical point of view.

3 Paradoxes of medical tourism

The logical contradictions that characterise medical tourism can be grouped under three themes: failures of health systems in richer countries, cultural affinities stemming from colonisation and respect/distortion for religious rules. Let us examine more closely each of these points.

3.1 An answer to the failures of the Western systems

Due to the globalisation of the healthcare market, tourism is developing largely by creating specialisations by geographical zone. Mass medical tourism is, therefore, one of the tourism specialties of emerging countries. South America, Asia and Maghreb (to name just a few), are developing real infrastructures and companies intended for resolving the failures of and/or to compete with the medical sector of major Western countries. The variable price of the marketing mix constitutes an important element in the choice of hospitalisation abroad. It is, nevertheless, advisable to associate this with the long waiting lists for surgical procedures and the problems relative to the non-coverage of care by Western insurers for certain types of operations (Connell, 2005).

Therefore, it is still rare to see British patients going to India to have a hip prosthesis or a knee reconstruction even though waiting times are between nine and eighteen months in British hospitals, while the patient can be admitted within a week to a private hospital in Kerala (Graham, 2005). An American can also use identical means for getting around a failing medical system. Therefore, the phenomenon becomes widespread in the middle classes. Table 8.1 presents an outline of the price of hospitalisations in the United States and in some countries specialising in medical tourism.

Table 8.1   Surgical options in the main medical tourism countries

Procedure	US insurer's cost	US retail price	India	Thailand	Singapore
Heart bypass	$54,741 to $79,071	$122,424 to $176,835	$10,000	$12,000	$20,000
Heart-valve replacement (single)	$71,401 to $103,136	$159,326 to $230,138	$9,500	$10,500	$13,000
Knee replacement	$17,627 to $25,462	$40,640 to $58,702	$8,500	$10,000	$13,000

Prices are in American dollars; benefits include at least one day of hospitalisation.
Source: PlanetHospital Inc. (Walker, 2006).

The emergence of this market, due to the absence of certain public services, brings about an everyday acceptance of medical services. The most precious things, health and life, are, from now on, considered simply as products. An individual can thus visit his dentist in Hungary, undergo knee surgery in India and recuperate in Morocco. Table 8.1 outlines vital surgical operations for the patient. We note that the prices of care practised in India or in Thailand are, on average, 70–80 per cent lower than the prices of care in the United States (Walker, 2006). To this must be added the favourable exchange rate with these countries, as mentioned by Connell (2005), inciting even more patients to benefit from these services.

On the other hand, if we linger over the case of aesthetic surgery (mainly plastic surgery), the variation of the price is less important, even if it remains very advantageous. As far as this market segment goes, for informational purposes only, a patient has the choice between a breast implant in Paris for an average price of € 5,000, while some private hospitals in Maghreb offer the same operation for an average of € 2,000. This globalisation of the healthcare market already highlighted by Horowitz et al. (2007) with regard to the medical aspect creates a risk that will most likely destabilise the current offers in Western countries and, consequently, provide a glimpse of serious competition to access consumers who are sensitive to the price and/or to the waiting period.

The map of the globalisation of the healthcare market (Map 8.1) presents interesting relationships between the concerned countries. The shaded areas represent the main countries where the request for medical care is very strong, considering key variables (price, waiting period, expectations, surgical procedures not covered by insurers and so on).

We have emphasised that a Westerner will seek care in a developing country. The opposite relationship has existed for a long time, since developing

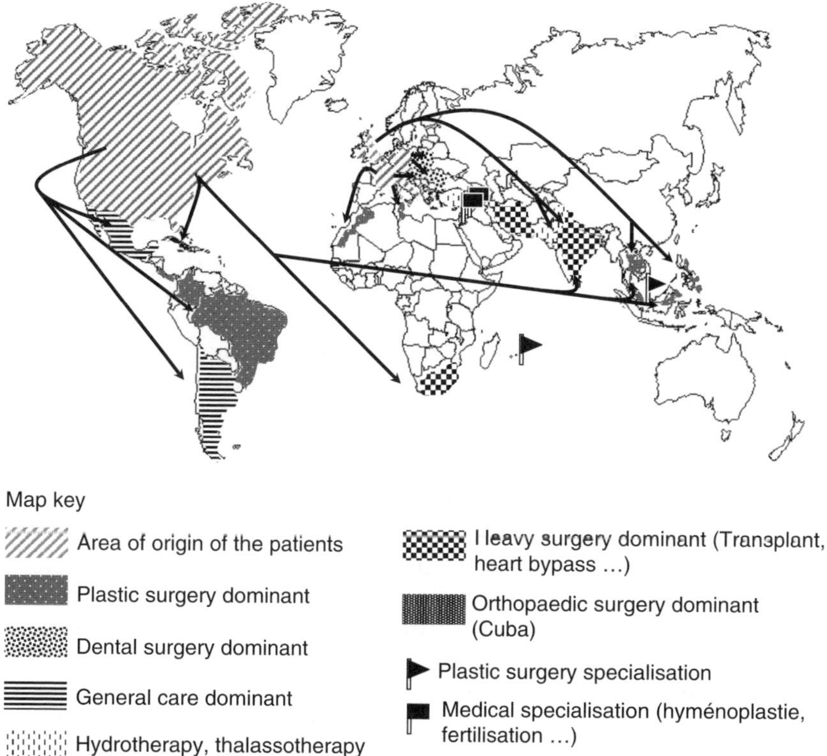

Map 8.1   Globalisation of the healthcare market
Source: Adapted from Courrier International (2008) and Connell (2005).

economies have been the recipients of diverse medical care from the wealthier countries. Also, the relationships between Europeans are not always mentioned. For example, Spanish abortions do not constitute medical tourism (there are no specific commercial offers that include the medical intervention and hotel infrastructure). The flow of British patients coming to France or Belgium for surgical procedures is not shown in the map because commercial offers do not generally integrate the idea of medical tourism.

Our analysis centres on the paradoxical idea of going to developing countries for surgical procedures, thus indicating the opposite of the usual business operations between North and South. Indeed, it is more surprising that people will go to countries for hospitalisation where the level of medical care is not the most successful and where the mortality rate of the young local population is high (Clift and Page, 1996). The illustration that follows proposes first and foremost the cases of North Americans, Britons and French, which illustrate the important paradox of the relationship of medical tourism, in particular, with regard to postcolonial relations. We will also illustrate, with the help of other examples, additional peculiarities of medical tourism motivated by religious questions.

North Americans regularly turn to the countries of South America (mainly for cosmetic and dental surgery or for medical checkups and evaluations). This area, with Brazil in the lead, represents in the minds of the general public a major destination for plastic surgery at a lower cost. On the other hand, few people tend to go there for medical checkups or to follow a particular treatment (even though it is less expensive than in the United States or Canada). Surprisingly, Cuba is a destination which is highly sought after by tourist-patients requiring orthopaedic or ophthalmological care. It is surprising that this destination is so popular since the country is marked by precariousness and poverty, and lacks medical means for the local population. This situation of building state-of-the-art medical facilities for tourists in Cuba partially underlines the gap engendered by the globalisation of healthcare.

A much less enjoyable perspective presents itself where the resident-patients of developing countries receive precarious medical care, while a few metres away, private hospitals (using the latest MRI, dialysis and retinal surgery technologies) improve the living conditions of the Western tourist-patients who come for treatment.

The imbalance of treatment that certain Westerners undergo in their own country, due to a two-tier medical system, migrates to developing countries when they buy medical tourism packages, hence reproducing the system that they tried to avoid at home. However, certain observers will notice that medical tourism allows young local clinicians to work with state-of-the-art tools, an experience that they would not have been able to obtain otherwise. As for the possibility of having the local population benefit from the latest medical technologies, nothing is certain for the time being.

There are three key areas of medical tourism for Westerners.

i. *Eastern Europe*. The opening up of Eastern European countries in free market economies is completely in line with the massive development of medical tourism. We can see a multitude of private hospitals and dental clinics flourishing in Hungary and Bulgaria, which offer very competitive services for those who cannot pay for the care that they need in their home country (Le Borgne, 2007).

ii. *Maghreb*. Maghreb represents a particularly interesting region for cosmetic surgery. The level of training of the staff, their language skills, the quality of the hotel infrastructures and so on lure numerous people (in particular the French) to seek treatment in Tunisia or Morocco. Compared with other destinations, these two countries display the most commercial ingenuity in seducing hesitant consumers.

iii. *Asia.* According to Connell (2005), and following a study by McKinsey, associated with the Confederation of Indian Industry (2006), this continent (India in particular) is emerging as a leader in the medical tourism market. The twenty-first century will be considered as a medical century (In fact, medical care demand will increase) and mass medical tourism will be concentrated in Asia. With regard to the increasing failures of health systems in the United States and in Britain, and with their strong connections with Asia, we suggest that the economic potential of this sector will be quickly confirmed in this area.

It is possible, therefore, to go on a scalpel safari in South Africa or dance a surgeon's-knife samba in Brazil. Even if these terms bring a smile, they are only a reflection of downplaying this type of tourism. They underline, however, a disturbing aspect of the everyday acceptance of surgery. Plainly, such misuses of language make a consumer who is worried about his image take risks with his physical integrity that he would otherwise probably not take in his own country. These risks are in total opposition to a positive self-image: a paradox in itself.

Is this phenomenon partially due to the commercial policies used in the area? A great number of patients tend to forget that the sun in southern countries, which is promoted in travel brochures, is only a simple incentive, a marketing argument of which they cannot take advantage in reality. How many people, avidly searching for cheap surgery in Maghreb, forget that they will not be able to take advantage of the sunshine or the magnificent swimming pool in the hotel for at least three or four weeks, before their return to their place of residence? This situation highlights the naivety of certain tourist-patients who do not consider the limitations and constraints of medical procedures, no matter which country. They forget that even cosmetic surgery is often a heavy and risky procedure which can result in complications, trauma and even death.

3.2 Postcolonial relations and the failure of a system

Two elements need to be clarified here. The first one concerns the relationship that exists between the former major powers and their ex-colonies. The second brings to light the failure associated with this type of tourism.

The planisphere of the globalisation of the healthcare market (Map 8.1) creates strong links between the former dominant powers and the territories which gained their independence during the twentieth century. It is interesting to note that these North–South relationships are important paradoxes in themselves. Being called into question is the 'old centre-suburb colonial axis' (Racine, 2006). This is shown through the slow integration of the 'heart of the former dominant powers' system', the numerous intellectuals of developing countries.[7] This situation most likely results from relationships stemming from postcolonialism, which is based on the idea of a sharing of common cultures, a sense of belonging and joint intellectual enrichments (between the West and the East, or between the North and the South) (Saïd, 2005). The medical sector is an important example. Often denigrated and relegated to the background, the medicine practised in developing countries (now, the medicine is emerging from developing countries) was often denigrated and relegated to the background. However, practitioners of such medicine knew how to take advantage of the knowledge of the colonising empires. For example, Moroccan, Tunisian and Indian fields of medicine have nothing to be ashamed of with regard to their older European counterparts. It must be admitted that a high proportion of the practitioners who operate on tourist-patients were trained in the United States, Britain or France, sometimes in the best schools of medicine.

Besides North–South relations, the ambiguity of the situation lies in the fact that the tourist-patient agrees to put their life and health in the hands of surgeons of whose skills or even working conditions they are not necessarily aware; even more surprisingly, they trust an unknown individual. This is the reality of medical tourism: to be looked after by doctors situated several thousands of kilometres away, without really knowing them, and meeting them for the first time a few hours before the procedure. This situation is occurring on a regular basis. Patients' behaviour may be considered extreme when it concerns incentive variables (such as the price or waiting period). For Page (2009), tourist-patients follow a paradoxical logic, leaving a protected environment to expose themselves to unusual problems in sometimes difficult conditions. A simple virus or ailment could prove fatal (Behrens, 1997; Clift and Grabowski, 1997), and the setting up of large medical tourism zones encounters sanitary problems (epidemics, tropical diseases) as well as security issues (kidnapping, conflicts). Surgical practices and sanitary conditions are not the issues being discussed here, contrary to what certain critics may believe. Certain individuals who, in their usual secure environment play it safe, admittedly adopt atypical behaviour in relation to medical tourism. How can a patient, in this case, be made aware of the risks connected with the medical intervention and of the context of the country in which they are treated? The answer to this question cannot be other than a paradox.

3.3 Medical tourism or the art of combining health and religion

In order to determine the dynamics of medical tourism it is necessary to take into account community and denominational dimensions. These dimensions incite certain patients to seek care in specific countries. As will be discussed, respect for religious rules definitely has a paradoxical effect on the development of medical tourism, which has as a mission the conciliation between the evolution of societies and the preservation of practices. For example, within the healthcare globalisation framework, certain young American Jewish couples (New Yorkers, for the greater part) avid to have children, travel to Israel to undergo artificial insemination (i.e. the Tel Aviv Sourasky Medical Center). This intervention is authorised by Halakha only in certain conditions, that is, only if the sperm intended for reproduction comes from future mother's husband.

However, Israel abounds in infertility, in vitro fertilisation and high-risk pregnancy specialists and experts. It is a destination of preference for these sterile men and women who wish to have children. This type of medical tourism (fertilisation) allows part of the Jewish diaspora to address, on the one hand, a real physical problem and, on the other, to comply with their spirituality. Although it is Jewish clientèle who are targeted, these health centres remain open to all.

Lebanon, which is completely under the influence of the pressures and incitements of religious rules, sometimes far removed from modern reality (Usta, 2000), benefits from the search for virgins in the Arabic world. During the last few years, Beirut has become the capital of hymenoplasty, the reconstruction of the hymen. In Lebanon, women are given a second virginity, far away from the critical glances that this subject can engender. Others prefer to go to Europe, particularly to the very popular and upmarket Regency Clinic in London (Appleyard, 2007), but the phenomenon remains, however, of more significance in Lebanon. It is important to note that, at the time of writing, the Lebanon First National Bank is developing credit options for those wishing to have access to plastic or dental surgery: plastic surgery loan (Shields, 2007).

We can determine that medical tourism is a rich and complex phenomenon that is essentially based on political, economic, historical and religious elements.

4 Conclusion

In this chapter, the main paradoxes connected to the globalisation of the healthcare market have been explored. Medical tourism raises ethical questions. The fact that patients choose according to how much they can pay goes against all medical ethics, as is the fact that reviewing a patient's file the day before the operation is unthinkable for some specialists. The development of high-speed medical care, the failure of hospital infrastructures, as well as religious obstacles, are inciting tourist-patients to cross oceans to obtain surgical procedures in India, South Africa or Cuba. The planet is becoming a health supermarket.

Medical tourism is also characterised by other paradoxes. At the host country level, hospitals propose sophisticated interventions to foreigners, while the local population sometimes suffers from serious illnesses, which can often be treated at little cost. At the patient level, there is a level of risk that is surprising when considering the attitude that the patient would adopt in their country of origin.

Medical tourism is a new industry which generates several billions of euros a year. The development of medical tourism invites the identification of current breaches in the system, especially at the level of postoperative risk management. In years to come, French practitioners fear that patients who have fallen victim to medical errors in emerging countries will be consulting them.

This sector is not presently controlled on an international scale. This is a problem that needs to be addressed internationally.

Notes

1. The loss of cultural norms and the modification of the lifestyles of local populations have resulted in a 'Disneyisation' of developing tourist areas. Admittedly, the arrival of tourists allows a new dynamism of the economy but the cost, in certain cases, is the destruction of the environment. Tourist activity has been condensed to enable the consumer to exist in 'an air-conditioned, sterilised and safe bubble in which what he sees, hears or breathes is carefully manipulated' (Cazes and Courade, 2004, p.250).
2. The integration of Hong Kong, returned to China in 1997 by the United Kingdom, supports to some extent this economic development, mainly in the sector of finance.
3. Statement of the preparatory meeting of the Committee for the Revival of Tourism, which was held in Sharm el Sheikh, 23–24 November 2008.
4. The A380 Airbus can carry between 555 and 840 passengers compared with its rival, the Boeing 747, which can carry only 450 passengers.
5. Some authors prefer to use the term 'tourism of economic discovery' regarding this, in order to integrate other concepts such as scientific and technical tourism; see Laliberté (2005).
6. See, for example, Boyer (2002).
7. These former colonies have been underestimated for a long time, and have also been considered by some as unable to compete worldwide.

References

Appleyard, D. (2007) 'The born again virgins'. *Daily Mail*, 17 December: 3.
Azarya, V. (2004) 'Globalization and international tourism in developing countries: marginality as a commercial commodity'. *Current Sociology*, 52 (6), pp. 949–67.
Bauer, R.A. (1960) 'Consumer behaviour as risk taking' in R.S. Hancock (ed.) *Dynamic Marketing for a Changing World*, Proceedings of the 43rd Conference of the American Marketing Association: 389–98.
Bendapudi, N. and Leone, R.P. (2003) 'Psychological implications of customer participation in co-production'. *Journal of Marketing*, 67 (1): 14–28.
Behrens, R. (1997) 'Important issues influencing the health of travellers' in S. Clift and P. Grabowski (eds) *Tourism and Health: Risks, Research and Responses*. London: Pinter.
Bianchi, R. (2006) 'Tourism and the globalisation of fear: analysis the politics of risk and (in)security in global travel'. *Tourism and Hospitality Research*, 7 (1): 64–74.
Boyer, M. (1996) *L'Invention du Tourisme*. Paris: Gallimard.
Boyer, A. (2002) *L'Impossible Ethique des Entreprises*. Paris: Editions d'Organisation.

Caire, G. (2004) 'Une évaluation critique de la politique de développement durable du groupe Accor' in C. Offredi (ed.) *La Dynamique de l'Évaluation Face au Développement Durable*. Paris: L'Harmattan.

Cazelais, N. (1991) 'Le tourisme industriel, une avenue pour réconcilier l'industrie et l'environnement'. *Téoros*, 10 (1): 35–8.

Cerina, F. (2007) 'Tourism specialization and environmental sustainability in a dynamic economy'. *Tourism Economics*, 13 (4): 553–82.

Clift, S. and Grabowski, P. (1997) *Tourism and Health: Risks, Research and Responses*. London: Pinter.

Clift, S. and Page, S.J. (1996) *Health and the International Tourist*. London: Routledge.

Cohen, E. (2004) *Contemporary Tourism: Diversity and Change*. Oxford: Elservier.

Connell, J. (2005) 'Medical tourism: sea, sun sand and…surgery'. *Tourism Management*, 27: 1093–100.

Conrady, R. and Buck, M. (2007) *Trends and Issues in Global Tourism 2008*. Berlin: Springer.

Courrier International (2008) *Pourquoi nous voulons un corps parfait*. January (900): 41.

Dworkin, R. (1981) 'What is inequality ? Part II: equality of resources'. *Philosophy and Public Affairs*, 10: 283–345.

Eiglier, P. and Langeard, E. (1987) *La Servuction*. Montreal: McGraw Hill.

Flipo, J.P. (1984) *Le Management des Entreprises de Services*. Paris: Les Editions d'Organisation.

———— (1988) 'On the intangibility of services'. *The Service Industries Journal*, 8 (3): 286–98.

Flipo, J.P. and Revat, R. (2003) 'Ethique et marketing'. *Cahiers de Recherche EM Lyon*, 11 (June).

Friedman, M. (1971) *Capitalisme et Liberté*. Paris: Laffont.

Garcia-Altes, M. (2005) 'The development of health tourism services'. *Annals of Tourism Research*, 32 (1): 262–6.

Gartner, W.C. and Lime, D.W. (2000) *Trends in Outdoor Recreation, Leisure and Tourism*. New York: Cabi Publishing.

Gilbert, E. (1954) *Brighton: Old Ocean's Bauble*. London: Methuen.

Goodrich, J.N. and Goodrich, G.E. (1987) 'Health-care tourism – an exploratory study'. *Tourism Management*, 8 (3): 217–22.

Graham, K. (2005) 'It was a big leap of faith'. *Guardian*, June 21: 8–9.

Grant, D., Mason, S., Khan, M. and Davis, R. (2005) 'Current issues in travel and tourism law' in J. Wilks, D. Pendergast and P. Leggatt (eds) *Tourism in Turbulent Times*. Oxford: Elsevier.

Grell, G.A.C. (1994) 'Ecotourism and health tourism in the Caribbean'. *Bulletin of Eastern Caribbean Affairs*, 19 (1): 39–45.

Hayek, F.A. (1944) *La Route de la Servitude* (1985 edn). Paris: Presse Universitaires de France.

Horowitz, M.D., Rosensweig, J.A. and Jones, C.A. (2007) 'Medical tourism: globalisation of the healthcare marketplace'. *MedGenMed*, 9 (4): 33–41.

Hut, A. (1996) 'Le tourisme industriel : à quelles conditions?' *Revue Théoros*, 15 (2): 19–22.

Keynes, J.M. (1936) *The General Theory of Employment, Interest and Money: The Collected Writings of John Maynard Keynes, Volume VII*. London: Macmillan.

Keynes, J.M. (2002) *La Pauvreté dans l'Abondance*. Paris: Gallimard.

Lansing, P. and De Vries, P. (2006) 'Sustainable tourism: ethical alternative or marketing ploy'. *Journal of Business Ethics*, 72 (1): 77–85.

Laroche, M., Bergeron, J. and Goutaland, C. (2003) 'How intangibility affects perceived risk: the moderating role of knowledge and involvement'. *Journal of Services Marketing*, 17 (2): 122–40.

Le Borgne, C. (2007) 'Le tourisme médical : une nouvelle façon de se soigner'. *Sève – Presses de Sciences Po*, 2 (15).

Lozato-Giotart, J.P. and Balfet, M. (2007) *Management du Tourisme* (2nd edn). Paris: Pearson Education.

McKinsey, associated with Confederation of Indian Industry (2006). http://www.thehindubusinessline.com/2006/03/07/stories/2006030702271900.htm (Accessed 2 February 2010).

Menvielle, L. (2009) 'Les paradoxes du tourisme medical et de la globalisation' in E. Milliot and N. Tournois (eds) *Les Paradoxes de la Globalisation des Marches*. Paris: Vuibert.

Menvielle, L. and Menvielle, W. (2007) 'Medical tourism: a new way of travelling', 3rd International Congress on Tourism, Athens Institute for Education and Research, July 5–6, Athens, Greece.

Mueller, H. and Lanz Kaufmann, E. (2001) 'Wellness tourism: market analysis of a special health tourism segment and implications for the hotel industry'. *Journal of Vacation Marketing*, 7 (1): 5–17.

Mowforth, M. and Munt, I. (2003) *Tourism and Sustainability: Development and New Tourism in the Third World* (2nd edn). New York: Routledge.

N'Goala, G. (1997) 'Vers une théorie générale en marketing relationnel'. *Cahier de Recherche*, GRECO, IAE Montpellier II: 34.

Nozick, R. (1974) *Anarchie, Etat et Utopie*. Paris: Presse Universitaires de France.

Page, S.J. (2009) 'Current issue in tourism: the evolution of travel medicine research: a new research agenda for tourism?' *Tourism Management*, 30 (2): 149–57.

Proulx, L. (2005) 'Tourisme, santé et bien-être'. *Revue Téoros*, 24 (3): 5–11.

Racine, J.L. (2006) 'L'Inde émergente, ou la sortie des temps postcoloniaux'. *Hérodote*, 1st trimester (120): 28–47.

Rawls, J. (1971) *Theory of Justice*. Cambridge, MA: Harvard University Press.

—— (1993) *Political Liberalism: The John Dewey Essays in Philosophy, Vol. 4*. New York: Columbia University Press.

Reddy, A.C. and Vyas, N. (2004) 'The globalisation paradox: a marketing perspective'. *International Journal of Management*, 21 (2): 166–81.

Saïd, E.W. (2005) *L'Orientalisme: L'Orient crée par l'Occident*. Paris: Seuil.

Shields, R. (2007) 'Banks court Beirut beauties with cosmetic surgery loans'. *Independent on Sunday*, 22 April.

Smith, M. and Kelly, C. (2006) 'Wellness tourism'. *Tourism Recreation Research*, 31 (1): 1–4.

Spindler, J. and Durand, H. (2003) *Le Tourisme au XXIe Siècle*. Paris: L'Harmattan.

Usta, I. (2000) 'Hymenorrhaphy: what happens behind the gynaecologist's closed door?' *Journal of Medical Ethics*, 26: 2217–18.

Walker, T. (2006) 'Consumers go abroad in pursuit of cost-effective healthcare'. *Managed Healthcare Executive*, 16 (7): 10.

World Tourism Organisation (2005) *World Tourism Barometer*, 3 (2).

—— (2008a) *World Tourism Barometer*, 6 (1).

—— (2008b) 'Réponse aux turbulences de l'économie et au changement climatique'. Conclusions de la réunion du comité de relance du tourisme, Sharm El Shiekh, Egypte. http://www.unwto.org/media/news/fr/pdf/Sharm.pdf (Accessed 12 January 2009).

Wheeler, M. (1995) 'Tourism marketing ethics: an introduction'. *International Marketing Review* 12 (4): 38–49.

Zeithaml, V.A., Parasuraman, A. and Berry, L.L. (1985) 'Problems and strategies in service marketing'. *Journal of Marketing*, 49: 33–46.

Further reading

Cazes, G. and Courade, G. (2004) 'Les masques du tourisme'. *Revue Tiers Monde*, xlv (178), April–June.

Laliberté, M. (2005) 'Le tourisme industriel, un volet du tourisme d'apprentissage'. http://veilletourisme.ca/2005/03/07/le-tourisme-industriel-un-volet-du-tourisme-pprentissage/ (Accessed 24 July 2008).

Sen, A.K. (1987) *Ethique et Economie, et Autres Essays*. Paris: Presse Universitaires de France.

9
The Impact of Sustainability on Global Logistics Strategies: Contradictory Issues

Corinne Blanquart and Valentina Carbone

Sustainable development permeates every area of a corporation. Although the notion of sustainability is now widespread and focuses energies on environmental issues, it is weakened by numerous paradoxes.

Some of these paradoxes are inherent in the notion of sustainability in general, regardless of which activities it is applied to. However, others are specific to the implementation of sustainability in well-defined areas. It is the same for logistics,[1] whose particular characteristics in the context of the globalisation of markets raise specific logical contradictions.

The following sections deal with these various paradoxes in order: those that are specific to the principles of sustainable development, those linked to the way sustainability is handled in global logistics practices, and finally those raised by the increasing complexity of the relations between actors in global chains. Our thinking revolves around one major question: is it possible to make minor modifications to global logistic strategies in the name of sustainability without fundamentally calling into question the current models of production and consumption? Lacking an immediate answer to this question, we propose to evaluate sustainability in the logistics field in a relative way, presenting the various possible solutions with regard to specific contexts.

1 Sustainable development and its internal paradoxes

Studies of the relation between the fields of economics and the environment are not new. In the fourth century BC, Plato was already exploring the relationship between man and nature.

Notwithstanding the age of the question, the Brundtland Report (World Commission on Environment and Development [WCED], 1987) is now the inevitable reference when one begins to take an interest in sustainable development. A victim of its own success, this reference has elicited numerous attempts to provide a definition of sustainable development – around sixty since 1989 (Allemand, 1999). Indeed, the Brundtland Report merely offers a framework within which the content can vary. It defines sustainable development as that which 'meets the needs of the present without compromising the ability of future generations to meet their own needs' (WCED, 1987). Of course this generality makes it possible for any actors to appropriate the content, but one can also reproach its imprecision and its general nature. Hence, some scholars argue that the vagueness of the concept of sustainable development attracts the risk of manipulation by corporations, given the opposition between economic, social and ecological approaches (Mounoud, 2000).

Without broaching the subject of manipulation, we can nevertheless observe that sustainability carries a value judgement; it has thus become the archetype of excellence for corporations, just as quality was in the 1980s (Larson et al., 2000). Still, the strategies that are implemented and defended in the name of sustainability do raise a certain number of paradoxes that are worth examining.

1.1   Sustainability and its implicit frames of reference

It is astonishing to observe that the assessment of sustainability can differ considerably depending on the points of view adopted.

- A single strategy might be sustainable for one company and yet impose on its partners choices that are not (the majority of discarded electric and electronic equipment collected in the US by large corporations is now disassembled and recycled in China, India and Pakistan by small and medium-sized companies in unhealthy and unregulated conditions).
- A strategy might be beneficial in the short term from a sustainable development point of view and yet generate harmful irreversible effects for the future (the choice between different energy sources, which differ in terms of pollution and renewability).
- A strategy might have a positive impact on the environment, but a negative social impact (relocation of factories which brings about a reduction in environmental pollution but causes a loss of jobs in the country of origin).

These illustrations show that evaluating sustainability involves making a judgement. This judgement functions in relation to certain frames of reference, but the frames of reference of sustainability are sometimes hard to reconcile. The incompatibility relates to the time scales chosen (short or long term), the dimension that is given priority (economic, environmental or social) and, finally, the level at which the judgement is made (a single actor, an entire sector). Thus, the characterisation of sustainability carries an implicit hierarchy of favoured dimensions, time frames and scales.

Depending on the angles adopted, the judgement can be fundamentally different.

In short, although seductive by virtue of its universality, sustainable development remains a victim of this quality: it is ambiguous because it allows free reign to numerous interpretations and appropriations (Harribey, 1998). Does sustainability mean, at best, the same quality of life and the same well-being? Does sustainability aim to reduce the pressure on the entire pool of resources we have at our disposal? Do we seek a reduction in negative externalities, an end to these effectsor an improvement in the state of our resources? In other words, how can we identify the most important objectives, determine the frames of reference for each objective, and define and measure the initial state that has to be improved?

In spite of this, in the particular area of logistics and transport there do seem to be absolute or optimal forms of sustainability that are tacitly recognised. Sustainable logistics and transport are often seen in terms of optimising route planning or flow consolidation, which allows the use of cleaner means of transport. Public policy options are structured around these good practices. For global flows, for example, intercontinental maritime shipping has been cited as one of the best strategies of sustainable mobility (World Business Council for Sustainable Development [WBCSD], 2007).

The challenge of sustainable mobility is to reconcile the growing transport requirements of people and goods with the necessity of reducing the impact of traffic on the natural and human environment. On the one hand, the movement of goods to ever more global markets is an essential element of competition. On the other, the growth of transport has its limits: beyond a certain level of traffic, even the best performing infrastructures get clogged. However, above all, the impacts on the environment and on health (increased greenhouse effect, harmful emissions, noise pollution, encroachment on public space and natural environments, etc.) demand that we rethink this endless growth.

1.2   The principles of sustainability are widely accepted but action is limited

The generalisation of the notion of sustainability may result in two opposing movements: appropriation by the entire range of actors (as we have already pointed out) and, at times, a superficial use of the associated principles (Alcouffe et al., 2002).

Initially concerned about their social acceptability *vis-à-vis* citizen pressure, companies have gradually seized the potential opportunities of a sustainable orientation for their strategy, without, however, wanting to or succeeding in exploiting it entirely.

This observation illustrates the fact that sustainable development is often nothing more than a device for corporate communication. Companies in several different industries structure their communication around this theme. In the retail sector, for example, Carrefour claimed in 2004 that *'mieux consommer, c'est urgent'* ('it's urgent to consume better'). As for Monoprix, they declared that they act 'for tomorrow, every day'. In terms of logistics, these brands publicise the use of non-road transport even though inland waterway and rail transport still represent a very small share of the total goods flow in retailing. In the auto industry, Daimler launched an advertising campaign in 2006 about Start-Stop automatic technology which helps to reduce fuel consumption, thus promoting a green image of the brand. At the same time, Toyota launched a pan-European communication campaign about its own technologies, which, thanks to the success of the Prius, made them the leader in the area of environmentally friendly automobile strategies.

With respect to this observation, we have the following three observations to make:

i. *The vagueness surrounding the notion of sustainable development makes it problematic to put into practice.* Despite a growing acceptance of the principles and culture of sustainable development, companies are often incapable of making it operational. A study on the handling of environmental constraints in global logistics strategies was carried out using a sample of 600 European, Japanese and American companies (Carbone and Moatti, 2008). Despite an elevated sensitivity to environmental questions (83 per cent of the companies take these questions into account during their strategic decision-making), only 35 per cent of the interviewees stated that they had implemented green global logistics strategies (aimed at limiting environmental impact all along the chain of actors from the raw materials producer to the end consumer). The two main obstacles (54 per cent of responses) were the complexity of the undertaking and the lack of information on available tools and possible actions to take. Geographically, the level of involvement is heterogeneous. The differences are particularly pronounced between Japan and the other countries. Indeed, the Japanese companies in the sample boast total involvement in a green logistics strategy approach, whereas the figure for Europe is only 38 per cent, with a large gap between the UK (45 per cent) and France (30 per cent). For the US, it is only 24 per cent. The variables accounting for such differences in company involvement relate to the regulatory contexts, to how long the approach has been in use and to the level of institutionalisation of the logistics and environment function.

ii. *There is difficulty in reconciling the numerous areas in which sustainable development is to be implemented, when no budget has been explicitly assigned to it.* In the best-case scenario, a single 'environment/safety' budget will have been allocated. It is used for a heterogeneous set of investments: installation of sites, bringing facilities up to standard, safety training, etc. Investments related to improving modes of transport from an environmental point of view (purchasing clean vehicles, equipment with embedded IT systems) also draw on the same budget. The efforts to achieve better environmental performance are often carried out within the framework of the budget allocated to the supply chain logistics department. Thus, right from the start, the ecological criteria are subordinated to the profitability criteria of the action in question. The short-term profitability of sustainable logistic strategies is now becoming the primary condition for launching these strategies.

iii. *Auditing capacities are very limited.* Only certain companies are obliged to disclose information about their environmental and social impact: all the listed companies whose shares are traded on a regulated market. However, although verifying the truth and accuracy of financial information is obligatory, this rule does not extend to social information. Several large corporations have freely chosen to have all or part of this information independently verified, but the lack of recognised frameworks of standards and the question of the auditors' competency in this area, still present obstacles to the harmonisation of procedures.

The proliferation of certifications and rating agencies and the lack of (or difficulty implementing) suitable audit systems undermine the credibility of non-financial evaluations.

Sustainable development should, in theory, simultaneously create value for the company, civil society and the natural environment. Logistics is chiefly oriented towards value creation at the company level but also the chain as a whole. That is why – and even more so at the international level – the specificities of global logistics activities engender a certain number of paradoxes as soon as they are confronted with the issues of sustainable development. Given these conditions, is sustainable logistics really feasible?

2   Sustainable development: paradoxes specific to logistics

Logistics is a vector of performance for the company, and logistic strategies have developed to take into account the structural changes of economies. In the global economic context, transport, logistics and the organisation of the supply chain have also become global and have taken on an increasingly strategic position. The stretching of channels in order to produce at low cost stems, in part, from increasingly distant purchasing, outsourcing, relocations and the globalisation of markets. It is also the result of improvements in transport, with the invention of containerisation and advances made in infrastructure and equipment. These trends raise numerous paradoxes when one analyses common logistics strategies from the perspective of sustainability.

2.1   The globalisation of flows and the concentration of production and warehousing sites

'Borderless consumption has accelerated since the end of the Second World War' (Fremont, 2007). In this context, logistics takes on a strategic function and supports the development of international trade. Figure 9.1 illustrates the magnitude of international flows in world trade.

The territorial implementation of logistics choices must also take into account the concentration of production sites. Indeed, production plants are undergoing two complementary movements: relocations in order to benefit from the low cost of labour in certain geographic areas, and the specialisation of factories to gain from the effect and, especially, economies of scale.

The role of storage has been profoundly altered by the impact of these two concomitant developments. There has been a massive centralisation of warehousing zones and a growing use of facilities for quickly routing goods coming from production sites to their end markets (cross-docking hubs). The growing size of production facilities has thus been accompanied by an increase in the size of warehousing facilities.

At the same time, there are many products and services for which purchasing accounts for more than two thirds of the cost price (automobiles, mobile phones, etc.). This economic weight, coupled with the ever-widening search for procurement markets, has conferred a notable strategic dimension on the procurement function and, in particular, the selection of suppliers.

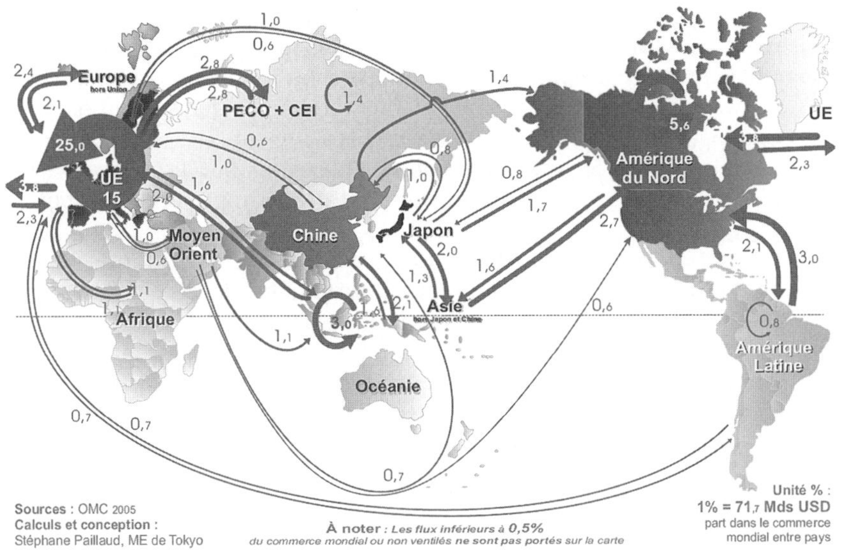

Figure 9.1   International flows in world trade

In this context, the organisation of logistics and transport is complex and depends heavily on industrial developments. Strategies and logistics networks are being reconfigured to adapt to the requirements of globalisation and their associated cost reduction pressure. Mounting concerns about sustainable development make logistic organisations even more complex. These concerns call for the reconciliation of environmental performance, social equity and economic efficiency. But is such reconciliation possible? Above all, is it achievable other than by piecemeal modifications to logistics organisations that are subordinated to industrial developments, which are in turn dictated by economic efficiency and cost reduction? This question is even more critical as the logistics strategies observed support modes of operation that contribute to upsetting equilibria – particularly environmental – throughout the world. In particular, they lead to a concentration of flows that is not without consequence.

2.2 The flipside of flow consolidation: traffic and congestion

The industrial organisation of the global economy is a very heavy user of transport, generating a very high volume of flows: between specialised factories, between those factories and consolidation hubs, and finally between those hubs and end distribution points. Because the logistic organisation adapts to the needs of the industrial organisation, it can only have a palliative approach to sustainable development. Faced with the increase in traffic (which itself generates negative externalities for the environment) and in search of sustainability, the logistic organisation turns to flow consolidation, the optimisation of load factors and co-modality.

At the same time, logistics organisations are supported by a network of hierarchically ordered national warehouses (central, regional, local), which is giving way to a concentration of very big warehouses that serve more than one country (Dornier and Fender, 2001). This acute concentration of storage facilities raises issues for town and country planning, but also increases the distances for supplying production sites and delivering to end distribution points.

One could, nevertheless, defend the idea that the concentration of production and warehousing is favourable to sustainable development because it allows for flow consolidation and, concomitantly, the use of alternative modes of transport. There again, the paradox lies in the fact that the number of journeys, mainly by road (the mode which pollutes the most), has increased around these poles: more traffic and more congestion around airports, seaports, factories and warehouses.

2.3 Production driven by demand: over-consumption of road transport

An economy of manufactured goods has developed since the 1970s based on demand-driven production, the reduction of inventories and Just in

Time (JIT). This has led to the increasingly frequent transport of smaller and smaller shipments: in the manufactured goods sector half of shipments weigh less than 30 kg. Traffic is dispersed. We are far from the tonnage of heavy goods for which rail would be most suitable. Fast and flexible, the truck is well suited to the transport of these products, especially given the vast network of motorways available. The trucking industry has modernised incessantly: improved productivity and high-performance organisations have been set up by big freight brokers. Today's trucks are cleaner than those of yesterday. Their involvement in accidents – currently only 3 per cent – is on the decrease. Finally and importantly, fierce competition ensures very low transport costs.

These points give perspective to the stigmatisation of road transport, which, for JIT logistics, is still the best-performing mode of transport. In recent years, its externalities have been reduced in terms of accidents while the vehicle stock has been upgraded with models that pollute less. Although putting the negative effects of road transport into perspective may seem to go against the grain, we mustn't forget that JIT logistics – a heavy consumer of road transport – is determined by JIT industry (Fassio, 2006).

Barring a complete overhaul of production and consumption modes, which depend on increasingly frequent and ever smaller shipments, sustainability will essentially focus on improving road transport productivity. On the one hand, this means creating conditions that are favourable to the development of intermodal transport by strengthening final-destination road journeys – the weak link in global rail/sea and inland waterway chains. On the other hand, the modernisation of roads, the development of eco-driving systems and related technological innovations will also help to reduce the environmental impact of vehicles.

Yet political leaders and civil society are in agreement today on the demonising of road freight. They see too many trucks on the road, safety hazards, various kinds of pollution and congestion, not to mention the fact that road transport is a very heavy consumer of energy. But how can one hope to reconcile JIT production systems with modal shift when one knows the competitive limits of the alternative modes of transport for small shipments and dispersed traffic?

Paradoxically, in order to reduce the environmental damage caused by transport, it is necessary to improve the operating conditions of road freight.

2.4   Other forms of logistic sustainability in a global context

Contrary to what some may think, encouraging sustainable logistics does not necessarily mean polluting less. The further logistic chains are stretched, branched out and diversified to include all types of flows and every continent, the more complicated it is to manage them in terms of security and safety. Security refers to measures taken to protect against malicious acts, delinquency and terrorism. Safety relates to technical malfunctions without a deliberate human cause.

The social pillar of any development intended to be sustainable requires that parameters besides respect for the environment be taken into account: consumers' health, the working conditions of employees, and the safety and security of flows.

Concerning the latter point, international flows of goods need to be protected. Theft and accidents (for example, the sinking of the *Erika*) jeopardise these flows. The vulnerability of physical infrastructures and distribution networks is another risk factor that must be managed. Dealing with this type of risk entails an increase in insurance spending and investments in product tracking systems. Companies present these developments in logistics as pro-sustainability initiatives.

With the modal shift from road transport to 'softer' modes, the forms that sustainability has taken in logistics may seem less ambitious than the reduction of greenhouse gas emissions. Yet are we really in a position to contest them? Under the surface we find the criticisms levelled by 'de-growth' proponents. Should sustainability challenge the current model of development? And, *a fortiori*, can sustainable logistics challenge the industrial organisation?

2.5 Towards an exacerbation of disparities: less pollution here, more pollution elsewhere?

There are significant disparities between various regions of the world in terms of climate, contamination and pollution. As far as climate is concerned, the main events will be played out in emerging economies (China, India, Russia and Brazil). The reason these countries are so critical is due to their economic development model and regulatory frameworks, which are less stringent than those of Western countries regarding environmental rules and social conditions. The relocation of numerous Western companies only exacerbates the difficulty these countries have in moving towards a sustainable production model. The result is an assault on the ecological balance in those regions, which casts a shadow on the progress made reducing carbon dioxide (CO_2) emissions in the countries where the factories came from. What will the net result of these phenomena be? At the time of the Nobel Peace Prize award in 2007, Al Gore paraphrased Martin Luther King in a press conference, arguing that increased CO_2 emissions anywhere are a threat to the future of civilisation everywhere.

3 Logistics and the interdependence of actors

The sustainable logistics approach is paradoxically limited. Very often we consider the result only in terms of transport. Hence, a logistic organisation is considered sustainable if the flows are. Can we speak of sustainable logistics without sustainable coordination between actors? Since the numerous studies in supply chain management (SCM) agree that logistic performance now rests as much on the optimisation of flows as on the improvement of relations between actors in the chain (Cox et al., 2002; Lamming, 1993), the same reasoning ought to be extended to the sustainable performance of logistic organisations.

These logistic organisations must adapt to the fragmentation of the value chain. Following Krugman (1991), the international fragmentation of the value chain is considered one of four most important characteristics of modern world trade (Defever and Mucchielli, 2005).

The case of manufacturing an electric toothbrush (Figure 9.2) illustrates this phenomenon (cf. article in *The Spiegel*, 'Globalization: the global toothbrush' by Ralf Hoppe, 31 January 2006). The end product, worth €130, is made up of thirty-eight components that have travelled an accumulated distance of 27,880 km. Japan and Taiwan supply the batteries, Malaysia the electronic components, China handles the assembly of the electronics and the Philippines provide the testing centre. This sub-assembly is shipped by plane to the United States.

The body as well as the steel and plastic components manufactured in Austria, Sweden and France are carried by road to Bremerhaven (Germany). They are then expedited by sea from Bremerhaven to Port Elisabeth (USA) and then by train from the east coast to the west coast (Washington state). Once the final assembly is done, the product and its packaging are shipped to the global markets for which they are intended. A global transport system is obviously indispensable for this geographically scattered production puzzle.

Within these very fragmented value chains, each company must carve out its own competitive advantage. For a firm, creating value depends not only on its own strategic choices but also on the choices of its partners, and it must know how they operate in order for them to coordinate as best they can. Increasingly complex production systems, the growing use

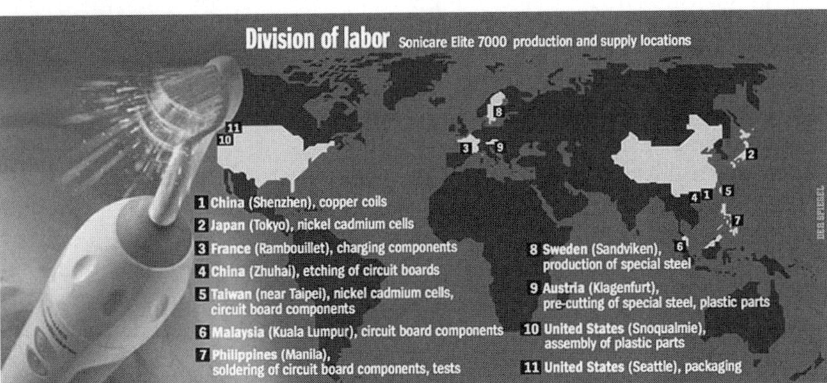

Figure 9.2 Manufacturing circuit for an electric toothbrush

of outsourcing and the diversity of forms that relations between actors take combine to make this a tricky operation.

Logistics provides the operational link between the various activities and the networked company, ensuring the coherence and reliability of flows in order to offer clients a quality service, while at the same time optimising resources and reducing costs (Paché and Spalanzani, 2007).

The value of studies in supply chain management (SCM), drawing on inter-organisational approaches, is to situate the corporation in an environment whose complexity derives from the multiplication and diversification of the relations between companies. The SCM approach entails the examination of the different kinds of relationship between actors in the chain: authority, trust, contract, etc. Given this context, the relative strengths of actors is a critical point worth studying.

3.1   The sustainability of relations: is restoring the balance of bargaining power conceivable?

The question of sustainable coordination must be handled with care. Large retailers make use of the relationship factor in the description of their sustainable practices. For products sold under the retailer's own brand, setting up partnerships with local suppliers – small and medium enterprises (SMEs) – is seen as an initiative inspired by the principles of sustainable development. In the annual reports of big retail chains, among their good practices one finds the development of projects to link local economic actors to retail outlets (for example, Carrefour's '*Pêche artisanale*' [traditional fishing] project in Portugal created long-term ties with local fish markets). Thus, 'suppliers' clubs' emerge with communication tools to share know-how. Other big retailers also offer assistance in exporting: ethics and the transparency of transactions are displayed at the signing of partnership charters.

We must not forget, however, that the principles of respect for human rights, food safety and the preservation of natural resources – which receive a great deal of attention in corporate communication – are often imposed on suppliers when contracts are signed. So what are we to think of the 'durability' of these practices? Does the uneven balance of bargaining power allow us to form an opinion? How can we avert the risk of idealising these collaborative practices?

Logistics and transport companies are emblematic in this area. What kinds of relations link these service providers to global clients who impose their globalisation strategies? Are balanced relationships conceivable?

3.2   Sustainability in relations with service providers

The quest for better performance in their core business drives companies to subcontract whatever lies outside their core competencies and know-how. Logistics and transport at the international level are two activities that are often contracted out. The various forms of outsourcing range from subcontracting basic operational activities (e.g. direct transport from one location to another) to the outsourcing of high added value activities (co-packing and co-manufacturing). Companies may also contract design services (planning distribution networks, reconfiguration of global chains). It is not enough to consider only the environmental and social characteristics of the service when evaluating sustainable logistics. The conditions under which this service emerges, and in particular the relative bargaining power of the shipper and service provider must also be taken into account.

The large investments needed to comply with environmental regulations can contribute to the marginalisation of small transport companies. Given the increasing complexity of providing a sustainable service, only the biggest logistics and transport service providers are able to keep up. The industry is characterised by a bipolar structure: on one side, a handful of global multi-specialist corporations, and on the other, myriad small operators with very limited bargaining power. Deutsche Post World Net (DPWN) embodies the trend towards immensity of a few large multinational companies that operate in every area of transport (sea, air and road) whether in traditional logistics (warehousing and distribution), express transport or integrated logistics consulting (supply chain management). The pursuit of a global strategy in terms of services, client sectors and geographic coverage, impels the group to respond to its clients' needs by updating its offer to take environmental issues into account (a fleet of clean vehicles, certified warehouses, modal shift, etc.).

Can small transporters modernise their offering in the same way so as not to lose their clients and, at the same time, maintain their (already small) profit margins? The costs of setting up a sustainable global transport service are very high. They include: material investments in new facilities and equipment (warehouses, vehicles), environmental certification procedures, IT links between production sites, means of transport and transit hubs. This undertaking is therefore the preserve of the biggest companies and excludes or eventually marginalises the smallest. All of this seems very far from the founding ideology of sustainable development, which, in its current form, tends to deepen inequalities.

4 Conclusion

This chapter analyses the complexity of sustainability, although its use is often distorted, reductive or dogmatic. The approaches used examine, typically, the three dimensions of sustainable development in a compartmentalised fashion. Thus the economic efficiency or profitability of sustainable strategies is studied separately from the reduction of environmental contamination and the improvement of working conditions.

We have shown that the analysis of sustainability in the field of global logistic strategies (as in others) suffers from a certain number of deficiencies and raises a certain number of paradoxes. Sustainability in the field of logistics appears to have little room to manoeuvre in view of the weight upstream in the chain, on the one hand, and the primacy accorded to productive efficiency on the other. At the operational level, sustainable development remains linked to the profitability of the strategies implemented. Similarly, the context of increased global competition for certain products prompts the pursuit of lower production costs, which in turn undermines the prospects of a sustainable orientation for logistics choices.

Our aim here is also to emphasise the fact that logistic and transport strategies are always the product of multiple constraints. This means that the quest for solutions of absolute excellence does not make much sense. Solutions cannot be identical for all companies; they have to be adapted to different contexts.

Transport and logistics are 'embedded' in the operating methods of companies. A certain number of studies (Burmeister, 2000) show that the logistic organisation – which will generate transport needs – does not exist in isolation from the company's production constraints. The procurement, production and distribution constraints are what will generate flow organisation and transport needs. These needs are also affected by the existence of multi-actor chains involved in the production process (suppliers, clients, subcontractors).

It is not very useful, therefore, to evaluate sustainability in logistics on an absolute basis. It is preferable to assess it on a relative basis, incorporating logistic and transport activities in the production process. This observation is summed up by Colin (2004), who writes 'there is no such thing as performance that is intrinsic to logistics'. Only the performance of activities (or functions) that are supported by logistics and the performance of the distribution-production process are of interest. Turnkey models of sustainable logistics do not exist.

The solutions may not be relevant or useful because questions about the sustainability of logistics are often poorly formulated, in particular those concerning responsibilities: production and consumption patterns are often the first to come under fire, are they not? The real question is to know whether a reorganisation of production and distribution systems is possible. Can the current practices in industry and distribution (JIT, relocation of production facilities, centralisation of warehousing, outsourcing, etc.) be rethought in order to implement sustainable logistics? All of this reorganisation would entail a change in the behaviour of end clients and consumers. Delivery frequency, times, locations and packing are some of the questions that ought to be reconsidered.... But are consumers ready for these changes?

These debates are, nevertheless, fundamental with respect to the political goal of decoupling transport from economic growth (i.e. where transport grows at a slower rate than production) even though the growth rate of international trade has been higher than that of world GDP since the end of the Second World War.

Note

1. Logistics refers to the management of all the flows and stocks as well as the management of resources and related information.

References

Alcouffe, A., Ferrari, S. and Grimal, L. (2002) Les enjeux du développement durable. *Sciences de la société*, 57, October, Footnote: 1.

Allemand, S. (1999) Développement durable et sciences sociales. *Sciences Humaines*, 92: 12–17.

Burmeister, A. (2000) Familles logistiques : propositions pour une typologie des produits transportés pour analyser les évolutions en matière d'organisation des transports et de la logistique. Rapport for *le PREDIT*, October.

Carbone, V. and Moatti, V. (2008) 'Institutionalising green supply chains: key findings of a global survey'. Paper presented at 22nd Conference of the Australian and New Zealand Academy of Management, Auckland (2–6 December).

Colin, J. (2004) 'La logistique du point de vue des sciences de gestion' in P. Lièvre and N. Tchernev (eds) *La Logistique entre Management et Optimisation*. Paris: Hermes Science.

Cox, A., Ireland, P. and Lonsdale, C. (2002) *Supply Chains, Markets and Power*. London: Routledge.

Defever, F. and Mucchielli, J.L. (2005) Décomposition internationale de la chaîne de valeur : une étude de la localisation des firmes multinationales dans l'Union Européenne élargie. *Revue économique*, 56: 1185–205.

Dornier, P.P. and Fender, M. (2001) *La Logistique Globale: Enjeux, Principes, Exemple*. Paris: Editions d'Organisation.

Fassio, G. (2006) Développement durable et organisation des réseaux industriels en juste à temps. *Logistique & Management*, 14 (2): 53–62.

Fremont, A. (2007) *Le monde en boîtes – Conteneurisation et mondialisation*, Synthèse INRETS N 53.

Harribey, J.M. (1998) *Le développement soutenable*. Paris: Economica.

Krugman, P. (1991) *Geography and Trade*. Cambridge MA and London: MIT Press.

Lamming, R.C. (1993) *Beyond Partnership: Strategies for Innovation and Lean Supply*. Hemel Hempstead: Prentice-Hall.

Larson, A.L., Teisberg, E.O. and Johnson, R.R. (2000) Sustainable business. *Interfaces*, 30 (3): 1–12.

Mounoud, E. (2000) Risques écologiques et discours idéologiques, Cahier spécial: L'art de la gestion du risque. *Les Echos*, 15 November.

Paché, G. and Spalanzani, A. (2007) *La Gestion des Chaînes Multi-acteurs: Perspectives Stratégiques*. Grenoble: Presses Universitaires Grenoble.

World Business Council for Sustainable Development (WBCSD) (2007) *Mobility for Development: Facts and Trends*. Geneva: Conches-Geneva.

World Commission on Environment and Development (WCED) (1987) *The Brundtland Report: Our Common Future*. Oxford: Oxford University Press.

Part III

Accounting and Finance

10
Paradoxes and Issues of the Globalisation of Accounting

Nadine Tournois and Robert Teller

Financial globalisation goes along with a strong change of the globalisation of accounting. This situation can be explained by several phenomena:[1]

- A multiplication of financial scandals (the Enron affair and WorldCom, for example) undermined the confidence of financial markets and led to a wave of reactions aimed at improving financial and accounting-information transparency.
- Europe's decision to make the International Financial Reporting Standards (IFRS) the mandatory standards for all listed companies.
- The accelerated power climb of the IFRS (resulting from this decision), which have now been implemented (or are being implemented) in more than 125 countries worldwide (Deloitte, Iasplus.com).
- The convergence process, engaged by Norwalk agreements between IFRS referential and the American standards Generally Accepted Accounting Principles (US GAAP), which is producing tangible results, especially regarding financial instruments, segment reporting and the restructuring of the Income Statement.

Following the Enron affair, the report prepared by the Economic Analysis Council for the French prime minister, pointed out the contradiction between the fast capital markets' globalisation and the fragmentation of national systems governing accounting and financial information. For companies operating in different countries and listed on different markets, '...this disparity of standards is at least, a cost, and at worst, a source of confusion in their communication strategy; for investors it is a factor of opacity which handicaps comparisons and represents an obstacle to mobility, and therefore to the proper capital allocation' (De Boissieu et al., 2003).

The European Commission (Regulation CE No.1569/2007) indicates that

'...the President of the European Council, the President of the Commission and the President of the United States have agreed in April 2007, to

183

promote and guarantee the conditions to ensure that, by 2009 or sooner, the Generally Accepted Accounting Principles (US GAAP) and the IFRS, are recognised in both jurisdictions without the need for reconciliation'.[2]

What best characterises this evolution is probably the strong emphasis of the accounting model's financialisation, which is particularly noted through the introduction of fair value and a new conception of performance. The main issues raised by this evolution are related to the following:

- limitations of the Anglo-Saxon financial model;
- legitimacy of the regulation process;
- theoretical legitimacy of the accounting model's financialisation;
- influence of the so-called Big Four auditing firms worldwide (Deloitte, Ernst & Young, PricewaterhouseCoopers and KPMG);
- conflict between standards based on principles and standards based on rules;
- difficulties in harmonisation and of the regulation of conflicts;
- consideration of other stakeholders.

In addition, this evolution could pose a problem of political legitimacy and governance of the accounting regulation.

Many authors have talked about the Accounting Big Bang referring to the introduction, in January 2005, of the IFRS in the European referential. This example, although significant, is just one amongst others that illustrates the convergence process towards the globalisation of accounting. Economic and financial globalisation definitely calls for the globalisation of accounting since it is about avoiding the distortions resulting from the use of international standards, as their impact differs from that of local standards (Hoarau, 2006). However, this evolution raises questions that go far beyond accounting aspects, given that behind the international harmonisation movement, the governance mode of corporations, markets and international financial capitalism, is at stake. We are dealing with a phenomenon that converges to what some authors call the tetra-normalisation (Savall and Zardet, 2005).[3]

Are we heading towards the globalisation of accounting induced by the financialisation of economies? What are the stakes of such an evolution for the accounting model? The purpose is to try to summarise these gradual steps towards the globalisation of accounting, to question the nature of this new international accounting regulation, to consider the impacts of this movement (or change) and to highlight the paradox of the governance of the regulations, provided by the Big Four.

1 Genesis of the globalisation of accounting movement

This hasty genesis is built around the large success of the standards produced by the International Accounting Standards Board (IASB). This success was amplified due to particular affairs such as Enron, as well as to the historical decision made by the European Union to make the IFRS compulsory.

1.1 The success of the International Accounting Standards Board

The International Accounting Standards Committee (IASC), established in 1973 and from 2000 known as the International Accounting Standards Board (IASB), has undergone an extraordinary and successful evolution. The IASC, as the first worldwide organisation for the standardisation of accounting (Scheid, 2008), is a private organisation that has a very unusual history. The Accountants International Study Group was set up in 1967 by a team of Canadian, American and English professionals. In 1972, at the 10th World Congress of Accountants in Sydney, Australia, Sir Henry Benson suggested the establishment of the IASC. This suggestion was approved by representatives of the accounting profession from Australia, France, Germany, Japan, Holland and Mexico. Led by a small team of accounting technicians working almost exclusively with professional accountants, the IASC produced, in less than ten years, the initial twenty-six standards that would become the future IFRS (Camfferman and Zeff, 2007). We have to look for the origin of international normalisation, not in any big international public institution, but among accounting professionals working with a tiny secretariat and a modest budget, initially financed by the professional organisations of the ten founding members[4] (Scheid, 2008).

For the first fifteen years, the IASC chose a flexible method of developing and disseminating the standards. The accounting standards that developed were related to generic concepts. Specific standards related to professions or sectors were avoided. Each standard draft included accounting treatment options, in order to avoid offending some countries or activity types. The final standards were well accepted, unlike the texts written by accounting committees selected by the United Nations (UN) or by the Organisation for Economic Co-operation and Development (OECD), both of whom were seeking some international harmonisation (UN, 2005).

From 1987, the IASC adopted a project to reduce the options in the existing twenty-six standards. However, the international exchange development pressed for the development of global accounting standards. Multinational companies found it increasingly expensive to have to adapt their financial statements to different national systems. Similarly, international financial investors wanted to be able to compare investment opportunities worldwide, which assumed that financial statements observe the same standards. Finally, the big auditing firms also pushed for this, since they could only benefit from the development of this globalisation of accounting. In this context, the IASC adopted a new strategic direction: from then on, the objectives were to '...build a comprehensive set of developed and directional standards applicable to all companies, but primarily to listed companies' (Scheid, 2008). These standards supposed the adhesion of stock exchange control organisations, regrouped within the International Organisation of Securities Commissions (IOSCO).

From 1995, the IOSCO asked the IASC to finalise a set of standards to impose on all listed companies. This required a change of work scale and a modification of the functioning structures of the IASC (a permanent general secretariat, a full-time team of technical assistants and so on). The agreement required IASC to build a standards basis, which was then adopted by the IOSCO in May 2000. When meeting in Venice, in November 1999, the IASC board decided to dissolve the IASC and start a new institution, the IASB. Formed by fourteen members appointed for five years (renewable once), the IASB is an international private and independent organisation of accounting standardisation, with its headquarters in London. It is supervised by the International Accounting Standards Committee Foundation (IASCF), a non-profit organisation based in Delaware state (the USA), which is responsible for providing finance to the IASB, as well as designating its members. The IASCF is formed by twenty-two trustees, in charge of the IASB's management and financing.[5]

This initiative, founded by private economic players, was receiving substantial political support in 2000, when the European Union took the decision to adopt these new standards, with effect from 2005. The IAS standards have acquired worldwide status, allowing them to extend their influence globally, particularly in the emerging countries. The United States then started to work towards the convergence of the American standards (US GAAP) with the IFRS. The IASB's success is mainly due to the initiative of a group of markets regulators (Arthur Levitt for Securities and Exchange Commission [SEC], Michel Prada for Stock Exchange Operations Commission [Commission des Opérations Boursières] and Andrew Sheng for Hong Kong Securities and Futures Commission [HKSFC]). This group pulled the international approach out of a rut, and, under the patronage of the president of IASC Foundation, Paul Volcker, transformed 'an inefficient IASC into a triumphant IASB' (De Boissieu et al., 2003).

1.2 Impact of the Enron affair and WorldCom etc.

The question related to the links between financial information and the globalisation of accounting re-emerges boldly in the context of a globalised and financialised economy that puts financial markets at the heart of the system. The world financial system is frequently crossed by serious crises that raise the fears of a chain effect that might end in a systemic crisis.

The current subprime crisis was preceded by the dot-com bubble in the 2000s, and the disclosure of a series of affairs related to accounting manipulations.

One of the most iconic was the Enron affair, which was recognised as a true earthquake that could undermine the markets' trust. Such affairs have exposed serious drifts on the whole chain of information production. The responsibility of all the players has been highlighted: managers, administrators, auditors, financial analysts, bankers, regulators and so on (Hoarau and Teller, 2006).

Many authors emphasised the risks linked to the uncontrolled development of financial innovations, in particular the one linked to derivatives. The complex financial products heavily contributed to the dematerialisation of operations of firms and have then favoured 'creative accounting' practices. The Enron affair also exposed the limitations of the corporate governance mechanisms, since its board of directors was made up of independent administrators. This affair has demonstrated the limits of self regulation within the financial community; it is incapable of reducing situations where there is a conflict of interests between auditors, bankers and managers. The Enron affair has finally illustrated the myth of the efficiency of the markets, which allowed, for more than a year, the survival of Enron and the postponement of its bankruptcy.

In order to try to restore the trust in accounting and financial information, public authorities advocated greater severity for accounting and financial infringements.[6] Beyond the trust issue, the purpose was to ensure better financial security. Regarding the globalisation of accounting, the Enron affair stimulated many theories related to the respective merits of standards based on rules, like those of the US, and those based on principles, like those of the IFRS (De Boissieu et al., 2003). The foundation of the two systems is completely different. We can either establish a number of principles organised in a conceptual framework (IFRS), or draw an exhaustive list of rules (US GAAP). The American system leads to a prescriptive set running to more than 140,000 pages, addressing almost every interpretation, but offering, at the same time, many opportunities for bypassing the rules. This system would be more susceptible to the manipulation of results than the IFRS, which are based on principles. This was the European Commission's position *vis-à-vis* an accounting-diversion risk similar to Enron in Europe; it pointed out the fact that adopting the IFRS, which are based on principles, greatly reduced the risks of creative accounting. Unfortunately, this argument was contradicted by the facts, since other affairs linked to European groups – subsequent to the Enron affair – have highlighted that the problem of reliability and control of financial information can be found in both standards' systems.[7]

This growing awareness has certainly served as argument in favour of the convergence process started by the Securities and Exchange Commission (SEC) and the European Commission. Other players in the financial markets advocate an even more forthright evolution towards the adoption of a unique standard of international accounting standards, applied to all listed companies. Thus, the vice-president of the American Institute of Certified Public Accountants (AICPA) announced that his organisation was in favour of a convergence of the two systems of standards, and that he wanted the US issuers to use the IFRS system. Similarly, 20 per cent of American companies would be willing to adopt the IFRS system if authorised by the SEC (Deloitte, Iasplus.com). Finally, the National Association of Securities Dealers Automated Quotations (NASDAQ) expressed its full support for the SEC's decision to authorise foreign issuers to use the IFRS without prior reconciliation to US GAAP.

1.3   Historical reach of European Union Regulation 1606/2002

Why did the European Union (EU) renounce adjusting the old accounting directives and opt instead for a mandatory implementation of an external body of standards, which is built by a private institution and predominantly controlled by the Anglo-Saxon accounting world? Did the EU have any other choice but to adopt the 2002 Regulation, which generalised the IFRS implementation to European-listed companies? Some authors were surprised by the European choice taken without prior impact study and without significant benefit in terms of governance (Capron, 2005). For them, the EU had somewhat hastily abandoned its accounting sovereignty to private players who have no political legitimacy.

This remark is true even though the EU's choice seems reasonable if we take into account the financial needs induced by the growth of big groups on the international markets, and if we consider the technical level of the 4th and 7th European Accounting Directives related to corporate financial statements and consolidated accounts. A consensus seems to emerge recognising this option as the only one that was politically viable considering the previous normalisation state. The Europeans could not agree on a common project, especially because of the British rejection. Moreover, were European standards really needed given that world standards were available to answer the growing internationalisation of companies? Big European firms started to raise their capital in the US, using the American accounting system. The Europeans then preferred to abandon their power to private international institutions rather than to model the European accounting standards on the US GAAP (Véron, 2007a).

This decision will have a heavy political impact, giving legal legitimacy to private international institutions that previously had only had a technical competency. The EU's decision to integrate these standards into the Community Law has thus conferred an institutional legitimacy that the IASB did not have before (Hoarau, 2008). It is highly probable that this decision played a major role in the progress of the standardisation of international accounting as can be noticed today.

1.4   The Norwalk Agreement and convergence process

It is likely that one of the positive consequences of scandals linked to the Enron affair is that it helped to weaken, in the minds of the American financial players, the belief in the general and indisputable supremacy of the US GAAP. From 2002, the American legislator asked for a reform of the US GAAP, in order for it to better converge with the IFRS. The president of the IASB, Sir David Tweedie, and the foundation president of the IASC, Paul Volcker, introduced a relevant project at the opening of the World Congress of Accountants in Hong Kong. The FASB and the IASB held a joint meeting and published a memorandum called the Norwalk Agreement, designed to make existing standards 'compatible and [...] to coordinate their future work programs'.

In early 2006, the American Financial Accounting Standards Board (FASB) and the International Accounting Standards Board (IASB) concluded a Memorandum of Understanding, defining a programme for a convergence of the American standards and IFRS. On 20 June 2007, the SEC published a final regulation that removes, under conditions, the obligation of reconciliation between the IFRS and the US GAAP. This regulation is applied to financial statements of years ended after 15 November 2007. The SEC now authorises foreign private issuers to introduce their financial statements prepared in accordance with IFRS, as they were published by the IASB, without the obligation of reconciliation with the US GAAP.

To summarise, this brief description of normative systems evolution allows us to suggest that the IFRS generalisation and the multiplication of convergence agreements of the IFRS and US GAAP, prefigure this new international accounting standard known as the globalisation of accounting. This evolution seems unavoidable, and probably denotes a departure from previous accounting models. We can then consider the consequences of such a phenomenon, especially at the governance level of this normative process.

2 The globalisation of accounting and governance of the normative process

The financial globalisation phenomenon is certainly one of the major causes of the evolution of the normalisation of international accounting. Given the impact of the standards, it creates a real problem of political and economical governance on the global level.

2.1 A globalisation of accounting induced by the financial globalisation

The more sophisticated a financial system is, the more complex are the issues of accounting information. A global financial system cannot live without universal accounting standards. Therefore, we can assume that financial globalisation implies a globalisation of accounting, i.e. a set of standards for transactions, contracts and relationships between economic agents within the global village (Véron, 2008).

Since the Norwalk Agreement on the convergence of the IFRS and US GAAP, the process of the globalisation of accounting has accelerated. This speeding up is explained by the significant success of the IFRS and by the recognition (under conditions) of these standards by the SEC.

The convergence process has already resulted in common texts or positions to each of the IFRS or the US GAAP referentials. Today, more than 100 countries require or allow the use of the IFRS, while there were only about fifteen in the late 1990s. This evolution is highly encouraged by the auditing giants who support the global acceptance of the IFRS worldwide (Gannon and Ashwal, 2004).

At the end of February 2008, the implementation status of the IFRS in the world confirms this evolution of globalisation (Table 10.1).

The phenomenon of the globalisation of accounting can be observed quantitatively since, of the first 500 global groups (Véron, 2007b),

- 37 per cent are listed in the US and communicate in US GAAP;
- 39 per cent are listed in other financial places (Europe, Australia, China, Hong Kong, Singapore) and communicate in IFRS standards;
- 20 per cent are listed in countries that entered the adoption process of the IFRS.

This statistic shows clearly that the IFRS are currently the dominant accounting system, rather than the US GAAP, even though the latter remains very important, especially in the development process of the IFRS. It is also evident that the European Union played an important role in the breakthrough of the IFRS, by obliging more than 7,000 European companies to adopt the IFRS referential from 1 January 2005. Similarly, the recognition of the IFRS on the American markets was decisive in the choices of emerging countries in favour of this referential (China, India, Brazil and Russia).

Table 10.1 IFRS adoption in 157 countries worldwide

The case of listed companies	The case of non-listed companies
<ul><li>Non-authorised IFRS: 32</li><li>Authorised IFRS: 24</li><li>Mandatory IFRS for some companies: 4</li><li>Mandatory IFRS for all listed companies: 82</li><li>Among 110 countries that authorise or oblige the use of IFRS, seventy five countries require the indication, in the auditing report, of compliance with IFRS</li></ul>	<ul><li>Non-authorised IFRS: 34</li><li>Authorised IFRS: 36</li><li>Mandatory IFRS for some companies: 19</li><li>Mandatory IFRS for all listed companies: 28</li></ul>

Source: Deloitte, Iasplus.com, February 2008.

This globalisation of accounting induced by financial globalisation can be a problem at the level of the political governance of normative process.

2.2 Political problem: the governance of the global normative process

The globalisation process, as it was depicted, highlights the strong development of standards enacted by the IASB worldwide, including in the Anglo-Saxon world. Despite this important progress, today we probably cannot assert that the IFRS are the global referential. However, it is certain that the convergence process launched between the IASB standards and the American standards forms the basis of the globalisation of accounting. This global normative base may generate many governance issues. On one hand, the IASB has very important economic power but is without political legitimacy. On the other, this global pedestal supposes a uniform implementation of standards, which is not currently the case.

2.2.1   *A great power without real political legitimacy*

The IASB enacted the standards whose dissemination worldwide has had a great impact, but this private international organisation has no political legitimacy. The institution in charge of its supervision (IASCF) is a private non-profit entity based in Delaware state. Although the IASB reports to the IASCF's college of trustees, which appoints its members and provides its financing, the legal status under private law of the IASCF may pose problems. Its current Constitution is subject to debate, especially regarding the trustees' representativeness to the financing mode and the degree of freedom of its members. At present, the IASCF is financed by the four big audit firms (the Big Four), the companies and the banks. Since 2008, the new mode of financing asks for voluntary contributions from different governments. The purpose is to provide a separation between the finance coming from different donors and the IASB's decisions, but we can question the political viability of this structure. Taking into account the significant stakes linked to this standardisation, it might not be desirable to lean this structure against an international institution such as the International Monetary Fund or the World Bank (Hoarau, 2008).[8]

The financial contributions review and the IASB members' distribution demonstrate a clear dominance of the Anglo-Saxon model, especially of the Big Four. Such dominance seems barely compatible with the universal vocation of this institution having an international vocation (Raffournier, 2007). In November 2007, the IASCF's trustees introduced propositions to strengthen the governance and political responsibility of their organisation. In particular, they retained the following propositions:[9]

- Establishing a formal link of reporting to official organisations, in particular the stock exchange regulators. This group would approve the trustees' designations and examine their supervising activities, including the adequacy of the IASCF's annual financing agreements and its overall budget.

- Designing a financing mechanism to ensure that the trustees would benefit from the contributions of interested parties while keeping their freedom.
- Pursuing the efforts to structure a sustainable financing system with a broad base.

The problem linked to the normative institution's legitimacy is also coupled with a central problem related to a standards system's accounting being based on a mix of principles and rules (Hoarau, 2008).

2.2.2 *Difficulties of a global homogeneous implementation of the IFRS standards*

Financialisation does not necessarily guarantee transparency and can even become an obstacle when the counterparts of the actual transactions are neglected. Moreover, if these standards are designed in and for an Anglo-Saxon environment, traditionally more familiar with a financialised context, this is not appropriate for the rest of the world, Europe included. The difficulties of implementing the IFRS remain. Hence, the initial assessments of the first adoptions of the IFRS in Europe highlighted many difficulties of implementation. Public-listed companies have underestimated the complexities of the IFRS, and the impact and the cost of compliance. Auditors have been greatly involved in this compliance with a risk of having to audit the information they basically contributed to develop (Hogendoorn, 2006).

The important place given to opinions and interpretation led regulators to implement coordination mechanisms in order to minimise the multiplicity of interpretations of the IFRS. In such a system, practice differences are inevitable and it is likely that more detailed rules will be required. The use of the International Financial Reporting Interpretation Committee (IFRIC), which is the interpreting committee of the IASB standards, will probably be more and more frequent. The question of the IFRS implementation's homogeneity remains unanswered and will require time and close monitoring in order to avoid a drive towards a local adaptation (localisation) of international standards. Finally, the implementation of the IFRS standards may lead to conflicts of interpretation because of the diversity of national environments (Hoarau, 2007). The establishment of a conflict resolution court or tribunal (or dispute resolution committee) remains something to address, while considering the issues of which framework and at which level.

2.3 The economic problem: the financialisation of the global accounting model

The global normative base that emerged on the international scene is the outcome of the needs of the international financial markets, which always claimed accounting standards that guaranteed transparency of financial information and comparability for the investors. This is central to the conceptual frameworks of the IASB and the US GAAP. The investor is the privileged beneficiary of financial reporting. They need the transparent information that best reflects the value creation expected from these investors. This objective directed the production of accounting standards towards a purely financial vision of the accounting model; for example, by highlighting the fair value principle (market value) and by advocating a new concept of performance based on the comprehensive income. The recent subprime crisis illustrates the accounting system mutation, which raises questions.[10]

2.3.1   *The limitations of the generalisation fair value*

The most significant point of the evolution of the financial and economic globalisation is certainly the rise of the fair value concept as the model's basis, which led the accounting model to converge to a balance sheet at market value. From the standards of financial assets, we notice the tendency to transpose this valuation principle to all assets and liabilities, which can ultimately lead to the end of the historical cost (Gelard, 1997). This approach favours the idea that any asset is comparable (at least conceptually) to a financial asset, the correct measure of which is the present value of the expected cash flows of this asset, given the risk (Tournois and Teller, 2004). The generated wealth results from the net variation of all assets and liabilities valued at their fair value. The balance-sheet orientation of the financial reports is preferred, and leads to the favouring of a new concept of performance.

2.3.2   *A new concept of performance*

One of the important challenges of the convergence project of American and international frameworks is the performance reporting, which is partly based on volatile and virtual market and stock exchange values. The IASB's project of performance reporting, initiated in 2001, aims to enact a standard that will focus on the communication of financial and accounting performances, referring to a wider notion of the comprehensive income (Ramond et al., 2007). This concept fundamentally differs from the classical net income, as it includes some changes in equity, such as realised or non-realised capital gains and losses. This new concept is consistent with the logic of the accounting model's financialisation, introduced by the IASB, with the gradual use of the agreement of valuation at fair value (Casta and Colasse, 2003). This approach does not seem to be producing significant results for the moment,[11] and has also made the IFRS into a system of hybrid standards which mix accrual accounting and value analysis principles. Such a system can lead to adding elements on a heterogeneous basis. However, the more the system is hybrid, the less it can provide relevant information

(Sleigh-Johnson, 2007). Besides, this accounting model's financialisation raises questions relating to the theoretical validity of this normative process.

2.4 The theoretical problem: the conceptual basis of global standards

Mirroring the global economy's financialisation, this significant evolution of the accounting model raises some questions. The emergence of the global normative base did not prevent the financial scandals such as Enron and WorldCom, or the subprime crisis. This global normative base is supported by a theoretical body coming from a conceptual movement of the value relevance, but does not solve the mix issue between standards based on principles and those based on rules.

2.4.1 *The arbitration between a global normative base, based on rules or principles*

It is evident that the worldwide dissemination of the IFRS is efficient, as it benefits from a convergence process with the American standards and from the SEC's support. This evolution, qualified as the global normative base, addresses the needs of the globalised financial markets but highlights an issue related to the internal coherence of the normative system itself. Indeed, as noticed beforehand, the IFRS approach is based on principles stated within a conceptual framework, while the development of the American standards remains mainly based on rules even though, following the Enron affair, the SEC requested that the American standardisation body reassess this issue. The recent evolutions show examples of reciprocal adaptation: a kind of alignment of the American position with that of IASB regarding the financial instruments, and an opposite position regarding the segment reporting standard. However, the influence of the Anglo-Saxon model remains significant in the IASB's normative process and might drive the IFRS alignment on the US GAAP. But what would then remain of the IFRS's originality based on principles, if an area was left open to substantial interpretation by the players (Hoarau, 2007)? This evolution may further reduce Europe's influence in this normative process at a time where a readjustment favouring continental European concepts would be desirable instead.

2.4.2 *The theoretical legitimacy question of the global normative base*

The IASB does not have a political legitimacy apart from the one occasionally granted, as in the case of the European Regulation 1601/2002. The theoretical legitimacy of these standards can also be questioned, being always introduced as standards favouring transparency and market functioning. The implicit frame of this approach is derived from the value relevance theory. This theory, predominant in the Anglo-Saxon milieu, produced much theoretical and empirical research, which sought to demonstrate the US

GAAP's supremacy over the other international standards, or even more, the IFRS's supremacy over the local standards.

The theoretical background of this hypothesise is based on the theory of market efficiency. Market efficiency gives to the fair value (market value) an almost sacrosanct character, so that any accounting information that gets closer to its market value would qualified as pertinent. Hence, any system of standards that converges the book value with the market value is considered to be more efficient. However, this logic, based on the validity of the perfect markets theory, is subject to disagreement. In addition, research related to this theory is producing contrasted outcomes (Holthausen and Watts, 2000). For example, the joint IASB-FASB project on the comprehensive income is supposed to have an informative content superior to the net income because it includes the non-realised capital gains and losses. It appears, therefore, that the result is currently yet to be seen (Ramond et al., 2007). The Institute of Chartered Accountants in England and Wales (ICAEW), as per the European Commission request, drafted a report on the implementation of the IFRS and the fair value directive. The report highlights the easiness of the financial statements' comparability following the implementation of the IFRS by the European listed companies. Almost all investors, preparers and certified public accountants judged the move to the IFRS as having improved the overall quality of financial statements. The study also examined financial statements during the transition to the IFRS. It showed that the explicative power of the accounting numbers for the market value measures is real, but this does not imply legitimacy to the value relevance theory (Sleigh-Johnson, 2007).

3 Conclusion

The establishment of a global normative base, formed by the dissemination over more than 100 countries of the IFRS, and by the speeding up of the convergence process with the American standards, addresses the needs of the international financial markets. This base, oriented according to investors' needs, is marked by an increased financialisation of the underlying accounting model, and by a new concept of performance. This first stage of the process of the globalisation of accounting is only one stage within an internationalisation process of the dissemination of financial information, a stage that will require more assessment and consolidation. It brings many implementation issues related to standards' complexity, and to cultural disparities of the countries that have adopted them. The key issue remains the political governance of such a process, taking into consideration the importance for companies and governments of accounting standards. Besides the aspects related to investors' financial information, the accounting standard carries out other important functions regarding contract representation, internal performance measurement and instruments of the structuring of organisations. The social, or even societal function of the accounting model, is also a key issue, in order to understand (otherwise to measure) the scale and impact of the externalities linked to the functioning of the current economic systems. We are, therefore, facing a wider issue of the measurement's governance, encompassing the environmental and societal information of public and private organisations. Today, we know that financial and accounting information has, in some respects, the character of public good, with a role going beyond past transitions' reporting and companies' valuation. This information plays a central role in the establishment of contracts and in the processes of value creation. It is the basis of incentive and coordination mechanisms that will help the modelling of the company and the building of responsibilities.

Financial and accounting information plays another key role in the societal governance of organisations, through providing an image of the formed relationships between companies and stakeholders. We have noticed the limits of an approach mainly oriented on the financial markets, in terms of economic performance as well as in social and societal aspects. On the economic side, the incentive mechanisms based only on the stock options revealed pernicious effects, encouraging the manipulation of information and creative accounting. On the social side, incentive models and oriented partnerships may have positive effects, especially by encouraging the membership of employees and executives with competencies and knowledge that represent genuine strategic assets to strengthen, in order to increase, the organisation's intellectual or intangible capital. Finally, on the societal side, the ability to take into account the environmental and ethical aspects is part of a company's reputation capital, and is a factor of value creation and sustainable development. When we consider the overall issues, we can welcome the progress made in terms of financial transparency and corporate governance, but we cannot avoid questioning the efficiency of the ongoing reforms, which is, in itself, a first order paradox. Isn't it the right time to look for improving the relevance of financial information by leaning it against internal mechanisms of value creation (management information) and by better integrating it into a wider set (stakeholder's report)?

Notes

1. In October 2005, the secretariat of the United Nations Conference on Trade and Development (UNACTD) prepared a document introducing an overall vision of the recent trends of the convergence processes towards the IFRS, which highlighted the main technical issues that emerged during their implementation. This document has been drafted to facilitate the debates of the International Working Group of Experts on International Standards of Accounting and Reporting (ISAR), in order to help countries to assess the effects of adopting the IFRS, and to examine all possible strategies related to their implementation.

2. The European Commission and the Securities and Exchange Commission (SEC) pursued their dialogue for the acceptance, in the US, of the IFRS, adopted in accordance with Regulation CE No. 1606/2002, which will exempt the issuers using the IFRS from costly reconciliation obligations. The Accounting Standards Board of Japan (ASBJ) is implementing its action plan jointly with the International Accounting Standards Board (IASB) in order to converge Japanese GAAP and the IFRS. The Canadian Accounting Standards Board (ACSB) published a plan for the integration of the IFRS into the Canadian GAAP, with effect from 1 January 2011.

3. For Savall and Zardet (2005) tetra-normalisation includes the four big poles of standards that correspond to trade exchange issues (World Trade Organisation), to social conditions (International Labour Organisation), to accounting and financial security (IFRS and US GAAP), and to quality and environment (ISO). These standards are made independently, which might engender some incompatibilities that are difficult to manage. Tetra-normalisation can be structured around three issues: the proliferation of standards, competition and conflicts between standards, and non-compliance with standards.

4. Australia, Canada, France, Germany, Japan, Mexico, the Netherlands, the United Kingdom, Ireland and the United States.

5. See Iasplus website: www.iasplus.com/restruct/iascf.htm

6. American authorities published the Sarbannes-Oxley Act (2002) and created the Public Company Accounting Oversight Board (2002), which was put in charge of controlling the accounting auditors. France followed with a financial security law (2003) (which is the origin of the Financial Market Authority) and the establishment of the High Council of Certified Public Accounts (2003) (le Haut Conseil du Commissariat aux Comptes).

7. In particular, the Ahold and Parmalat affairs, and even Vivendi.

8. Since November 2001, the World Bank has prepared reports on the observation of levels and codes of the accounting standards' compliance by state members. The objectives are to ensure the comparability of the accounting standards with the IFRS and the audit standards ISA. The reports examine the standards' implementation level by the companies of different countries (UNCTAD, 2005).

9. IASCF *Constitution Review*, 2008; Deloitte, Iasplus.com, February 2008.

10. Hence, Jean-Louis Mullenbach wonders if the financial crisis does not hide an accounting-standards crisis (*Les Échos*, 25 January 2008, p. 21).

11. The study conducted by the ICAEW (2007) insisted on the fact that academic research on the relevance of accounting figures in the IFRS are not significant for the moment.

References

Camfferman, K. and Zeff, S. (2007) *Financial reporting and global capital markets, A history of the International Accounting Standards Committee (IASC):1973–2000*. Oxford: Oxford University Press.

Capron, M. (2005) 'Les enjeux de la mise en œuvre des normes comptables internationales' in M. Capron, È. Chiapello, B. Colasse, M. Mangenot and J. Richard (eds) *Les normes comptables internationales, instrument du capitalisme financier*. Paris: La Découverte.

Casta, J.F. and Colasse, B. (2003) *Juste valeur: enjeux techniques et politiques*. Paris: Economica.

De Boissieu, C., Lorenzi, J.H. and Mistral, J. (2003) *Les normes comptables et le monde post-Enron*. Paris : La Documentation Française.

Gannon, D.J. and Ashwal, A. (2004) Financial Reporting Goes Global. *Journal of Accountancy*, September: 43–7.

Gelard, G. (1997) La normalisation comptable en quête de cohérence. *Revue Française de Comptabilité*, 290: 37–40.

Hoarau, C. (2006) Convergence IFRS US GAAP: vers une hybridation des modes de normalisation. *Revue Sciences de Gestion*, ISMEA ISEOR, 54 : 39–51.

——— (2007) *Comptabilité et Management*. Paris: Foucher Enseignement Supérieur.

——— (2008) La gestion des résultats comptables, IFRS vs US GAAP. *Revue Française de Comptabilité*, 406 (January): 20–2.

Hoarau, C. and Teller, R. (2006) L'évolution du rôle des outils comptables. *Comptabilité, Contrôle, Audit*, 2 (13).

Hogendoorn, M. (2006) Accounting in Europe. *European Accounting Association*, 3: 23–6.

Holthausen, R.W. and Watts, R.L. (2000) 'The relevance of the value relevance literature for financial accounting standard setting', available online at http://papers.ssrn.com/paper.taf?abstract_id=228950.

Institute of Chartered Accountants in England and Wales (ICAEW) (2007) 'EU Implementation of IFRS and the Fair Value Directive, A report for the European Commission', available online at www.icaew.com/ecifrsstudy.

Raffournier, B. (2007) Les oppositions françaises à l'adoption des IFRS : examen critique et tentative d'explication. *Revue Comptabilité Contrôle Audit*, Special edition: 25 et sq.

Ramond, O., Batsch, A. and Casta, J.F. (2007) Résultat et performance financière en normes IFRS: Quel est le contenu informatif du comprehensive income? *Revue Comptabilité Contrôle Audit*, Special edition: 95 et sq.

Savall, H. and Zardet, V. (2005) *Tétranormalisation: défis et dynamiques*. Paris: Economica.

Scheid, J.C. (2008) IASC 1973–2000. *Revue Française de Comptabilité*, 406 (January): 12.

Sleigh-Johnson, N. (2007) IFRS in Europe: a successful transition. *Accountancy Magazine*, December: 97.

Tournois, N. and Teller, R. (2004) 'From financial value creation to substantial value management in French banks' in Matthias Fischer (ed.) *Handbook Value Management in Banking and Insurance*. Weisbaden: Gabler Publishing.

Véron, N. (2007a) *The Global Accounting Experiment* (Bruguel Blueprint Series). Brussels: Bruegel. www.bruegel.org.

——— (2007b) Les comptables de la mondialisation. *Alternatives Economiques*, 260 (July/August): 39–48.

——— (2008) Le triomphe fragile des normes comptables internationales. *La Tribune*, 15 Septembre.

Further reading

Colasse, B. (2005) 'La régulation comptable entre public et privé' in M. Capron, È. Chiapello, B. Colasse, M. Mangenot and J. Richard (eds) *Les normes comptables internationales, instrument du capitalisme financier*. Paris: La Découverte.

Ernst and Young (2005) *Passage aux IFRS : les pratiques des grands groupes européens*. Paris: CPA.

Gornick-Tomaszewski, S. and McCarthy, I.N. (2003) Cooperation between FASB and IASB to achieve convergence of accounting standards. *Review of Business*, Spring: 52–61.

Hoarau, C. and Teller, R. (2005) 'Information financière et responsabilité sociale des entreprises' in *Mélanges en l'honneur de Roland Pérez, La responsabilité sociale de l'entreprise*. Colombelles: Edition EMS.

Mullenbach, J.L. (2008) La crise financière cache-t-elle une crise des norms comptables? *Les Echos*, 30 January.

ONU (2005) *Commission on Investment, Technology and Related Financial Issues, Intergovernmental Working Group of Experts on International Standards of Accounting and Reporting*. (22nd session), November, Geneva.

Teller, R. (1998) *Un modèle comptable de la valeur peut-il restaurer la valeur du modèle comptable? Valeur, marché et organisation*. Nantes: Actes des XIVèmes Journées des IAE.

Tweedie, D. (2007) Simplifying global accounting: IASB Chair discusses the future of IFRS, U.S. GAAP and the global accounting profession. *Journal of Accountancy*, September: 56–60.

11
The Paradox of Globalised Accounting in the Public Sector: An Analysis of the Reform of Public Accounting in Madagascar

Evelyne Lande, Harimino Oliarilanto Rakoto and Sébastien Rocher

In a move to reform their public administration, more and more countries implement international public sector accounting standards released by the International Public Sector Accounting Standards Board (IPSASB). It is a surprising paradox that many developing countries are, as a priority, and even though they lack the necessary human, material and financial resources, developing the application of these standards, originally created by and for developed countries. Parallel goals such as addressing illiteracy, infant mortality, epidemics of infectious diseases, malnutrition, access to water and so on, appear to be higher priorities. This discovery raises a fundamental question: why do countries in the developing world apply the international benchmark?

To answer this question, the reform of public accounting in Madagascar is discussed in interviews with officials of the institutions concerned by the standardisation process, and through the analysis of political speeches and official documents. The results obtained show that the modernisation of the Malagasy government accounting, through the application of accrual accounting advocated by the International Accounting Standards, is linked to the phenomena of normative isomorphism, mimetic and dependence on resources.

The IPSASB transposed the accounting framework proposed by the International Accounting Standard Board (IASB) for the private sector into the public sector through the diffusion of the International Public Sector Accounting Standards (IPSAS). These standards come from the application in the public sector of International Accounting Standards (IAS) and International Financial Reporting Standards (IFRS) accounting standards on a semantic basis only.

Since the beginning of the 1990s, a keen interest in applying the IPSAS has been observed on an international level. This interest is contributing to a movement of accounting globalisation. In 2007, the International Federation of Accountants (IFAC) listed seventy-one developed or developing countries that had adopted, or were in the process of adopting, the new accounting framework. Now, with regard to the reforms begun by these countries, a surprising paradox can be observed: developing countries are applying the IPSAS in their entirety without questioning their applicability in relation to their socio-economic and legislative environment, whereas in developed countries these same standards are the object of intense debate, and are considered to be difficult to adopt as they stand.

The developing countries' strategy[1] is surprising as the IPSASB advocates giving up cash-based accounting in favour of accrual-based accounting,[2] as seen in the private sector model. Numerous developing countries do not have a reliable information system based on receipts and disbursements, even though mastering cash-based accounting is often a prerequisite for introducing the accrual accounting model (Hepworth, 2003; Lande and Rocher, 2008). Nor do they have the necessary human, material and financial resources for modifying their accounting system. In addition, many developing countries make accounting reform an important priority, even though the fight against illiteracy, endemic sickness, infant mortality or malnutrition seems to be a far greater priority. Arising from this contextually paradoxical environment, the main question dealt with in this study focuses on the reason why developing countries have decided to introduce international accounting standards in the public sector. This chapter answers the question of why developing countries apply the international benchmark, by studying the decisive factors which have motivated the Malagasy government to apply the accrual accounting model to comply with the international accounting framework. This case study is interesting for two reasons:

i. the Malagasy government officially promoted the new plan of accounting;
ii. the implementation of the new plan failed because of the lack of involvement of the related parties (Rakoto, 2007).

The first section of this study deals with the stimuli required for adopting international accounting standards within developing nations. The second section focuses on the Malagasy public sector case study.

1 The incentive for the adoption of international accounting standards

Firstly, the will to improve public management has stimulated many countries to adopt the international accounting framework. It is assumed that if international accounting standards are used, better financial information will be available. Secondly, the international recognition of these standards by developed countries legitimises the change to accrual accounting.

1.1   The search for better financial information

The lack of relevant financial information and the unsuitability of financial control mechanisms hinder the action of a state: the costs of goods and public services are underestimated, and corruption is not always controlled. Consequently, governments are called on to install rigorous procedures aiming to promote managerial accountability and the transparency of public finance management. This is the reason why several OECD countries, in particular those in the Anglo-American zone of influence, have reformed their public management and have adopted management rules similar to those of the private sector. However, this evolution cannot succeed without improving the accounting system and without implementing appropriate procedures. Many states have also become aware of the necessity of adopting an accrual-based accounting model – which is more adapted to these new stakes – replacing the cash-based accounting system.

With cash-based accounting, the role assigned to public accounting was to measure the performance of the administrators on the basis of budget conformity. The objective of the controls was to know if the allocated resources were used in accordance with arrangements foreseen in the budget. With accrual accounting, the objective is to weigh the invested resources (and not only those disbursed) against the results. This method should allow management efficiency to be measured above and beyond its budgetary conformity.

This is how, from the 1990s onwards, accrual-based accounting spread progressively to the public sector. Several countries, including developing countries, have opted for this accounting model in order to modernise their public management. They have largely based the reform on the international accounting standards elaborated by the IPSASB and backed up by the main international financial institutions such as the International Monetary Fund, the World Bank, the Asian Development Bank or the European Union. This international public sector accounting framework is itself inspired by that drawn up by the IASB for commercial entities.

Madagascar has also undertaken a reform of its public management. Since 2000, the Malagasy government has been carrying out a complete revision of its public sector accounting in order to integrate the international accounting standards as drawn up by the IPSASB. This reform has been carried out in two stages:

i. adoption of the Public Sector Chart of Accounts 2000 (PSCOA, 2000), which recommends revised cash-based accounting for public entities;

ii. adoption of the Public Sector Chart of Accounts 2006 (PSCOA, 2006), which introduces accrual-based accounting for public entities, with the international accounting standards laid out by the IASB and the IPSASB.

Better financial information and an improvement in the management of public resources are expected to result from this reform. Nevertheless, the reform highlights the myth of the comparatively better management of the private sector, which becomes a byword of quality and an inescapable reference point whenever deficiencies in public management are noted. It seems necessary, therefore, to enquire into the existence of other factors that would explain the adoption of the accrual accounting basis and international accounting standards.

1.2　The search for institutional legitimacy

According to the neo-institutional theory, the environment, as a social construct, dictates the behaviour of organisations and their members. Indeed, institutions are composed of expertise, cultures, structures and routines that formalise, standardise and legitimise the models of behaviours of the members of the organisations (Glynn and Murphy, 1996; Lande, 2006; Scott, 1995). Thus, the more practices are externalised, the more well known they become, and the easier they are accepted by other members or other organisations. In this respect, the neo-institutional theory can be activated to explain the adoption of international accounting standards within the public sector. The choice of a given accounting system finds its legitimacy through the institutional values that dictate and allow the actions of various stakeholders:

- users of the governments' financial information;
- producers of information, such as administrators;
- recipients of the information, such as political leaders, legislative bodies and the public in general.

Social behaviour can be analysed through the interactions existing between the members of an organisation and their environment. They act as a signpost outside which dealings are not legitimate and are considered irrational. Thus, according to neo-institutional theory:

- at the individual stage, behaviour is legitimised by conformity to values, beliefs, incentives or expertise;
- at the organisational stage, behaviour is guided by mutually shared values or policies;
- at the environmental stage, behaviour obeys external pressures, such as the respect for regulations or conformity to standards dictated by professionals.

Nevertheless, behaviour, whatever the level of legitimisation, satisfies three forms of isomorphism: normative isomorphism, mimetic isomorphism and coercive isomorphism.

Isomorphism is defined as a process of copying or adjusting to a collective rationality to legitimise actions (DiMaggio and Powell, 1983). In other words, it is a process in which organisations tend to adopt the same practices and the same structures in response to institutional pressure (Carpenter and Feroz, 2001). This explains how the technological, social and organisational innovations undertaken by successful entities are taken up by other entities.

1.2.1   Normative isomorphism

An organisation's practices are legitimised by their generalisation and backed up by intellectual authorities that formulate rules (Burns and Scapens, 2000; Carpenter and Feroz, 2001). These rules are adapted internally, becoming routine and shaping social life. The degree of conformity to these rules justifies the actions undertaken and offers a basis of comparison between the different existing structures (Scott, 1995).

In addition, the dissemination of practices, rules, norms and values is essential: the more widespread they become, the more legitimate they are. The most reassuring generalisation is the one observed at national or even international level (Meyer and Rowan, 1977). Moreover, academic institutions and professional organisations facilitate the recognition of the reforms (Carpenter and Feroz, 2001; DiMaggio and Powell, 1983).

The intellectual and professional legitimacy assigned to the organisations of accounting harmonisation, although questionable, may justify the adoption of accrual-based accounting. The underlying incentive is economy and market globalisation, rendering management disciplines and accounting practices dependent on international rules and prerogatives.

1.2.2   Mimetic isomorphism

Mimetic isomorphism relies on the legitimisation of practices or ideas by imitation: the practices of the organisations are endorsed by the success of other well-known and valued organisations (Bealing et al., 1996; Carpenter and Feroz, 2001). Imitation offers an answer to the uncertainty and the ambiguity attached to the realisation of a given activity (for example, the undertaking of reform).

In addition, a country's accounting system is affected by historical, political and socio-economic factors (Chan, 2006). Thus, the public sector accounting of formerly colonised countries is no exception to this phenomenon, as demonstrated by the case of Madagascar. Indeed, after independence, ex-colonies continue to use the practices instituted by the former colonising country, and remain influenced by them for a long time after independence (Merrouche and Devlin, 2005). The adoption of an accounting framework conceived by and for developed countries can, therefore, be considered by developing countries as legitimate.

1.2.3   Coercion

Coercive isomorphism is based on the legitimisation of practices by reason of pressures exerted by more powerful organisations on which the survival of the less powerful organisation depends. In this case, the reforms are carried out from a survival perspective. Coercion implies the existence of sanctions in accordance with which the connection to power is crucial (Pfeffer and Salancik, 2003). Non-profit organisations, such as associations, are the most vulnerable. Due to the insufficiency of financial resources, they are obliged to conform to the rules of their backers (Galaskiewicz and Bielefeld, 1994). Developing countries are also subject to the pressures of international investors. The standards decreed by the latter apply to various fields of public administration: control, information systems and the budgetary process. The objective underlying their acts is the promotion of the transparency of management and the accountability of the leaders at all levels of public administration (Matthew, 2003). For Madagascar, financial dependency on investors certainly influences the decisions of political leaders, in particular the incentives to adopt accrual-based accounting.

2   The adoption of accrual-based accounting by the Malagasy government

The research methodology is presented in the first section. The various influences that led the Malagasy government to adopt accrual-based accounting are then analysed in the second section.

2.1   Research methodology

Several methods of compilation of data have been used in the setting-up of this study: the compilation of opinions, documentary analysis and the multi-angulation of data (Hlady Rispal, 2002; Wacheux, 1996). This study is based on interviews, carried out at the end of 2005 and the beginning of 2006 with representatives of the central government institutions involved in Malagasy public sector accounting. These were the Ministry of Finance and the Budget, the Ministry of Decentralisation, the Ministry of the Interior, the Superior Accounting Council and the World Bank. These formal and informal semi-guided interviews were carried out with the ministers, the general secretaries, the managers within both the ministries and the Superior Accounting Council. The results were then compared with political speeches, with ministries' and the World Bank's financial reports, and with opinions given by representatives of the communes, in order to find response elements that would explain the incentives of the reform in spite of the existing constraints. The data obtained from the interviews was validated by comparing it with that from the documentary analysis, the political speeches or other opinions.

2.2   The Malagasy case study

The study of the motivation of the Malagasy government to adopt accrual-based accounting highlighted three major phases:

i. the influence of the accounting professional body, initiators of this reform;
ii. the conception and the development of the framework where institutional ties between Madagascar and France played a major role and largely influenced the normative content;
iii. the promotion of the framework that underlined the influences exerted by the international investors.

During these three phases, different actors – promoters or catalysts of the reform – influenced Madagascar's choice of adopting accrual-based accounting.

2.2.1   *Phase 1: the decision to adopt the accrual-based accounting model and the role of the chartered accountants*

The conferences organised by French Chartered Accountants were decisive factors in the Malagasy public sector accounting reforms. From 2000 onwards, the conference proceedings refer constantly to the works of the IASB, by pointing out the necessity of applying the international accounting standards in answer to the globalisation of the economy. These would reduce the gaps between countries and would contribute to the transparency of financial information. These conferences have struck a chord with the president of the Superior Accounting Council and the Association of Malagasy Chartered Accountants:

> Every time that they come back from a conference of chartered accountants organised in France, the President of the Superior Accounting Council, himself a chartered accountant, and the President of the Association of Chartered Accountants, never fail to report and to make us aware of the necessity of reforming our accounting system. The conference reports refer to the necessity of harmonising accounting practices on an international scale. I am sure that it is what persuaded them.
>
> Interview with the manager of the observation unit
> of the Superior Accounting Council, 2004.

A speech given by the president of the Superior Accounting Council confirms this position:

> The Chart of Accounts 2005 (COA 2005) is the result of an evolution process of accounting in the world and in Madagascar [...]. The Chart of Accounts 2005 is the outcome of a period of internal group work lasting over three years. The participants were constantly supervised by members of the Association of Chartered Accountants and occasionally by French specialists of international accounting standards.
>
> Speech of the president of the Superior
> Accounting Council, 2004.

These remarks underline the important implication of the chartered accountants in the development of the new chart of accounts. The manager of the observation unit of the Superior Accounting Council emphasises the influence of the conferences of chartered accountants organised in France on the actions of reform in Madagascar. In the same way, the views held by the president of the Superior Accounting Council highlight the crucial involvement of professional accountants in the technical development of the new Malagasy chart of accounts.

At the same time, the progressive generalisation of international accounting standards had a strong influence on the reform of the different Malagasy charts of accounts.

> The new chart of accounts must conform to the standards decreed by the IASB of which the Superior Accounting Council has been a member since 1999. The national harmonisation body is thus obliged to find solutions that are not contrary to international standards, while at the same time answering the specificities of the situation that prevails in the country. It is not possible to stand aside from the important world currents and especially to ignore the IAS/IFRS standards.
>
> Speech of the minister of the Economy,
> Finance and the Budget, 2003.

> Madagascar must imperatively adopt an accounting system that is completely coherent with international standards: namely with the standards set out by the IASB.
>
> Speech by Rahabison, chartered accountant and member
> of the Association of Chartered Accountants and
> the Superior Accounting Council, 2003.

The awareness of the necessity to standardise the accounting practices persuaded the Superior Accounting Council, an institution presided over by a chartered accountant belonging to the Malagasy Association of Chartered

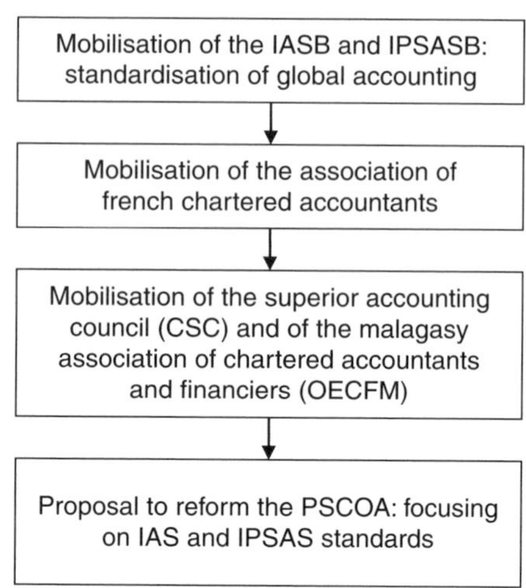

Figure 11.1   Motives for reform from the point of view of the Superior Accounting Council and of the Malagasy Association of Chartered Accountants and Financiers

Accountants and Financiers, to reform the public sector accounting framework. The Superior Accounting Council thus drew up a new public sector chart of accounts based on the standards promoted by the IPSASB and the IASB.

Accounting harmonisation on a global scale has motivated the adoption of accrual-based accounting in Madagascar. Figure 11.1 is an organisational flow chart of the professional influences directing the reform of Malagasy public accounting.

2.2.2   *Phase 2: drawing up the normative framework and the role of France*

On the eve of the independence of Madagascar, technical support was provided by France. The objective was to allow the new Malagasy civil servants to acquire the necessary expertise to manage the country. To this effect, the practices and the systems of the former coloniser were taken literally, and applied to Malagasy administration. So, for example, the Malagasy organic budget law is inspired by the French Loi Organique des Lois de Finance (LOLF) (Ralamboson and Randrianasolo, 2005). In the same way, accounting standards and the Malagasy chart of accounts are almost identical adaptations of the French documents:

The Malagasy organic budget law is inspired by the French experience. We did a lot of training moreover, and we visited France, to prepare the reform of Malagasy public finance.

Interview with a consultant of the
Ministry of Finance, 2005.

The structure of the development of Malagasy accounting standards is comparable to that of France. The preparatory work in the drawing up of the present draft of the new Chart of Accounts involved the steering committee, ten sector groups and a French international consultant.

> Speech of the president of the Superior
> Accounting Council, 2003.

Our new Chart of Accounts, at the root of all sector account charts, is a revival of the new French Chart of Accounts. You can verify that besides at the level of certain parts of the chart: the chart of accounts is a literal copy of the French Chart. For further proof, the experts who helped us in the conception of the 2005 Chart of Accounts were French.

> Interview with the leader of the work group for the
> 2006 public sector Chart of Accounts, Superior
> Accounting Council, 2004.

The French experience, therefore, formed the basis for drawing up the new Chart of Accounts. This is also confirmed in the public sector Chart of Accounts 2006:

The net expenses statement, the state tax and fines statement and the statement of determination of the balance of transactions within the last financial period were inspired by models of French financial states, proposed by no other existing international frameworks.

> 2006 public transactions Chart of Accounts,
> presentation notes.

This phenomenon of replication appeared to be a decisive factor in the adoption of the accrual-based accounting system in the Malagasy public sector, since the texts and standards come from the basis of the French experience (through the LOLF), from private entities' charts of accounts: the Plan Comptable General of Madascar (PCG 2005), and from the French public sector Chart of Accounts.

2.2.3 Phase 3: the adoption of accrual-based accounting and the role of the World Bank

According to the perception of those questioned, the role of the World Bank in the adoption of accrual-based accounting does not appear to be one of pressure. This idea is validated by senior civil servants and managers of the Malagasy state, and the World Bank itself.

Why believe that the World Bank always brings pressure to bear on developing countries? If leaders want to initiate reforms, they do as they please.

> We are there only to back financially the initiatives that we judge relevant for the development of the country.
>
> Interview with a World Bank manager, 2005.

> If the private sector Chart of Accounts is modified, I think that the public sector Chart of Accounts also deserves to be modernised. There is no pressure exerted by the backers for this reform initiative.
>
> Interview with the chief of staff of the Ministry of the Economy, Finance and the Budget, 2005.

> The reforms of public finances and public sector accounting had no pressure from our investors. The initiative comes from the government with the help of experts: the Superior Accounting Council and the Malagasy Association of Chartered Accountants. Having seen its inspirational text modified, the COA 2005, it is logical that the public sector Chart of Accounts must very quickly change. However this decision has been backed by the investors, who were quick to provide us [with] the financial help necessary for our choice of accounting reform.
>
> Interview with the minister of the Economy, Finance and the Budget, 2004.

For the respondents in agreement with Phase 1, the fact that the Superior Accounting Council and the Chartered Accountants Association are behind the idea of reforming Malagasy public sector accounting is not seen as the consequence of pressure from the backers.

However, while the different actors questioned do agree on the absence of influence of the World Bank in the choice of adopting accrual-based accounting in the Malagasy public sector, they claim at the same time that globalisation and the necessity for transparency in public management are the events causing this accounting reform.

The arguments put forward by the respondents correspond to those of IASB, which says that the necessity of reducing gaps, of possessing more detailed, relevant and transparent financial information, and of being able to give the leaders a sense of responsibility are the main incentives for the reform.

> The LOLF (organic budget law) has been adopted because the former management framework was judged too rigid and of such a nature as not to make leaders accountable enough. The main objective of the administrators was to spend credit lines because of the risk that they would not be renewed the following year. The government must promote the efficiency of public spending on behalf of general interest. The LOLF, through the budget programme, facilitates the rational allocation of scarce public resources to the different governmental actions considered to have priority [...] The contribution of the LOLF is the establishment

of a legal framework to promote efficiency, the transparency of public management, performance culture and result-oriented budget practice.

> Manager from the Ministry of Finance and
> the Budget, 2005.

This interlocutor underlines the necessity of establishing a more accountable management mechanism and rational management of public finance through the LOLF and the accrual-based accounting model. However, some contradictions have been raised in different texts and speeches.

> The ministries still have problems in appropriating the principles of the LOLF, and they are only at the starting point of the reform: the development of the budget programme. I am persuaded that it is even more difficult for the communes, which are almost completely lacking in the human and financial means for operating such a reform. Besides, it is not necessarily so that, because that particular reform worked for the French government, it will automatically succeed for the Malagasy government.

> Interview with a consultant of the Ministry of the
> Economy, Finance and the Budget, 2005.

These contradictions put forward by the same representatives show that there is incoherence between the apparent incentives and the discerned reality; the representatives seem unconvinced by the reforms that they have themselves supported. Other undeclared decisive factors affecting the decision to adopt the LOLF and the accrual-based accounting model at the level of the Malagasy public sector could well exist. The analysis of other speeches helps to understand such contradictions.

> Financial information should present a triple character from now on. It should be more economic and oriented toward the measure of performance, more transparent and more detailed.

> Speech of the minister of Finance
> and the Budget, 2003.

> The restoration of the state under the rule of law and of well-governed society appears among the strategic axes of the Document of Strategy for the Reduction of Poverty (DSRP). This axis regroups a set of actions which relate to improvement, to modernisation and to the reinforcement of an institutional framework of good governance. It will allow the state to assume its roles of facilitator and leader of the economy efficiently and transparently.

> Document of strategy for the reduction
> of poverty, 2005.

The improvement of governance appears among the priorities of Structural Adjustment Credit 3.

World Bank, Structural Adjustment
Credits (SAC), 2004–06.

The national programme of good governance and the reform of the financial system are national programmes financed by investors.

General State Policy, 2005 and 2006.

To continue the efforts expended in the framework of the Programmes for the Reduction of Poverty (Poverty Reduction Support Credits – PRSC) 1 and 2, the World Bank allocates a credit, by means of PRSC3, to support the Ministry of the Economy, Finance and the Budget in continuing the reform of public finance management.

World Bank, Report Number AB2298, 2006.

The structure of public finances is characterised by extremely poor revenue and a strong dependence on external financial aid.

Malagasy government, Document de Stratégie
Pays (DSP) 2008–2013 (2007).

Certainly, these texts have been drawn up in different contexts: Chart of Accounts reform, reduction of poverty and so on. Nevertheless, they are based on management transparency, good governance and financial dependence in relation to external financial aid.

The will to increase management transparency has motivated the policymakers to support the reform of public accounting. In addition, this reform complies with the priorities of the World Bank. The support provided by the leaders conveys a type of *political consulting*, of which the objective is to improve the government's image in the eyes of the World Bank. Finally, it is necessary to note that various measures, such as the conception of training modules in public sector Charts of Accounts or training for Inland Revenue personnel, have benefited from World Bank financial aid.

3 Conclusion

It is a surprising paradox that the international accounting framework is considered legitimate by developing countries such as Madagascar, even if it was designed, taking into account the constraints of developed countries, on the private model. The setting-up of the accrual-based accounting model thus makes it necessary to monitor the operations recorded by installing an information system, although, most often, software and computing material are found wanting in the majority of developing countries. In the same way, the introduction of accrual-based accounting requires training the accountants and other administrative and financial managers beforehand. This often represents a cost for these countries that is hard to bear. However, in the Malagasy case, these constraints apparently have no influence on the content of accounting reform.

The presumed and real benefits of the introduction of the accrual-based accounting model seem sufficient in justifying this reform. The legitimacy of this framework is reinforced by the number and importance of the instigators who are, either directly or indirectly, backing it:

- the Superior Accounting Council and the Malagasy Association of Chartered Accountants and Financiers: they *triggered* the reform, have actively taken part in the drawing up of the accounting framework and have even succeeded in mobilising other actors such as the prime minister, the finance minister, not to mention the president of the republic, in launching the reform;
- the implicit participation of the World Bank: this reform must allow the World Bank to better guarantee the integrity of accounting management by an improved monitoring of commitments and heritage;
- the measures of cooperation from France, a relic of the colonial past, which reinforce the phenomenon of imitation.

As the following diagram shows, the three forms of isomorphism are present in adopting the international accounting standards and, in this case, accrual-based accounting. Dependence on resources and normative isomorphism acted simultaneously as a motive to legitimise the actions of politicians, the Superior Accounting Council and the Malagasy Association of Chartered Accountants. In addition, mimetic isomorphism has strongly influenced the technical design of the charts of accounts (Figure 11.2).

The necessity of adopting the accrual-based accounting model has been actively backed by the Superior Accounting Council and the Malagasy Association of Chartered Accountants and Financiers; and, in an implicit manner, by the investors. The latter, however, do not possess sufficient power to launch the reform process. In a country like Madagascar, where the body of accounting harmonisation is under state authority, all acts of reform require political validation and backing. Political leaders are, therefore, becoming pivotal actors. Thus, in 2003, the reform proposals were presented and approved by the Cabinet. Simultaneously, the organic budget law (LOLF) was passed without difficulty by the parliamentarians (and without real incentive) because most of them have little interest in accounting: from the moment a bill is carried by the government and the presidential majority, the passing of the law goes without saying.

Malagasy accounting reforms are closer to being a game of power, fuelled by political interests, than to being a rational process of decision-taking primarily in order to improve public management. Indeed, even though this incentive is present, it tends to become blurred as the reform process goes

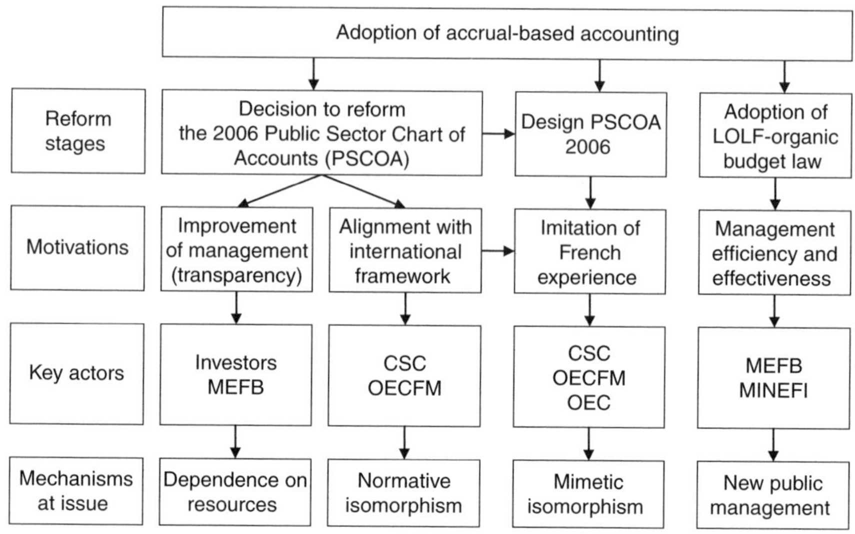

Figure 11.2   Reform of Madagascar's accounting system and institutional pressures

Key: CSC: Conseil Supérieur de la Comptabilité (Malgache); MEFB: Ministère de l'Économie, des Finances et du Budget (Malgache); MINEFI: Ministère de l'Économie et des Finances (France); OEC: Ordre des Experts-Comptables (France); OECFM: Ordre des Experts-Comptables malgache.

on. This then becomes an accounting reform that has lost sight of its initial objective. This could largely explain the paradox whereby, on the one hand, the adopted accounting reforms are not really carried out or, at the very least, are carried out in a very basic manner, and on the other hand, why these reforms are analysed as administrative and statutory constraints, and not as opportunities for improving public management.

Notes

1. The introduction of international accounting standards in newly created countries (the Balkan countries or republics created after the fall of the former Soviet Union) can be explained by the lack of competence and the financial means to set up their own accounting system. Nevertheless, in adopting accrual-based accounting, these countries often benefit from European Union aid. Some of them prefer to adopt a robust cash-based accounting system in view of the difficulties encountered (IPSASB standards also exist for this). Conversely, in developing countries, there are no real difficulties to be found in adopting international standards.
2. The accrual-based accounting system has three objectives: recognition of the occurrence of events (while with the cash-based method, the operations are recorded on the basis of receipts and disbursements), the connection between the different components of the cost to the revenues, and the separation of assets from liabilities.

References

Bealing, J., Fogarty, T. and Dirsmith, M.W. (1996) Early regulator actions by the SEC: an institutional theory perspective on the dramaturgy of political exchanges. *Accounting Organization and Society*, 21 (4): 317–38.

Burns, J. and Scapens, R.W. (2000) Conceptualizing management accounting change: an institutional framework. *Management Accounting Research*, 11 (1): 3–25.

Carpenter, V. and Feroz, E. (2001) Institutional theory and accounting rule choice: an analysis of four US state governments' decisions to adopt generally-accepted accounting principles. *Accounting Organization and Society*, 26: 566–96.

Chan, J.L. (2006) 'Government accounting reform in developing countries', in E. Lande and J.C. Scheid (eds) *Accounting Reform in the Public Sector: Mimicry, Fad or Necessity*. Paris: Edition ECM.

DiMaggio, P.J. and Powell, W. (1983) The iron cage revisited: institutional isomorphism and collective rationality in organizational fields. *American Sociological Review*, 48 (2): 147–60.

Galaskiewicz, J. and Bielefeld, W. (1994) *Non Profit Organization in an Age of Uncertainty: A Study of Organizational Change*. Hawthorne, New York: Aldine De Gruyter.

Glynn, J.J. and Murphy, M.P. (1996) Public management: failing accountabilities and failing performance review. *International Journal of Public Sector Management*, 9 (5): 125–37.

Hepworth, N. (2003) Preconditions for successful implementation of accrual accounting in central government. *Public Money & Management*, January: 37–43.

Hlady Rispal, M. (2002) *La Méthode Des Cas – Application À La Recherche En Gestion* (Perspectives Marketing Collection). Brussels: De Boeck.

Lande, E. (2006) 'Accrual accounting in the public sector: between institutional competitiveness and search for legitimacy' in E. Lande and J.C. Scheid (eds) *Accounting Reform in the Public Sector: Mimicry, Fad or Necessity*. Paris: Edition ECM.

Lande, E. and Rocher, S. (2008) 'Apports et difficultés de l'introduction de la comptabilité d'exercice dans le secteur public'. Séminaire européen dans le cadre de la présidence française de l'Union Européenne, *L'importance des systèmes de contrôle dans la réussite des réformes comptables des Etats européens*. Ministère de l'Economie, des Finances et de l'Industrie, September.

Loi Organique des Lois de Finance (LOLF) Number 2004-007, 26 July 2004 sur les lois de finances malgaches.

Matthew, O. (2003) Deploying financial management systems in developing nations. *The International Consortium on Governmental Financial Management, Public Fund Digest*, 3 (2): 8–20.

Merrouche, C. and Devlin, P. (2005) *Local Government Accounting in Algeria: Anarchy or Modernity*. Paper given at the Comparative International Governmental Accounting Research Conference, Poitiers (May).

Meyer, J.W. and Rowan, B. (1977) Institutionalized organisations: formal structure as myth and ceremony. *American journal of Sociology*, 80: 340–63.

Pfeffer, J. and Salancik, G.R. (2003) *The External Control of Organizations: A Resources Dependency Perspective*. California: Stanford University Press.

Ralamboson, P. and Randrianasolo, A. (2005) 'Budget de programmes de Madagascar'. Actes du Colloques Institut National des Sciences Comptables et de l'Administration des Entreprises (INSCAE) *Les sciences de gestion au cœur du développement*, Antananarivo.

Rakoto, H. (2007) *Innovation Comptable au sein des communes : le cas de l'adoption de la comptabilité d'exercice*. Unpublished doctoral thesis, Sciences de Gestion, Université de Poitiers.

Hlady Rispal, M. (2002) *La méthode des cas, application à la recherche en gestion*. Brussels: De Boeck University.

Scott, W. (1995) *Institutions and Organizations*. Thousand Oaks, CA: Sage Publications.

Wacheux, F. (1996) *Méthodes qualitatives et Recherche en Gestion*. Paris: Economica.

Further reading

Macmillan, G. (2003) Improving government financial reporting: the window to good governance, *The Governance Brief*. Manila: Asian Development Bank.

12
Interests and Limits of Globalisation as an Investment-Creating Process

Sophie Nivoix and Dominique Pépin

National financial systems of both developed and developing countries have experienced a serious wave of deregulation during the last thirty years. This was implemented by the countries' governments, in order to promote investment, growth and employment in stabilised macroeconomic conditions (Aglietta et al., 1990). Barriers to international mobility of capital have, therefore, been erased in many countries, something which leads to financial markets being far better integrated today than they were thirty years ago.

From the point of view of the countries that are concerned, financial globalisation means the integration of their financial systems into the international capital market (Das, 2006). In order to reach this situation, the governments of these countries have to allow foreigners to invest in their economies: this is financial liberalisation (Chari and Henry, 2004). For the countries that receive capital flow, globalisation provides major advantages that justify the financial deregulation process (Obstfeld, 1994). The access to international markets makes it possible for them to borrow in order to smooth consumption in case of negative shocks; it also enables borrowers to build up new investment projects that would not have found any financing otherwise, and therefore it sustains growth.

From a more general point of view, financial globalisation is defined as the liberalisation of financial assets transactions (Stulz, 2005). This liberalisation modifies the nature of systematic or non-diversifiable market risk, as it no longer comes from the local but from the international market. This is what motivates investors to globalise, as they look for new investment and risk diversification opportunities (Solnik, 1974). Wealth gains enabled by better risk sharing are another inducement for governments to enter the financial globalisation process.

Have all these governments succeeded? Have investment, growth and macroeconomic stability been favoured inside integrated financial markets? To these questions, which go beyond the scope of this chapter, we will nevertheless attempt to provide a partial answer that is specifically related to the issue of firms' investment. Just reviewing the following questions today is already an ambitious goal. Has financial globalisation, which was called 'the compulsory adventure' by Aglietta et al. (1990), helped firms' investments? What effect has financial market integration had on the investments of firms? And how has financial globalisation influenced share value and the cost of capital among firms?

The first section of this article sheds light on the concepts we use and describes the historical evolution of the financial globalisation process. The second section contradicts the first, while showing that the answer, whatever it may be, is not a unanimous one from either the theoretical and empirical points of view, it thus insists on the paradoxical aspects of financial globalisation. And finally, if it is possible to contemplate financial globalisation that really sustains firms' investments, it can be conceived of only under certain conditions that will be discussed in the conclusion.

1 Globalisation as a help for firms' investment: theoretical analysis and empirical evidence

1.1 Financing constraints and financial globalisation

Financial globalisation has brought about huge changes in the structure of domestic and international financial markets, and has opened new investment perspectives for fund providers. Before detailing more formal analyses, which are usually built within neoclassical models whose hypotheses have sometimes been criticised, it is necessary to present pro-globalisation arguments that go beyond the scope of the dominant economic point of view. A favourable theoretical aspect of financial globalisation that is recognised by many economists is the provision of better efficiency in resource allocation, to the benefit of firms looking for financing sources. By definition, globalisation creates a larger market and enables some asks and bids to meet each other, as they could not have done otherwise.

To this argument of higher efficiency, we have to add a quantitative one that is probably the most obvious and the one that surely motivated governments to liberalise their markets. Financial globalisation in all its forms creates an inflow of funds from abroad. An economy open to foreign investors receives more funds that are added to domestic ones. However, the availability of financing sources is a key element of every investment decision. In this way, Evans and Jovanovic (1989) showed that wealth constraints can theoretically negatively affect entrepreneurship. The effect on investment demand of the credit bid increase is a now a well-known argument. Flows of funds from abroad enable sustained growth while increasing the amount of available funds to finance domestic projects. Wasn't it Schumpeter's view (1935) that growth is possible only if 'new productive combinations' are financed? According to Schumpeter, previous savings would not be able to finance these new combinations. As he was reasoning within a closed economy, Schumpeter saw monetary creation as the only source of financing these investment projects. However, within an open economy the use of foreign investors is another way of finding new financing sources.

Alongside purely financial flows that sustain domestic investment, we have to add direct investments, which also help to enlarge in both quality and quantity the production capacities of the receiving economies. It is also interesting to point out the role of multinational firms, which can appear to be major agents of globalisation.

When markets are imperfect, liberalisation of stock markets can have other effects. The financing constraints (Hubbard, 1998) make inside financing (equity and self-financing) more costly than outside financing (loans) and, as a consequence, make investment more sensitive to firms' funds. The liberalisation of asset markets directly reduces these financing constraints as more foreign funds become available. Moreover, foreign investors willingly invest their funds outside their own economies only under certain conditions, which sometimes lead to better management rules and to better governance of the company, and which indirectly reduces the cost of inside and outside investment. Thus, the cost of capital can decrease thanks to the reduction of financing constraints (Bekaert et al., 2005).

Not only can international financial integration increase the total amount of available capital for an economy, it also improves capital intermediation. The penetration of foreign banks into the domestic market is another argument favouring financial globalisation. Levine (1996) and Caprio and Honohan (1999) argue that the entry of foreign banks into the domestic market creates advantages for numerous reasons. Firstly, the entry of foreign banks is an obvious way of finding new access to the international capital market. Secondly, it increases the banking services and raises the competition level between banks. Thirdly, it sometimes enables new banking techniques and more sophisticated technologies to be introduced. All this contributes to the reduction of many kinds of costs (such as acquisition and information analysis costs), and to improvements in the quality and availability of financial services of the domestic market. Fourthly, the entry of foreign banks can stimulate the development of banking supervision, more specifically when foreign banks are supervised in their home countries and domestic banks less so. Fifthly, foreign banks are said to ensure greater financial stability (through a decrease of short-term capital volatility). Indeed, in case of financial turmoil in the domestic economy, instead of transferring their funds abroad, savers may prefer to transfer them to foreign institutions that are established in the country and are perceived as less risky than domestic banks. Finally, we can add that the improvement of financial intermediation and the borrowing facility of larger firms (making domestic funds more available for other firms) improve financing conditions even for small firms unable to borrow on international markets, despite their being more accessible nowadays, thanks to financial liberalisation (Alfaro and Charlton, 2007). Foreign banks particularly represent a godsend and play a major role in the creation of new firms for countries whose stock markets are underdeveloped, where shareholders are poorly protected, and where investment financing of small firms is essentially based on loans, and more precisely on bank credit (Gianetti and Ongena, 2005).

Considering development theory, it has often been said that financial globalisation has made it possible to support the growth of less developed countries. This is because rich countries could invest their funds in economies with little savings but many investment opportunities. Indeed, it should be remembered that financial integration enables assets to go from economies where they are abundant (and where the expected return is low) to economies where they are rare (and where the expected return is high) (Obstfeld and Rogoff, 1995). Moreover, in countries with an underdeveloped financial system, financial integration may increase the finance bid and thereby develop the financial system of these countries, consequently backing growth and the investment of firms. Indeed, the existence of a large and solid financial system appears a necessary condition for development, as has been shown by many authors in the line of Schumpeter (for example, King and Levine, 1993a, 1993b).

1.2 Theoretical consequences of globalisation on the cost of capital and stock prices

Although the terms 'globalisation' and 'financial integration' are often considered as synonymous, it is possible to draw a distinction between them and offer a more accurate definition. Capital markets are known as 'integrated' when assets seen as equally risky are also perceived as providing the same expected return, whatever the national market in which they are issued (Stulz, 1981). This is a technical definition, which simply assumes that if investors use the minimum of common sense, the liberalisation of financial exchanges will lead to a rational standardisation of financial asset pricing processes. In a world where agents can freely buy and sell financial assets, we can rightfully assume that assets similar in terms of risk should likewise be similar as far as return is concerned. If not, arbitragers could trade and benefit from these abnormal returns. Thus integration appears as a consequence of globalisation (which justifies the possible confusion of the concepts, as one state implies the other).

The stability of the norms of valuation coming from globalisation is thus a direct argument in its favour. When a firm has to finance an investment, it has the choice between self-financing and external financing. The latter essentially consists of equity or loan contribution. If markets are economically and financially integrated, financing from the same country as the firm is equivalent to financing from another country. So, as we mention in Section 2.1, except for the transaction costs, if the risk level of an investment is the same wherever the shareholder or the lender comes from, its expected return will be the same. This means that the weighted average cost of capital[1] of the firm should stay the same, and that the firm's capacity to create value through annual economic value added (EVA),[2] spread between the firm's return on investment (ROI) and the cost of its resources, and MVA (market value added: market expectations of future EVAs that can be estimated from the spread between market value and book value of equity) remains stable. Such stability can favour investments because it reduces uncertainty related to return.

The financial theory of the valuation of financial assets represents a well-developed research field. It is, therefore, interesting to put forward again the opinion of theoreticians about globalisation, in particular concerning the effects of financial liberalisation on the cost of capital and stock prices. This question is, indeed, directly related to the problem of the investment of firms, considering that when the cost of capital decreases, investment increases, as firms maximise profit and lower marginal productivity of capital at its new weakest cost (which, in relation to a declining productivity, is possible only through an increase in investment). This is, at least, what the neoclassical model of the firm predicts in a world of pure and perfect competition. Another justification, which is more pragmatic and leads to the same conclusion, is to notice that some negative net present value investment projects can, after a decline in the cost of capital, show a positive net present value. As these projects become profitable they are carried out and they strengthen the increase of the investments of firms. It is not surprising, therefore, to read in academic studies that authors analyse the relation between globalisation and the cost of capital, or between globalisation and stock prices (because of the inverted relation between cost of capital and stock value).

So, let us consider which arguments have been presented to justify the decline of the cost of capital as a consequence of financial liberalisation. First of all, as we have already mentioned, financial integration makes international sharing of risk easier, thanks to international portfolio diversification. As a consequence, investors require a smaller risk premium, which induces a decline in capital cost. Thus, global diversification favours the investment of firms and growth (Obstfeld, 1994).

Arguments other than that of international portfolio diversification have been presented to suggest that the risk premium of stocks should decrease thanks to financial globalisation. Indeed, the increase of net capital inflows raises stock market liquidity (Levine and Servos, 1998), which enables risk premium to be reduced (Ahimud and Mendelson, 1986).

According to these arguments, the cost of capital declines when a country liberalises its stock market. We have to recall, though, that there are two elements in the cost of capital for a country: the risk-free rate and the risk premium. In the case of a developing country, theory suggests that both should decrease thanks to liberalisation (Stulz, 1999). The risk premium declines, as we have explained before, and the risk-free rate is reduced because the international rate is theoretically lower than the rate of a less-developed country. Concerning more developed countries, the risk premium of each country is also weakening, and the risk-free rate may also decrease if, at first, the domestic rate is higher than the rate of the international market.

An argument that is closely related to the decline of risk premium is the rise in demand for the domestic financial asset when the domestic market opens to foreign investors. As the market opens to foreign investors (or when this opening is anticipated), domestic asset prices rise because of the increase in demand from foreign investors. From this viewpoint, market liberalisation has an unequivocal way of increasing the effect on asset prices. In this perspective, Stapleton and Subrahmanyam (1977), Errunza and Losq (1985) and Alexander et al. (1987) have shown the harmful aspect of the segmentation of capital markets. Indeed, the general effect of market segmentation is to decrease the prices of assets that are accessible only to domestic investors. The effects of market segmentation explain the motivation of firms willing to enter the corpus of investment opportunities of the most numerous investors possible, in order to enlarge the demand they can face. The direct opening of the domestic market is not the only way to capture some of the foreign demand. Other policies enable firms to reduce the effects of segmentation: direct investments abroad, mergers with foreign firms (as analysed by Adler and Dumas, 1975) and, finally, dual listings of firm's stocks in foreign stock markets.[3]

During the first stages of financial liberalisation, all domestic firms are usually not accessible to foreign investors, and an important distinction has to be drawn between domestic assets that can be acquired by foreign investors (corresponding to firms in which foreigners can invest) and assets that can't (firms in which foreigners can't invest). Indeed, the history of financial liberalisation shows that domestic markets always open up progressively, as some fractions become accessible to investors while others remain closed, at least in the first step of liberalisation (a step that can last for a short or long time). In the model of Alexander et al. (1987), who value dual-listed stock prices, some assets are listed on a foreign market (besides a domestic listing, of course) while no foreign stock is listed in the domestic market. The other domestic stocks are listed on the domestic market. Such a situation has often characterised the first step of financial integration of many markets, notably with the appearance since the 1960s of what have been called 'country funds'. These were foreign stock portfolios that were globally listed on the American market while their stocks were also individually listed on their domestic markets. Alexander et al. (1987) showed that under certain conditions[4] the expected return of a stock is lower (or put another way, the stock price is higher) when a stock is dual listed only when the markets are fully segmented (then the stock is listed on its domestic market only). This, of course, corresponds to the advantage sought by the firm that wants to reduce its capital cost.

To finish, let us mention a less obvious way in which financial globalisation can benefit certain firms. After liberalisation, some stock prices can increase, not because of a better share of risks but because of pressures on prices after the integration of stocks in a market index, which raises the demand for them and thus their price (Harris and Guerel, 1986; Shleifer, 1986).

1.3   The effect of financial globalisation on the country-risk

Investments flows move between countries under several kinds of constraints. They are notably of an institutional, legal, economic and fiscal nature, and exist in spite of partial harmonisations prevailing in some areas like the European Union. The characteristics specific to a country create monetary and financial conditions that influence the forming and allocation of resources in firms. We can explain the various characteristics of the risk related to a country, which is called 'country-risk'.

Firstly, the country-risk is primarily linked to the volatility of international transaction returns, but the consequences have to be defined with the globalisation of markets and the sophistication of asset management instruments since the 1990s. Thus, the development of hedging and arbitraging, thanks to complex theoretical models, has enabled investors to diversify their assets and then reduce a mostly specific type of risk.

Country-risk contains an economic dimension defined as real GDP or GNP volatility. Indeed, the macroeconomic situation of a country markedly determines the results of investments that are made there. A diversified economy that is ready for international competition, and that offers a wide range of services and products, is less volatile than an economy whose business activities are less diversified. And, of course, lower volatility favours more investments of firms towards or from the given country.

Secondly, financial risk expresses the ability of a country to comply with the repayment schedule of its debt. The repayment of the principal and interest of the debt is mostly based on the country's capacity to export in order to more than offset imports in the long run, as no country can live without imports. Therefore, the higher the economic risk, the higher the risk that exports will not be able to balance the import outflows, thus creating an increase in financial risk. It is the same for firms, where default risk reduces both external financing and the use of self-financing in order to invest.

Another dimension of country-risk is currency risk, which is measured with the currency rate volatility of a country. This risk has an influence on investment return when the investor is located in another country. Indeed, a currency rate variation can increase or reduce to nothing an investment return in the country where the investment is made. As firms need to reduce their currency risk as much as possible for the sake of their investment, anticipations and the optimisation of their risk-return couple, the economic areas sharing a common currency create a valuable advantage. Not only does the currency risk disappear between the area's countries, but it is lowered in regards to outside area currencies. This globally reduces costs related to currency risk hedging. As investment reduces one of these risk factors, it can bear the increase of another (economic risk, for example), which enables an easier world asset allocation.

Finally, political risk has no unanimous definition (Marois, 2000). At least two distinctions have already been suggested (Clark et al. 2001). The first one separates the global political risk concerning a firm owning subsidiaries in several countries and the specific political risk related to a particular investment in a given country. The second distinction separates macro-risk coming from measures or events to which investments are sensitive (industry strikes, legal constraints, nationalisations, wars etc.), and micro-risk concerning a particular firm in a particular country (and related to the firm's country, its industry and its history). For internationalised firms the effect of political risk can be seen in both operating risk increase and return decrease. Operating risk can be measured with operating result volatility (unexpected price increases on raw materials, costs of strikes, losses due to expropriations) and net income volatility (the same causes plus an unexpected variation of interest rates or fiscality). The decrease of return comes from the weakening of these two results because of excessive expenses compared with all the invested funds (equity or long-term financing). Can these risks lead to the renunciation of investment? The factors contributing to such a decision are briefly presented below.

During an investment decision the firm factors in the discount rate it applies to its expected cash flows, a factor related to country-risk. The higher this factor, the lower the Net Present Value (NPV) of the project, which can lead the firm to reject the project. Then if I_t represents investments occurring within n years and creating annual cash flows F_t, the discount rate is composed of an r factor without country-risk and an s factor representing this risk. Thus, we can write:

$$NPV = \sum_{t=0}^{n} \frac{(F_t - I_t)}{(1 + r + z)^t}$$

As for the estimation of s, which indicates the excess return required by investors because of the systematic, and thus non-diversifiable, country-risk, it can be given straightforwardly with a two-beta CAPM:

$$r + s = R_f + \beta_i \beta_c (R_s - R_f)$$

where R_f is the risk-free rate, R_s is the worldwide index return; β_i is the investment-return sensitivity to the economy return of the country where the investment has been made; β_c is the economy-return sensitivity of the country compared with the worldwide economy return; $\beta_i\beta_c$ thus evaluates the global economic and operating risk of the project.

As economic globalisation increases interdependence of national economies, it increases β_c value and reduces β_i value at the same time, because the purely national economic conditions have less influence on the result of investment. Thus, the global risk investment and its return requirement are higher during international economic turmoil, but lower during other periods because of the smoothing effect of domestic risks inside β_c. And risk reduction leads to a more frequent acceptance of projects evaluated with the NPV criterion.

To sum up, there are numerous theoretical reasons that show a positive effect of financial globalisation on stock prices, or a negative effect on the cost of capital, and thus a favourable effect on the investment of firms. We can now add some empirical evidence leading to the same result as these theoretical arguments.

1.4   Financial globalisation: backing from empirical evidence

Evans and Jovanovic (1989) showed, in a theoretical model, the importance of wealth constraints for investors. In the same light, but from an empirical perspective this time, Evans and Leighton (1989) showed that credit constraints are a critical factor in the creation and survival of firms. Investment financing is of major importance, which is not surprising and represents that upon which financial globalisation can have an influence. Thus, the OECD (1996) points out the orientation changes of many countries during the 1980s. They evolved from a situation where foreign investment and private sector investment were limited, to a development strategy that included the participation of foreign multinational firms. They have experienced a widening of their scope of investment with privatisations, deregulations and public policy liberalisations, as shown in Table 12.1.

While FDI in developed economies reached $857 billion in 2006, flows to developing countries and the transition economies attained their highest levels ever: $379 billion (21 per cent increase over those in 2005) and $69

Table 12.1   Foreign Direct Investment (FDI) inflows (billions of dollars)

	1980	1985	1990	1995	2000	2003	2006
Developing economies	10	15	30	110	240	190	379
Developed economies	70	65	170	240	1170	370	857
World total	80	80	200	350	1410	560	1236

Source: UNCTAD (2007), World Investment report.

Table 12.2   Reinvested earnings: share in total FDI inflows

	1990	1995	2000	2003	2006
Share in world FDI inflows	−2%	16%	8%	25%	30%
Share in developing economies' inflows	32%	22%	28%	35%	45%
Share in developed economies' inflows	−3%	15%	4%	20%	27%

Source: UNCTAD (2007), World Investment report.

billion (68 per cent increase), respectively. In the period 2000–06, FDI inflows accounted for 56 per cent of all net capital flows into developing countries, whereas the shares of portfolio, other capital transactions (e.g. bank loans) and official flows were 16 per cent, 19 per cent and 10 per cent, respectively (World Bank, 2007).

Moreover, income on FDI (i.e. repatriated profits and reinvested earnings as recorded in host countries' balance of payments) rose 29 per cent in 2006, following a 16 per cent rise in 2005. Indeed, there are three components of FDI: equity investments, reinvested earnings and other capital (essentially intra-company loans). Reinvested earnings in 2006 reached a peak: they accounted for 30 per cent of world FDI inflows and for almost half of total inflows to developing countries (Table 12.2).

More recently Alfaro and Charlton (2007) explored the relation between international financial integration and the level of entrepreneurship activity. With a database of 24 million firms in about 100 countries in 1999 and 2004, they noticed that international financial integration is associated with higher levels of entrepreneurship activity. This influence applied through larger direct investments from abroad or through a greater availability of credit and capital. They showed that countries with weaker barriers to international capital flows have a larger proportion of small firms, and that firm age tends to be higher in less-integrated economies. According to these results, small firms, which are proportionately the most innovative, find more favourable development conditions in economies that are open to foreign capital.

Gianetti and Ongena (2005) have also studied the impact of financial integration on small investing firms, a category of firms they consider to be crucial for economic development. They investigated a panel of 60,000 firms from Eastern Europe. They analysed the impact of foreign bank loans on the growth of these firms and their financing, and then studied the effect of foreign bank penetration. They found that foreign loans have a positive effect on firms, and a stronger effect on larger firms. Even if larger firms benefit more from the presence of foreign banks, small investing firms also benefit from them to a smaller degree.

Other authors have examined the impact of the entry of foreign banks on banking system efficiency. Demirguc-Kunt and Huizinga (1999) showed that competitive pressures created by the entry of these foreign banks lead to an improvement in banking system efficiency. However, this kind of study is based on the average of a large group of countries and estimations are made using a mix of industrial countries and developing countries. A specific study on Argentina carried out by Clarke *et al.* (2000), which used data from 1995 to 1997, analysed the impact of the entry of foreign banks on Argentinian domestic banks. They found that foreign bank penetration increased the global efficiency of the banking sector and raised competitive pressures on domestic financial institutions.

Some papers have also examined how financial liberalisation affects the cost of capital and financial constraints. Henry (2000a; 2000b; 2003), Kim and Singal (2000) and Bekaert, Harvey and Lundblad (2005) showed that stock market liberalisation decreased capital cost, generated rise in investment and led to an increase in aggregated wealth. In a more comprehensive study, Chari and Henry (2004) examined the effects of stock market liberalisation in eleven emerging countries. Their results suggested that firms owned by foreigners experience a rise in their stock price and a decline in their capital cost. On average this increase reaches about 15 per cent. They also showed that firms with a larger floating and more liquid stocks better attract investors' attention and experience a larger decline of capital cost than other firms. More recently, Mitton (2006) showed, from a sample of 1100 firms from twenty-eight countries from 1980 to 2000, that liberalisation leads to higher levels of firm investments (2.2 points higher on average) and larger profitability ratios (2.4 points more).

These empirical analyses clearly seem to sustain the point of view according to which financial globalisation backs firm investment. However, as we will see in the following section, there are some contrary arguments and some empirical objections to this viewpoint, which may be too optimistic.

2   Limits of globalisation as an investment and growth-creating process

2.1   Financial globalisation and fragility of international capital markets

Financial globalisation is not really a new phenomenon. Indeed, the history of asset flow movements is at least a century old,[5] and the world has gone through two globalisation periods since then (Schularick, 2006). The one we are currently experiencing is only the second one, the first one having begun during the 1870s and finished with the First World War. This gold exchange standard period, that occurred at the same time as strong European imperialism, was characterised by large net flows of assets (in percentage of gross domestic product or GDP), even larger than those of today's economies.[6]

Investment in poor countries (usually colonies at that time) was a key element of financial globalisation in the nineteenth century, whereas today it plays a smaller role. The present financial globalisation is characterised by a massive diversification of flows between high income economies, and a relative marginalisation of less-developed economies (Schularick, 2006). Going a little further, we could say that today's globalisation concerns mostly rich countries (or at least does not concern the poorest countries). Indeed, we can see that Africa is not part of this process.

The present financial globalisation should not be confused with the globalisation of the colonial period, for which the question raised in the introduction has a straightforward answer. Flows of assets from the home country towards colonies were obviously allocated to production investment that produced the expected effects. Can it be claimed that it is the same for the second globalisation era? We can doubt it. Even if it is unquestionable that some of the capital coming from developed countries surely helps to finance productive investments, a significant fraction of these funds is invested in the very short term, and is purely speculative or has secondary financial goals.

The history of financial markets has led many economists and political leaders to recognise that financial liberalisation also generates high costs. Such costs include the high degree of capital flow concentration[7] and the lack of financing access for small countries, either permanently or when they most need it. They also include an inadequate domestic allocation of these flows, which can worsen previous imbalances,[8] as well as the loss of macroeconomic stability.

From an empirical point of view it is not obvious that the advantages of integration prevail over its costs. What really happens? As far as small countries are concerned, historical evidence has shown that integration brings huge net gains (Obstfeld, 1998), because these small countries have more to gain from financial globalisation than large ones. Indeed, nowadays, financial crises can pass very quickly from one market to another, because of the close links created by financial globalisation. According to some authors, financial globalisation has emphasised speculative behaviours. Moreover, as the first studies on the topic pointed out, if moderate speculation tends to stabilise the working of markets, particularly if it concerns goods and services, the increase in this speculation and its generalisation to finance may create instability (Kaldor, 1940). The extension of global finance, which is supposed to ease operations for large industrial firms, can thus be harmful for them. It creates instability of product markets and capital markets, which leads to phases of excessive credit bid or, on the contrary, to credit crunch. This leads to considerable damage for consumption and investment.

Contagion and crises represent the major drawbacks of financial globalisation. The international mobility of capital can increase the likelihood of a financial crisis, all the more so since domestic economies already showed distortions and a weak institutional frame before financial liberalisation. Under these conditions, greater volatility and higher financial risk may considerably slow down entrepreneurship and the innovative activity of firms. These economic and financial crises lead to the idea that financial globalisation is not an 'everybody wins' game. Thus, emerging economies suffered from capital fickleness after the Asian and Russian crises, since capital flows can quickly leave when the markets feel a change in an economy's solvency.

The pro-cyclic nature of short-run capital flows and the risk of their sudden withdrawal, as well as volatility of capital flows associated with major contagion problems, has led some authors to criticise financial globalisation during recent years, as it was considered to be responsible for all troubles. Even some of the greatest economists have written about the dangers of financial globalisation, as it increases hot money and raises the probability of financial crises with no significant effect on investment or growth (Bhagwati, 1998; Rodrik, 1998; Stiglitz, 2002).

The infrastructure of international financial organisation is clearly questioned. Financial globalisation might be too fragile. However, even without that, globalisation raises other doubts that are presented in the two following sections.

2.2 Risks related to international investments and paradoxical effects of globalisation

Firms that make foreign direct or indirect investments incur several kinds of risks, which have an impact on the decision to invest through their influence on the return level required by investors. Meanwhile, financial globalisation may influence the size of these risks, as it gives more importance to some of them, which paradoxically slows down investment.

Exchange globalisation has modified the balance between commercial areas, those which have a legal basis (European Union or Mercosur, for example) as well as those that arise from the development of a particular country (the growing influence of China in the Japanese or American balance of trade, or the breakthrough of India outside its initial area of influence). Thus, the emergence of such areas, which favours the signature of bilateral or multilateral agreements, has created favourable conditions for the investment of firms. Such evidence is all the more convincing in that exchanges are made in a common currency and with common custom tariffs. Moreover, the lowering of tariff barriers removes a protection firms could benefit from, particularly the most fragile companies, the start ups and declining firms. As a consequence, the development of economic and trade integration areas potentially increases risk for the firms least strongly rooted in their markets (among which there are many innovative firms).

Here the risk is linked to retaining market shares, and to the capacity of firms to attract investment flows. Indeed, a situation that is globally favourable to investment doesn't mean that it will help all firms the same way. Commercial risk means a higher operating risk for some firms, and therefore a higher volatility of their commercial return and return on investment. This leads to a higher uncertainty of return on equity for the financially weakest firms. Indeed, firms with little financial power have to compensate for their lack of self-financing with loans, and then increase their leverage and the risk of their return on equity.[9]

We also have to add the notion of liquidity risk, which is more related to emerging markets' volatility. This risk creates a locking of funds invested by companies in firms in emerging countries, because of lack of counterpart enabling to sell financial assets. Such a situation is obviously discouraging for investors in some economic areas.

2.3   Financial globalisation can harm firm investment

Detractors of financial liberalisation usually criticise the ambiguous aspect of some characteristics of globalisation. In this way, instead of being added to their domestic counterparts, foreign investors can supplant them and eventually have little impact on the domestic economy. For example, Grossman (1984) showed that international capital, and particularly foreign direct investment, can exclude domestic entrepreneurs.

The idea that too much openness harms investment and entrepreneurship is developed by certain authors (Hausman and Rodrik, 2003). It is an old idea among development specialists that foreign direct investment can harm economies, and was already explained by Hirschman (1958). Some other famous authors have supported the idea that opening capital markets can impair economic development (Bhagwati, 1998; Rodrik, 1998; Stiglitz, 2000). Thus, when we look at the relative levels of investments among the main industrialised countries, we do not see any increase in the last thirty years (Figure 12.1). However, constant or current monetary data values are on the rise.

According to Agénor (2003), the appraisal of financial globalisation is quite dull. Only direct foreign investment could bring some benefit and might stimulate investment and growth. As for the empirical research about the entry of foreign banks, it is far from presenting very clear conclusions. Thus, these foreign banks can shorten credit to small firms on a wider scale than domestic banks, in order to concentrate on the largest and strongest ones (which are more involved in the exchangeable goods sector). When banks experience a lowering of their operating costs, they can put some pressure on domestic banks and induce them to merge in order to be competitive. This concentration process (backed by the possible acquisition of domestic banks by foreign banks) can create banks that are 'too big to fail', which can increase moral hazard problems. Therefore, domestic banks become less careful in credit allocation and in selecting borrowers (and their follow-up). Concentration can also lead to situations of monopolies

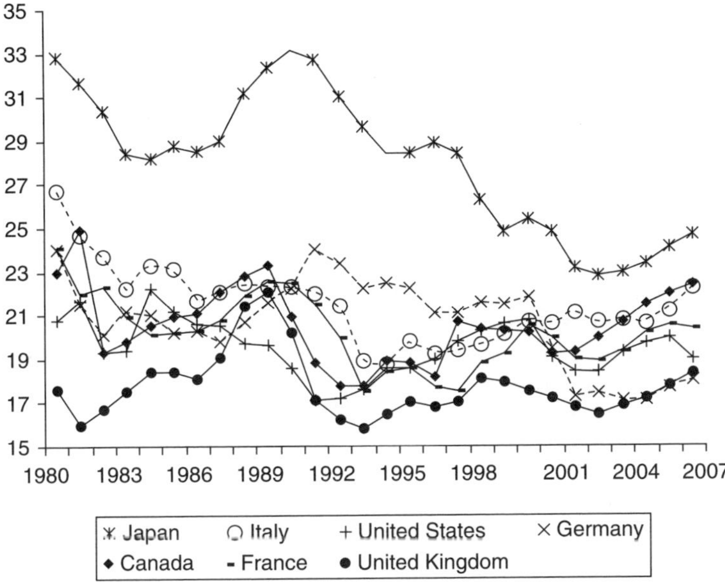

Figure 12.1   Investment as a percentage of GDP
Source: FMI, World Economic Outlook Database, April 2007.

or oligopolies, which reduce the global efficiency of banking systems and
the availability of credit. Finally, these foreign banks are not a stabilising element from a macroeconomic point of view, because of their 'cut and run'
behaviour during a crisis.

On the empirical side, the question of the influence of foreign banks
remains open. Claessens et al. (2000) studied the cost and profitability of
foreign banks in both developed and developing countries. Their banking sample was composed of eighty countries during 1988–95, with 7800
commercial bank observations. The impact of the entry of foreign banks
on interest rate spreads, which can be seen as a financial intermediation
efficiency measure, is not statistically significant according to them. The
conclusion of their study is a serious impairment to the idea that the entry
of these banks may increase banking system efficiency and could back the
investment of firms.

We can add that there are numerous other reasons why small firms
cannot benefit from financial integration, even when foreign banks are
present. These foreign banks can encounter more serious information asymmetry problems than domestic banks. Furthermore, as Stiglitz (2000) pointed
out, misleading information may prevent capital from being invested
profitably.

2.4   The limits of globalisation

During the last few decades, barriers to international mobility of capital have been removed in many countries. Despite this tendency to reinforce financial globalisation, there are still some major restrictions on international financial transactions. Indeed, the international net flows of capital remain small relative to those predicted by the theoretical models. In spite of this limit which is known as 'home bias', national financial markets worldwide are today far better financially integrated than they were thirty years ago.

Table 12.3 shows that, despite a declining tendency of the home bias, this characteristic of investors' portfolios remains a topical problem.

Today a typical investor portfolio is still mostly composed of domestic assets,[10] and the investment of a country still strongly depends on its savings. In 2003, the fraction of foreign assets in the average portfolio of American investors was only 12.5 per cent, whereas it was supposed to be 52.8 per cent if they held a worldwide market portfolio (Table 12.3). Thus, in 2003, the American investors owned only 23.6 per cent (12.5/52.8) of what it should have been had they held a worldwide market portfolio.[11] The measure of the American domestic bias might then have been about 76.4 per cent, which is tremendous. In 1990, American investors owned only 8.4 per cent of the benchmark amount, meaning a 91.5 per cent bias. However, such a situation

Table 12.3   Fraction of foreign stocks in portfolios and comparison with the benchmark

	1990	1995	2000	2003
Canada				
number	2.0	20.6	25.5	19.3
benchmark	97.4	97.9	97.4	97.5
Germany				
number	13.2	13.6	23,9	26.3
benchmark	96.2	96.8	96.1	97.1
Japan				
number	2.2	4.2	9.1	10.6
benchmark	69.0	79.4	90.2	90.9
United Kingdom				
number	29.5	30.1	38.4	45.7
benchmark	91.0	92.1	92.0	92.0
United States				
number	5.7	9.1	10.4	12.5
benchmark	67.5	61.4	53.1	52.8

Number: Proportion of foreign stocks among all stocks held. Benchmark: proportion of foreign stocks among world stocks.
Source: IMF (2005), *World Economic Outlook*.

is not specific to American investors. In 2001, the average measure of the domestic bias in a sample of eighteen developed countries was 63 per cent (Sorensen *et al.*, 2004). This demonstrates that the achievement of financial globalisation is not as comprehensive as one might have thought. Moreover, it must be emphasised that financial globalisation remains the concern of rich countries. Taking this into consideration, Stulz (2005) gave a significant figure of this amazing reality: despite what neoclassical theory forecast concerning developing countries (that they should have experienced large inflows of capital into their economies), we see that the amount of net flows was negative between 1996 and 2004 (-67.4 billion dollars). Indeed, capital transfers went from the poorest countries towards the richest ones, where investment opportunities were the most numerous. Thus, financial globalisation may not have the characteristics it is supposed to. Firstly, the globalisation process is still being finalised. Secondly, it does not even benefit the countries that most need it.

What about the effects of liberalisation on stock prices and capital cost? One cannot contest the results of the studies of Kim and Singal (2000), Bekaert and Harvey (2000) and Henry (2000b), which seem to back the viewpoint of the theoretical analyses of Stapleton and Subrahmanyam (1977), Errunza and Losq (1985) and Alexander et al. (1987). Liberalisation may, therefore, have a negative effect on capital cost. However, an important weakness of these studies lies in the value of their results: even when they go in the right direction significantly, they are very weak from a practical viewpoint. Stulz (1999) noticed the effects of globalisation on capital cost that were shown by these studies did not have the expected magnitude. According to him, this is a puzzle to be solved.

Among Stulz's attempts to explain this puzzle, one seems particularly relevant. Contrary to what is assumed in theoretical models, globalisation does not occur after a unique transformation that would completely integrate all markets. It happens progressively, as the persistency of a phenomenon such as the home bias shows. In order to fit this reality, the conclusions of theoretical models have to be modified. Another very important limit to theoretical models is that they consider a univariate liberalisation. They consider the liberalisation effect on prices among one market only, with the usual *ceteris paribus* hypothesis. Financial globalisation, though, is a global phenomenon that concerns many countries simultaneously. This is where the theoretical analysis of globalisation reaches an important limit because we have to recall that, for political leaders and from the viewpoint of economists, the main objective of financial globalisation is to attract (in the long-run if possible) foreign capital. Financial globalisation cannot be an 'everybody wins' situation according to this viewpoint, because if assets arrive in one place it means that they have just left another place. Furthermore, if many countries experience financial liberalisation during the same period, this race for foreign capital creates harmful competition that sharply reduces the interest of globalisation (for them, as well as for the countries that provide this foreign capital). In a world where capital bid doesn't increase, the price increases generated in one place by capital inflows simultaneously create price decreases in other places because of outflows. According to this logic, everyone cannot win. In a theoretical model including the multivariate aspect of globalisation, meaning that it concerns several economies simultaneously, Pépin (2004) showed that the results of simple models are no longer true. So capital cost may rise or decline during the financial globalisation process.

3 Conclusion: the need to discipline finance

To conclude, these developments raise two questions. Is globalisation irreversible? And does it really sustain the investment of firms?

Although the globalisation phenomenon developed and intensified throughout the decades at the end of the twentieth century, a partial and limited return to protectionism is never excluded for a given country. Indeed, on the one hand there is a strong correlation between 'collective joining to border opening and economic growth', and on the other hand, 'a real risk of withdrawal or protectionism as soon as there is an economic, political or sanitary crisis' (Leersnyder, 2001). In this light, the mad cow or avian flu crises clearly show the reflex to ask for domestic traceability or for food safety based on local production rather than on imported products. Does it come from the relevance of health considerations, or is it a pretext to favour domestic producers over international competitors? Whatever the reason, governments of many industrialised countries do not hesitate to reduce the opening of their markets when they believe there is a threat.

The answer to the second question depends on two particularly important factors. Firstly, financial globalisation does not have the same interest for all countries. The countries that know that they experience savings deficit and have profitable investment projects are the only ones that can benefit from the liberalisation of their financial system in order to attract foreign capital. Such countries may experience huge net inflows of capital that can help investment. Then, in order for these capital inflows to back the investment of firms and be productive, they have to be long lasting and based on solid roots. This condition refers back to the structure of the international financial system. On the worldwide level, a number of measures must be taken in order to avoid the repetition of too many major financial crises. As Boyer (2000) pointed out, there are two challenges for the twenty-first century: to discipline finance and to organise internationalisation. However, at the level of each domestic economy, financial liberalisation also has to be carefully prepared.

Thus, the amplitude of some recent financial crises,[12] in the case of some less-developed countries, simply came from the delay in implementing prudential rules. For these less-developed countries, financial opening didn't occur with the corresponding modernisation of risk-management tools (Mahar and Williamson, 1999). Governments of all these countries now have an important role to play in the financial liberalisation process, with the creation of prudential rules and control structures that administrate more solid financial systems such as those of the United States or the United Kingdom. As Agénor (2003) wrote, prudent macroeconomic management, relevant supervision and prudent regulation of the financial system, greater transparency and an increased capacity of the private system to manage risks are the necessary conditions for a successful integration, whose major risk is the sudden reversal of short-term capital.

Nevertheless, the recent example of the American crisis of subprime loans shows that the existence of an efficient, prudent infrastructure does not protect an economy, even the most prosperous one, from all risk of bank or financial crisis. After all, the existence of this infrastructure may lead to more risky behaviour as it makes people believe that systemic risks have disappeared. As financial globalisation can be destabilising in a world capital market that is badly organised, it may have the same effect on a better-organised market, simply because it may change the behaviour of agents towards risk.

Finally, we have to add some shade to the flattering portrait of globalisation that some advocates of financial liberalisation have drawn. The finance world has changed in the last thirty years. Several old problems have been solved or eased, and some new ones have appeared. This is probably where the paradox of financial globalisation lies, in that we have ignored a quasi-universal truth of any change in any human organisation: how could we seriously imagine that a redefinition of the frame and the rules would not create new problems? Is it not the case of any change?

Notes

1. Defined as $WACC = cS/(D+S) + iD/(D+S)$ with c the cost of equity, S the amount of equity, i the after-tax cost of debt and D the amount of financial debts.
2. Economic Value Added and Market Value Added (see Stewart, 1991).
3. Later, when the domestic market opens more directly to investors, these ways to attract foreign investors lose some or all of their interest. When markets are perfectly integrated dual listing is no longer attractive as foreign investors can come into the domestic market in order to invest more directly.
4. These conditions are that both domestic and foreign investors should have the same risk aversion, and that asset returns should usually be less correlated between markets than inside a given market.
5. For a more precise analysis of financial globalisation, see Das (2006) and Schularick (2006).
6. Concerning France, leader of the second colonial empire at that time, assets net flows represented 2.4 per cent of GDP between 1870 and 1889, 1.3 per cent between 1890 and 1914, v. 0.8 per cent between 1974 and 1989, and 0.7 per cent between 1990 and 1996. As for the United Kingdom, leader of the first colonial empire, net flows represented 4.6 per cent of GDP between both 1870 and

1889, and 1890 and 1913, v. 1.5 per cent and 2 per cent between 1974 and 1989, and 1990 and 1996 (Obstfeld and Taylor, 1998).

7. Few receiving countries get the large majority of capital flows. For example, at the beginning of the 1990s, this was the case with some Latin America and Asian countries.

8. In countries where banks have a small net wealth (or a negative one), where capital/risk ratios are low, and where banking supervision is insufficient, direct or indirect intermediation of funds by banks can aggravate the important moral hazard or selection-adverse problems that existed previously. Then lenders tend to engage more in concentrated and higher-risk loans operations.

9. This link between return on investment ROI and return on equity ROE can be directly written with D/S the leverage level, i the interest rate of financial debts D, and T the income tax rate: ROE = (ROI + (ROI–i)D/S) (1–T).

10. See Karolyi and Stulz (2003) for more information about the persistency of home bias.

11. The worldwide market portfolio represents the ideal portfolio of risky assets owned by any investor, according to the mean-variance analysis principles.

12. Mexico suffered in summer 1982 and then all emerging countries: Mexico again in December 1994, Thailand in 1999–98 and then Asia and Russia in August 1998, followed by Brazil and Latin America, Ecuador in 2000, Argentina and Turkey in 2001 and Uruguay in 2002.

References

Adler, M. and Dumas, B. (1975) Optimal international acquisitions. *Journal of Finance*, 30: 1–19.

Agénor, P.-R. (2003) Benefits and costs of international financial integration: theory and facts. *World Economy*, 26: 1089–118.

Aglietta, M., Brender, A. and Coudert, V. (1990) *Globalisation financière: l'aventure obligée*. Paris: Economica.

Ahimud, Y. and Mendelson, H. (1986) Asset pricing and the bid-ask spread. *Journal of Financial Economics*, 17: 223–49.

Alexander, G.J., Eun, C.S. and Janakiramanan, S. (1987) Asset pricing and dual listing on foreign capital markets: a note. *Journal of Finance*, 42: 151–8.

Alfaro, L. and Charlton, A. (2007) International financial integration and entrepreneurial firm dynamics. *Harvard Business School Working Paper*, Number 07-012.

Bekaert, G. and Harvey, C. (2000) Foreign speculators and emerging equity markets. *Journal of Finance*, 55: 565–613.

Bekaert, G., Harvey, C.R. and Lundblad, C. (2005) Does financial liberalisation spur growth? *Journal of Financial Economics*, 77: 3–55.

Bhagwati, J. (1998) The capital myth. *Foreign Affairs*, 77: 7–12.

Bouchet, M.-H. (2005) *La Globalisation*. Paris: Pearson Education.

Boyer, R. (2000) Deux défis pour le XXI$^\text{è}$ siècle: discipliner la finance et organiser l'internationalisation. *Cepremap Working Paper*, 2000–08.

Caprio, G. and Honohan, P. (1999) Restoring banking stability: beyond supervised capital requirements. *Journal of Economic Perspectives*, 13: 43–64.

Chari, A. and Henry, P.B. (2004) Risk sharing and asset prices: evidence from a natural experiment. *Journal of Finance*, 59: 1295–1324.

Claessens, S., Demirguc-Kunt, A. and Huizinga, H. (2000) 'The role of foreign banks in domestic banking systems' in S. Claessens and M. Jansen (eds) *The Internationalisation of Financial Services*. The Hague: Kluwer Books.

Clark, E. (1997) Valuing political risk as an insurance policy. *Journal of International Money and Finance*, 16: 477–90.

Clark, E., Marois, B. and Cernès, J. (2001) *Le Management des Risques Internationaux*. Paris: Economica.

Clarke, G., Cull, R., d'Amato, L. and Mollinari, A. (2000) 'On the Kindness of Strangers? The impact of foreign entry on domestic banks in Argentina' in S. Claessens and M. Jansen (eds) *The Internationalisation of Financial Services*. The Hague: Kluwer Books.

Das, D.K. (2006) Globalisation in the world of finance: an analytical history. *Global Economy Journal*, 6: 1–22.

Demirguc-Kunt, A. and Huizinga, H. (1999) Determinants of interest margins and profitability: some international evidence. *World Bank Economic Review*, 13: 379–408.

Errunza, V. and Losq, E. (1985) International asset pricing under mild segmentation: theory and test. *Journal of Finance*, 40: 105–24.

Evans, D.S. and Jovanovic, B. (1989) An estimated model of entrepreneurial choice under liquidity constraints. *Journal of Political Economy*, 97: 808–27.

Evans, D.S. and Leighton, L.S. (1989) Some empirical aspects of entrepreneurship. *American Economic Review*, 79: 519–35.

Feldstein, M. and Horioka, C. (1980) Domestic saving and international capital flows. *Economic Journal*, 90: 314–29.

Fontaine, P. (1988) *Arbitrage et Évaluation Internationale des Actifs Financiers*. Paris: Economica.

Gianetti, M. and Ongena, S. (2005) Financial integration and entrepreneurial activity: evidence from foreign bank entry in emerging markets. *ECB Working Paper Series*, Number 498.

Grossman, G. (1984) International trade, foreign investment, and the formation of the entrepreneurial class. *American Economic Review*, 74: 605–14.

Harris, G. and Guerel, E. (1986) Price and volume effects associated with the new S&P 500 list: new evidence for the existence of price pressure. *Journal of Finance*, 41: 815–29.

Hausman, R. and Rodrik, D. (2003) Economic development as self-discovery. *Journal of Development Economics*, 72: 603–33.

Henry, P.B. (2000a) Do stock market liberalisations cause investment booms? *Journal of Financial Economics*, 58: 301–34.

——— (2000b) Stock market liberalisation, economic reform, and emerging market equity prices. *Journal of Finance*, 55: 529–64.

——— (2003) Capital account liberalisation, the cost of capital, and economic growth. *American Economic Review*, 93: 91–6.

Hirschman, A. (1958) *The Strategy of Economic Development*. New Haven: Yale University Press.

Hubbard, G. (1998) Capital market imperfections and investment. *Journal of Economic Literature*, 36: 193–225.

Kaldor, N. (1940) Spéculation et stabilité économique. *Revue Française d'Economie*, 2: 115–64.

Karolyi, A. and Stulz, R. (2003) 'Are assets priced locally or globally?' in G. Constantinides, M. Harris and R. Stulz (eds) *The Handbook of the Economics of Finance*. New York: North-Holland Publishers.

Kim, H.E. and Singal, V. (2000) Stock market openings: experience of emerging economies. *Journal of Business*, 73: 25–66.

King, R.G. and Levine, R. (1993a) Finance and growth: Schumpeter might be right. *Quarterly Journal of Economics*, 108: 717–37.

King, R.G. and Levine, R. (1993b) Finance, entrepreneurship and growth: theory and evidence. *Journal of Monetary Economics*, 32: 513–42.

Leersnyder de, J.M. (2001) 'Les nouveaux risques commerciaux' in P Chaigneau (ed.) *La Gestion des Risques Internationaux*. Paris: Economica.

Levine, R. (1996) 'Foreign banks, financial development, and economic growth' in C.E. Barfield (ed.) *International Financial Markets*. Washington DC: American Enterprise Institute Press.

Levine, R. and Servos, S. (1998) Capital control liberalization and stock market development. *World Development*, 26: 1169–83.

Mahar, M. and Williamson, J. (1999) A survey of financial liberalization. *Princeton Essays in International Finance*, 211.

Marois, B. (2000) Le risque-pays revisité. *Revue Française de Gestion*, 133.

Mitton, T. (2006) Stock market liberalisation and operating performance at the firm level. *Journal of Financial Economics*, 81: 625–47.

Obstfeld, M. (1994) Risk-taking, global diversification and growth. *American Economic Review*, 84: 1310–29.

—— (1998) The global capital market: benefactor or menace? *Journal of Economic Perspectives*, 12: 9–30.

Obstfeld, M. and Rogoff, K. (1995) *Foundation of International Macroeconomics*. Cambridge MA: MIT University Press.

Obstfeld, M. and Taylor, A.M. (1998) 'The Great Depression as a watershed: international capital mobility over the long run' in M.D. Bordo, C.D. Goldin and E.N. White (eds) *The Defining Moment: The Great Depression and the American Economy in the Twentieth Century*. Chicago: University of Chicago Press.

OECD (Organisation for Economic Cooperation and Development) (1996) *Tendances des marchés de capitaux*, 64 (June): 47–50.

Pépin, D. (2004) Globalisation des marchés de capitaux et valorisation des actifs financiers. *Revue Économique*, 55: 207–26.

Rodrik, D. (1998) Who needs capital account convertibility? *Princeton Essays in International Finance*, 207: 55–65.

Schularick, M. (2006) A tale of two 'globalizations': capital flows from rich to poor in two eras of global finance. *International Journal of Finance and Economics*, 11: 339–54.

Schumpeter, J.A. (1935; original edition 1926) *Théorie de l'évolution économique, recherches sur le profit, le crédit, l'intérêt et le cycle de la conjoncture*. Paris: Dalloz.

Shleifer, A. (1986) Do demand curves for stocks slope down? *Journal of Finance*, 46: 579–90.

Solnik, B. (1973) *European Capital Markets*. Maryland: Lexington Books.

—— (1974) Why not diversify internationally rather than domestically? *Financial Analysts Journal*, 30: 48–54.

Sorensen, B.E., Wu, Y.-T., Yosha, O. and Shu, Y. (2004) Home bias and international risk sharing: twin puzzles separated at birth. *Working Paper*, University of Houston.

Stapleton, R.C. and Subrahmanyam, M.G. (1977) Market imperfections, capital market equilibrium and corporation finance. *Journal of Finance*, 32: 307–19.

Stewart, B. (1991) *The Quest for Value*. New York: Harper Business.

Stiglitz, J. (2000) Capital market liberalization, economic growth, and instability. *World Development*, 25: 1075–86.

—— (2002) *Globalization and its Discontent.* New York: W.W. Norton.

Stulz, R.M. (1981) A model of international asset pricing. *Journal of Financial Economics,* 9: 383–406.

—— (1999) Globalization of equity markets and the cost of capital. *NBER Working Paper,* 7021. Cambridge MA: National Bureau of Economic Research.

—— (2005) The limits of globalization. *Journal of Finance,* 60: 1595–638.

UNCTAD (United Nations Conference on Trade and Development) (2007) *World Investment Report, Transnational Corporations, Extractive Industries and Development.* Geneva: United Nations.

World Bank (2007) *Global Development Finance 2007: the Globalization of Corporate Finance in Developing Countries.* Washington DC: World Bank.

13
Banks and Globalisation: The Sorcerer's Apprentices

Guy Tournois

Globalisation is not a new phenomenon. Nevertheless, we are witnessing important developments either in its shape or in the nature of its process.

At the beginning, we noticed this globalisation in trade exchanges, then through cross-border investment flows. We found it again inside companies that are going global, and from now on, in the financial flows that are becoming worldwide.

Globalisation was initially trade's prerogative, then one of direct investments. Nowadays, it concerns the free circulation and strong mobility of capital.

This natural evolution reveals paradoxes that are particularly surprising and symptoms of a feeling of helplessness when faced with strategic choices. Bankers became adventurers, a profound metamorphosis that we will analyse while trying to find explanations and justifications. Financiers became the sorcerer's apprentices, inventors of unmanageable alchemies, causing devastating explosions. This is a fact of the paradoxical behaviours of rational bankers who have lost their minds.

Financial globalisation has materialised through the liberalisation of financial markets, the opening of economies to international capital flows, the building of integrated economic areas, the universality of the exchanges of products and services, the privatisation of companies and the systematisation of free competition. Financial companies play a key role in this process, which combines technology transfers, movements of goods and capital flows.

It is worth noting that this globalisation followed the recommendations of the World Bank and the International Monetary Fund, commonly named the 'Washington Consensus'.

On the one hand, we may be delighted with these globalisation concepts, which promise new perspectives either for the old countries with traditional economies, or for the new emerging economies. On the other, we notice the existence of a supranational state, the one of finance. Hence, it is undeniable that the explosion in the economic and financial connections worldwide carries risks up to the volumes exchanged, for all the players, whatever their geographical, sector or socio-cultural origins.

Based on the information above, we can conclude that banks, financial institutions and insurance companies manage information and allocate capital without taking into account either the origin or characteristics of that information and capital. The current financial crisis exhibits the ease with which toxic financial products were disseminated with complete impunity. The controlling authorities worldwide were not mistaken in multiplying the safeguards for more than thirty years, through the Bale Committee established in 1975 by the G10's central banks.

The first agreement was in 1988 instituting the 'Ratio Cook', still named Bale 1. The objective, at a time of a globalisation context targeting a solid and stable international banking system, was to prompt banks to maintain a high level of equity and to strengthen the fairness of the competition conditions among international banks. Since 1999, the Bale Committee has been working to improve these rules and, in 2004, it implemented the Bale 2 standards that instituted a new plan intending to evaluate the risks and prevent possible incidents.

The stakes are huge. The distortions between regulatory, and national and international accounting approaches demonstrate the difficulty of coordinating a policy of major financial risk prevention. The American Federal Reserve decided to scrutinise the financial statements of the largest American banks, a mission that was started but has not taken place for the last ten years. The objective is to strengthen the financial intermediaries' legislation as well as the banks' prerogatives. The Swiss national bank also decided to tighten the control on banks after the serious setbacks faced by the Confederation's two major banks, namely Crédit Suisse and Union des Banques Suisses (UBS). The recent case of the subprime mortgages, with the estimated losses of hundreds of billions of dollars by banks and financial institutions worldwide, illustrates, if it was needed to, that international markets carry unmanageable risks; risks, moreover, that cannot be controlled within a feebly regulated international financial sphere with inexperienced or incompetent players and controllers. The German banking control authority estimates the worst scenario of the impact of the crisis is up to \$600 billion, while hoping this would be around \$430 billion. The International Monetary Fund (IMF) estimates the crisis has cost to up to \$945 billion for the whole international financial system. The potential losses of banks and other financial institutions, due to risky mortgage loans, were estimated to up to \$565 billion and up to \$380 billion for other closely related loans.

The authorities of several countries noticed from then on a contamination of other financial institutions such as assurances, speculative funds, insurance companies and pension funds. All the institutions have lender/borrower relationships, which create a total interdependence. All the interbank markets are connected. If, on the top of that, trust no longer exists between different players, the system falls into crisis. This is what we call the 'systemic crisis'. In a sector in which the activities have a non-physical character, the importance of information processes intensifies that of control and diversification (the universal bank and bank insurance principle).

One cannot help but notice that risk/return is still not well handled, and is sometimes hidden or ignored. In finance, however, one has to choose between risk and return. Globalisation creates a quest for performance and thus risk taking.

Access to financial markets worldwide is made easier, indeed is encouraged, through the convenience offered by the new information and communication technologies (ICT). Paradoxically, players have to bear high transaction costs to acquire the information. Additional costs related to the reduction of an asymmetry in information also have to be borne, as well as those induced by the creation of an additional clientèle.

Are we going to witness the shift of financial systems dominated by the banks to those dominated by the financial markets? Where is the border between the traditional professions of bank and insurance? How could an international finance system, perfectly organised, led by inherently conservative players, come to such extremes?

To address these questions, we will, in the first section, analyse the current crisis. In the second section, we will identify the answers to facing this crisis, in order to avoid being confronted by it again.

1   The global financial crisis and its paradoxes

1.1   The subprime mortgage crisis

In order to understand the current situation, it is important to list the main characteristics of the banking and financial environment. Several observations can be made.

- *Significant shocks in the global economy.* In the subprime mortgage case, there are hundreds of billion of dollars of high risk loans, with a loss probability of outstanding debts of around 30 per cent. Almost all banks worldwide are involved, not only through providing bad loans, but also because of their seeking of returns outside their borders, through securitisation. One must remember that the instruments of risk transfer in the markets, the securitisation and loans derivatives, became the terrible driving belts of the crisis. The mechanisms are not themselves at fault. Since the 1970s, good quality loans baskets have been transformed into negotiable securities and these operations allow the giving up of several slices of risk to qualified investors. Banks compress thousands of debts that are in their accounts. These operations are highly profitable: they are the source of important commissions, allowing banks to write off risky debts from the balance sheet, as well as increasing the opportunity to provide new loans. With an abundance of savings worldwide, banks have no difficulty in investing in those products that offer a higher return than those available in the various domestic markets of interested investors. The phenomenon is the same with the 'Credit Default Swaps' (CDS), which entail hedging contracts against the risk default of a debt issuer. At the first default of a big bank, or when these contracts are treated in a way that artificially triggers the stock market's fall, the bad risks are spread among all the counterparts that provided the guarantees. The origin of the crisis has to be identified in the source: mortgage loans have been offered on a massive scale, without sufficient guarantees to poor solvent borrowers who have been unable to withstand the effect of the upward adjustment of the loan's payments with variable rates (not capped) with a thirty-year maturity. One has to add to this the lenders' lack of judgement and their speculation that real estate can only gain in value. Although the American real estate prices reached their highest level in autumn 2005, before starting to fall, the loans' chain in the US is now broken up. Whatever the quality of the acquirers'/borrowers' track records, commissioned brokers played an important role in this. In October 2008, the assets depreciation of major banks worldwide were estimated to having reached up to $600 billion since the beginning of the crisis, knowing that the first elements of a real estate crisis became apparent in February 2007. Many large banks have to be recapitalised while admitting that investments funds or emerging countries' sovereign funds bring them money in order to secure their liberty and survival. More than $200 billion have been infused into the American, Swiss, British, German, Dutch and Belgian banks facing trouble. Since February 2008, the UBS issued 13 billion Swiss francs' worth of convertible bonds underwritten by Singapore's sovereign funds and by an unknown investor from the Middle East. Because of the weight and influence gained by sovereign funds, the IMF intends to circulate a guideline of best practice for sovereign funds in general. China's exchange reserves – the most important in the world – reached up to $1,900 billion. Here is again a paradoxical situation: how can one expect to commercially enter a market of more than a billion inhabitants and at the same time, not fear opportunistic predatory funds?

- *A wild battle among the major stock exchanges worldwide, looking for supremacy, leadership and maximum profitability.* Deregulation will make monopolies disappear and drive the competition among the financial markets, which will no longer be protected by their private preserve. The winners will probably be investors and savers whom the battle of prices will benefit. However, this battle will leave some players scarred, whether they are institutions (banks, financial and management companies, all intermediaries, brokers and so on) or simply employees after substantial restructurings (20 per cent of Citigroup's total staff).

- *The grouping of financial institutions.* These institutions are looking for external growth and profit maximisation for higher shareholders' satisfaction, and are more attracted by a distribution policy of important dividends than by the institution's culture (Tournois and Fischer, 2008). The search for the maximum dividend is often the investor's primary motive, making them ready to relocate their funds from one country to another, following the opportunities and the expected benefits. International finance is moving and will keep on doing so, as borders become less distinct. Large companies are now worldwide and financial patriotism is no longer expected. A company from one country can make its profits from a manufacturing or trading activity in other countries or continents. In addition to this, the logic of internationalisation and the distribution of activities smooth the effects of technical cycles, dilute the exposure to major risks, optimise the allocation of assets and limit the effects of monetary cycles, and arbitrate the development of the various activities of the enterprise.
- *The failure of several mergers.* These occurred because of the players' cultural and organisational differences (the human dimension, administrative issues, policy, economic and geographic distances, and compatibility of the applied technologies).
- *The internationalisation of large banking groups.* These groups were established in countries of former Eastern Europe, and also in Asia and the Middle East. Large scale manoeuvres started within these countries, as well as from one country to another, or one continent to another. Billion of dollars or euros can be transferred in few minutes from one financial place to another without any trouble, following the strategic or tactical choices of their holders.
- *The emergence of new important players.* Chinese banks, whose capital will soon exceed that of Western banks, could acquire equity in Western banks; for example, the China Development Bank has acquired equity in Morgan Stanley and Barclays. The sovereign funds of countries exporting raw materials, and often having considerable reserves, can take over any large occidental company or at least become a majority shareholder, allowing them to seek board membership and to request high dividends. The assets of sovereign funds increased by 18 per cent in 2007 to reach $3,300 billion. Experts from the International Financial Services Institute of London (IFSL) estimate that these funds will attain $10,000 billion by 2015. The US treasury estimates this will be $15,000 billion. The situation becomes extremely paradoxical: where are international finances' players now? In Wall Street? In London? Officially, and in the media, yes. However, in fact, historical players are no longer the leaders, being at the mercy of foreign capital actors, who are predators of

a collapsing Anglo-Saxon finance, rather than white knights riding to save it. The growing power of some countries is changing the nature of markets. As an example, countries such as China or India are accumulating hundreds of billion of dollars as reserves each year. The wealth and liquidity distribution in the world has changed: a source of bigger vulnerability for the occidental financial or industrial companies. Some protectionist coalitions are worried about the risk of companies becoming involved in strategic areas such as arms or the nuclear energy industry, through a takeover bid or a capital increase under a foreign flag. These sovereign funds came from China, the Gulf states, Singapore and so on. They invested a lot in 2007. They are currently in a standby position: the intervention of only one of them rescued Lehman Brothers from bankruptcy.

- *Globalisation reinforces the interdependency of economies.* Capital markets, better integrated than before, are the factors of instability at the origin of the crisis, for example, the Enron Company, the Long-Term Capital Management speculative fund, or economic crises like those in Russia, Argentina or in South-East Asia.

1.2 Analysis of the crisis and its paradoxes

How can we explain this explosion of financial flows on a global scale? Several explanations can be given.

Low interest rates, the lowest in about forty years, drive the players to take greater risks. The search for performance is worldwide and capital flows are moving, forgetting, as mentioned above, any financial or economic patriotism. Following the bursting of the Internet bubble and the 9/11 attacks, the US Federal Reserve eased access to credit by lowering, on several occasions, its short-term key (intervention) rates, reaching 1 per cent in 2003 and nearly 0 per cent in 2009. The banking profession is changing and the transformation risk takes its true position: banks borrow short-term and lend long-term. While the prices of both money and merchandise sold have weakened, banks have paradoxically become distanced from their core business.

The increase in the price of domestic real estate generates gain in the medium term, but no longer provides sufficient revenue. The players concerned in real estate put their funds into countries and markets with high returns. Generally speaking, the price increase of assets drives capital towards other, more highly profitable, devices. The recent price increase of agricultural or industrial commodities demonstrates the sector and geographic volatility of capital that is looking for performance. This observation highlights the paradox of capital – traditionally invested in real estate, a secure value – now suddenly seduced by the sirens of commodities placements, who are volatile by nature.

The increase in household debt carries risks. Any break-up of a speculative bubble, whether securities or real estate, weakens everybody by a high level of debt. The subprime mortgage crisis in the US illustrates this kind of risk. Bankers, basically prudent, took thoughtless risks, speculating on rises in securities and real estate.

The price increase of commodities, and more specifically of oil prices, worsens the deficits of importing countries and inversely enriches the exporting countries. It is not surprising to notice capital movements between several parts of the world. Almost 50 per cent of the capital of the companies which lead the index of the Paris stock exchange is owned by foreign funds, a significant sign of the mobility of capital. Are industries of industrial countries going to be under funds' guardianship, often coming from the emerging countries? What a U-turn situation, particularly as globalisation was initially driving towards the rich countries having a higher grasp, to the detriment of the poorest countries!

The sudden emergence of financial devices within the insurance sector pressured the insurers to cease being satisfied with making only safe or low-risk investments, as was their tradition, but to go further and use all the tools of speculation.

This saw the advent of a new generation of overpaid 'traders', receiving commission based upon accumulated performance, working on behalf of institutions looking for super profits, and succeeding the 'golden boys' of the 1980s that we thought had disappeared. New York and London bankers shared more than $35 billion as bonuses in 2005. Regulators finally decided to handle the bonuses control issue, and it became one of the conditions demanded by the public authorities before implementing their rescue plans.

International monetary authorities and, more specifically, the European Central Bank and US Federal Reserve, believed in market supremacy. They have been too accommodating with their key/intervention rates and allowed speculative bubbles to develop: a paradoxical situation, as these institutions are supposed to be the guarantors of orthodoxy. Capital movements attracted by rapid-gains perspectives have naturally multiplied. Because of the important volume exchanged, authorities gave complete freedom to speculative funds, which lacked transparency and destabilised the markets. In early 2008, the only alternative solution would be the $1,700 billion of outstanding, discounted bills. The quasi-absence of regulation and the lack of human resources, data treatment and the capacity to process information enables cross-border transactions. These funds have their proper rules, codes and strategies, making them beyond the reach of the classical controls. Capital movements are, therefore, both easier and encouraged. Financial centres do not share the same analysis of these funds. Some, like London, advocate a *laissez-faire* attitude in order to achieve enormous turnovers in returns.

Banking havens sheltered and intensified speculation, the source of the crisis. The complete absence of their cooperation with the tax, stock exchange and judiciary authorities cultivated the banking secret, and was used by banks to bypass regulations such as the prudential ratios. Bad debts could be then written off in the balance sheets of banks, through Structured Investment Vehicles (SIV) subtly hidden in offshore structures. Several toxic financial products found refuge in tax havens, with the complicity of interested banks worldwide. There are between thirty and fifty offshore centres in the world, nourishing a lack of transparency that eases substantial and unidentifiable movements of funds. Capital volatility is in opposition to the primary objective of banks, which is to secure and fix clients' deposits in order to exercise their capital-lender profession. Paradoxically, banks seem publicly concerned by anti-money laundering issues but, at the same time, they indirectly encourage obscure speculation.

The scarcity of regulation in the markets allowed short selling strategies that eased and then amplified the fall of markets. The practice of 'naked short selling' allows the selling of simply borrowed securities, while having three days to provide the guarantee that these securities really have been borrowed. The combination of disastrous rumours about companies doing these transactions and massive sales leads to downwards speculation that can be dramatic. In the US, more than 1,000 companies, all connected to financial activities, have been subject to authorised attacks from speculators worldwide. Today, the historical bastions of international finance are asked to be more rigorous, a reversal of roles that is paradoxical.

Rating agencies did not play their role in the quality assessment of players. They overestimated the quality of issuers and products that were proposed to investors and savers. Available funds travelled from one country to another, responding to the call for savings that were financially attractive as well rated. The AAA ('Triple A') rating, the best, has sometimes been attributed to companies having a bad financial situation. The role and mission of the rating agencies will be one of the crucial issues to address once the financial crisis under control. Here again, we are in a paradoxical situation with the incompetence of evaluators to measure the real capacity of the players to honour their signatures making these evaluators to act as pyromaniac fire fighters.

All these combined aspects can only contribute to a permanent international financial instability, consensually maintained by the demand of naïve clients and by the cynical offers of financial institutions. The recent Madoff story illustrates how far clients' credulity, even with an entry ticket of at least one million dollars, can be maliciously exploited, over decades, by unscrupulous financiers, thanks to (or because of) a globalised financial system unable to control the nature and content of funds that have been sailing from one financial market to another.

If the globalisation of trade flows has been managed progressively, it is because discrepancies are identified and evolutions are predictable. Several international organisations governing the world trade destiny seek to regulate the exchanges as well as the fragile North/South equilibrium.

This is not the case for the more important financial flows, which operate with virtually no regulatory framework and no genuine world governance.

We have already discussed the volatility of these funds, looking for the best return. This volatility may only stress the negative effects of the globalisation of markets. The past financial crises, like that which occurred a few years ago in South-East Asia, have led to severe adjustments, with consequences on the equilibriums of the countries affected.

This volatility of capital markets will lead to complex and interwoven consequences of various natures, such as the banking sector's deterioration and lost of credibility. The currency risk is, among others, an increased factor of vulnerability.

Deficiencies in the financial systems have been at the heart of the recent economic crises: they are the detonators of the current economic crisis. Nobody believes any longer in the valuation of each other's assets. This is as a result of vigilance, particularly on the structures of the balance sheets of banks and financial institutions, on the transparency of their activities and on the development of regulatory, supervision, and prudential control systems.

In this context, the banking sector is witnessing changes in its profession. Its activity is resolutely separated into two parts. The traditional activity of collecting deposits and granting loans remains the basis of the business. It is the bank's historical profession, in which margins are going to diminish because of the double effect of price competition in the mortgage markets, on the one hand, and the practice of a rather high return-policy for collected savings, on the other. The savings part is called 'regulated savings', with rates of return fixed by governments. It is usual to find in the mortgage market rates that are 1 per cent higher than those for savings. The generated margin cannot sufficiently feed the income statement. We can easily find in deposits banks rates of return of some savings accounts or time deposits that are largely higher than the interbank (money) markets' rates. The banking margin is negative, which disturbs the standards of the profession, where the return on credits should be largely higher than the costs of resources needed to put them in place.

How is it possible to see banks like the National Bank of Paris (BNP) exhibiting an operating income of €8 billion in 2007, despite some losses in the subprime area? This situation seems even more paradoxical since financial globalisation should, due to the development of the disintermediation, affect the profitability of banks. The financing of the economy is done more and more through financial markets, involving more and more investments funds, pension funds and, more generally, institutional investors. We can observe a process of linked diversification, which leads banks to explore the areas of activity that show the links with their core activity, thanks to the removal of regulatory barriers that previously compartmentalised the markets. We can also qualify linked diversification as economic diversification.

We have to conclude, therefore, that, paradoxically, banks make money in the areas of activity that should, *a priori*, condemn them to vegetate, that is, the area of market finance. Financial globalisation thus proves to be a major source of profits for the banks, the determinant contribution to the income statement. What a paradox this is – that we finally discover that banks and financial markets are not so very different!

Hence, do we conclude there is an erosion of the traditional role of banks? Or do we notice an enhancement of the financial intermediary function? In fact, the explosion of markets does not occur to the detriment of the historical intermediaries. Traditionally, a bank-based financial system is opposed to a market-based one. The reality is more complex and is sweeping away this dichotomy between the two approaches, due to the structural heterogeneity of the financial systems.

The explosion of capital markets turns out very profitable for banks that are becoming indispensable intermediaries, taking advantage of the windfall effect to multiply product- development. From now on, banks will be key players of the capital markets. In 1995, the banks' equity profitability was, on average, 3 per cent. Today, thanks to the activity of the financial markets, this profitability peaks at 15 per cent. How can we explain these spectacular results? Can we now discuss new strategies?

2   Towards a new strategy

2.1   Banking strategies

Two findings become obvious when observing banking strategies.

i. Life-insurance and securities have become very dynamic. Their savings offer more income than those of a bank's basic balance sheet. Moreover, both visible and less visible commissions (i.e. performance fees, management fees of life-insurance agreements, admission fees and management fees of the Undertakings for Collective Investments in Transferable Securities [UCITS]) are all recurrent and very profitable.

ii. International development, especially the acquisition of banks in emerging countries such as Russia, Romania or Turkey, where banking activities are still very weak, has become a dominant strategic axis that is, in itself, is a factor in profit-making. Banks are internationalising their activities through subsidiaries and affiliates.

The banking sector, therefore, now shows two diametrically opposed faces.

i. The financing of the economy through credit, the classical activity called balance intermediation: profitability is guaranteed by the flow found in the credit or debit side of the balance sheet and the intermediation margin (gross interest margin); in this case, resources are permanently locked.
ii. The intermediation in the capital (money) markets, which is the creation of new savings and speculation products, and operations outside of the balance sheet (signature commitments, finance commitments, forward and options contracts/fixed-term finances): profitability is made through collecting the commissions generated by commercial operations based on an indisputable and proved competency and reputation.

The verdict is convincing and, before the financial crisis, banks did better than survive thanks to the activity that, theoretically, was supposed to condemn them to collapse. Furthermore, this market intermediation is taking an important position in the structure of the gross financial margin, which is, beside the intermediation margin, the traditional basis of the profession. Therefore, the off-balance sheet value exceeds the in-balance sheet value. Globalisation is showing us a spectacular example of a paradoxical situation.

Naturally, the balance sheets of banks evolve. The share of the loans provided decreases significantly in favour of the purchase of securities. Also, clients' deposits are decreasing in favour of the creation of securities, a financial technique that is now unavoidable based on the volumes processed. The corollary is that income structure also changes. The traditional activity of collecting deposits and providing loans contributes less than 50 per cent of the result. The bulk of profitability is mainly due to several products, mostly extracted from the market's activities. This new intermediation is, in addition, easily mobilised thanks to the steadying (*mobiliérisation*) of the supports.

In contrast, the recent loss of €5 billion caused by a single, badly supervised 'trader', who took hazardous and speculative risks, of which the Société Générale was the victim, illustrates how considerable the amounts can be and, as a consequence, the sensitivity to the risk market is very important. The decision taken by the bank's management to close in a single day its risky positions is probably somewhat responsible for the crash of the markets on 'Black Monday', 21 January 2008. A single individual holding few responsibilities caused losses that are far in excess of the €2 billion of consecutive reserves (provisions) to the subprime mortgage crisis.

Thus, banks do not see the capital market as a competitor but rather as a wonderful opportunity to multiply their profits; however, there are risks, as we have discovered.

2.2   The relationship between the banks and the markets: competition or partnership

It is certain that, in any event, this movement of banks towards the markets was unavoidable, with an effective risk of having to notice a gradual decline of goodwill. The erosion of interest margins should be largely compensated for by the multiplication of commission. Financial intermediation both develops and relies on banks.

We can see that intermediation of savings remains the major activity compared with the direct investment of savings in the markets. The process of disintermediation of savings seems to have stabilised. We can even foresee a temporary slowdown of the use of disintermediation as a result of people's distrust of online banking and all virtual institutions.

Retail banking remains at the heart of the profession, allowing a network of agencies to capture all types of clients, whether at home or abroad. Field coverage by this network is still essential and the location of point-of-sale remains strategic.

Based on this core business, which allows the gaining of a clientèle that needs a chequebook, an address for their invoices and bills, and facilities for services and savings, banks have the means to engage in new and far more profitable businesses.

2.3   The new technologies

Globalisation has contributed to the emergence of new technologies, which highlights yet another paradox. These new technologies could give rise to severe competition through the possible emergence of modern online banks, which are both less costly and available 24/7. If these technologies are now in the picture, however, they have not yet produced significant competition.

The reverse is also true. Banks are able to exploit new technologies, through multiplying computer links with their clients, who thus find themselves more entangled with their bank than previously. Thanks to these new technological tools, banks have a more intimate knowledge of their customers' consumption habits and savings patterns, so allowing them to better serve their customers, and also to make additional profits.

2.4   The formation of large international banking groups

Financial globalisation also has other impacts, such as the gradual formation of international banking groups, through mergers-acquisitions that often are cross-border and represent a substantial part of the Gross Domestic Production (GDP) worldwide. If the industrial sector of the new technologies remains the primary area of these groups, today the banking and insurance areas occupy the second rank. This situation is also paradoxical. The rationale of banks aims for a strong corporate culture and systematic customer loyalty, while globalisation pushes towards the acquisition of institutions with different strategies and clients, by definition, who are completely unknown. The quest of growth, therefore, entails the abandonment of the profession's standards.

The logic of enlarged groups has the same requirements as those of industry: to research development through external rather than internal growth (less spectacular and probably more onerous), to correlate the increase of market shares and hence of turnover, to search for rapid diversification, to be concerned with economies of scale, to gradually remove competition and so on.

Banks internationalise their activities and globalise their operations.

i. The internationalisation phase corresponds to the search for resistance to the existing competitive pressures, in either foreign or domestic markets.
ii. The globalisation phase has the objective of organising the resources to both obtain the highest efficiency and to reinforce competitiveness. Globalisation and the building of integrated economic zones have strongly stressed mergers that are started within the industrial sector before extending to the service sector.

The strategy for banks during the period 1980–2000 was to collect deposits in their domestic markets and to re-lend part of them in other foreign markets. Twenty-five years ago, the World Bank and the International Monetary Fund recommended the opening of economies to international capital movements. This increasing international mobility of capital was then labelled as financial globalisation. From then on, collection of deposits could take place on foreign markets with concomitant credit activity within the same territories. This is why we can talk about 'globalisation'. However, in reality, we notice a double strategy.

i. The strategy of wholesale, investment and financing banks is to think about internationalisation. Wholesale banks are those whose core business is with investment banks and who want to expand their retail activities.
ii. The strategy of retail banks is to think locally. These banks practise in close proximity with their clients, and their multi-speciality means that they want to diversify on all the markets, particularly on the capital (money) markets.

This new approach is justified by the fact that clients move, either for private or professional reasons. Before trying to attract new clients, banks start by working on retaining their current clients, regardless of location, through intensifying their network. Today, the private client wants to do business with a major financial institution that has local branches. Companies want to use international banks established close to them. To summarise, therefore, banks need to be everywhere in the world in order to serve their clients.

Moreover, a conquest strategy leads the banks to try to capture additional clients, often complementary to the existing ones. European banks benefit from a competitive advantage over the banks of target countries, which is their know-how. These banks have more than twenty years of advancement in terms of facilities for clients of products or services, as well as offering administrative facilities at the point-of-sale.

Independent of this commercial aspect of the client relationship, we also particularly find that the profit growth areas are at international level. The potential for gains in these markets is important and becomes more so when entry barriers are reduced. The contribution from activities abroad to the profits result of the major French banks exceeds 50 per cent. The growth potential of the French banks in their traditional retail activities with their domestic clients is almost non-existent. In a climate that leaves little space for growth, the banking population is almost 100 per cent, with a high level of service and product facilities. Development within this saturated mar ket can be done only at the expense of the competition, which is also in a defensive standby position.

Geographical diversification is imposed on banks due to lack of potential within their own market. This diversification will be done in markets with limited banking facilities, competing with domestic players that are unaccustomed to competition and efficiency, and speculating on an anticipated future growth similar to the one previously known in Western economies. It is certain that banks, motivated by a conquest desire, can legitimately aspire to profitability and competitiveness using these new opportunities.

This international mesh concerns almost all the profession's business areas, with a selective internationalisation practice, based on the chosen development axes: investment bank, retail bank, private banking or asset-management bank. We can, therefore, speak of the global banking firm.

These developments are facilitated by several main phenomena:

- The relaxation of legal barriers, such as abandoning the concept of exchange control.
- The advent of a global shareholder, made possible by computerised access to all the world's financial markets in real time.
- The internationalisation of staff, and the research into the cultures, professions and profiles of these new countries, in order to facilitate integration. This process begins at the level of students who, in their academic curriculum, have periods of internship abroad. The French banks can easily integrate into their teams foreign personnel, or send French staff collaborators to their branches abroad.

- The relocation of the financial sector, especially within emerging countries, which hosts back-office services and call centres of banks from all countries.
- The capital mobility among the major financial centres, facilitated by the development of information technologies and data transmission.
- The place taken by information technologies in the production process of banking and insurance companies.
- The competition for the supply of prices and products, generating both creativity and diversification.
- The search for economies of scale and spread.
- Customer loyalty, the source of new attractive products.
- Deregulation, which facilitates capital movement and allows banks to practise all their monetary business. The legal framework of various European banking systems, including the European directive of 1993 on investment services, opens the door to universal banking. Depending on the country, the directive may cover the entire banking operation and allow diversification, liberalisation, de-specialisation and involvement in the investment and insurance sectors.
- The achievement of the single European market.

This paradoxical situation of retail banks seeking access to new profitable markets leads them to want to conquer at the international level in all areas: access to securities' primary market (stocks or bonds), the design and promotion of new financial products, the advisory business to issuers, the fundraising operations, the complex financing arrangements and the development of private banking, middle-office and back-office.

Banks cultivate their paradoxical management in order to develop their profession. They continue to offer loans, but also underwrite securities. Their balance sheet becomes more oriented towards working in the markets evolving from the usual structure of deposits and loans. It is ultimately hard to distinguish financial systems based on financial markets from financial systems based on the banking system. To be convinced, one should look at their operation in different countries. This paradoxical equilibrium, banking system-capital markets, depends on the size of banks, their level of specialisation or universality, the level of concentration, the corporate governance system, the original characteristics, the historical background and so on.

Analysts distinguish in a systematic way between the Anglo-Saxon countries, which are more oriented towards markets, and countries like Germany and Japan, which are more oriented towards traditional banking. The former are funded by shareholders and creditors involved in a large number of listed companies in a liquid financial market. The latter are funded by a less scattered ownership, financial holding companies. Latin systems leave a major control role to shareholders, the state and owner-families. According to governance models, one can expect strategies that are differentiated at the international level. According to their market orientation, the Anglo-Saxon institutions can engage in external growth operations such as the acquisition of shares or take-over bids.d The other players are motivated more by a negotiated-partnership approach than by hostile takeovers.

The paradox generates from the multiplication of products, services and, more importantly, the players. These are the source of capital flow worldwide, flow that is much larger than that identified in the international trade of goods and services. The subprime mortgage crisis is a dramatic although unexpected result, but one of the important flows initiated by actors seeking to maximise performance.

This same crisis demonstrates, moreover, that the financial system works with actors who all have commitments, *vis-à-vis* others, and use as support products that are often innovative with consequences that can be dramatic, in the case of failure. The financial press qualifies this phenomenon as 'the domino effect'. For example, the collapse of the US bank Bear Stearns was hastened by its colleagues, who refrained from lending it money on contracted interbank markets. This institution was in a paradoxical situation: on the one hand, it had to respect the obligation to have security reserves and so have significant equity; on the other, it could not raise cash even though it had quality assets as collateral. This normally solid bank was in extreme difficulty through being the victim of a trust crisis and a 'bank run' (customers in a panic who rush to immediately remove their assets and/or cash deposits). In the emergency the US central bank was forced to buy $30 billion of very poor-quality assets before merging the institution with one of Bear Stearns' colleagues, J. P. Morgan. The system relies on trust between its various protagonists. Since banks are failing in their role as lenders, there is a break in the refinancing chain. Failure of one bank can automatically lead to failure in the next in line, and so on. There is a liquidity crisis worldwide, since all banks, in a classic scenario, lend to one another. This is a new effect, and not least one, which has been created by globalisation.

3 Some answers and new perspectives

The only remaining solution to the banking liquidity crisis is the massive intervention of central banks and governments of all the countries affected. Central banks are flooding liquidity markets with hundreds of billion of dollars. Governments are committing their signature to and guaranteeing loans made between banks, in the expectation that the process will be restarted.

In some cases, states implement rescue plans to save their strategic financial bastions. For example:

- Fortis and Dexia in Belgium and the Netherlands
- the US insurer AIG
- the refinancing mortgage agencies Freddie Mac and Fannie Mae, from which the Federal Reserve has bought, for $500 billion, securitised mortgages products, since early 2009
- the bad debts being accumulated in the balance sheets of Japanese banks, which the Central Bank of Japan plans to buy back, for €78 billion, using the Deposit Insurance Corporation of Japan.

However, rescue by the state is not always the case. The US government allowed the fourth major US bank, Lehman Brothers, to go bankrupt. It was 160 years old, and had over 25,000 employees. This was the biggest bankruptcy in US history.

3.1   Towards a review of international accounting standards

We are in the middle of paradoxical situations that might lead to criticism of the international accounting standards, and particularly the concept of 'intrinsic value', translated from the American term 'fair value'. These rules provide that complex derivative products, traded over the counter, should be given their market value at the time and not their historical value established over a specific period. As a result, the balance sheets of financial institutions lose their significance, due to the absence of markets for particular toxic products. However, this absence is partially due to the crisis of trust in assets valuation. We can then question the accounting rules of 'mark to market'.

Richard Bove, a well-known analyst of the US banking system, noted that the CMBX index, which reflects the value of securitised products related to commercial real estate, provides a default rate of 30 per cent, while in fact it is around 1 per cent. This raises the question whether the problem lies upstream, i.e. at the governance level of these standards and the absence of real control. It should be emphasised that, starting from the implementation of these new international rules on 1 January 2007, many financial institutions took the opportunity to raise the value of their securitised products and boost their results. Today, it is the strictly opposite movement that is produced, and assets value remains unrealistic. A few months ago, both American and European authorities formulated recommendations for improving this concept of fair value. Some structured products can now get out of 'trading books' and be classified in the 'banking books', which slightly inflates the balance sheets. The only modifications allowed by European authorities have produced a gap of €1 billion for the third quarter of the Deutsche Bank alone.

Globalisation has led to the implementation of international standards, applied by all institutions; the effects of these have been found to have contributed to the disaster. The paradox is that the primary concern of the legislation was to make assets situations transparent, and to allow a correct comparison of accounts.

The response of governments not only dictates accounting standards, but also addresses issues of risk control and compliance with legislation.

3.2 Towards a better risk management

The Banking Committee of the US Senate interviewed the major stakeholders of the New York financial industry to shed light on these unusual collapses. This helped the Federal Reserve to reconsider its position through ensuring that it has the authority and necessary power to respond to any systemic risk threatening financial stability. In 2008, the British bank Northern Rock faced a cash shortage that forced the UK Central Bank, being the last resort lender, to save the bank, the first time in forty years this has occurred. The bank was ultimately rescued by the state itself, through public support of £50 billion.

German banks BayernLB, WestLB and SachsenLB put rescue plans into place, solicited their shareholders (often, the Länder, i.e. the equivalent of US states), and established quarantine structures for the doubtful assets estimated for BayernLB alone at €24 billion. UBS (Union des Banques Suisses), one of the world's leading private banks, announced a further assets depreciation of $44 billion in its investment bank. Its cumulated provisions (reserves) reached more than $37 billion, a world record to date. The US bank Merrill Lynch exceeded $52 billion in depreciation and losses. Its colleague, Citigroup, reached $60 billion; Britain's HSBC exceeds $27 billion. Others records are Morgan Stanley, JP Morgan Chase, Wachovia, Washington Mutual, Deutsche Bank, Crédit Suisse, Bank of America, Capital One, Royal Bank of Scotland and Crédit Agricole.

Some institutions create Assets Management Companies (AMCs) to isolate bad assets from the remaining activity that was considered profitable. Many managers demanded the creation of a 'bad bank' which would bring together €800 billion of toxic assets, a structure deemed necessary to restore trust between institutions and to revive the offer of loans. Others, such as USB, yield debt portfolios. On 15 September 2008, the financial community witnessed the unexpected, record bankruptcy of Lehman Brothers. The Californian credit institution Fremont General corporation filed a voluntary petition under chapter 11 of the US bankruptcy code. As part of measures taken jointly by the European Central Bank (ECB) and the Federal Reserve (FED) to restore the calm on the currency markets, the ECB has injected on several occasions, dozens of billions of euros of liquidity. Interdependence is, in this case, clearly established and demonstrates the consequences of the domino effect.

It is interesting to observe that, affected by the financial crisis, the banks have announced strict plans, particularly a reduction of the scope of their market activities. This shows a reorientation towards a gradual return to core businesses. They recognise that it is not enough to accumulate assets to make money, and in reality they are no longer able to understand all their activities. They have to ask themselves about their key competencies and their comparative advantages. Are we, therefore, going to witness a massive return to the core business, as did many industrialists in the recent past? Are we going to become spectators of the end of the paradox of bankers who want to manage businesses that are not theirs?

3.3   Towards a refocus of the bank's core business

Globalisation upsets the usual classification of banks. The activities of retail banks are traditionally in the local market, as the banks look for proximity to customers, to minimise the chances of misinformation between them. The banking market's scope has always been based on geographical criteria, for obvious reasons of convenience and culture. Conversely, investment banks practise their activity at a worldwide level, i.e. the global scope. In recent years, major French banks have been working to engage both sectors, with the objective of increasing their gross financial margin via capital markets activities, mergers and acquisitions, brokerage and analysis, derivatives and structured finance. Obstacles to this strategy are real, particularly entry barriers in foreign markets. Among these are contractual implementation costs, lack of reputation, new consumers' capture costs, adapting techniques used in the territories invested, technology costs, cultural barriers, managerial practices, the distortion of organisational practices, regulatory barriers, protectionist vigilance of some central banks and political interference.

However, globalisation is followed by national policies of deregulation in favour of supranational regulations. In many cases, states withdraw from economic and financial affairs, in particular from the privatisation of the banking sector. In addition, since 1992, the opening of the European banking system was established with regulations that authorise free establishment of banks and free provision of financial services within the European Community. We can now talk about the harmonisation of banking rules in Europe, thanks to a number of guidelines that remove obstacles to the development of companies in Europe, particularly the single banking licence. The EU Markets in Financial Instruments Directive (MIFID) has been in force since 1 November 2007. This directive answers the requirements of the structural changes of markets, such as the emergence of the euro, the weakening of national barriers, the growing use of corporate capital markets, the exponential increase in transaction volumes, the numerous financial innovations or the emergence of new trading systems. These are all factors that required the establishment of a truly integrated market for the benefit of investors, issuers and for the European economy. MIFID addresses the following objectives:

- to establish a healthy competition between the different methods of carrying out clients' instructions;
- to harmonise and strengthen the protection of investors, particularly during the marketing of financial products;
- to ensure the integrity of the European banking system.

A directive on payment services was also adopted in 2007 to make payments within the EU easier and safer. In 2008, the Single Euro Payments Area was established.

Beyond these regulatory aspects, the partitioning of financial practices has been removed, products and services have been simplified, and the businesses of banks have converged.

The universal bank is gradually establishing itself, the heart of its business being retail banking, openness to other businesses and skills, and cross-border freedom.

Banking market in Europe is saturated and highly concentrated. Actors are cramped in their domestic market. Therefore, growth depends on international development. It is the big banks, specialists in asset management and investment banking, which have global ambitions, obviously related to the search for improved productivity and performance, value creation, efficiency and, of course, return on equity.

The possible failure of external growth operations abroad is usually due to a lack of synergies between the regrouped entities, to errors in communication both internally and externally, to the telescoping of strategies far distant from each other and to the oversizing of some players.

The paradox is that failure for the banks is success for customers who take advantage of tough competition on prices, quality services, products and overall performance from all points of view. The happy compromise would obviously be a win-win between banks and customers.

The primary purpose of searching economies of scale and range through growth often encounters problems caused by the management of too-complex organisations. Size is not a key to success. Cost control is much more a managerial problem than a technical matter.

This paradoxical situation of banks, which we strive to highlight, is illustrated by the opposition retail/wholesale banking and the research, not of global economies of scale, but of specific economies of scale. It is in this spirit that the changing role of the banker now operates. Banks are looking for activities that create value and are considering each area individually.

Business-oriented markets benefit from savings related to transaction costs and operational expenses. New technologies in the field of transferring and processing information can process many transactions at a controlled cost. They help manage a growing volume of transactions at a decreasing cost. It is interesting to note in this regard the contribution of computing platforms, call centres, video-texts servers and so on. A stock market order routed over the Internet costs almost nothing but is cosily invoiced. In addition, the systematic exploitation of information collected allows 'middle-office' services to process data utilisable by the 'front-office' service in the pursuit of the achievement of business development and objectives.

It is therefore important to explore the sources of economies of scale resulting from the use of new technologies. The new business of the bank, oriented towards the capital markets find there pockets of new profits. The finance market is a competence centre that creates value.

4   Conclusion

Banks are at a crossroads. What conclusions will they draw, what consequences will they realise from this financial crisis? Are we going to witness the questioning of the strategies of maximising profits by adopting new businesses? Is this paradoxical situation of institutions that are no longer doing well in their traditional banking business, as it is defined by the first article of the banking law of 24 January 1984, going to persist? At what point will the influence of shareholders, who primarily expect higher dividends, become decisive, even at the risk of seeing the most prestigious companies lose billions or even lose their identity?

What will be the limits of uncontrolled globalisation without effective governance? The coming months will reveal the choices made by leaders of the major players in international finance, whether commercial banks, investment banks or investment funds.

The financial crisis of 2007–2009 may have contributed to a resituating of the issues and a return to reason.

Reference

Tournois, N. and Fischer, M. (2008) *La Création de Valeur dans la Banque*. Paris: Vuibert.

Further reading

Borderie, A. and Lafitte, M. (2004) *La bancassurance, stratégies et perspectives en France et en Europe*. Paris: Revue Banque Edition.
Comité Consultatif du Secteur Financier (2007) Les enjeux économiques et sociaux de l'industrie bancaire. *Alternatives Economiques*, January: 254.
Gannon, Martin J. (2007) *Paradoxes of Culture and Globalization*. California: Sage Publications.

Lamarque, E. (2005) *Management de la banque, risques, relation client, organisation*. Paris: Pearson Education.

Montel-Dumont, O. (2007) *Mondialisation et commerce international*. Paris: Les Cahiers Français.

Pastré, O., Blommestein, H., Jeffers, E., de Pontbriand, G. and Noyer, C. (2005) *La nouvelle économie bancaire*. Paris: Economica.

Plihon, D., Couppey Soubeyran, J. and Saïdane, D. (2006) Les banques, acteurs de la globalisation financière. *Les études de la documentation française*, November–December.

Saïdane, D. (2006) *La Nouvelle Banque*. Paris: Revue Banque Edition.

14
Concluding Chapter – Globalisation and Scenarios: A Paradoxical Navigation

Anne Marchais-Roubelat and Fabrice Roubelat

When a strategy that was efficient yesterday is counter-efficient today, the decision-maker often invokes complexity and time acceleration. When companies have become a nexus for contracts concluded between geographically separated stakeholders, the manager speaks of globalisation. Looking for a methodology enabling him to manage the dynamics of interacting stakeholders, a futures-thinking approach may well come to mind. From its inception, this approach takes as a given the fact that decisional contexts are likely to be increasingly unstable and interdependent. The futures approach developed from the post-war period attempts to mix the long-term visions of decision-makers, managers and academics with the aim of enlightening decisional processes. Such a futures-oriented thinking outlines several possible worlds, the existence of only one of which would be promoted (Berger, 1964: 226). The objective here is to highlight the gaps between these worlds and the one in which the decisions are made.

Designed for geopolitical futures (Kahn and Wiener, 1967) and disseminated via issues of globalisation and the transformation of the environment of energy companies (Lesourne and Stoffaës, 2001; Wack, 1985a; 1985b), futures scenarios propose representations, for managers, of these possible worlds. Founded on visions of structurally different futures (Van der Heijden, 1996), they propose at the organisational scale as many competing rationalities – alternative scenarios – as may be imagined and thereafter integrated into the decision-making process. Paradoxically, because of the very instability and acceleration of the change and decision-processes themselves, the modelling of temporal dynamics is tending to disappear from futures thinking (Gonod, 1996; Roubelat, 2001). Scenarios, in this case, favour alternative world-based thinking; that is to say, based on the nature of the gaps, instead of questioning decisional processes and, consequently, the patterns of these gaps.

At a time when globalisation (which should be thought of as a process and not a state) lends its full meaning to Berger's initial proposition (this deformation of the global system caused by the differentiated acceleration of the evolutionary dynamics of its interacting sub-systems), the evolution of futures methods leads us to preach Berger's 'far sight', setting aside time and action in the construction of scenarios. Thus, within the scope of a globalisation making any vision of the future unstable, we may question the interest of integrating a temporal dynamic in 'thinking the unthinkable' (Kahn, 1962) and even assume the illusory nature of futures studies (McDermott, 1996). We may also consider some of the dilemmas of the futures methodology (Gaspar and Novaky, 2002: 373), including that which consists in questioning the opportunity of researching different alternative scenarios given that firstly, the 'existence of only one of them will occur', and secondly, given the growing complexity and instability of the world, the scenarios imagined will never really correspond to this occurring future.

We thus reach a paradox: it is precisely when the manager has the greatest need to navigate his way through globalisation that the thinking on the processes is abandoned and that the modelling of temporal dynamics disappears, as well as the analysis of systems and the uncomfortable paradoxes it reveals (Barel, 1973). Although the futures approach was designed for a globalisation that was merely a possible future, must it stop just as the scenario that seems to be unfolding today proves to be precisely that for which it was created?

On closer inspection, is a paradox any more than a purely abstract construction? Does the futures approach really generate the impossibility of conceptualising the future in the context of globalisation? Or may we re-examine the scenarios (namely, their alternative character) at the expense of a rethink on their insertion into the action (since what fundamentally interests the manager is neither the decision nor the forecast, but essentially the action)?

In fact, the paradox stems essentially from the disappearance not only of time but, above all, of the action in the representations produced by futures thinking, despite the fact that these were invented upstream to evaluate the consequences of gaps between the time of making the decision and the action. Are scenarios merely a paradoxical illustration of the paradoxes they raise, or an actual management tool tailored to globalisation and to managers engaged in action? This issue firstly needs to be examined from the perspective of the two component characteristics of globalisation, instability and interdependence, so as to determine the relative importance of the principles underlying the approach and the historical development of the methodological practices. Returning to these principles, scenarios may be designed in which the conditions under which the rules of the game are changed are substituted for the search for structures that no longer exist. In this case, the scenarios are no longer considered as rigid and necessarily alternative structures, but as historical processes able to succeed one another and combine. Work is no longer done on the developments leading to such scenarios, the scenarios are themselves this development. Instability and interdependence (characteristics of globalisation), far from constituting an impediment for the manager, on the contrary appear to be his strategic instruments.

By way of a conclusion, we will develop the research perspectives generated by this reversal for decision-makers, particularly with respect to the emerging issue of the individual will, which we imagine may, in the future, form the hub of the action in this process that constitutes globalisation.

1 Globalisation and foresights: the search for the action in scenarios

Originators of futures thinking, Berger (1964) and Jouvenel (1964) were interested in the relation between the content and the consequences of the decision. Classically, the decision is conceived as both the choice and the content of this choice; the futures problems coming from the fact that the consequences may have effects in a world that is totally different from that in which they were prepared (Berger, 1964). In other words, decisions must be justified in order to apply them, since the justification enabling their implementation can be based only on a past or on a future that prolongs them, whereas the application itself will take place in conditions that are radically different from those that enabled this justification. As an aid to decision-making, the futures approach tackles both the problem of the decision as a choice, and the monitoring over time of the consequences of the decision.

However, the time in question for futures is not the linear time of the mathematician, nor that of the philosopher. It is that of the decision-maker (today, the managers) engaged in the action. Jouvenel evokes a process that seems to him important enough to be precisely defined as the 'development of a phenomenon that has not been selected as a goal by human will but which is the effect of a complex combination of actions that do not deliberately strive to be so' (Jouvenel, 1964: 144). If reference is made, therefore, to the founding fathers of the concepts of 'prospective anthropology' and 'futuribles' (i.e. possible futures), futures thinking is firstly considered within the context of a dynamic temporal process (that is developing), eminently complicated, constructed via human interactions to which it is, nevertheless, an exception. This definition of the process – given well before the advent of the present-day concept – incorporates elements of constructivism and globalisation (instability and interdependence). Because of its interest in the process, futures thinking is thus inherently within the logic of globalisation. The issue of time and interaction is, therefore, central, but not for reasons of intellectual speculation: on the response made depends not only the actual tools that are put into practice, but also the sense that is made of our actions.

1.1   Long term, instability and globalisation: from alternative worlds to interacting scenarios

For Berger, the contemporary period is marked by the differential acceleration of time: our environment constitutes a system whose multiple sub-systems evolve at different rhythms. Consequently, the decision cannot be justified by the projection of the past towards the future, since the global system deforms in the meantime. If everything were to evolve at the same pace, projections could be made to simulate the future and the validity of our decisions could be established. On the contrary, in as much as time evolves differentially, temporal ruptures or shifts are to be expected and navigated (Grove, 1997). However, while it is not known either when or which new rules of the game will emerge, it is precisely within this unknown world that the consequences of our present actions will be felt. From a temporal perspective, the articulation between the action and the prospective future raises the question of the voluntary orientation of a future that we cannot conceive either by analogy or by extrapolation (Berger, 1964), but only by the imagining of possible futures. In that the futurible – deriving from the construction of an imagining of possible futures (Jouvenel, 1964) – is a concept equivalent to that of a scenario (Kahn and Wiener, 1967), we should firstly concentrate on the conception of the future and its consequences on the construction of scenarios, before exploring the question of the voluntary orientation of the future within the context of globalisation.

At the turning point between the anticipation and the historical course of the action, futures-thinking scenarios, considered as a body formed from the description of a future situation and the unfolding of events, and taking us from the initial situation to the future situation (Bluet and Zémor, 1970), thus propose alternative visions of a world that enable the connection to be made between the decision-justification process and the anticipation of possible futures. From this perspective, they appear not only as lists of hypothetical events made to attract attention to the important points and their causes (Kahn and Wiener, 1967), but also as sets of reasonably plausible but structurally different futures, as mentioned in the introduction (Van der Heijden, 1996), and enable the effects of a decision to be envisaged in different possible futures.

In a scenario-based futures-thinking exercise, the aim is firstly to bring the actors to project the events of the ongoing action towards possible futures, and secondly, to lead these same actors to construct imaginary alternative futures, to interpret the future unfolding of these events. In this case, they must be made to change their attitude with respect to the future by bringing them to opt either – to use a distinction well established in game theory – for the principle of forward induction, where the game is solved starting from the beginning, or for the principle of backward induction, where the game is solved from its ending (Jungermann, 1985). Yet, depending on which principle is selected, the game is not solved in the same way, leading us to consider two separate paths developed from two different ways of viewing the action.

In a globalising world, these two approaches are doubly advantageous. Firstly, using a forward induction approach by means of projective scenarios the consequences of ongoing or even incipient processes can be shown. These projective scenarios can be obtained either by simply pursuing the phenomena observed or by amplifying them. Thus, without changing the nature of the ongoing action process, the decision-maker will see the consequences of his decisions, or absence of decisions. Projective scenarios may, in this case, prove unacceptable, as in the Datar (French regional planning agency) scenario of the same name (Durand, 1972). They may also cause a major rethink, such as those scenarios of continuous change which, continuing past structures in the future, highlight their very obsolescence, or such as the strategic scenarios of Electricité de France (EDF), the public utility, in *EDF in 2025*, which amplify the vast movement of the deregulation of public services under the effects of globalisation (Roubelat, 2006). This logic of projective scenarios amounts to an extrapolation, sometimes taken to extremes, of the processes linked to globalisation, such as the liberalisation of the economy, the spread of western democracy after the collapse of the Soviet bloc and the structuring of the world around totally fluid transport and communication networks, leading some to wonder about reaching an end of history (Fukuyama, 1989) and others to suggest an end to geography (O'Brien, 1992) as the number of possible futures becomes increasingly limited.

However, these projective scenarios are not the only ones imaginable since the other approach, that of backward induction, proposes surprise scenarios linked to accidents of history, such as 11 September 2001 (so-called '9/11'), that enable these same thinkers to question the return of history (Fukuyama, 2002) and that enable those observers of management practices to proclaim the return, in view of 9/11, to the use of contingency-planning scenarios: 'companies recognising the greatest risks and opportunities linked to globalisation, and the increasing need to anticipate crises and to develop robust contingency plans' (Rigby and Bilodeau, 2007: 22).

The scenario-construction methodology is an attempt to respond to the paradox of the decision in action raised by Berger, by comparing the possible decisions with the scenarios – be they projective or surprise – in which they could develop. Indeed, the issue of the justification of the decision supposes an approach that moves from the present to the future and that is comparable with that of forward induction. On the contrary, the anticipation of a world in which the effects of the decision will unfold supposes that any surprises, or even accidents, are imagined in the form of ruptures that can lead from modes of control that are presently known, or at their onset to future modes of control that are not known at present, or that are considered as implausible. Thus, any representations envisaged for the future must be used as a basis to form a link with ongoing processes as in backward induction. Indeed, if 9/11 may be considered as an unexpected event, it is equally true that 'thinking the unthinkable' echoes the processes that enabled this unexpected event to modify the course of history. Thus, the logic of backward induction consists in reconstructing the countdown of a process, to which no attention was previously given, and whose effects are felt only when this process leads the course of history to be suddenly called into question, that is to say that of projective scenarios with which these unexpected event or surprise scenarios appear to be competing. For example, for the *EDF in 2025* scenarios, European surprise scenarios, in which a Europe is constructed that is deregulated with respect to energy, appears to counter the principle of subsidiarity, which justified all the other visions of the world and enabled the globalisation of the electricity market to be rejected as a surprise.

Once these surprises have come to pass, are those scenarios that did not include them simply swept aside, eliminated through the change of course? If we consider, to borrow from Berger once again, that from among several possible worlds, only one would be promoted into existence (Berger, 1964: 226) and that the changes of course must be deemed irreversible, the decision-maker faces the risk of his decision being implemented in a world for which it was not intended. To avoid this risk, he must look for robust contingency plans, as mentioned by Rigby and Bilodeau, which will enable him to maintain a certain latitude with respect to the zones of uncertainty revealed by the scenarios (Schoemaker, 2002). Such an attitude assumes, from a strategic perspective, the capacity of constructing options compatible with a large number of scenarios, the modalities of occurrence in time of these scenarios being now of little importance. Besides the difficulties that the decision-maker may encounter in designing an incremental strategy in a world where ruptures have become commonplace, such an attitude assumes that the scenarios unfold regardless of the wishes of the actor on whom they are imposed: these are the constraints of his external environment. If, however, the future is understood constructivistically, the strategy of the actor will interact with the remainder of his environment: even if a single world occurs, it is the construction of that specific world to which he will have contributed. The art of his strategy will rely on his capacity to recognise when several scenarios interact, and when one of them is emerging or may be purposefully promoted, even if it means the irruption of a world that is unknown but about which he has great expectations. From a strategic point of view, the interaction taken to its limits makes it necessary to look back at the relation between scenarios and the notion of what constitutes the long term.

In globalisation, the relativity of the temporal horizon justifies the approximate choice of durations (twenty years, 100 years and so on) or dates (2025, 2100) for most studies, since the idea is simply to place the deadline in an 'after' when the rules operant today are no longer valid. It also explains why this notion related to duration is particularly judicious, since even tomorrow is located in the long term: 'in the game we must play today, rules are being modified incessantly, whereas the pieces change their number and properties even during the game itself' (Berger, 1964: 223). If we then push this notion to one side in order to focus on the content by event of alternative scenarios, it then becomes pointless; especially as we neglect the second difficulty inherent in globalisation, which is the interaction between the different dimensions of the process. Focusing on scenarios as exclusive situations effectively over-simplifies this complexity by reducing it to a set of simple dimensions for which zones of latitude merely have to be defined. Since each zone corresponds to one or several scenarios, we can wonder, on the contrary, about the interactions between these dimensions over time, as well as about the dynamics that will enable the strategy to produce creative irreversibility or to maintain latitude in its irreversibility. However, is this not precisely the role of the strategist subjected to globalisation – to continue to navigate through known waters that have been foreseen, at the risk of being drowned by a tsunami submerging his flexible strategies; or to venture between Charybdis and Scylla into new waters of which he knows neither the currents nor the sirens?

1.2   Exacerbation of the interactions in globalisation: the prospective imaginary as an instrument in the sense-making

As highlighted by Jouvenel (1964), action is a process without purpose, that is to say it is constructed by actors in pursuance of projects but is itself so complex that it escapes them. This does not mean that actors behave as simple variables dependent on their environment: their behaviour is oriented by their will. It is also the will of actors acting with a view to a purpose *to come*, and consequently necessarily imaginary, that constructs the action in practical terms. It is generally useful to distinguish between the construction of the actors' imaginary by futures thinking (in terms of method) and the result sought after in this type of construction in the potential orientation of the action, and thus forecasting's function in aiding strategic decision-making, which means questioning the ideological and scientific functions of scenarios. However, this distinction will thereafter need to be re-examined in the light of the exacerbation of the interactions within the context of globalisation and their consequences on the decision and the action itself.

Technically, the construction of the imaginary of the actors by futures thinking is a process in itself: it is the collective process of scenario construction. From this perspective, the result will depend on the method by which the group of actors made to interact is constituted, as well as how it acts. The idea is to integrate in a global vision the beliefs with regard to the future of actors from different domains; that is to say, going back Berger's (1964) initial objective to get 'a philosopher, a psychologist, a sociologist, an economist, an educationalist, several engineers, a doctor, a statistician, a demographer' to work together (p. 224). Similarly, the pre-visional forum advocated by Jouvenel (1964) is designed as an institution intended to combine, by way of global forecasts, the specific forecasts of experts from different fields. Thus, in the prospective imaginary, the world can no longer be considered as being segmented, but must combine the beliefs of actors that could have been, even yesterday, treated separately.

Futures thinking is thus applied to the cross expression of implicit and explicit beliefs with respect to the future, even more than to expert knowledge. These beliefs are those of the different actors linked either to the issue of futures thinking, or to the organisation and its environment, leading futures thinking to be cautious in its consideration of the notion of expertise and to discuss in an interactive process the individual and collective representations that are constructed by the collective process. This evolution towards futures thinking as the result of collective thinking appeared very early, in the review *Prospective* from Berger's Centre International de Prospective. The prospective views of the great names featured at its onset were rapidly followed by collective productions that expressed the interactions assumed by ongoing globalisation. This was particularly the case for the aircraft engine manufacturer Snecma, with their applied futures-thinking experiment that accompanied the emerging structuring process of the aeronautic industry in Europe (Roubelat, 2000). In addition to being an instrument for analysis, futures thinking has thus become an exercise in sense-making, of mobilisation around a project (Lesourne, 1985).

As an exercise in sense-making, futures thinking fulfils a certain number of different functions that may be classified (Barel, 1971) according to whether or not they seek to construct knowledge (scientific function) or to influence the construction of the future (ideological function); these two function types being complementary rather than antagonistic. From this perspective, scenarios appear to be constructed beliefs that can challenge strategic paradigms (Roubelat, 2006). The scenarios thus find their equivalence in emerging ideologies; such ideologies being defined in the particular meaning of belief systems that explain the way the actors act and that lead to actions that are consistent with these beliefs (Van Dijk, 1998). These belief systems may be compatible with the dominant paradigm, and the scenarios will thus contribute to its corroboration. When the scenarios contradict the dominant paradigm they will, on the contrary, serve to challenge it. This contradiction explains the fact that the scenarios are more often than not considered as alternatives, even if the temporal shifts allow for periods of confrontation between the different visions of the future, and consequently for coexistence between scenarios.

The function of the created imaginary is to have the actors validate the required images of the future thereafter. The efficiency of this function depends, at this stage, on the capacity of the scenarios to emphasise the possible paths between the perceived present and the foreseen futures. It also depends on the number of scenarios foreseen, since the more numerous the scenarios, the greater the number of foreseeable paths.

These scenarios are ideologies also in the sense that they describe virtual states (in that they are not real) (Granger, 1995), which are both utopian and uchronical, the paths often being absent so as to leave the way clear for surprise scenarios that allow few interactions with the present action. Validating such scenarios thus corresponds to adopting an ideology. That they challenge existing ideologies by creating new ones does not pose a problem in itself to the manager, who is accustomed to strategic intent (Hamel and Prahalad, 1989). On the contrary, they constitute an exercise in sense-making, which – if it works in time – will avoid those strategic errors generated by the managers' possible blindness to the evolutions of their environment: since they do not foresee the rules changing, they do not always adapt in a timely fashion. Nevertheless, if this conception of scenarios is suited to a world (the end of the twentieth century) when periods of stability still reign, can the same be said when the only constant is that of change?

In this conception, where worlds are considered as alternatives, the scenario essentially indicates a state corresponding to a given system of beliefs. The improbable path that leads there assumes a certain stability in the development logics until such time as the proposed image is attained, otherwise the progression would become illogical. A second constraint stems from the fact that the scenarios are, in fact, states. The events composing them cannot belong to two different states at the same time, which would be paradoxal. These two constraints (stability of the development logic for each scenario and the mutual exclusion of the scenarios) necessarily makes them alternative. If the scenarios are alternative, it is not by choice, it is consequent to their mode of construction. Is this mode of construction still adapted to a globalised world where the development logics are precisely unstable and interactive? Is it relevant to seek paradigms to compete with the paradigms of globalisation? Is it possible to replace the existing methodology for scenario construction with one that specifically targets interdependency between scenarios in a globalised world?

2   Futures thinking within the scope of globalisation: a dissolution of time in action

If the idea of the relativity of the duration (from the perspective of the short/long-term relation) is present from the start in futures thinking, the scenarios have difficulties in translating this as the instability increases. In fact, the scenarios assume that the existing rules will last a relatively long time before becoming irreversible, such irreversibility being translated by a certain independence in the alternative images that they propose. The problem that arises is thus not that of futures thinking, but that of the design of scenarios methodology in the second half of the twentieth century, in an era when change is accelerated, undoubtedly, but not continuous. Henceforth, rather than imagining globalisation in the vein of Wiener's theory on plate tectonics, with coherent periods of evolution (the scenario paths) punctuated by catastrophic frictions and shocks (changes, of course), under the pressure of the deep uncontrollable movement of the underlying magma (the system strained by the differential accelerations of the sub-systems composing it), it is more appropriate to think in terms of the durable (and more importantly enduring) plates fusing. Thus, the manager now has to navigate directly on a magma where there remain no hardnesses to create friction, hence a situation that is totally unstable. In this idea of a world in fusion vehicled by globalisation, we no longer know if reversibility or irreversibility can exist outside the actors' representation of it. In this case, designing alternative scenarios is pointless, as is designing them on the basis of their event content, as for surprise scenarios.

What we are highlighting here is not, however, the paradox of futures thinking: obsolete before the advent of the world for which it was created. It is merely the necessary discussion of prospective scenarios methodologies under pressure of the conditions that justified them being challenged at a time when, despite the uncertainties already prevalent, a certain stability enabled the limits of the sub-processes of the global action to be recognised in space and time, immobilised in the scenarios images and marked out by lists of events. On the contrary, globalisation implies logics of transformation and interaction between the action processes.

2.1 Scenarios in globalisation: processes of action in interaction

From the first works of the Datar (Bluet and Zémor, 1970; Durand, 1972), and excluding the work on the application to scenarios of mathematical formulisations, such as Markovian processes (Eymard, 1977) or neural networks (Canarelli, 1995), the thinking on methodology has only rarely taken into account the issues of the modalities of transforming scenarios. Even methodologies such as those made popular by the Global Business Network (Schwartz, 1993; Van der Heijden, 1996) induce binary change logics leading to the construction of a number of scenarios reduced *a priori* (namely, four scenarios corresponding to the junction of two axes, each incorporating two possible states) that give global scenarios founded, not on logics of interaction, but on antagonistic logics. Even if new modes of representation are appearing, as in Shell's global 2025 scenarios, those scenarios are still founded on oppositions (Shell, 2005). Thus, the Flags scenario, nationalistic and communalist, assumes a slowing down of globalisation such as that developed in the Open Doors scenario. This results in a presentation of the future in the form of dilemmas and even trilemmas (a choice between three directions); that is to say, once again the necessity of choosing between alternative logics translated in the form of scenarios arises.

From this follows the paradox of the disappearance of time and, above all, of action in futures-thinking methodology, leading us to consider scenarios as action processes (Marchais-Roubelat, 2000), namely by delving more deeply into the conceptual aspects of retro-futures thinking (Lesourne, 2001) with a view to proposing a methodological frame within which the multiple aspects of globalisation may be made to interact. If we return to the concept at the origin of futures thinking – the action – this complex temporal process integrating the interactions of the actors in globalisation must be distinguished from the wishes of the actors themselves. The action has no goal whenever the actors may have ones; it is constructed by them and acts as a constraint on them at the same time.

Within this context, if instability makes the limits of a scenario ever more uncertain, it also makes its re-conception as a *phase* increasingly interesting. The latter is defined as a period during which a rule remains valid, the *rule* being understood as having the precise meaning of behavioural constraint or of the relation between variables (Marchais-Roubelat and Roubelat, 2008). We are thus faced once again with the idea of irreversibility and long-term changes at the basis of Berger's decisional paradox: as soon as the phase changes, the implementation of the decision follows other rules than those that governed its establishment. On the other hand, instability approaches the pace of strategy and futures thinking: the far horizon is no longer expressed in decades, from now on it is tomorrow for all the stakeholders as soon as the pieces change (the stakeholders present) and the rules are modified (the modalities of interaction between the stakeholders).

As a result, the construction methodology for imaginaries (namely the choice of stakeholders and their being made to interact) is not neutral, in that it is not detached from the ongoing action but, on the contrary, participates in its creation: 'the basic idea of sense-making is that reality is an ongoing accomplishment that emerges from efforts to create order and make retrospective sense of what occurs' (Weick, 1993: 635). From a constructivist point of view, therefore, futures thinking participates directly in action since, by creating their imaginary, the actors – as long as they are also stakeholders – agree on the sense of events that are happening, and on the sense of their own interactions. Thus, they organise themselves and construct the action by their imaginaries and their wishes, such action being punctuated by concrete events whose sense they agree on.

Nevertheless, the fact that the action has no goal does not justify the actors being 'short-sighted and interactive' (to borrow a term from game theory) and simply reacting to ongoing events. If they want to attain the goals they have fixed for themselves they must anticipate, or even create, the following rules, either in order to apply them or to facilitate (or avoid) their emergence. Instability and the interactions that characterise globalisation do not release the actors from the need to think about the scenarios, on the contrary, they render such thinking strategic.

Taken as phases in the action process, the scenarios can be constructed from three components:

i. a rule defining each scenario in an action logic;
ii. the differential evolution of the principle dimensions of the action (in particular, political, economic, societal, environmental);
iii. the strategies following the actors' behaviour (the state, which can, if need be, be broken down into different ministries or services, local authorities, European institutions, companies, associations and so on); the actors not necessarily being the same from one scenario to another.

In this type of scenario, the rule structuring the action is the fundamental element, in that it explains the evolution of the dimensions of the environmental context as well as the strategies of the actors, which are analysed not as detached from the action, but within the scenario, since they play a role in its evolutionary logic. When this rule changes, the scenario is changed, the different scenarios being able to constitute not only a before and/or an after, but also multiple phases in interaction as long as certain rules are enacted at the same time.

2.2   Globalisation and risk management: navigating between strategic scenarios

As the investigation by Rigby and Bilodeau (2007) has shown, one of the characteristics attributed to globalisation by decision-makers is that of the risks and crises that it is likely to generate. Rather than listing the innumerable unexpected events likely to occur, and trying to establish an infinite typology of the risks (nuclear, political, biological, social, alimentary, financial and so on), which would amount to their segmentation, the manager would prefer a global analysis of what risk management or crisis management may constitute since, in a globalised world, these risks, local at the origin, are likely to propagate and interact with one another. In this case, we have to wonder why, when and how we can move from one management mode to another, or even how to make the different management modes interact, which would imply a navigation between risk management modes suggested in scenarios on the risk management research-intervention for 2020 (Table 14.1; Pivot and Rychen, 2004; Marchais-Roubelat and Roubelat, 2008).

Within this perspective, the actors' strategies, as well as the evolutions in the dimensions of the action, are likely to make the different scenarios interact. The latter do not, in this case, simply constitute alternatives, but

Table 14.1   Risk management forecasting: scenarios and rules of action

Scenario	Rule of action in the scope of the scenario
Old Maid	The public authorities make society safe but pass on the risks to other actors when they become difficult to manage.
Monopoly	Society favours an individual response to risk.
Happy Families	The regional authorities become specialised in the management of those risks for which they have the necessary competency.
Meccano	The decentralised state administers the risks (with a European variant).
Tarot	The local actors manage the risks via negotiation.

Source: Marchais-Roubelat and Roubelat, 2008.

may be combined with one another, the actor being able to choose one rule rather than another or even enact several rules at once, depending on the risk undertaken and on the actor's strategic preferences or on the unfolding of the action.

Thus, the Old Maid can give way to the Meccano scenario if the state or Europe takes over the management of the risk, since the rule of this Meccano is that the decentralised state – or Europe – administers the risks. If the distribution of competency between the state and Europe creates a blockage, the Meccano scenario reverts to the Old Maid, when the state has to manage the constant oneupmanship of the stakeholders or an over-radical challenge to the techno structure.

In Monopoly, society favours an individual response to risk. Companies take over the management of risks by proposing innovative products and by fulfiling society's expectations. Any deceptions with regard to such risks can jeopardise this scenario via a loss of confidence in the market thus leading to the Tarot scenario, for example, where the local actors manage the risks via negotiation.

Besides the actors' strategies, events may cause the passage from one scenario to another. In Monopoly, for example, the outbreak of high-intensity events may lead to a development of the non-trader, or may force the public institutions out of the role as regulators by reverting to an Old Maid or Meccano scenario. As for the Tarot, it favours crisis prevention, feedback and learning from experience, but is difficult to adapt to crisis management.

Considered classically, these different scenarios could have been treated as alternative management modes. Thus, analysis of the different elements likely to trigger, accelerate or slow down scenarios reveals the fact that the actors' strategies may lead to the rule itself being challenged. As long as the rule is respected or imposed on the actors, the actors' dimensions and strategies characterising the scenario remain stable or, more specifically, are characterised by continuous evolution. On the other hand, once these dimensions and strategies have been challenged, the rule of the game can no longer be followed and we move into another scenario. This situation is likely to cause problems in the management of risks when, in a crisis situation, the different actors must be coordinated. This explains why the failings of an actor, or a major catastrophe, can lead to a Meccano scenario where the state administers the risks and eventually makes its decisions alone. Lastly, the passage from one scenario to another can generate malfunctioning when the actors, who do not consider themselves to be in the same phase, are not following the same rule.

Therefore, depending on the intensity of the risks in question, there appears to be a form of fluctuation between the Old Maid, in which the actors push the management of a risk onto one another, leading to its being moved back in time by means of legal process, and the other scenarios such as Meccano, where the urgency, linked to the immediate impact of the risk, imposes the intervention of a dominant actor such as the state. The latter may thus choose, interactively, between one or other of the two scenarios, that is to say either to retain or pass on the Old Maid.

For the manager, different navigation strategies between the scenarios appear possible as long as, in a globalised world, the friction that rigidifies the rules has disappeared. First of all, the increasing constraints linked to the risks can be assumed by the consumer if they are willing to pay the corresponding price, either via the taxation of such risks (fluctuation between the Old Maid and Meccano scenarios) or via innovation (Monopoly scenario). However, innovation can also consist in postponing the problem in time, when the risks have not been assessed *a priori* or when they have been incompletely assessed, as with the controversial genetically modified organisms. This amounts to managing the uncertainties linked to innovation in the Old Maid scenario whilst making the management of other risks, such as chemical risks, pay the price of such innovation as a solution, as in the Monopoly scenario. Lastly, thanks to the specialisations of the local actors in the Happy Families scenario, the manager is able, by means of delocation, to transfer the problem in space so as to avoid the constraints of the Old Maid or the Meccano, whilst profiting from the Monopoly, in the sense that globalisation enables us to change our game by passing with little or no constraint from one space to another.

3   Conclusion

In a globalised world, the manager must be able to adapt to the exacerbated instability and interdependency of the contexts in which management decisions are made. Futures thinking, conceived in the idea that action is a complex, dynamic but directionless process constructed by the interaction of actors but escaping their control, might appeal to him. In trying to implement concepts, he would thus become interested in the methodology. However, the scenarios were constructed at a time when globalisation, had it even begun, was far from having reached its present intensity. Much rigidity remains, thereby justifying the conception of scenarios as alternative images describing an environment outside of action. Disappointed in his search for the necessary tools to know how to evolve in a world where pieces and rules change ceaselessly, the manager might come to the conclusion that futures thinking is not all it is claimed to be. This contradiction between the principles and the method is only superficial: it simply illustrates the fact that the methodology has to evolve with the world that it is intended to observe, as demanded by Bourbon-Busset (1963) who refused the idea of a futures-thinking methodology frozen for all time.

If we abandon the idea of a distant image and its corollary (the fact that the scenarios are mutually exclusive), we can imagine that a scenario is defined by rules, that is to say, by constraints or relationships respected by the actors more or less durably. The instability and interaction that are characteristic of globalisation no longer represent risks but rather mere particular circumstances. In fact, the actors are free to choose to move from one rule to another, or to follow several rules simultaneously, and thus to make it possible for several scenarios to be played out at the same time. In this case, a decision no longer has to be justified with respect to possible futures, the existence of only one of which will be promoted; it is rather a case of navigating between systems of rules, which, according to the meaning they have for the stakeholders, will form as many futures interacting within the scope of an action process.

From a methodological point of view, futures research should concentrate on the work of modelling transfers, that is to say the passages from one scenario to another, or even fluctuations between scenarios, which appear to be determining elements in the integration of actors' strategies and decision-making processes in scenario construction. The study of relations of dominance (Marchais-Roubelat, 1999) in particular, within the network of actors, enables the conditions of such transfers to be defined, as has been highlighted in research-intervention for the French army high command. The modelling of these relations of dominance and their dynamics needs to be examined more deeply so as to study the emergence and implementation of simultaneous scenarios.

Finally, the disappearance of structural rigidities does not lead merely to the obsolescence of classical scenarios; it provides a major challenge to limits hitherto unquestioned, in particular those of companies, organisations and institutions whose transformations cannot be limited to a search for greater flexibility, but which must integrate, in addition to the relations of dominance, the role of individuals in action. What remains, in effect, is the individual, of which the manager is one. Over and above the technical responses to the management issues that concern the manager, the issue of the place of the individual engaged in the globalisation process makes itself increasingly felt. Shall we have to resort to seeking clones, their very flexibility a direct result of the multicultural varnish with which they are fashioned, or does navigation, on the contrary, require individuals whose classical culture enables them to try out multiple games before deciding to which new rules they want to play or even create? Can futures thinking really limit itself to an exercise by specialists left to manage the Old Maid, or should it revert to its philosophical and anthropological origins, which is perhaps more useful to the problem of the individual within globalisation?

References

Barel, Y. (1971) *Prospective et analyse de systèmes.* Collection Travaux et recherches de prospective, No. 14. Paris: La documentation française.
———— (1973) *Le paradoxe et le système. Essai sur le fantastique social.* Grenoble: Presses Universitaires de Grenoble.
Berger, G. (1964) Sciences humaines et prévision. *Revue des deux mondes* in G Berger (ed.) *Phénoménologie du temps et prospective.* Paris: PUF
Bluet, J.C. and Zémor, J. (1970) Prospective géographique: méthode et direction de recherches. *Metra,* 9 (1): 111–27.
Bourbon-Busset de, J. (1963) Réflexions sur l'attitude prospective. *Prospective,* 10: 5–16.
Canarelli, C. (1995) Analysing the past and managing the future using neural networks. *Futures,* 27 (3): 325–38.
Durand, J. (1972) A new method for constructing scenarios. *Futures,* 4 (4): 325–30.
Eymard, J. (1977) A Markovian cross-impact model. *Futures,* 9 (3): 216–28.
Fukuyama, F. (1989) The end of history? *The National Interest,* 16 (Summer): 3–18.
———— (2002) Has history started again? *Policy,* 28 (2): 3–7.
Gaspar, T. and Novaky, E. (2002) Dilemmas for renewal of futures methodology. *Futures,* 34 (5): 365–79.
Gonod, P.-F. (1996) *Dynamique des systèmes et méthodes prospectives.* Collection Travaux et recherches de prospective, Futuribles International, No. 2. Paris: La documentation française.
Granger, G.-G. (1995) *Le probable, le possible et le virtuel.* Paris: Odile Jacob.
Grove, A.S. (1997) Navigating strategic inflection points. *Business Strategy Review,* 8 (3): 11–18.
Hamel, G. and Prahalad, C.K. (1989) Strategic Intent. *Harvard Business Review,* 67 (3): 63–77.
Jouvenel de, B. (1964) *L'art de la conjecture.* Monaco: Editions du Rocher. (English translation: (1967) *The art of conjecture*). New York: Basic Books.
Jungermann, H. (1985) Inferential processes in the construction of scenarios. *Journal of Forecasting,* 4 (4): 321–7.
Kahn, H. (1962) *Thinking About the Unthinkable.* New York: Horizon Press.
Kahn, H. and Wiener, A. (1967) *The Year 2000.* New York: MacMillan.
Lesourne, J. (1985) Vers un retour en grâce de la prévision et de la prospective. *Revue Française de Gestion,* 54 (September–December): 17–21.
———— (2001) *Ces avenirs qui n'ont pas eu lieu.* Paris: Odile Jacob.
Lesourne, J. and Stoffaës, C. (eds) (2001) *La prospective stratégique d'entreprise.* Paris: Dunod.

Marchais-Roubelat, A. (1999) 'Le rapport à l'autre dans le temps: le jeu et l'action'in J. Thépot (ed.) *Gestion et théorie des jeux: regards croisés*. Paris: Vuibert.

———— (2000) *De la décision à l'action. Essai de stratégie et de tactique*. Paris: Economica.

Marchais-Roubelat, A. and Roubelat, F. (2008) Designing action based scenarios. *Futures*, 40 (1): 25–33.

McDermott, W.B. (1996) Foresight is an illusion. *Long Range Planning*, 29 (2): 190–4.

O'Brien, R. (1992) *Global Financial Integration – The End of Geography*. London: Pinter.

Pivot, C. and Rychen, F. (eds) (2004) *La gestion des risques à l'horizon 2020*. La Tour d'Aigues: Datar-Editions de l'Aube.

Rigby, D. and Bilodeau, B. (2007) A growing focus on preparedness. *Harvard Business Review*, (July–August): 21–2.

Roubelat, F. (2000) Scenario planning as a networking process. *Technological Forecasting and Social Change*, 65 (1): 99–112.

———— (2001) Réseaux prospectifs et stratégie d'entreprise. *Revue Française de Gestion*, 133: 14–22.

———— (2006) Scenarios to challenge strategic paradigms: lessons from 2025. *Futures*, 38 (5): 519–27.

Schoemaker, P.J. (2002) *Profiting from Uncertainty*. New York: The Free Press.

Schwartz, P. (1993) La planification stratégique par scénarios. *Futuribles*, 176: 31–50.

Shell International (2005) *Shell Global scenarios to 2025*. London: Shell International.

Van der Heijden, K. (1996) *Scenarios: The Art of Strategic Conversation*. Chichester: John Wiley and Sons.

Van Dijk, T. (1998) *Ideology: A Multidisciplinary Approach*. Thousand Oaks, Cal.: Sage.

Wack, P. (1985a) Scenarios: uncharted waters ahead. *Harvard Business Review*, 63 (5): 73–89.

———— (1985b) Scenarios: shooting the rapids. *Harvard Business Review*, 63 (6): 139–50.

Weick, K (1993) The collapse of sense-making in organizations: the Mann Gulch disaster. *Administrative Science Quarterly*, 38: 628–52.

Glossary

Acquisition: A cooperation operation whereby one company takes control of another, which is then integrated into the first company. This is a strategic manoeuvre whose consequence is loss of independence for the company that is acquired. The objectives of the acquirer may be multiple; for example, procuring an increase in economic and technical efficiency, strengthening market power or creating financial synergies.

Alliance: A cooperation agreement associating several companies who pool their resources with a view to achieving objectives together, while retaining their independence. The cooperation may concern various elements in the value chain. The commitment of the partners is not definitive, and the duration of the signed agreement is often limited in time.

Communitarian (and communitarianism): A liberal political theory (and a corresponding political ideology for communitarianism) in which the community is the primary level of identification and the expression of freedom.

Control: The process by which one entity (for instance, the headquarters of an MNC) influences the behaviour and output of another entity (for instance, their subsidiaries abroad) through the use of power, authority and a wide range of bureaucratic, cultural and informal mechanisms.

Cooperation: An agreement of a strategic nature between at least two independent companies who choose to pool some or all of their resources (human, technological, production, commercial, etc.). Cooperation agreements can cover a wide variety of links between companies, from purely contractual arrangements to the total integration of the associated entities. They may bring together companies who are in competition with each other, but also businesses who are linked vertically in the production process or companies in different areas of competition.

Cosmopolitism: An internationalist political ideology designed to move beyond a citizen-based identification with the nation.

Cost of capital: The weighted average cost of the various financing sources of the firm, meaning equity and financial debts. It is useful for investment selection through the NPV criteria, as well as to assess the required rate of return for investors.

Country-risk: The risk that a country may not make all the payments related to its external debt. This can be measured with the volatility of deal returns of this country. Country-risk also includes financial risk, currency risk, political risk or liquidity risk.

Deregulation/financial liberalisation: The rules that restricted financial transactions have been suppressed (they concerned mostly credit controls and administrative rates). Beyond investors' behaviour, they modified the economic and monetary policies of the countries.

Differentialism: A particularist political ideology that establishes difference as a superior political value.

Economies of experience: The reduction in unit added costs achieved thanks to cumulated production. The concept was developed by the Boston Consulting Group. The experience curve shows that the total unit cost of a product decreases by a constant percentage each time the cumulated production of the production is doubled.

Economies of scale: The reduction in unit costs in a given activity, associated with an increase in production capacity and sales volume. Economies of scale are achieved by the spreading of overhead costs over longer production series, and by the reduction of the cost of investment per unit of capacity, when the total capacity increases.

Economies of scope: These result from the joint management of several types of product. The sharing of resources, skills, external relations and so on, enable lower management unit costs than those the company would have if it managed different products separately.

Efficiency: Producing goods or services effectively, with a minimum of waste, expense or unnecessary effort, leading to the highest ratio of output to input.

Ethnocentrism: The excessive promotion of the country of origin's cultural standards and values. The latter are seen as superior to those developed in other contexts (countries, regions and so on).

Foreign Direct Investments (FDI): The investment flows leaving a country or a specific geographic area, or going inside it. These investments aim to have a sizeable influence in the firms that are located outside the country or the domestic area of the investor.

Franchise: The concession to a network of franchisees of the right to use a brand or a retail name. The company that wishes to develop via a franchising system can choose to recruit the local franchisees itself, or to recruit a principal franchisor who will be responsible for the organisation and control of a sub-network of franchisees in a given geographical territory. The franchisees benefit from the technical and commercial resources of the franchisor's brand or retail name in return for a fee (in the form of an entry charge and the payment of regular licence fees).

Fund allocation: Allocation and use of rare resources (capital, commodities and so on). This is made by private economic agents (enterprises, investors, individuals) as well as by governments (through taxation and expenses).

Geocentrism: An opening up to the cultural standards and values developed in different regions of the world. Analytical and operational methods are then based on numerous international references and not on the country of origin's references alone.

Geographic functionalism: Geographic resources (raw materials, human capabilities and so on), which are a means of prosperity for businesses (mainly multinational corporations).

Governance: Principle-based processes and techniques for designing a government (or a firm, in which case one refers to 'corporate governance').

Heckscher-Ohlin-Samuelson Model (HOS): The specialisation of countries, at the level of international trade, which results from the differences of allocation in production factors (capital and work). This specialisation is not absolute; for various reasons countries may continue to produce a certain quantity of goods and services for which they are relatively less well equipped.

Home bias: Contrary to what is forecast by financial theory, international diversification of financial asset portfolios is insufficient, because of an overweighting of the domestic assets of the investor.

Hypermarket: A retail outlet with a surface area greater than 2500 m^2, which offers a wide assortment of products (between 25,000 and 40,000 items). The hypermarket format was developed in France and was then exported by several retail groups into international markets.

Impartition or Out-sourcing: Companies who are complementary on the vertical level (partnerships earlier or later in the chain). Concretely, it concerns sub-contracts or the out-sourcing of peripheral activities.

Infra-national: Whatever is located inside the nation. The representative authorities of the nation must share the sovereignty of the nation with this 'interior' political level, which is constructed independently of the existing administrative constituencies (for example, in France, association of local governments, local missions and so on).

Integration/financial globalisation: The development at the international level, or worldwide, of financial transactions according to the rules of market economy. It goes along with a lowering of the barriers to free trade in capital and to financial services deals.

Key success factor: An element on which competition is based, which corresponds to the resources and competences that must be mastered in order to achieve good performance in a specific business. The resources are both tangible and intangible assets that are associated in a semi-permanent way with the company. The competences are the company's ability to deploy resources in order to attain a fixed objective.

Local responsiveness: The willingness of multinational firms to make adjustments to their products, services and ways of conducting business at the local level, taking into consideration local institutional context, culture, needs, opportunities and constraints.

Multinational company (MNC): A company or enterprise that manages production, sales or services in more than one country; an MNC has its headquarters in a home country and operates in several other countries known as host countries.

Risk premium: The spread between the expected return of the market (the share) and the risk-free rate. Switching from the market risk premium to the share risk premium is done by multiplying the market risk premium by the beta coefficient of the share.

Specialised superstore: A self-service shop specialising in a specific field such as do-it-yourself, household electrical goods, furniture or sports equipment. The sales area is generally between 1,000 and 3,000 m^2.

Authors' Biographies

Corinne Blanquart is a doctor in Economics and a Researcher at INRETS (French National Institute for Transport and Safety Research) and she is qualified to supervise doctoral thesis. She is part of the SPLOTT research unit (productive systems, logistics, transport organisation and work). Her research in industrial economics analyses the link between production systems and the logistic and transport choices. She is the author of many articles, book chapters and communications at international conferences. Her work is based on surveys in France and abroad and she is involved in several European projects with other European universities.

Valentina Carbone is an associate professor at ESCP Europe, in Paris. She is also an Affiliate Professor at the ESCE Business School. She is Italian and worked for Procter & Gamble and Finseda for three years before starting an academic career. After earning her Doctorate from the École Nationale des Ponts et Chaussées (Paris) she became a Research Fellow at INRETS (National Research Institute of Transport). Dr Carbone's main research interests concern the organisation and coordination of global supply chains. Her current research area is green and sustainable supply chain management. She is the author of articles, book chapters and communications at international conferences. She often hosts courses and seminars abroad (Vietnam, the United States, Italy, Bahrain, Lebanon, England, Portugal, Thailand, Sweden, Norway).

Mitsuyo Delcourt-Itonaga is a graduate of ESCP Europe. She specialises in advertising, specialising in international media consultancy and international brand management, in particular, automotive, high-tech sectors and hotel business in Europe and Middle-East. She is also involved in intercultural coaching for companies dealing with Asia.

Jacques Jaussaud is Professor of Management, and Director of the CREG research team in Management at the University of Pau (France). His research interests are in the areas of business strategy, organisation, control and human resources management, with a particular focus on Japan, China and other Asian countries. He has published widely in these areas, including papers (*Journal of International Management*, 2006; *International Management*, 2006, both co-authored with Johannes Schaaper) and several books, some of which are in English. The most recent of these is *Evolving Corporate Structures and Cultures in Asia*, edited with Bernadette Andreosso-O'Callaghan and Sam Dzever (ISTE Publishing, 2008). He has also published a book in Portuguese (Brazil), *Expatriação de Executivos: Coleção Debates en Administração* (2007) with Leni Hidalgo Nunes and Isabella F. Gouveia de Vasconcelos.

Evelyne Lande is Professor at the Business Administration Institute (IAE) of the University of Poitiers (France). She is the Dean of IAE and a member of the CEREGE, IAE's research laboratory. Her research interests are focused on public sector accounting and audits. She supervises doctoral research done in collaboration with the Supreme Audit Institution, such as the *Cour des Comptes* in France, the French Ministry of

Finance, and those financed by international institutions like IMF, World Bank, AUF. She has published several articles about government accounting in academic and professional journals. She is a member of the Comparative International Governmental Accounting Research (CIGAR) network board.

Jean-Paul Lemaire teaches International Business with a multidisciplinary approach at ESCP Europe (France). He holds degrees in political science, sociology, international economics and international law. He earned his Doctorate in Economics from Paris I and is also qualified to supervise research at universities (DHDR). With his focus on cross-border and overseas expansion of profit and non-profit, public and private organisations in a large diversity of sectors, he is invited on a regular basis to teach and give talks by various institutions in fast-growing economies (Indian Institute of Management Ahmedabad, EGADE/TEC Monterrey Mexico, Royal University of Law and Economic Sciences, Phnom Penh, Centre FrancoVietnamien de Formation à la Gestion, Ecole Supérieure des Affaires de Beyrouth). He is the author of numerous articles, publications and case studies. His book *Stratégies d'Internationalisation, Développement International de l'entreprise* (2003, with Gérard Petit) was awarded the Grand Prix de la Stratégie et du Management (AFPLANE, *l'Expansion Management Review* and McKinsey. With his colleague Jean Klein he recently published *Financement International des Entreprises* (2006). He is currently president of Atlas/Association Francophone de Management International.

Anne Marchais-Roubelat is Associate Professor at the Cnam-Paris. She supervises doctoral theses and she is in charge of the research methodology seminar of the PhD in foresight-strategy-organisation. Her research areas include strategic management of action processes in public and private organisations. She is a board member of *Flux*, an international journal of research in networks and territories. She has written (in French) *From Decision to Action* (2000) and recently co-authored in *Futures* a paper on the design of action-based scenarios.

Marin A. Marinov is Professor in International Business and Management at the Business School of the University of Gloucestershire (the UK). He has held a number of professorial appointments all over the world, including Bulgaria, Germany, the USA, Denmark, Finland, Sweden, France, Spain and Portugal. His research focuses on the role of multinational corporations in the international business area, internationalisation of business, firms from emerging markets and internationalisation challenges in firm management and marketing. He has published six books, numerous chapters in books and more than fifty papers in refereed academic journals.

Svetla T. Marinova is a senior lecturer at the Business School of the University of Birmingham (the UK). She is Director of the MSc in International Business programme. Her research interests focus on the internationalisation and globalisation of businesses from developing economies. She has published many articles in academic journals, including *International Marketing Review, European Journal of Marketing, Advances in International Marketing, Research in Marketing* and *Thunderbird International Business Review*. Dr Marinova has contributed chapters to a number of books and has also co-edited books.

Ulrike Mayrhofer is Professor of Business Administration at the Institut d'Administration des Entreprises (School of Business) of the University Jean Moulin

Lyon 3 (Magellan Research Centre, Euristik team), and an Affiliated Professor at Rouen Business School (France). Her teaching and research activities concern international marketing, international management and strategic management. She has published five books, including *Marketing International,* (2004) and *Management Stratégique* (2007), several case studies and many articles published in journals such as *European Management Journal, European Management Review, Finance-Contrôle-Stratégie, International Business Review, Journal of International Marketing, Management International* and *Revue Française de Gestion.*

Loïck Menvielle is a lecturer in Marketing at the EDHEC Business School of Nice (France). He collaborates closely with the University of Quebec in Three-Rivers and with the University of Nice. He has taken part in many international congresses such as those organised by American associations: Travel Tourism Research Association (TTRA), Athens Institute for Education and Research (ATINER), and the French Association of Marketing. He has contributed to four books about marketing.

Eric Milliot is Associate Professor of Management Science, Head of the Department of Strategy and Marketing at the Institut d'Administration des Entreprises (School of Business) of the University of Poitiers (France). As a member of the research laboratory CEREGE, his studies principally concern the strategic and organisational systems developed by companies in the face of globalisation. On this topic, he has published various academic works. This field of research has led to his giving classes and seminars at institutions in several countries (University of California at Berkeley, University of Nanchang, Universidade de Fortaleza, Aïn Shams University, Thang Long University, University of Mauritius, European Management Institute at New Delhi, Ecole Supérieure des Affaires de Beyrouth, INSCAE d'Antananarivo).

Bertrand Monnet is Professor at Edhec Business School, Lille, France, and the Manager of the Edhec Chair 'Management of Criminal Risks'. He is the author of several articles about crimes committed against companies. He is often consulted by television and radio channels as an expert. He conducts investigations in many countries on the studied topic (Columbia, Nigeria, Sierra Leon).

Sophie Nivoix is Associate Professor at the Faculty of Law and Social Sciences of the University of Poitiers (France), and coordinator of the Master in Law and Marketing at the Faculty of Law and Social Sciences of the University of Poitiers. She is a member of the CEREGE laboratory (IAE of Poitiers), and works on risk and return analysis of listed firms in various countries, including Japan. She has contributed to several collective books, published numerous academic papers and lectures in several universities (University of Nanchang, University of Warsaw, Ecole Supérieure des Affaires of Beirut, European Management Institute in New Delhi). Before working in the university, she was a quantitative analyst in the banking sector (CIC banking group).

Dominique Pépin is Associate Professor at the Faculty of Economics of the University of Poitiers (France). Formerly coordinator of the Statistic-Insurance-Health department of the IRIAF institute in Niort, he is now in charge of the statistics speciality module of the Economics Degree in the Faculty of Economics. He is a member of the CRIEF laboratory (Economics Faculty). He works on monetary and financial theory and he has written several papers about the globalisation of capital markets.

Yvon Pesqueux is Professor at the Conservatoire National des Arts et Métiers (CNAM) in Paris, and he holds the Chair of the 'Développement des Systèmes d'Organisation'. He holds a PhD in Economics from the University of Paris 1 Panthéon-Sorbonne, and his special interests are management, philosophy and ethics, business and society, and corporate social responsibility. He has published several scientific articles and his book publications link the concepts of organisation and politics. The latter include *Management de la Connaissance: Knowledge Management & Apprentissage Organisationnel & Société de la Connaissance* (2006); co-authored with Michel Ferrary, *Gouvernance et Privatisation* (2007) and *Management de la Qualité, une Analyse Critique* (2008). He is editor of *Society and Business Review* and a member of the Société Française de Management (SFM).

Nathalie Prime is Associate Professor of International Marketing and Cross-Cultural Management at ESCP Europe (France). Her teaching and research are focused on four main areas: managing cultures in the global environment, corporate culture and the internationalisation process, and international marketing and strategies of business internationalisation. Her geographical interests are especially focused on fast-growing emerging economies and her industry work relates mainly to the automotive and the retailing sectors. Her publications include several articles and international academic communications. A book in collaboration with Jean-Claude Usunier, *Marketing International, Développement des Marchés et Management Multiculturel* (2004), was granted an award by the Académie des Sciences Commerciales in 2004. Professor Prime has taught in India, South Africa, Vietnam, Lebanon, Italy, Algeria, Madagascar and Russia. Over the last ten years, she has developed extensive links with the Indian Institute of Management Ahmedabad, in India.

Harimino Oliarilanto Rakoto is Professor at the Institut National des Sciences Comptables et de l'Administration d'Entreprises (INSCAE) of Antananarivo, Madagascar. She is a member of the Bureau de Recherche pour les Activités Innovatrices (BRAIN), INSCAE's research laboratory. Her doctoral thesis is about the adoption of accrual accounting by Malagasy local government. She is a member of the Comparative International Governmental Accounting Research (CIGAR) network.

Sébastien Rocher is Associate Professor at the Institut d'Administration des Entreprises (School of Business) of the University of Poitiers (France). He is a member of the CEREGE, IAE's research laboratory. His doctoral thesis is about the development of a risk-consolidation method in the public sector, in partnership with the French Ministry of Finance. He won the 2006 best doctoral thesis award of the French Accounting Association. He has published several articles about public accounting harmonisation at the international level in academic and professional journals. He is a member of the Comparative International Governmental Accounting Research (CIGAR) network.

Fabrice Roubelat is Associate Professor at the University of Poitiers (France). He is currently engaged with research and supervises doctoral theses in scenario planning, business strategy and risk management. He is also a consultant in scenario planning and strategy in public and private organisations. He has published many papers in the field of scenario planning in journals such as *Futures*, *Technological Forecasting and Social Change* and *Long Range Planning*.

Johannes Schaaper is Senior Professor at the Bordeaux Management School (France). He has a PhD in Economics from the University of Bordeaux, and a Research Habilitation Degree in Management Science from the University of Poitiers. He taught management at various Universities in France, China and several African countries. He was attached to the French Embassy of Lebanon to develop management teaching and research in Beirut. His research interests concentrate mainly on the control that French and Japanese multinational companies exert over their subsidiaries abroad, especially in China and South-East Asia, and he mixes face-to-face interviews with expatriates and quantitative surveys. His second field of interest concerns Chinese consumer behaviour, with a special focus on the influence of Chinese cultural values. He has published several articles, co-authored with Jacques Jaussaud, in academic journals including *Asian Business and Management*, the *Journal of International Management*, the *Journal of Asia Pacific Economy*, *Management International* and *Finance-Contrôle-Stratégie*.

Robert Teller is Professor of Sciences of Management at the Institut d'Administration des Entreprises (School of Business) of the University of Nice Sophia Antipolis (France). He has held several administrative and scientific posts including President of the French Accounting Association and member of the Reading Committee of the *European Accounting Review*. He has published several books and articles, all dealing with accounting, finance and company management.

Guy Tournois is an associate professor at the Institut d'Administration des Entreprises (School of Business) of the University of Nice Sophia Antipolis (France). He is the Director of a Masters 2 degree course, and holds a PhD. He has specialised in international wealth management and private banking. He has worked for different banks and asset management companies and, ten years ago, he formed his own company specialising in wealth management and seminars for banking executives. He has published academic articles, most recently discussing value creation in banks.

Nadine Tournois is Professor in Management Sciences at the Institut d'Administration des Entreprises (School of Business) of the University of Nice Sophia Antipolis (France), and also Director of International Studies at IAE. She has published books and articles concerning marketing management, strategy and value creation in banking. She is regularly invited to teach in various foreign universities (University of California at Berkeley, Virginia Commonwealth University, University of Exeter, University of Tianjin, Gulf University at Bahrein). Before becoming a professor, she worked in the high technologies industry, and she has been a consultant to French and foreign banks.

Philippe Very is a professor at Edhec Business School, Nice, France, and the Scientific Director of Edhec Research Centre on mergers and acquisitions. He is also involved in the research projects of the Edhec Chair 'Management of Criminal Risks'. He is the author of numerous academic publications in top-ranked journals, and has also written four books and several book chapters. He was recently acting as President (2008–09) of the French-speaking Academy of Management (AIMS: Association Internationale de Management Stratégique).

Atlas/AFMI Presentation

(Association Francophone de Management International)

In 2008 the idea of Atlas/AFMI emerged from the group of contributors to this book, all teachers and researchers in International Business, originating from more than ten management-education institutions, universities and business schools, in France and abroad. This academic and professional association aims at promoting International Business and International Management as a recognised management discipline in France[1] and in French-speaking countries, as is already the case in many other regions.[2]

Objectives

Atlas/AFMI aims to achieve the following:

- The acknowledgement of International Business and International Management as a specific domain of managerial science. This domain develops a transversal approach of management's various functional areas in close connection with fundamental disciplines, such as economics, sociology, anthropology, geography and so on.
- A close relationship with companies and organisations operating beyond their national boundaries, in order to relate international business research and teaching to problems stemming from international realities.
- Inductive approaches leading to the conceptualisation of observed international business situations, to seek qualitative and/or quantitative validation, to identify managerial implications stemming from these, and to transfer them to a diversity of sectors and geographic contexts.
- A privileged focus on emerging countries, as major actors gaining a progressively increasing share of the international trade and investment flows, the challenge being to better understand their dynamics, conditions and forms of their world economic integration in relation to the mature economies.

Activities

In search of these objectives, Atlas/AFMI tries to maximise synergies among various types of activities:

- Studies and research related to the opening of economic areas, as well as to internationalisation of corporations and organisations (case studies, conceptual models, action-research, decision-making tools) in an academic and/or professional perspective.
- Their exploitation and diffusion through publications (academic and professional articles, books) and contributions (international conferences), as well as through

participation to assignments and missions sponsored by public authorities at national or international level.

- Organisation of events (forums, conferences, round tables and so on) with the support and cooperation of academic and professional national and international associations, major business education institutions, international organisations.
- Coaching and support of young researchers sharing their doctoral research with international business as facilitation of their academic and/or corporate placement.
- Networking among the various stakeholders (private and public) of international corporate development in order to better inter-connect them and build a community of converging interests, leading to the identification of new needs, generation of common initiatives and gathering of resources to serve and support them.

Position

Beyond its major objective of developing international business as a specific management discipline, Atlas/AFMI is eager to cooperate with existing academic associations through partnerships (round tables, joint events, contributions to conferences and so on) and/or more permanent relationships (research on specific issues or subjects, on particular geographic zones or industrial sectors, on international dimension of managerial functional areas).

As well as working with the professional organisations which regroup companies (by activities, geographical zones), Atlas intends to contribute to international data-gathering and analyses, to internationalisation, decision-making processes and to action research.

The position of Atlas would then be at the crossroad of the various stakeholders of international corporate development.

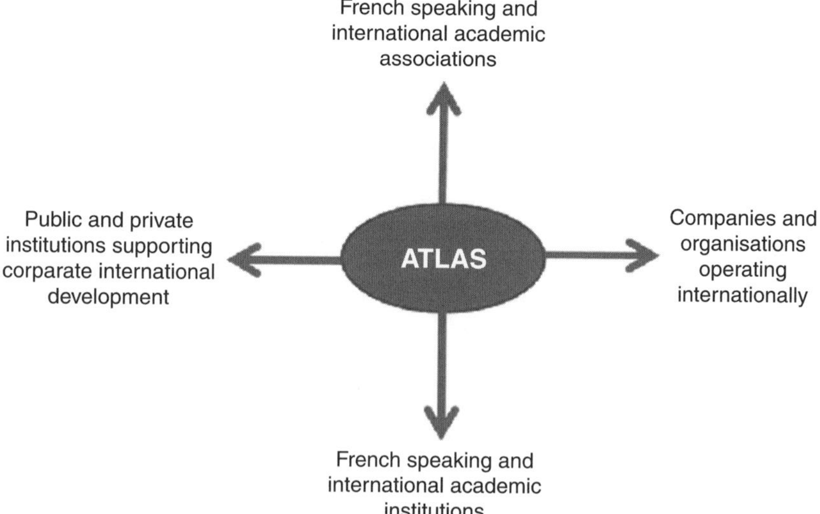

Notes

1. In France, unlike various other Western countries (such as the USA, the UK, Germany or Scandinavia) international business departments almost all disappeared from the organisation chart of management schools during the 1980s. The international functional contents are now hosted by functional departments (marketing, finance, strategy and organisation, human resources, etc.), which do not offer the transdisciplinary and environmental approach that was formerly the backbone of this discipline.
2. Some organisations promoting international business exist at world level (Academy of International Business) as well as at European level (European International Business Academy).

Index

Note: Page numbers with '*b*', '*f*', '*m*' and '*t*' in the index denote boxes, figures, map and tables in the text.